PRAISE FOR *ACCOUNTING AND FINANCE FOR MANAGERS*

This book provides an easy-to-understand essential guide for managers to learn key concepts and systems of financial accounting, management accounting and corporate finance. With balanced coverage of practical applications of preparing financial statements, financial analysis and related questions and exercises, the book gives managers the necessary skills in understanding and using accounting information for decision-making in the real business world. I strongly recommend this book for anyone interested in accounting and finance.

Aly Salama, Professor of Accounting and Head of Accounting Subject Group, Northumbria University

This is a useful and elaborate overview of the principles of financial accounting and management accounting. A well-written, comprehensive volume. This textbook is very informative, the chapters are well organized and the learning goals are highlighted and illustrated in a straightforward and understandable fashion. The basic formulas, concepts and theories associated with managerial finance including solved examples are very well designed and presented.

Neveen Abdelrehim, Senior Lecturer in Accounting and Finance, Newcastle University

This book has been a key resource in the preparation of lecture and seminar sessions, as it is well written and easy to comprehend. I highly recommend *Accounting and Finance for Managers* to those interested in understanding how accounting and finance informs business decision-making by organizations, whether you are a student or manager within the business world. The illustrative examples provided facilitate a deeper understanding of the topic areas covered in each chapter, whether you have a background in accounting and finance or are new to the subject.

Paul Brewster, Programme Leader – Football Business and Finance, UCFB Wembley

D0528177

Third Edition

Accounting and Finance for Managers

A business decision-making approach

Matt Bamber and Simon Parry

KoganPage

Publisher's note

Every possible effort has been made to ensure that the information contained in this book is accurate at the time of going to press, and the publisher and authors cannot accept responsibility for any errors or omissions, however caused. No responsibility for loss or damage occasioned to any person acting, or refraining from action, as a result of the material in this publication can be accepted by the editor, the publisher or the authors.

First published in Great Britain and the United States in 2014 by Kogan Page Limited
Second edition published in 2018
Third edition 2021

2nd Floor, 45 Gee Street
London EC1V 3RS
United Kingdom

www.koganpage.com

122 W 27th St, 10th Floor
New York NY 10001
USA

4737/23 Ansari Road
Daryaganj
New Delhi 110002
India

Kogan Page books are printed on paper from sustainable forests.

ISBNs

Hardback   978 1 78966 753 0
Paperbook   978 1 78966 751 6
Ebook   978 1 78966 752 3

British Library Cataloguing-in-Publication Data

A CIP record for this book is available from the British Library.

Library of Congress Control Number

2020948768

Typeset by Integra Software Services, Pondicherry
Print production managed by Jellyfish
Printed and bound by CPI Group (UK) Ltd, Croydon CR0 4YY

CONTENTS

05   Business planning 168

06   Budgets and performance management 200

09   Investment decisions   314

Bonus online-only materials are available at the following URL

(please scroll to the bottom of the web page and complete the form to access these):

www.koganpage.com/afm3

Introduction

In this book we hope to show you that, despite some imperfections and limitations, accounting information can help you make better-informed decisions as individuals and as managers. Though we talk about accountants and accounting, we hope that you will begin to understand and appreciate that this group of people do not produce all the accounting information. More importantly, the information they produce needs to be interpreted at an operational, tactical and strategic level by employees from across the organization regardless of background. You might think that certain professions are naturally exempted from the push and pull of accounting, but this is not true. Just ask any marketing director, for example, how he or she feels about this year's budget, or sales team managers what they think of their 'on-target earnings' bonus!

Despite the broad reach of the subject matter, accounting and finance as a discipline is often viewed with unease as students commonly have a pre-existing belief that it requires a strong grounding in mathematics, that it comprises a set of impossibly convoluted and complicated rules, or that it is simply boring! But these presuppositions are unfounded and ultimately untrue. What *is* true is that much of accounting and finance is a 'building-block' exercise, ie one issue sets the foundation upon which the next can be built. Therefore, we have provided exercises throughout the text. Some of these are follow-my-lead 'worked-through exercises', while others give you the opportunity to practise for yourselves. We urge you to attempt these. They provide an opportunity to reflect on what you've learnt and question the underlying purpose of the process and/or result. We have also given a number of real-life examples and illustrations to help you get a better grasp of the material. We try to take you beyond the mechanics of generating 'an answer' and towards an understanding of why that 'answer' might be important.

To make the book as accessible as possible we have divided it into two broad sections: financial accounting (Chapters 1 to 4); and management accounting (Chapters 5 to 11). These are the two major sub-disciplines of accounting and finance in professional and academic life. The chapters vary quite considerably in length and to a certain degree this can be interpreted as a reflection of our view of their relative importance to a subject novice. Throughout each topic, the following advice pervades: the more you put in, the more you will get out. Only the tip of the iceberg is revealed during each chapter and therefore we urge you to pursue other sources as far and as wide as you can. That might be in the form of media releases, academic and trade journals, discussion forums, and so forth. The deeper you engage, the more you will understand and the greater the likelihood that you will ultimately be able to make better-informed decisions.

You might already be familiar with some of the more common terms such as 'annual report', 'financial statements', 'accountant' and 'auditor', but you might not know what they mean. That is fine. The financial accounting section expands on these and other related topics. The management accounting section introduces some practical and useful tools, methods and techniques to help you deliver solutions and suggestions to some major business problems.

The financial accounting section presents some common business vehicles, ie sole traders, partnerships, limited liability companies and public limited companies. The advantages and disadvantages of each are subsequently explained and explored. Though the first few chapters focus on *corporate* reporting practices (as it is simpler to extrapolate these to simpler forms of accounting than the other way round), much of the information and advice provided within both the financial accounting and management accounting chapters can also be mapped to other organizations, including those within the not-for-profit sector.

How to approach the content

Our objective has been to include key (or core) information in the body of the text. Alongside this, we have also included a number of examples and exercises. If you follow the primary exercise on the first run through, that is excellent and you might like to simply move on. Many, however, won't and if you fall into this camp there is no harm in following it through in more detail in your own time. We have also provided some supporting examples which run alongside the main text. These secondary and supplementary examples are different enough to stop even the most advanced students from becoming bored. It has always seemed strange to us that accounting and finance are portrayed as subjects which are passively learnt, on a surface level, facilitated by a teacher-led approach. We do not concur. You should see these examples the same way as you might learn to catch a ball, take a penalty, undertake an experiment, choose the right chemical etc. The examples help you to grow in experience and guide your future decision-making behaviour. Indeed, we have an advantage over other academic disciplines as our examples are interesting because they are real! You can see them in your everyday life, often panning out before your eyes. Once you begin to understand the subject, you will never see the world in the same way again.

We have also included notes which we have called '*expert view*'. The idea behind these is to encourage you to think more broadly and present you with further issues and questions that you could consider pursuing. Though these are non-essential, they bridge the gap between this introductory text and other, more advanced sylla-buses. Solutions in accounting are not binary as many uninitiated believe. There is plenty of scope for discretion in practice and behaviour (normally legal but occa-sionally illegal!). Even at this first step into the discipline, we hope to show you some interesting arguments, conflicting viewpoints and how they (have) arise(n).

A note on terminology

We feel it is worth making clear at this early stage that this is a textbook designed for an international audience. Throughout, therefore, we have adopted International Financial Reporting Standards (IFRS) terminology. Occasionally we have referenced the relevant document produced by the International Accounting Standards Board (IASB), eg an International Financial Reporting Standard (IFRS), an International Accounting Standard (IAS) or the Conceptual Framework (F). Though we don't rec-ommend *beginners* to pursue these references, there are some who might want to. If you are interested, a site which is well worth a visit and which we strongly recommend is IASplus.com. This site is maintainedby one of the *Big Four*[1] accounting firms – Deloitte. It is generally recognized as the go-to site for international financial reporting updates.

Proposed course outline

We fully expect lecturers who adopt this text to adopt different approaches to the con-tent and the method of delivery. The book is designed to aid a standard 'lecture series followed by tutorial' approach, but the material and exercises have also been trialled in workshops and smaller seminar groups and found suitable for all sizes and formats.
    University course lengths differ by institution and jurisdiction. Some standard course outlines are provided below.

*Twenty-four-hour course (12 weeks * 2-hour lectures)*

Week 1	Chapter 1
Week 2	Chapter 2
Week 3	Chapter 3
Week 4	Chapter 3
Week 5	Chapter 4
Week 6	Chapter 5

Week 7	Chapter 6
Week 8	Chapter 7
Week 9	Chapter 8
Week 10	Chapter 9
Week 11	Chapter 10
Week 12	Chapter 11

Sixteen-hour course (8 weeks * 2-hour lectures)

Week 1	Chapter 1
Week 2	Chapter 2
Week 3	Chapter 3
Week 4	Chapter 4
Week 5	Chapters 5 & 10
Week 6	Chapters 6 & 7
Week 7	Chapter 8 & 9
Week 8	Chapter 11

Twenty-four-hour course (24 weeks * 1 hour lecture; or 12 * 2-hour lectures)

Week 1	Chapter 1
Week 2	Chapter 1
Week 3	Chapter 2
Week 4	Chapter 2
Week 5	Subsidiary bookkeeping appendix
Week 6	Chapter 3
Week 7	Chapter 3
Week 8	Chapter 4
Week 9	Chapter 4
Week 10	Chapter 5
Week 11	Chapter 5

Note

1 Deloitte, PricewaterhouseCoopers, Ernst & Young (EY), KPMG.

Introduction to accounting

OBJECTIVE

To provide an overview of the conceptual and regulatory framework that underpins financial accounting and an understanding of the content and structure of the financial statements.

LEARNING OUTCOMES

After studying this chapter, the reader will be able to:

- Discuss the role of the financial accountant and the information which they prepare.
- Describe the relationship between the statement of financial position, income statement and statement of cash flows.
- Understand the elements and structure of the annual report and primary financial statements.
- Describe the conceptual and regulatory framework of accounting.
- Evaluate what information the financial statements cannot provide.

KEY TOPICS COVERED

- Why do businesses need financial accountants and financial statements?
- The type of information financial accounts record.
- The concepts of assets and liabilities, income and expenditure.
- Introduction to the three primary financial statements: the statement of financial position, income statement and the statement of cash flows.
- Introduction to the accounting regulatory system and the way it has shaped the informational content of financial statements.
- Discussion of some key problems and issues with financial statements.

MANAGEMENT ISSUES

Managers need the skills to be able to 'read' or 'interpret' financial statements rather than prepare them. Equally importantly, they need an understanding of what financial statements can and cannot tell them about a business.

Introduction

Though it is incredible to us, there are always a minority of newcomers to accounting and finance who believe that our discipline is dull! Yet nothing could be further from the truth. Accounting, and accountants' work, is fascinating, not least because it is dynamic. The role of the accountant is constantly being redefined by innovation. The information we are about to share guides individual and corporate decision making at every level of an organization. This combination of importance and dynamism means that accounting workplaces – whether in practice or industry – are almost always vibrant, energetic and intellectually stimulating.

Chapters 1–4 of this book discuss the role of the financial accountant alongside the purpose and usefulness of the information they produce. We outline some basic preparation rules, propose several analysis and interpretation techniques, and introduce some broader questions about financial accounting and its role. Chapters 5–10 are concerned with management accounting and the sub-discipline financial management.

In this chapter we open by addressing some of the questions most frequently asked by those who are new to the world of accounting and finance, namely: What is an accountant? What is the accountant's role? What is the broad purpose of this function in an organization? We introduce the key elements of the conceptual and regulatory frameworks and follow this by identifying the most common types of business vehicle. This chapter therefore outlines who the preparers and users of financial information are. In addition, we introduce the standard-setters and describe their role in the accounting community. We conclude this chapter by providing an overview of some of the commonly perceived key problems associated with the main information product output of the financial accountant: the annual report and financial statements.

Throughout this text, we have dedicated our efforts to presenting the material in a meaningful and enjoyable way. To this end, we have broken up 'hard facts' by bringing in other issues, such as who uses the information and why it might be important (necessary?) for there to be a legitimate and credible standard-setting body. A further problem is that this material can feel disjointed. While, there isn't enough space in an introductory textbook to consider every issue that underlies the development, refinement, purpose and importance of accounting, we have tried to capture the core themes and present them in an exciting and enjoyable way. Furthermore, as with so many other disciplines, in accounting there are often no right or wrong answers to complex organizational questions. As such, we would like to take this opportunity to ask you to think critically as you make your way through the material. For example: Do you think a global financial reporting system is desirable? Do you think it is right that accountants should be allowed to be self-governing? Do you think domestic governments should intervene to make rules *fairer* to their jurisdiction? Do you think accounting systems should comprise a set of restrictive rules or do you think they should be based on principles? Why is there a vibrant accounting and finance academic community? What do accounting scholars study, and why? Additionally, given the rapid pace of change in practice (in real life), how can a relatively slow-moving research community help the profession?

Who and what is an accountant?

One thing that has remained unchanged for millennia is that every day, in our private and work lives, we rely on accountants and accounting information to make better-informed decisions. To put this in context, some examples of decisions you might face include whether to: buy an asset, rent it, or make it; price a product higher or lower than your competitors; outsource a product, project, department or operation; take on a new contract; acquire a competing business. Needless to say, there are many more!

The Oxford dictionary defines accounting (noun) as 'the process or work of keeping financial accounts' while an accountant (noun) is 'a person whose job is to keep or inspect financial accounts'. This definition, however, is overly simplistic. For a long time, accounting has been considered a process of collecting, analysing and communicating financial information to allow users to make better-informed decisions. This work remains at the forefront of the role but more recently accountants have been asked to expand their remit into new areas. For example, accountants are now deeply involved in the preparation of non-financial information, including corporate social responsibility reports. The image of the staid, conservative, grey-suited accounting drone is outdated. The job has changed. We now need to be communicators as well as doers. We need to be client facing rather than just hit buttons on a calculator from the safe distance of our office. There is a new breed of accountant and whether you believe this is a change for the better or worse, it seems to be a change that is here to stay. Also, audit and accounting firms are at the cutting edge of digital technologies.

The good news is that learning the procedural forms of accounting is reasonably straightforward because often the systems represent a refinement of common sense. Among other factors, relative levels of reliance on financial information, increased regulation and professionalization have driven increased sophistication of presentation and methods, but at the heart of all accounting is the idea that financial data should be converted into useful information for decision making. If either the process or the output were to become overly complex or burdensome, the profession might risk damaging this core objective.

Expert view 1.1: Seeking definitions – what is an accountant?

The subtleties and complexities of the definition of an accountant are illustrated by the recently drafted consultation paper produced by the International Federation of Accountants (IFAC) in 2011, entitled 'A proposed definition of "professional accountant"'. This work drew attention to a number of important problems exacerbated by a lack of specificity in the term 'professional accountant'.

IFAC organized their definition into three descriptive levels:

1 Initially, the term 'professional accountant' is defined by emphasizing some form of official accounting qualification (eg formal education, certification, or chartering).

2 IFAC then state what a professional accountant *does* by outlining the core responsibilities that imply the application of skills in the context of society's expectations. Thus, their definition recognizes the public-interest responsibilities of accountants and their profession.

3 Finally (which is optional and contingent upon the characteristics of each jurisdiction), the definition states that professional accountants can be differentiated from one another by certain factors, such as types of responsibilities (eg public-sector accounting, auditing role) and the level of formal training or education generally.

A simple way to understand the role of an accountant is through an illustration. As you work through the paragraph, try to picture yourself as the protagonist. You will see *how* and *why* the simplest forms of accounting developed.

WORKED EXAMPLE 1.1 Climb On!

For a long time, you have been wondering how to convert your passion for rock climbing into a business opportunity. During a recent climbing trip you met Chris, a climbing-gear designer. He agreed to give you 100 chalk bags and 100 climb-oriented t-shirts for $4 and $5 each, respectively. You came to an agreement with him that you'd make payments on an ad-hoc basis as the goods were sold. As soon as you arrived home you listed the first 30 chalk bags and 50 t-shirts on an internet-based auction site. These sold within three days of their listing for $8 and $10 respectively. Half of these customers paid immediately. You offered 20-day credit terms on the sales and your past experiences tell you that customers tend to take full advantage of this policy.

You are keen to work out your *financial position* before you proceed any further.

Table 1.1   Solution to Worked Example 1.1

What do you own?		What do you owe?	
70 chalk bags which you bought for $4 each	$280	You owe Chris money for the 100 chalk bags at $4 each	$400
50 t-shirts which you bought for $5 each	$250	You owe Chris money for the 100 t-shirts at $5 each	$500
You received $8 per chalk bag, and collected 15 units worth of sales immediately	$120		
You are owed for (the remaining) 15 chalk bags sold at $8 per unit	$120		
You received $10 per t-shirt, and collected 25 t-shirts worth of sales immediately	$250		
You are owed for (the remaining) 25 t-shirts sold at $10 per unit	$250		

Through the medium of this example, we have introduced many of the basic tenets of accounting. Your mind should be racing with the same questions as business owners and their stakeholders have been asking for millennia. From an *internal* perspective, you were simply interested in your financial position:

- How much more (or less) wealthy am I?
- Who do I owe money to?
- How much do I owe?
- Who owes me?
- How much do they owe me?
- How much cash have I got?
- How much are my inventories (unsold goods) worth?

However, given this analysis your interest might have been piqued and you are now pondering other associated questions about your performance, future position and cash flows, plus any constraints and opportunities which you might face. These might include:

- Have I excluded any costs?
- Have I made a profit?
- Am I charging a sensible price?
- Will all my customers pay?
- How long will Chris be willing to wait for his payment?
- Will Chris allow me to buy more inventories?
- Can I negotiate the purchase price down?
- Will the goods Chris sells me be manufactured to the same quality?
- ... and so forth.

Extract 1.1: Perspectives from accounting research

Many people who first start studying accounting and finance cannot believe that there is a large, thriving, active research community. The problem is that, more often than not, all that people know of accountants comes through the media who like to portray us, and the information we produce, in binary terms. They lead casual audiences to believe that it is 'right' or 'wrong'. What they don't tell you is that accounting-related decisions are rarely so clear cut.

Maintaining and cultivating the link between practice (ie the accounting profession) and academia is important. There needs to be a vibrant academic community in the same way that the academic community needs a strong, credible and socially responsible accounting profession. There are those who argue that the gap has never been wider, while others argue that it's never been narrower. Kaplan (2011) has a more balanced view and suggests in his paper, 'Accounting scholarship that advances professional knowledge and practice', that though research (academic scholarship) has helped craft the direction of professional decision making and contributed to professional knowledge, there are many areas where the community could do more. He states:

> As accounting scholars have focused on understanding how markets and users process accounting data, they have distanced themselves from the accounting process itself. Accounting scholarship has failed to address important measurement and valuation issues that have arisen in the past 40 years of

practice. This gap is illustrated with missed opportunities in risk measurement and management and the estimation of the fair value of complex financial securities.

Kaplan (2011)

Let's not be too disheartened, though, for when a community recognizes a performance gap and there is a positive attitude towards change, this is normally the first – albeit tentative – step on the pathway to finding solutions.

The two forms of accounting: financial accounting and management accounting

Broadly speaking, accounting as a discipline can be sub-divided into two forms: financial accounting and management accounting. The principal differences can best be summarized into four categories as shown in Table 1.2.

Table 1.2 Differences between financial accounting and management accounting

Key differences	Financial accounting	Management accounting
Users	External, principally owners of the business eg shareholders	Internal management of the company
Format	Governed by region-specific law, exchange-specific regulation and accounting standards	Can take any form depending upon the purpose of the information
Frequency	Normally annually. Large listed entities sometimes report quarterly or half-yearly dependent upon regulation	As required. Some information is produced and some exercises are performed, as a matter of course, daily, weekly, monthly, quarterly and annually. Other information is required on an *ad-hoc* basis
Content	Dominated by historic information based on past transactions	Forward-looking perspective. Detailed analysis of past results and incorporation of known changes, in order to plan for the future

Exercises: now attempt Exercise 1.1 on page 42

Expert view 1.2: The origins of accounting

We are about to learn the underlying basis of financial accounting – bookkeeping. It is often claimed that bookkeeping, as we know it today, was first documented by Luca Pacioli (often referred to as the 'Father of Accounting') in his text *Summa de arithmetica, geometria, proportioni et proportionalita* (Venice, 1497). Within this mathematics textbook was a section describing the method of double-entry bookkeeping employed by Venetian merchants. Pacioli described a system of journals and ledgers which accounted for assets, liabilities, gains and losses. For more information on the genesis of double entry bookkeeping, see Sangster's work (eg 2016). However, systems of recording assets and liabilities, income and expenditure have existed for millennia. For example, clay tablets which appear to record financial transactions have been found in Egypt and Mesopotamia dating to before 2000 BC. Indeed, Jones (2011) dates the first accounting scandal to the same period.

The financial accountant

There are marked differences between the sub-disciplines of accounting, namely: financial accounting and management accounting. Let's now look more closely at where one would find financial accountants and what they are responsible for producing and preparing. It is common for financial accountants to work within accounting practices that provide external services and advice to entities about their financial reporting and related matters, eg audit and accounting services. They can also be found within organizations, preparing in-house accounting records and associated information.

Expert view 1.3: Professional accounting qualifications

To the uninitiated, it might be natural to presume that when people refer to themselves as 'an accountant', they mean 'Chartered Accountant'. However, to be able to call oneself a Chartered Accountant it is necessary to be a member of the Institute of Chartered Accountants in England and Wales (ICAEW), Scotland (ICAS), Ireland (CAI), Australia (ICAA), Zimbabwe (ICAZ), New Zealand (ICANZ), The Canadian Institute of Chartered Accountants (CICA) or The South African Institute of Chartered Accountants (SAICA).

Job adverts in the UK commonly specify 'CCAB qualified accountant required'. The Consultative Committee of Accountancy Bodies (CCAB) is an umbrella group and has five member bodies: Association of Chartered Certified Accountants (ACCA); Chartered Institute of Public Finance and Accountancy (CIPFA); ICAEW; CAI; and ICAS.

NOTE The Chartered Institute of Management Accountants (CIMA) gave notice to withdraw from this group in March 2011.

It is common for financial accountants to be trained by, and work within, accounting partnerships. These range from sole practitioners working in isolation to global organizations generating tens of billions of dollars in revenue per annum. There are a number of so-called *elite* professional accounting firms which have become household names. Collectively they are known as the Big Four: PricewaterhouseCoopers; Deloitte; KPMG; and Ernst and Young (now known as EY).

There are fears about the long-term viability of this dominance and most in the profession expect changes (see Extract 1.2). However, the accounting services marketplace is competitive. There are hundreds of accounting firms outside of these Big Four. Organizations regularly put work out for tender as they are not obliged to stay with one firm. Indeed, from a commercial perspective, there is no better way of being offered a lower fee from your current auditor than by asking others to bid competitively against them!

Extract 1.2: Big Four dominance

UK Competition Commission Says Big Four Audit Dominance Not Best for Investors

March 4, 2013
Accountingweb
By Frank Byrt

The United Kingdom's Competition Commission (UKCC) says that the nation's audit market is dominated by the Big Four accounting firms, which has stanched competition for audit work from public companies to the detriment of their shareholders. The UKCC, in its 'Statutory Audit Services Market Investigation' report released on 22 February 2013, suggested that among the possible remedies is mandatory rotation of audit firms.

UKCC's report is a major milestone in a 16-month probe that was set in motion by a critical report from the House of Lords Economic Affairs Committee in 2011. The UKCC's inquiry focused on Big Four firms KPMG, Deloitte, Ernst & Young (EY) and PricewaterhouseCoopers (PwC).

'Essentially, we identified two clusters of issues,' UKCC Audit Investigation Group Chair Laura Carstensen told AccountingWEB UK. 'The first was "stickiness" and propensity of companies not to switch auditors and adverse issues that can result. And the second was to make sure auditors are more squarely aligned with what shareholders want.'

UKCC Recommendations

- Mandatory tendering.
- Mandatory rotation of audit firms.
- Expanded remit and/or more frequent audit quality reviews.
- Prohibit 'Big Four only' clauses in loan documentation.
- Strengthen accountability to the audit committee.
- Better shareholder–auditor engagement.
- Extended reporting requirements.

The UKCC concluded that Big Four firms hold most of the big company audits and that those organizations rarely change auditors, which hurts the competition for public company audit work and results in higher prices, lower quality, and less innovation and differentiation than would be the case in a more open market.

The lack of competition creates a risk of auditors being insufficiently independent from executives and insufficiently sceptical of their attempts to present the accounts in the best possible light, the report said.

How can this be interpreted and why is it relevant to you?

The existence of a Big Four has benefits but there are also drawbacks. Extract 1.2 identifies two potential issues: *stickiness*; and a threat to goal congruence. There is some debate about whether audit firms should be forced to rotate after a fixed term has been served, ie the job should be mandatorily put out to tender every five years, maybe with the incumbent firm not being allowed to engage in the process. The former has recently been proposed in the UK by the Competition Commission in a series of measures to limit the dominance of these élite firms and increase competition in the market. It is clear, however, that though this will solve one set of problems, it creates another: eg set-up costs, learning curve effects, a risk that sector/industry audit specialism won't be developed. There is no doubt that an audit firm who 'is in the pocket' of the senior executives (or vice versa) is an unhealthy situation, but none of the proposed solutions is perfect.

Ultimately, the central function of the financial accountant is to prepare (review or audit) the annual report and financial statements. Traditionally this document acts as a summary of the organization's performance and position. More recently it has become a repository for other information, and this point will be discussed in more detail later.

Alongside providing accounting support, the range of services provided by financial accountants (an accounting firm) can be summarized as follows:

- *assurance services*, including auditing and regulatory compliance;
- *taxation services*, including taxation planning, developing taxation strategies and taxation compliance work;
- *transaction work*, including advice to help businesses grow, prosper or reinvent themselves on issues such as obtaining funding, or mergers and acquisitions;
- *advisory services*, including internal audit, risk management advice and corporate recovery (insolvency).

Discussion point

Did you know that accountants provide this wide range of services? But they are not the only professional service providers – can you list any others? Why do managers need accountants and other external advisors to provide these services?

Who are the users of financial accounting information?

If financial accountants are responsible for the preparation of the annual report and financial statements, it is worth asking the follow-on questions: 'who uses this information?' and 'what do they use this information for?' (Figure 1.1).

Figure 1.1 Users of financial reporting information

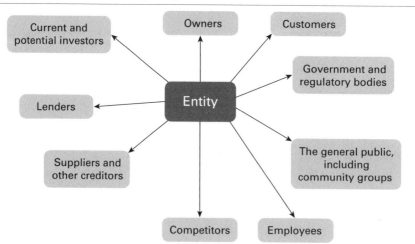

The Conceptual Framework for Financial Reporting (Conceptual Framework or 'F') identifies the primary users of general-purpose financial reporting as present and potential investors, lenders and other creditors. They use this information to make decisions about buying, selling or holding equity or debt instruments and providing or settling loans or other forms of credit [F, objective {OB} 2]. The information is intended to allow these stakeholders to assess an entity's performance and position as well as gauge future cash-flow prospects. These users will probably be keen to assess how well management have discharged their responsibilities in the use of the entity's resources [F, OB4].

The Conceptual Framework notes that there are also other stakeholders who might find general-purpose financial reports useful. Among these are regulators, the public, the government, customers, employees and competitors. The IASB notes that interested parties should not limit themselves to the financial report; there is other information available which would be useful when undertaking a full assessment of an entity's position and performance.

Exercises: now attempt Exercise 1.2 on page 42

The regulatory and conceptual framework

There are a limited number of professions that can claim to be self-governing, but accounting is one of them. The government has ceded responsibility to a group of experts whom they have deemed to be credible, reliable and socially responsible. In many ways, this is a great benefit. It does mean, however, that the central coordinating body (or bodies) need to be able to respond to any problems quickly and efficiently and with the requisite levels of ability and skill when challenged by economic, political, social and technological complexities.

The profession needs a strong, robust and fair conceptual and regulatory framework. The following paragraphs aim to introduce the main players in the environment as well as outline some of the processes.

Expert view 1.4: A current problem for the accounting standard-setters

A recent example of the type of problem faced by the profession is the case of financial instruments reporting standards. These are being regularly updated to take account of financial developments in the use and complexity of derivative financial instruments, eg what value should these be shown at: cost or market value? This decision is made more difficult when you know that the cost of these commonly economically significant assets/liabilities is normally $nil (or close to $nil). Standard-setters need to ask themselves: 'How do you value an instrument where there is no market?' 'And how do you create a rule that would be fit for all purposes?' 'How do you allow management to explain to the reader the risks faced by the entity as a result of holding these instruments?' 'Is there a minimum amount they should disclose?' It is amazing to think that a decade or so ago, companies were able to hold massive amounts of highly volatile derivative financial instruments without it being mandatory to declare how much they were worth. Though the rules we have now may not be perfect, they are certainly more useful than what we had before.

Principles-based versus rules-based standards

The IASB, in their role as standard-setter, aspire to create principles-driven requirements rather than rules-driven regulations. This is thought to alleviate some of the problems created by hard rules (eg de jure compliance, or organizations being willing and able to 'work around the rules') and allow organizations to be able to meet requirements even when faced with a situation not previously encountered. This does, however, mean that organizations frequently need to make judgements because the reporting code is not completely rigid and immovable.

The Conceptual Framework

The Conceptual Framework for accounting provides supplementary guidance when there are no specific reporting requirements or regulations governing the reporting area. There are a number of reasons why this might happen, eg because a reporting issue is brand new – and hence no regulation has been written, or a firm has a very complex reporting issue – and the regulations do not provide adequate guidance. That means that this document can be used to guide preparers when there isn't a standard that tells them what to do. The Conceptual Framework is a frame of reference which has two purposes: first, it is used by companies to aid their financial reporting decision making; and second, it is used by the IASB to help them to develop new accounting standards and revise old ones.

The Conceptual Framework deals with the following key issues:

a the objective of financial reporting;

b the qualitative characteristics of useful financial information;

c the definition, recognition and measurement of the elements from which financial statements are constructed; and

d concepts of capital and capital maintenance.

The objective of general-purpose financial reporting is to provide financial information about the reporting entity that is useful to key stakeholders. The concept of usefulness is subject to great debate. Accounting and finance research has attempted to define and refine the notion of financial reporting quality. The key problem, however, is that *quality* is a nebulous term and thus the integrity and robustness of any definition is questionable.

The qualitative characteristics of useful financial information

Defining a nebulous concept such as 'quality' has proved to be difficult for everyone who has ever approached the subject. For example, how easy is it to say what makes Shakespeare's *Hamlet* such a wonderful play? What contributes to its quality? Can those characteristics be mapped to other texts? Accountants and their representative bodies have had the same problem. What characteristics ensure that information is of sufficient quality; or useful for decision making? In response, the IASB state that for financial information to be useful, first and foremost it must be relevant and faithfully represent what it purports to represent. There are then four further enhancing characteristics: comparability, verifiability, timeliness and understandability. These are summarized in Figure 1.2 and some definitions of these characteristics follow.

It is almost impossible to define quality, but it should be noted that it is also difficult to fully define these other terms. We thought it would be useful to set out how the standard-setters have chosen to define them (F, Qualitative Characteristics {QC} 6–20):

The fundamental characteristics

- **Relevant** financial information is capable of making a difference in the decisions made by users. Information may be capable of making a difference in a decision even if some users choose not to take advantage of it or are already aware of it from other sources. Financial information is capable of making a difference in decisions if it has predictive value, confirmatory value or both.

- Financial reports represent economic phenomena in words and numbers. To be useful, financial information must not only represent relevant phenomena, but it must also **faithfully represent** the phenomena that it purports to represent. To be a perfectly faithful representation, a depiction would have three characteristics. It would be complete, neutral and free from error.

The enhancing characteristics

- Users' decisions involve choosing between alternatives, for example, selling or holding an investment, or investing in one reporting entity or another. Consequently, information about a reporting entity is more useful if it can be compared with similar information about other entities and with similar information about the same entity for another period or another date. **Comparability** is the qualitative characteristic that enables users to identify and understand similarities in, and differences among, items.

- **Verifiability** helps assure users that information faithfully represents the economic phenomena it purports to represent. Verifiability means that different knowledgeable and independent observers could reach consensus, although not necessarily complete agreement, that a particular depiction is a faithful representation. Quantified information need not be a single-point estimate to be verifiable. A range of possible amounts and the related probabilities can also be verified.

- **Timeliness** means having information available to decision-makers in time to be capable of influencing their decisions. Generally, the older the information is the less useful it is. However, some information may continue to be timely long after the end of a reporting period because, for example, some users may need to identify and assess trends.

- Financial reports are prepared for users who have a reasonable knowledge of business and economic activities and who review and analyse the information diligently. Classifying, characterizing and presenting information clearly and concisely makes it **understandable**.

Discussion point

Do you think this list of characteristics is all-inclusive?

Figure 1.2 The qualitative characteristics

The usefulness of financial information is determined by the following qualitative characteristics:

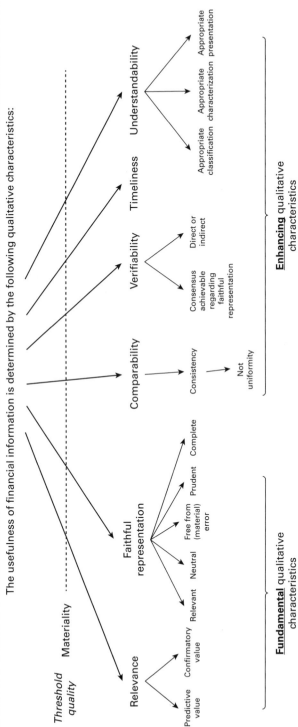

Materiality

You will often hear accountants refer to the separate notion of **materiality**. This concept is critical to an understanding of the aims and objectives of financial reporting and auditing. An item is deemed material if its omission or misstatement could influence decisions that users make on the basis of financial information about a specific reporting entity.

Materiality therefore is an entity-specific variable. It is based on the nature or magnitude (or both) of the item(s) to which the information relates in the context of an individual entity's position. Consequently, there is no single specified measure or quantitative threshold for materiality. Each item must be reviewed on its own merits and in the broader context.

Discussion point

Can you think of two 'material' items that you own: one which is material by size, and the other because of its nature?

Exercises: now attempt Exercise 1.3 on page 43

The regulatory framework

We have briefly introduced the Conceptual Framework and therefore it is now time to turn to the regulatory framework. It is not essential at this level of study for you to know the intricacies of the accounting standard-setting process or the wider regulatory framework. However, an outline of the structure of the major bodies and processes forms both interesting and worthwhile knowledge. An outline of the structure of the IFRS Foundation is shown in Figure 1.3. Figure 1.4 provides a brief overview of the phases of the standard-setting due process.

Figure 1.3   The structure of the IFRS Foundation **(www.IFRS.org)**

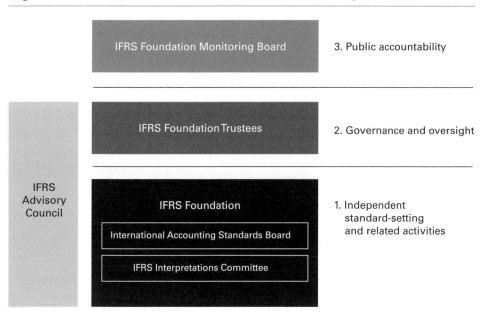

The IFRS Foundation

The IFRS Foundation is an independent, not-for-profit private-sector organization. The IFRS Foundation sets at its core the notion of public interest which is mirrored by the definition of accountants and their work (eg, IFAC, 2011). The principal objectives of the IFRS Foundation are as follows:

- to develop a single set of high-quality, understandable, enforceable and globally accepted International Financial Reporting Standards (IFRSs) through its standard-setting body, the IASB;

- to promote the use and rigorous application of those standards;

- to take account of the financial reporting needs of emerging economies and small and medium-sized entities (SMEs); and

- to promote and facilitate adoption of IFRSs, being the standards and interpretations issued by the IASB, through the convergence of national accounting standards and IFRSs.

Source: **www.IFRS.org**

The IASB

The IASB acts as an independent standard-setting body on behalf of the IFRS Foundation. The IASB currently has 15 full-time members who are responsible for the development and publication of IFRSs. Interestingly, all meetings of the IASB are held in public and are webcast. The IASB and the IFRS Foundation heavily stress the notions of comparability, inclusiveness and consultation. They actively engage with stakeholders from around the world, including investors, analysts, regulators, business leaders, other accounting standard-setters and the accountancy profession.

The IFRS Interpretations Committee

The 14 members of the IFRS Interpretations Committee are responsible for reviewing, on a timely basis, widespread accounting issues that have arisen within the context of current IFRSs and to provide authoritative guidance (IFRICs) on those issues. The members are drawn from different professions and countries.

Expert view 1.5: Is this an unfair or biased system?

Though there is research which finds limited evidence of varying levels of relative influence among stakeholder groups during the standard-setting process, the IASB have put in place a system which has the potential to be fair and rigorous (see Figure 1.4). There is a combination of observable and non-observable phases and though it has been argued that these 'dark' periods impair transparency, they also allow the Board to take, behind closed doors, valuable expert advice which otherwise might not be provided. In order to make the process more transparent, the Board has recently opened up Board meetings to the public, made minutes available and also webcasts them.

Exercises: now attempt Exercise 1.4 on page 43

The standard-setting process

Figure 1.4 outlines the standard-setting process in financial reporting. This is the template for accounting requirements' innovation and implementation. As you can see, the process is designed to be robust, involved and transparent as the outcome needs to be agreed among stakeholders. Agreement between constituents – including preparers, users, auditors, representative bodies and so forth – helps to ensure the continued legitimacy of the standard-setter. It should also mean that the requirements are likely to be met by preparers and their value understood by users.

Figure 1.4 IASB standard-setting due process

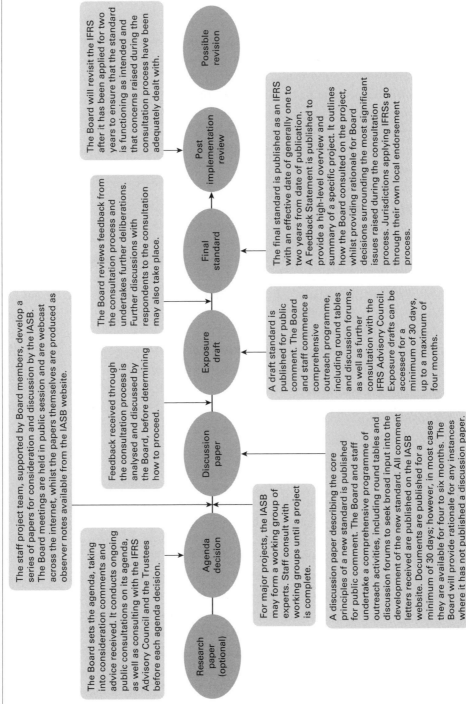

The staff project team, supported by Board members, develop a series of papers for consideration and discussion by the IASB. The Board meetings are held in public session and are webcast across the internet, whilst the papers themselves are produced as observer notes available from the IASB website.

The Board reviews feedback from the consultation process and undertakes further deliberations. Further discussions with respondents to the consultation may also take place.

The Board will revisit the IFRS after it has been applied for two years to ensure that the standard is functioning as intended and that concerns raised during the consultation process have been adequately dealt with.

Post implementation review

Possible revision

Final standard

The final standard is published as an IFRS with an effective date of generally one to two years from date of publication. A Feedback Statement is published to provide a high-level overview and summary of a specific project. It outlines how the Board consulted on the project, whilst providing rationale for Board decisions surrounding the most significant issues raised during the consultation process. Jurisdictions applying IFRSs go through their own local endorsement process.

Exposure draft

A draft standard is published for public comment. The Board and staff commence a comprehensive outreach programme, including round tables and discussion forums, as well as further consultation with the IFRS Advisory Council. Exposure drafts can be accessed for a minimum of 30 days, up to a maximum of four months.

Feedback received through the consultation process is analysed and discussed by the Board, before determining how to proceed.

Discussion paper

The Board sets the agenda, taking into consideration comments and advice received. It conducts ongoing public consultations on its agenda, as well as consulting with the IFRS Advisory Council and the Trustees before each agenda decision.

Agenda decision

For major projects, the IASB may form a working group of experts. Staff consult with working groups until a project is complete.

A discussion paper describing the core principles of a new standard is published for public comment. The Board and staff undertake a comprehensive programme of outreach activities, including round tables and discussion forums to seek broad input into the development of the new standard. All comment letters received are published on the IASB website. Documents are published for a minimum of 30 days; however, in most cases they are available for four to six months. The Board will provide rationale for any instances where it has not published a discussion paper.

Research paper (optional)

Types of business entity

We are now at the crossroads between topics being covered in this chapter. The first part considered the role of the accountant and the systems and processes that have grown up around them. The conceptual and regulatory framework has been described. For accounting to exist, there must be something to account for. Therefore in terms of basic background information, we address two further questions: 'What is a business?' and 'What is the purpose of a business?'

The answer to both questions is far from straightforward. Indeed, they often overlap and intertwine.

What is a business?

One could argue that in its simplest sense a business should be defined by its legal form. Therefore, we shall briefly review the most common types of business entity that exist.

There are a wide range of business vehicles, or forms of business ownership, available. Each has their relative advantages and disadvantages. In the UK, the government has developed an excellent resource which explains the major differences between the various business vehicles available. The site also offers advice on how one might set up a business (**https://www.gov.uk/browse/business/setting-up**). There are three business organizational types which it is useful to be aware of:

1 sole trader;

2 partnership;

3 limited company.

Sole trader

As the name suggests, a sole trader is someone opting to work for themselves. As seen in the example above – Climb On! – we put 'you' in the position of running your own business. The business is not incorporated, ie it is not a limited liability company. You do not share the ownership of the business with anyone else, ie you have no business partner(s). This doesn't mean that you cannot have any employees, it is just not common. Businesses of this type are normally quite small in terms of assets, liabilities, revenues and expenses. There are many everyday examples of people going into business on their own, such as plumbers, electricians, hairdressers, private tutors, artists, photographers and so forth.

The financial accounting information a sole trader is *required* to produce is limited. It is normally required to satisfy tax authorities' purposes. Occasionally financial institutions might request specific information, particularly for lending purposes.

Establishing oneself as a sole trader, therefore, is frequently the first step for many entrepreneurs. The main advantage of this business vehicle is the retention of control.

The owner is solely responsible for all decision making. The other key advantage is the reduced accounting and legal regulatory burden. The major disadvantage is the unlimited liability! In other words, a sole trader is wholly responsible for all liabilities of the business.

Partnership

A partnership occurs when *two or more people* decide to run a business together. As with establishing a business as a sole trader, the regulatory burden is low, especially in comparison with limited companies. Partnerships range considerably in size. It is probably more common that they have low assets, liabilities, revenues and expenses; however, they can be huge global businesses. Examples again include hairdressers, plumbers, tutors and so forth. They also include businesses such as medical practices, legal practices and accounting practices.

The advantage of forming a partnership is that you can share responsibility and the burdens of ownership. It is also likely that the skill-set available will be more varied and expertise could be easier to channel towards specific projects. In an accounting partnership, for example, you might want the skills of both a financial accountant and a tax accountant; it is rare that one person is an expert in both. The disadvantages largely stem from behavioural issues. Sharing ownership often places significant burdens on pre-existing well-functioning relationships. Also, there are some people who simply like making all the decisions, not sharing this role!

Limited company

In the UK, a privately held business is referred to as a limited company; this is commonly abbreviated to 'Ltd'. The equivalent term used for a private company in Australia is Proprietary Limited Company (abbreviated to Pty. Ltd.). In India and Pakistan the designation Pvt. Ltd. (Private Limited) is used for all private limited companies. In South Africa the term Pty. Ltd. is used. In the United States, the expression 'corporation' is preferred to limited company and it is common to see the abbreviation 'Inc.' (short for 'Incorporated'), but in many states 'Ltd.' is also permitted.

The word 'limited' relates to the level of financial exposure. An entity can be incorporated as a limited liability company, at which point, in law, it becomes a separate legal entity. Therefore, while sole traders and partners are personally responsible for the amounts owed by their businesses, the shareholders of a limited liability company are only responsible for the amount to be paid for their shares. A limited liability company conducts all activities in the name of the entity, eg invoices are issued in the company's name, bank accounts need to be set up in the company's name (not directors' or managers' names). Note, however, that it is not uncommon for lenders and trading partners to ask the directors of companies for personal guarantees, which, of course, negates much of the advantage associated with incorporation.

As with partnerships, companies can range in size from small to huge. Most companies which are household names are public limited companies. There are several advantages and disadvantages to incorporating. Some of these are shown in Table 1.3.

Table 1.3   Advantages and disadvantages of incorporation

Advantages	Disadvantages
Limited liability reduces the personal investment risk.	The regulatory burden is far greater on limited liability companies than on sole traders and partnerships. A limited company has to publish annual financial statements. These are public statements of account, meaning, of course, that anyone (including competitors and employees) can see how well (or badly) the entity has done. As stated above, sole traders and partnerships do not have to publish their financial statements. *Note: the regulatory burden on public limited companies is far greater again!*
It is theoretically more straightforward to generate funds for a limited company because new shares can be sold when additional financing is required. With no cap on the number of different shareholders, investors could come from anywhere and everywhere. Indeed, most of the world's major companies are public limited companies (plc), which means their shares are publicly traded.	Limited companies accounts must comply with the relevant domestic or international financial reporting requirements.
The existence of a partnership or sole trader is dependent upon the owners. A limited liability company, on the other hand, has a separate legal identity from its shareholders which means that directors, management and owners can come and go but the company will continue to exist regardless.	It is a common requirement in domestic law that large companies' financial statements are audited. In other words, they are subject to an independent review to ensure that they are true and fair, and comply with all relevant legal requirements and accounting standards. This process can be both time-consuming and expensive.
There are potential tax advantages. A company pays corporate income tax whereas sole traders and partners pay personal income tax.	Though raising finance is listed as an advantage, note also that share issues are regulated by law and a public sale of shares on a stock exchange can be an extremely expensive affair (and sometimes an expensive failure). It is also quite difficult to reduce the level of share capital or to get rid of shareholders who are deemed to be standing in the way of management objectives.
Assuming liquid secondary markets, leaving your position as an owner of share capital in a limited liability company is far simpler than exiting your position as a partner.	

What is the purpose of a business?

The second question has no clear-cut response. The neo-classical economic perspective holds that a corporation's objective is 'to maximize shareholder wealth'. However, this financial objective should be balanced against a set of non-financial objectives.

Non-financial objectives are typically clustered under three broad sub-headings:

1 ethical;

2 social;

3 environmental.

A business can be a commercial organization, involved with manufacturing, designing, developing, selling and so forth. Shareholders will likely remain satisfied provided that the risk–return relationship continues within their accepted bounds. However, there are other stakeholders who must also be satisfied. It has been argued that 'the customer is king', ie the entity exists both 'for' and 'because of' its customers. The community which the entity serves might be a crucial factor in relation to performance. Thus, social and environmental policies could dictate relative levels of success (failure). Investment in plant, property, equipment, employees and so forth is a function of a business and these investments will, it is hoped, generate jobs and profits which, in turn, will yield tax revenues which are essential to the economy of the country of residence as a whole.

The annual report and financial statements

Every business should (and will) produce a summary of their position and performance for a period of account. There is a set of primary financial statements which is included in the annual report and financial statements. Their contents and a basic preparation guide will be slowly introduced to you over the coming pages and chapters.

The IASB reported in the Conceptual Framework for Financial Reporting 2018 (Conceptual Framework) that 'the objective of financial statements is to provide information about the **financial position, performance** and **changes in financial position** of an entity that is useful to a wide range of users in making economic decisions'. The Conceptual Framework requires any IFRS reporting entity to produce the following information about its economic resources, claims, and changes in resources and claims:

a Economic resources and claims

- Economic resources and claims are recorded in the entity's *statement of financial position.*

   - Chapter 2 includes a series of exercises and examples which are designed to show you how to prepare a basic set of financial statements which includes a statement of financial position and a statement of comprehensive income (income statement). Chapters 3 and 4 provide a summary of how these statements can be used as tools to interpret the performance and position of the entity.

- Economic resources and claims are the entity's assets and liabilities (see below for definitions). These can either be current or non-current in nature.

- Users need to be aware of the nature and value of an entity's economic resources and claims to aid an assessment of the financial strengths and weaknesses, liquidity and solvency position, and its need and ability to obtain financing [F, OB13].

b Changes in economic resources and claims

- An entity should make users aware of, and allow them to distinguish between, any changes in economic resources and claims which result from either: i) the entity's performance; or ii) other events or transactions [F, OB15].

    - Changes in the entity's performance: economic resources might change, for example, as a result of an increase in production during the period of account. It is likely that at the end of the year the business will hold more non-current assets (to meet the production requirements), inventories (unsold units will increase because the size of order will have comparably increased), trade receivables (ie amounts owed by customers at the end of the period), trade payables (ie amounts owed to suppliers), and so forth.

    - Other events or transactions: a company might, for example, issue new share capital in order to fund the business. This is, by definition, not a performance-related event.

- The changes in an entity's economic resources and claims resulting from performance are presented in the *statement of comprehensive income* [See International Accounting Standard 1 *Presentation of Financial Statements* {IAS 1}, paragraphs 81–105].

    - The preparation of financial statements is covered in Chapter 2 while interpretation of this financial information is considered in Chapters 3 and 4.

- The changes in an entity's economic resources and claims resulting from other events and transactions are reported in the *statement of changes in equity* [See IAS 1,106–110].

- Changes in economic resources and claims could impact on users' assessments of past performance and a company's ability to generate future cash flows.

c Financial performance reflected by past cash flows

- The statements of financial position, comprehensive income and changes in equity are prepared on an accruals (accounting) basis. As results reported under accruals accounting and cash accounting are likely to be different, entities are also asked to prepare a statement of cash flows [See IAS 7 Statement of Cash Flows].

- This statement details how the entity generates cash and spends it [F, OB20].

The elements of financial statements

As we know, the financial statements present information about an entity's economic resources, claims, and changes in resources and claims. However, these terms can be confusing because they are not in everyday use. Instead, it might be more helpful to rephrase these into the following more commonly known terms (extracted from the Conceptual Framework).

i) Financial position terminology

> *Asset* – a resource controlled by an entity as a result of past events and from which *economic benefits* are expected to flow to the entity.

- On the face of the statement of financial position these are separated into current (due within one year) and non-current assets (due in more than one year).

- Examples of current assets include inventories, trade receivables and cash held at bank and in hand. Non-current assets include property, plant and equipment.

> *Liability* – a present obligation of the entity arising from past events, the settlement of which is expected to result in an outflow from the entity of resources embodying *economic benefits*.

- On the face of the statement of financial position these are separated into current (falling due within one year) and non-current liabilities (falling due in more than one year).

- Examples of current liabilities include trade payables and a bank overdraft. Non-current liabilities include long-term debt (eg bank loans) and provisions for future costs.

The definitions of an asset and liability contain reference to *future economic benefits*. This is the potential to contribute, directly or indirectly, to the flow of cash and cash equivalents to the entity.

> *Equity* – the residual interest in the assets of the entity after deducting all its liabilities.

> *Provision* – a present obligation which satisfies the rest of the definition of a liability, even if the amount of the obligation has to be estimated.

ii) Income statement terminology

The IASB has adopted a balance sheet approach to accounting. This means that gains and losses are measured in terms of changes in assets and liabilities. In other words, an increase in an asset will give rise to a gain, while an increase in a liability will give rise to a loss. Equally, a decrease in assets equates to a loss and a decrease in a liability equates to a gain.

Gains – increases in economic benefits.

Losses – decreases in economic benefits.

WORKED EXAMPLE 1.2 Burberry plc

Burberry plc has developed a global reputation for excellence as a designer, developer, maker and seller of luxury goods. Product design and development are centred in Burberry's London headquarters. Finished products are manufactured in the UK and through an external supplier network predominantly located in Europe. The company seeks to engage and connect the brand and its products with consumers through internally developed marketing content and programmes. Burberry products are sold globally through its stores and online at Burberry.com, as well as through third-party wholesale customers, both offline and online. These activities are executed by a worldwide team of over 10,000 employees.

Expert view 1.6: Complex financial statements

The financial statements presented here are for illustration purposes. Presenting the financial statements of a fictional entity lacks integrity and risks masking some of the complexities. However, seeing the financial statements of one of the world's largest businesses creates issues as well. Do not concern yourself with jargon you do not recognize but rather embrace the fact that at this stage, you can draw out an elementary understanding. Once you have completed the financial accounting sections you might want to come back to this section to see how far your learning has progressed.

Let us work through the introductory pages of their annual report together. It is common for large listed entities such as Burberry plc to provide an initial summary that brings together the key indicators related to performance and position related to the current and prior years. Burberry plc have called this section 'Financial Highlights' (Table 1.4)

Table 1.4   Burberry's financial highlights*

	Revenue (£m)	Adjusted profit before tax (£m)**	Adjusted diluted earnings per share (pence)***	Net cash (£m)	Dividend per share (pence)	Capital expenditure (£m)
2019	2,720	438	82.1	837	42.5	110
2018	2,733	467	82.1	892	41.3	106
2017	2,766	459	77.4	809	38.9	104
2016	2,515	418	69.9	660	37.0	138
2015	2,523	455	76.9	552	35.2	156

Notes

* All figures year to 31 March
** Adjusted profit before tax is stated before adjusting items.
Reported profit before tax £416m (2015: £445m)
*** Adjusted diluted EPS is stated before adjusting items.
Reported diluted EPS 69.4p (2015: 75.1p)

The annual report typically follows a standardized format that is presented within the first couple of pages (see Burberry plc's annual report contents page, Figure 1.5). This allows you to navigate around what is a lengthy document quickly and easily. Of course, technology is making these lengthy documents ever more navigable, which in turn improves their usefulness. The annual report is designed for a variety of user groups and their needs are fluid, shifting according to context. As such, sections relevant to one user might not be relevant to the next.

Figure 1.5 Burberry's contents page

It is common for a firm's senior executives to provide an analysis of the performance and position of the business (see pp10–20). There is no prescribed format for these disclosures. Here, to accompany the executives' narrative, Burberry plc has also chosen to include an update on their strategy (pp 22–41), an Investment Case (pp 56–57) and a brief explanation of their business model and some guidance on the luxury market environment (pp 17–21).

The financial statements and accompanying notes have become increasingly lengthy and complex. In response, and to shelter the user from the need to delve into the detail, the entity will often highlight certain key performance indicators, provide a financial review and a summary of the principal risks (pp 66–91).

The annual report has also become a repository for certain regulatory compliance disclosures, including those related specifically to corporate governance issues and directors' remuneration (pp 92–151).

Strategic report	Governance report	Financial statements
4 Chairman's Letter	92 Chairman's Introduction	152 Statement of Directors' Responsibilities
8 CEO's Letter	94 Board of Directors	153 Independent Auditor's Report to the Members of Burberry Group plc
13 Driving Positive Change	100 Corporate Governance Report	
14 Financial and Operational Highlights	101 Executive Committee	160 Group Income Statement
17 Business Model	103 Board Roles	161 Group Statement of Comprehensive Income
18 Luxury Market Environment	114 Report of the Audit Committee	162 Group Balance Sheet
22 Strategy	120 Report of the Nomination Committee	163 Group Statement of Changes in Equity
42 Responsibility	123 Directors' Remuneration Report	164 Group Statement of Cash Flows
56 Investment Case	145 Directors' Report	164 Analysis of Net Cash
58 Key Performance Indicators		165 Notes to the Financial Statements
62 Stakeholder Engagement		211 Five Year Summary
64 Non-Financial Information Statement		214 Company Balance Sheet
66 Financial Review		215 Company Statement of Changes in Equity
72 Capital Allocation Framework		216 Notes to the Company Financial Statements
74 Risk and Viability Report		224 Shareholder Information

It is not uncommon for a company to provide financial and non-financial disclosures regarding its ethical, social and environmental philosophy and actions. In this case, Burberry have provided a 'Responsibility' agenda (pp 42–55), which sets out a series of goals split into three focus areas: (i) communities; (ii) company; and (iii) product.

Most large listed entities conclude their annual report with a summary of the last five years' performance (p 211).

Unlike the front-end of the annual report, which is not subject to rigorous auditing, the financial statements and notes to the financial statements are (pp 152–232).

A statement of directors' responsibilities (p 152) is followed by the auditors' report (pp 153–159).

Following this are the primary financial statements (pp 160–164) and the notes to the financial statements (pp 164–210).

As Burberry plc reports on a consolidated basis (ie all results from entities within the group are brought together in this single report), the parent company's financial statements are also presented here (pp 214–232). Separate financial statements will be prepared independently for all the entities in the group, often for tax purposes as well as compliance.

The income statement

Figure 1.6 Burberry's Income Statement

	52 weeks to 30 March 2019 £m	Year to 31 March 2018 £m
Revenue	2,720.2	2,732.8
Cost of sales	(859.4)	(835.4)
Gross profit	1,860.8	1,897.4
Net operating expenses	(1,423.6)	(1,487.1)
Operating profit	437.2	410.3
Financing		
Finance income	8.7	7.8
Finance expense	(3.6)	(3.5)
Other financing charge	(1.7)	(2.0)
Net finance income	3.4	2.3
Profit before taxation	440.6	412.6
Taxation	(101.5)	(119.0)
Profit for the year	339.1	293.6
Attributable to:		
Owners of the Company	339.3	293.5
Non-controlling interest	(0.2)	0.1
Profit for the year	339.1	293.6
Earnings per share		
Basic	82.3p	68.9p
Diluted	81.7p	68.4p
Reconciliation of adjusted profit before taxation:	£m	£m
Profit before taxation	440.6	412.6
Adjusting items:		
Adjusting operating items	0.9	56.3
Adjusting finance items	1.7	2.0
Adjusted profit before taxation – non-GAAP measure	443.2	470.9
Adjusted earnings per share – non-GAAP measure		
Basic	82.7p	82.8p
Diluted	82.1p	82.1p
Dividends per share		
Interim	11.0p	11.0p
Proposed final (not recognized as a liability at 30 March/31 March)	31.5p	30.3

Notes

- The income statement follows a standard pro-forma.
- It is designed to allow a user to assess the performance of the entity over the period of account.
- It is only a relatively recent phenomenon that companies are forced to disclose more than their revenue and profit before tax.
- Key line items include: revenue, gross profit, operating profit (otherwise known as profit before interest and tax [PBIT] or earnings before interest and tax [EBIT]) and profit for the year (otherwise known as retained profit or net income).

The statement of financial position

Figure 1.7   Burberry's Statement of Financial Position (balance sheet)

	As at 30 March 2019 £m	As at 31 March 2018 £m
ASSETS		
Non-current assets		
Intangible assets	221.0	180.1
Property, plant and equipment	306.9	313.6
Investment properties	2.5	2.6
Deferred tax assets	123.1	115.5
Trade and other receivables	70.1	69.2
Derivative financial assets	–	0.3
	723.6	681.3
Current assets		
Inventories	465.1	411.8
Trade and other receivables	251.1	206.3
Derivative financial assets	3.0	1.6
Income tax receivables	14.9	6.7
Cash and cash equivalents	874.5	915.3
	1,608.6	1,541.7
Total assets	2,332.2	2,223.0
LIABILITIES		
Non-current liabilities		
Trade and other payables	(176.5)	(168.1)
Deferred tax liabilities	(3.4)	(4.2)
Derivative financial liabilities	(0.1)	(0.1)
Retirement benefit obligations	(1.4)	(0.9)
Provisions for other liabilities and charges	(50.7)	(71.4)
	(232.1)	(244.7)

(Continued)

Figure 1.7   *(Continued)*

	As at 30 March 2019 £m	As at 31 March 2018 £m
Current liabilities		
Bank overdrafts	(37.2)	(23.2)
Derivative financial liabilities	(5.5)	(3.8)
Trade and other payables	(525.7)	(460.9)
Provisions for other liabilities and charges	(34.6)	(32.1)
Income tax liabilities	(37.1)	(32.9)
	(640.1)	(552.9)
Total liabilities	(872.2)	(797.6)
Net assets	1,460.0	1,425.4
EQUITY		
Capital and reserves attributable to owners of the Company		
Ordinary share capital	0.2	0.2
Share premium account	216.9	214.6
Capital reserve	41.1	41.1
Hedging reserve	3.5	3.8
Foreign currency translation reserve	227.7	214.7
Retained earnings	965.6	946.1
Equity attributable to owners of the Company	1,455.0	1,420.5
Non-controlling interest in equity	5.0	4.9
Total equity	1,460.0	1,425.4

Notes

- The statement of financial position is commonly referred to by its previous title, the balance sheet. You will notice that this balance sheet *balances*: net assets are £1,460 million and the total equity is also £1,460 million (ie net assets equals total equity). Interestingly, however, the balance sheet was named thus because it is a rephrasing of the 'list of balances'.

- It has been said that the statement of financial position is like a financial photograph. It is a snapshot of an entity's position at a certain point in time capturing summarized details of assets and liabilities. In modern terminology, it might be more appropriate to refer to it as a 'selfie'!

- Though there are several formats permitted under financial reporting regulations, the above format is the most common in the UK.

- The statement is structured in order of liquidity, ie how quickly the asset or liability will be translated into cash.

The statement of cash flows

Figure 1.8   Burberry's Statement of Cash Flows

	52 weeks to 30 March 2019 £m	Year to 31 March 2018 £m
Cash flows from operating activities		
Operating profit	437.2	410.3
Depreciation	87.2	105.8
Amortization	28.6	25.5
Net impairment of intangible assets	3.9	6.5
Net impairment of property, plant and equipment	7.9	10.7
Loss on disposal of property, plant and equipment and intangible assets	1.2	2.7
Gain on disposal of Beauty operations	(6.9)	(5.2)
Gain on derivative instruments	(2.4)	(3.5)
Charge in respect of employee share incentive schemes	15.7	17.1
Receipt from settlement of equity swap contracts	2.5	0.5
(Increase)/decrease in inventories	(59.3)	37.2
(Increase)/decrease in receivables	(54.6)	68.1
Increase in payables and provisions	54.9	115.5
Cash generated from operating activities	515.9	791.2
Interest received	8.1	7.2
Interest paid	(1.8)	(1.6)
Taxation paid	(110.8)	(118.4)
Net cash generated from operating activities	411.4	678.4
Cash flows from investing activities		
Purchase of property, plant and equipment	(62.6)	(57.5)
Purchase of intangible assets	(48.0)	(48.5)
Proceeds from disposal of Beauty operations, net of cash costs paid	0.6	61.1
Acquisition of subsidiary	(14.5)	–
Net cash outflows from investing activities	(124.5)	(44.9)
Cash flows from financing activities		
Dividends paid in the year	(171.1)	(169.4)
Payment to non-controlling interest	(11.1)	(3.0)
Issue of ordinary share capital	2.3	3.2
Purchase of own shares through share buy-back	(150.7)	(355.0)
Purchase of own shares by ESOP trusts	(12.8)	(11.9)

(Continued)

Figure 1.8 *(Continued)*

	52 weeks to 30 March 2019 £m	Year to 31 March 2018 £m
Net cash outflow from financing activities	(343.4)	(536.1)
Net (decrease)/increase in cash and cash equivalents	(56.5)	97.4
Effect of exchange rate changes	1.7	(14.5)
Cash and cash equivalents at beginning of year	892.1	809.2
Cash and cash equivalents at end of year	837.3	892.1
	As at 30 March 2019 £m	As at 31 March 2018
Cash and cash equivalents as per the Balance Sheet	874.5	915.3
Bank overdrafts	(37.2)	(23.2)
Net cash	837.3	892.1

Notes

- The format of the statement of cash flows is governed by its own financial reporting standard – International Accounting Standard 7 *Statement of Cash Flows*.

- Cash generated/spent is categorized between three sections: operating activities; investing activities; and financing activities. The cash flow generated from operating activities is increasingly being used by analysts as a measure of performance, alongside traditional income statement measures.

Expert view 1.7: The financial year-end

Organizations can set their year-end to whatever date they prefer. There are many determinants including: when the financial director/controller is least busy (for example, a toy manufacturer would look to avoid the busiest times of the year, eg Christmas), when asset values are maximized (for example, inversely it is possible that a toy manufacturer might call their year-end around traditional gift-giving periods when their inventories are most valuable, eg Christmas), at a time when it is most convenient for your external accountant (possibly reducing your bill slightly).

Exercises: now attempt Exercise 1.5 on page 43

The articulation of the financial statements

Though this might seem a little confusing to get your head around at first, the following illustration (Figure 1.9) shows how the financial statements fit together. Feel free to refer back to this as you're working through some of the exercises in Chapters 2, 3 and 4.

Figure 1.9   How the financial statements fit together

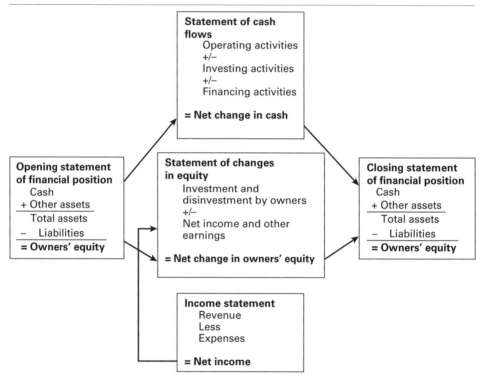

A brief guide to some key problems and issues with financial statements

We do not want to finish this chapter on a negative note, but it seems timely to consider some of the problems with financial statements. You might think that some of these are more important than others and you'd be right. We will reflect on some of these over the next few chapters but, for the time being, a summary is sufficient:

● Trade-offs between the qualitative characteristics, especially between the enhancing characteristics. A position might be inherently complex, therefore making it less verifiable, comparable and understandable.

- Owing to the nature of the financial reporting and auditing process, financial statements generally suffer from not providing timely information. The information contained therein is based on past transactions and when it is published, it will relate to a period that has already passed. This is why many argue that the annual report is simply a regulatory document which carries confirmatory value rather than a positive economic one.

- The cost–benefit issue. In other words, at what stage do the reporting requirements become overly complex and burdensome? Is there a point where the costs of preparation outweigh the benefits of the information produced?

- There is a wide range of users and the potential for conflict between them is worrisome. The IASB has promoted the idea that current and potential investors are the primary user group; however, the annual report and financial statements has not significantly altered to reflect this. It has been found that the participation of investors in the standard-setting due process has been extremely limited. Therefore, if an annual report's first audience is supposed to be the investor community, then why do they not get more involved?

- The conflict between accounting firms' varied interests means that their participation in the standard-setting process and in the audit, preparation and presentation of financial statements leads to potential difficulties. They must take decisions which potentially create disunity between their varying interest concerns, namely their own self-interest, the public interest, client interests and the institutional interest.

- Standard-setting is a complex process and full agreement is unlikely to be reached given the conflicting and competing interests of the varied stakeholder groups.

- Despite the benefits inherent in the notion, is international accounting an aspiration rather than an achievable reality?

- Selecting appropriate recognition and measurement methods will vary dependent upon the class of asset (liability) and the information available. For example, derivative financial instruments (eg forward exchange contracts, options, swaps) cost little to purchase but have the potential to expose entities to material obligations. Which is a preferable measurement method? Mark-to-market or historic cost?

Exercises: now attempt Exercise 1.6 on page 44

COMPREHENSION QUESTIONS

1 What are the two main forms of accounting? List the principal differences between the types of information that practitioners of each discipline produce.

2 What is meant by the terms trade receivables and trade payables?

3 Potential and current investors are the primary users of financial statements but there are others. List four different users aside from investors and explain their information needs.

4 List the two fundamental qualitative characteristics of financial reporting and provide a brief description of both.

5 List the four enhancing qualitative characteristics of financial reporting and provide a brief description of each.

6 Who are the IASB and what is their role within the IFRS Foundation and standard-setting framework?

7 There are several advantages to incorporating your business, but can you list some of the commonly perceived disadvantages?

8 Define the three terms: asset; liability; and equity.

Answers available at **www.koganpage.com/afm3**

Exercises

Answers available at **www.koganpage.com/afm3**

Exercise 1.1: A comparison between financial and management accounting

Reflect on the supplementary questions raised in Worked Example 1.1. Do you think it is straightforward to ascertain accurate and reliable answers? Try to write in jargon-free terms an example of the information that might be prepared by a financial accountant versus a management accountant.

Exercise 1.2: Identifying the users of financial reports

Using the information presented in Figure 1.1, list THREE key user groups for each of the following organizations and briefly explain what each group might hope to ascertain from the publicly available financial information prepared by the entity:

(a) Compartmentalized Inc is a company that specializes in making self-fold boxes for storage and transportation purposes. The entity was founded in 1923. It has grown in a slow but structured and organic fashion from a family-run business with four staff to an international organization generating revenues of $85 million with a workforce of over 400 people. The company has no debt and is still family owned.

(b) Gronk plc is a ferry company boasting Europe's second-largest fleet. The company provides services to almost every major port on the continent. During the last five years, the company has acquired four competitors who were in financial distress and facing bankruptcy. This has led to high levels of borrowing.

(c) Worldwide Water is a not-for-profit charitable organization. Their objective is to provide safe drinking water across Zambia.

Exercise 1.3

Can you provide a suggestion for each of the following, briefly explaining your rationale:

(i) A balance which could be material owing to its magnitude?

(ii) A balance which could be material owing to its nature?

(iii) A balance which could be material owing to its context?

Exercise 1.4

The internationalization of financial reporting has attracted significant attention. There are many in favour and, equally, many opposed. The United States (US), for example, has continued to use US Generally Accepted Accounting Principles (GAAP) as opposed to adopting international standards.

(a) Briefly list the key advantages of international financial reporting harmonization.

(b) Briefly outline what you think the key barriers to international reporting adoption might be.

Exercise 1.5

This is a simple exercise to familiarize you with the kind of information that is presented in the financial statements. Examine the three primary statements presented above to discover the following information:

(a) What is the value of Burberry plc's property, plant and equipment for the year ended 31 March 2019?

(b) What is the value of its amounts owing to trade and other payables for the year ended 31 March 2019? (Note: Burberry plc has long-term and short-term trade and other payables.)

(c) How much cash and cash equivalents did Burberry plc hold at the end of the most recent financial year?

(d) How much revenue did Burberry plc generate during the year to 31 March 2019?

(e) What was the operating profit for Burberry plc during the years to 31 March 2018 and 2019?

(f) What was the sum of current assets at 31 March 2019? And, as far as possible, can you provide a breakdown of this balance?

(g) How much cash did Burberry plc generate through operating activities during 31 March 2019?

Exercise 1.6

The IASB acknowledges within the Conceptual Framework that general-purpose financial reports cannot provide all the information that users may need to make economic decisions. They suggest that users will need to consider pertinent information from other sources as well.

(a) Briefly outline what you feel the financial statements cannot tell an external user.

(b) List examples of further information (ie beyond the annual report and financial statements) which a potential investor would require before making an investment (or disinvestment) decision.

References

Burberry plc (2019) [accessed 18 February 2020] Burberry Annual Report 2015/2016 [Online] www.burberryplc.com/en/investors/results-reports.html_Reports/2016/5-annual_report_2015_16/Report_burberry_annual_report_2015-16.pdf (archived at https://perma.cc/Q239-A77J)

International Federation of Accountants (2011) A Proposed Definition of 'Professional Accountant', Agenda Paper 7-B

Jones, M (2011) *Creative Accounting, Fraud and International Accounting Scandals,*

John Wiley & Sons Ltd, Chichester, UK

Kaplan, R S (2011) Accounting scholarship that advances professional knowledge and practice, *The Accounting Review*, **86** (2), pp 367–83

Pacioli, L (1497) *Summa de arithmetica, geometria, proportioni et proportionalita*, Venice, Italy

Sangster, A (2016) The genesis of double entry bookkeeping, *The Accounting Review*, **91**(1), pp 299–315.

Supplementary reading

Carnegie, G D and Napier, C J (2010) Traditional accountants and business professionals: portraying the accounting profession after Enron, *Accounting, Organizations and Society*, **35** (3), pp 360–76

DeCoster, D T and Rhode, J G (1971) The accountant's stereotype: real or imagined, deserved or unwarranted, *Accounting Review*, **46**, pp 651–64

International Accounting Standards Board (2010) The Conceptual Framework for Financial Reporting 2010, IFRS Foundation Publications Department, London

Accounting concepts and systems

02

OBJECTIVE

We use this chapter to introduce the types of financial accounting information you will encounter in your daily managerial lives. We provide a basic guide to bookkeeping and outline how to prepare a straightforward set of financial statements. Some key measurement rules and accounting concepts are also explained.

LEARNING OUTCOMES

After studying this chapter, the reader will be able to:

- Describe the key elements of an accounting system.
- Identify the different types of accounting adjustment.
- Assess the impact of accounting adjustments on reported results.
- Prepare basic primary financial statements.

KEY TOPICS COVERED

- What accounting systems record, and how.
- Cash-based accounting, accruals and other accounting adjustments.
- The impact of accounting adjustments on the statement of financial position and on profit.
- Practical issues of adjustment, for example dealing with tangible non-current assets.

MANAGEMENT ISSUES

This chapter will deal specifically with the management skills of understanding and assessing the impact of accounting adjustments on the reported results.

Introduction

During this chapter we try to show you why financial statements are important, describe their contents and show you how to prepare a straightforward set. Appendix A deals with double-entry bookkeeping and works through the same examples using this method.

Even though the material presented in this chapter represents only the tip of the iceberg in relation to financial reporting, it is extremely helpful to know how the various items of information are combined to become financial statements. In turn, the series of exercises contained herein should show you that the quality, complexity and context are crucial to understanding a firm's position and performance.

This chapter also introduces some key accounting concepts and conventions. These show that interpreting – and to an extent, preparing – financial statements can be as much an art as a science. This chapter also highlights how accounting procedures and policies can have an impact on reported results. As managers, you need to be aware that accounting is not a system of rigid or fixed rules where output is predefined. Rather, there is flexibility within the regulations which allows scope for presentational, recognition, measurement and disclosure differences.

What is the purpose of the financial statements?

We hope that you will agree that an attempt to identify the purpose of the financial statements is the most obvious starting point for this chapter. To this end, towards the end of the previous chapter we showed you Burberry plc's financial statements. We hope that you have also gone away and looked at a number of other companies' annual reports. Annual reports are often more interesting if you have a special interest in them and/or are predisposed to their activities, products or services. For Burberry plc, we showed you three primary financial statements: the statement of comprehensive income (income statement); the statement of financial position (balance sheet); and the statement of cash flows. This chapter will focus on these and walk you through the double-entry bookkeeping process which is used for accounting purposes. To illustrate, we start with a few basic transactions around buying and selling goods.

Statement of comprehensive income (income statement)

The income statement shows how much profit the business has made during a specific period of time. We told you that the 'period of account' is normally a year, but large organizations are often required to produce interim statements, eg quarterly.

The layout of the income statement will depend on the entity, but there are a selection of headings which are typical, including:

- **Gross profit**: A company generates revenue by undertaking its normal operating activity, eg selling goods and/or services. The costs that directly relate to selling these goods are called 'cost of goods sold' (or 'cost of sales'). The net of revenue and cost of sales gives the gross profit figure.

  The gross profit is stated before the deduction of indirect expenses – such as operating expenses, finance costs or taxation – and before adding any 'other' income generated, not arising from the normal operating activity – such as finance income.

- **Operating profit**: Business expenses which are not directly incurred in relation to the generation of revenue are deducted after the gross profit line. These indirect costs might include items such as rental costs, business rates, heating and lighting costs, administrative expenses, wages and salaries, depreciation and so forth.

  Finance income and/or costs (which include interest receivable/payable) and taxation are deducted from the operating profit, which is why the operating profit is sometimes referred to as profit before interest and tax (PBIT) or earnings before interest and tax (EBIT).

- **Profit for the year (period)**: The profit for the year is arrived at by deducting all other expenses from the operating profit. This total is transferred to the statement of financial position on a rolling basis each year. The balance on this account accumulates under the heading 'Retained earnings'.

Figure 2.1 shows an income statement for a fictional entity – Malambo Inc. – for illustration purposes.

Expert view 2.1: Comprehensive income

The statement of comprehensive income is actually subdivided into two parts. The top part is the 'income statement' and the bottom part is the section that captures the 'comprehensive income'. As a basic rule of thumb, the income statement shows an entity's realized gains and losses whereas the statement of comprehensive income as a whole identifies those which are both realized and unrealized. Examples of unrealized balances include gains and losses arising from issues such as revaluing property to its open market value, cash-flow hedging gains and losses, and foreign exchange translation gains and losses.

Online content

Listed companies such as Burberry plc are subject to greater levels of scrutiny and regulation. We have provided a couple of examples (available online) which show that there is still freedom to present information differently. Go to **www.koganpage.com/afm3**

Figure 2.1   Malambo Inc

Malambo Inc. is a fictional entity. The example exists simply to illustrate the various components of an income statement. You will note that the company generates revenue of $900,000, gross profit of $600,000, operating profit (PBIT) of $366,000 and profit for the year of $267,000. The statement includes the organization's name, the statement's title and the period covered.

Malambo Inc.
Income statement
For the year ended 30 September 2020

	$
Revenue	900,000
Cost of sales	300,000
Gross profit	600,000
Operating expenses:	
Heat and light	25,000
Rent and rates	50,000
Motor running costs	8,000
Wages and salaries	100,000
Insurances	40,000
Postage, packaging and stationery	4,000

Depreciation	6,000
Amortization	1,000
Operating profit	366,000
Finance income	5,000
Finance costs	14,000
Profit before taxation	357,000
Taxation	90,000
Profit for the year	267,000

In order to engage with this process, we would recommend that you locate the financial statements of a company whose goods, services or products you know and like (or dislike, if you prefer). Archived annual reports (in the US, 10-Ks) can be easily traced through the entity's website (often through the investor relations link). You can also search for 'Company X annual report' and this will often link you directly to the relevant pdf. Summarized statements are also available through other platforms, such as Yahoo Finance or Google Finance. If you feel a connection with a company or organization through some form of personal involvement, then you are more able to contextualize – and hence, make sense of – the information you are presented with.

The statement of financial position (balance sheet)

The statement of financial position (commonly referred to as the balance sheet) is akin to a financial photograph: a snapshot of the current worth of an organization at one moment in time.

Financial statements are prepared according to one golden rule, as follows:

- Every **debit** entry in the ledger accounts must be matched by a corresponding **credit** entry.

And nowhere is this rule more visible or understandable than in the statement of financial position. The **accounting equation** is as follows:

- Assets – Liabilities = Capital (shareholders' funds).

Both assets and liabilities are categorized as either current (due within one year) or non-current (due in more than one year). Below is a brief description of each category and a few examples:

- **Non-current assets** are bought with the intention to use them to generate revenue over a number of years. There are two forms of non-current assets – tangible and intangible. The former are those which it is possible to touch, see and feel. Intangible assets are assets that have a realizable market value despite not having a physical presence. The rules governing the capitalization (ie bringing onto the statement of financial position as an asset) of intangible assets are quite strict. Analysts typically reassess the value of an entity's intangible assets, as they are commonly a key driver of the difference between market value (ie the share price) and book value (ie the notion of net worth shown at the foot of the statement of financial position).

  - Examples of tangible non-current assets include: property (land and buildings), plant, equipment, fixtures, fittings, motor vehicles and so forth.

  - Examples of intangible non-current assets include: (purchased) goodwill, patents, royalties, computer software and so forth.

- **Current assets** are expected to be sold or converted into another form within one year.

  - Examples include: inventories, trade receivables, cash held in hand or at bank, cash equivalents, prepayments.

- **Non-current liabilities** are amounts owed by the business which it is not obligated to repay within the next 12 months.

  - Examples include: bank loans, mortgages, debentures, loan stock, provisions and so forth.

- **Current liabilities** are obligations which need to be settled within the next 12 months.

  - Examples include: bank overdraft, short-term borrowings, trade payables, taxation owed and so forth.

Online content

We have provided a couple of examples (available online at: **www.koganpage.com/ afm3**) which show some complex entities' statements of financial position to mirror the income statements provided. As before, we recommend that you search for brands and companies you are acquainted with and have a look at their annual reports.

The statement of cash flows

The statement of cash flows shows whether we have earned or spent cash (and cash equivalents) during the year. The focus of the statement of cash flows is, as the name suggests, cash inflows versus cash outflows. The statement is divided between three activities: operating; investing; and financing.

Expert view 2.2: Preparing a statement of cash flows

Students of financial accounting commonly find this the most difficult of the three primary statements to prepare. This is surprising because you often know the answer before you start – if you know the opening and closing cash position (available from the statement of financial position or from your books and records), then preparing the statement of cash flows is simply a reconciliation exercise where you organize movements in balances and allocate to appropriate categories (ie decide whether they are operating, investing or financing).

Note that the income statement and balance sheet are prepared on an **accruals basis** whereas this statement is prepared on a **cash basis**. This is important because organizations can be profitable (or loss-making) but be losing (or generating) cash. A recent example is Amazon Inc. The firm has huge cash inflows from operating activities but small – often negative – net income. We will explain this in more detail later. Ultimately, the accounting profits and the cash profits will reconcile, but the chances of them being identical year to year are negligible.

Discussion point

Do you think the 'cash flow from operations' figure disclosed in the statement of cash flows is more, less or equally important as the 'net profit' figure disclosed in the income statement?

The key differences between profits on an accruals basis versus those measured on a cash basis relate to:

- **Timing differences.** For example, goods might be sold to an entity, delivered immediately and an invoice for payment raised at the same time. However, if you grant a credit period then you should expect your customers to take advantage of it (after all, this is essentially an interest-free loan for them). Therefore, the revenue can be booked to the income statement as the transaction took place during the period, but if the cash has not been received by the end of the period then it will show as a balance being owed to you. In other words, the cash follows the sale.

- **Accounting estimates**. It is necessary for accountants to make accounting estimates during the preparation of the financial statements. One example is the accounting for depreciation against tangible non-current assets. Depreciation acts as a proxy for the costs related to wear and tear of an asset over time, so assets classified as non-current must be written off to the income statement as their revenue-generating potential is consumed (more on this later). In cash terms, however, the payment will often occur up-front.

- **Accounting transactions that bypass the income statement**. For example, capital expenditure, sale of share capital, repayments of loans and so forth.

- **Changes in the working capital position**. For example, an increase in inventories means that an entity has invested cash in inventories, which it hopes to translate back into cash through the sale of these goods. Figure 2.2 shows the working capital cycle and reveals how the process of investment and re-investment in working capital makes the management of short-term resources crucial. It also shows the importance to a business of focusing on the cash cycle.

Expert view 2.3: Financial reporting regulation

Financial reporting is governed by many regulations, foremost of which are the International Financial Reporting Standards (IFRS). The predecessor to the IASB was called the International Accounting Standards Committee (IASC). This body released International Accounting Standards (IAS). Though IASs are continuously being developed and refined, it is intended that they will all be replaced by IFRSs. This exercise is far from being complete and many still exist. Therefore, you will commonly see references to IAS as well as IFRS. For a full list see Appendix B.

We will come back to this idea again in later chapters but, for the time being, it is worth noting that the concept of cash is important in both financial and management accounting. Cash is often described as the 'lifeblood' of the business because without cash, a business cannot expect to survive for long.

Figure 2.2 illustrates how a traditional manufacturing business operates while also serving to highlight the importance of cash to the process. While a company holds inventories or they are owed money, the cash balance is reduced. This can be offset by owing others money (payables), but if management extend their credit

Figure 2.2   Working capital cycle

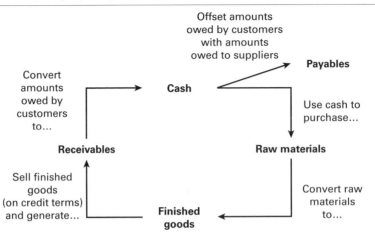

terms too far, beware the consequences. This is, of course, an over-simplification but it does highlight the importance of efficiency.

Discussion point

There are two important components to generating a high return on assets: profitability and efficiency. Thinking about balances such as inventories, trade receivables or trade payables, can you describe why and how there might be a trade-off between these profitability and efficiency components?

When preparing a statement of cash flows, you will notice that an increase in a current asset (eg inventories) will lead to a decrease in cash. We hope that Figure 2.2 makes it obvious to see why.

Exercises: now attempt Exercise 2.1 on page 84

Preparing a set of financial statements

Even though it may never be necessary for you to be called upon to prepare a full and detailed set of financial statements, an understanding of the basics is essential to any interpretative study of financial information. During this section, our aim is to cover only the basic, but most valuable, tenets.

Double-entry bookkeeping: an introduction

Double-entry bookkeeping is a system adopted by accountants to help us record financial transactions. The underpinning principle is that every debit entry must have an equal and opposite credit entry. Recognizing amounts in a timely and structured manner has helped owners and managers organize their day-to-day business since records began. Today, there are many computerized bookkeeping packages which are extremely useful in assisting accounting staff to produce key reports. These accounting packages, however, do not teach you accounting *per se*; they just simplify the process of data entry.

Expert view 2.4: Mastering the basics of financial accounting

Financial accounting should be seen as a building-block exercise. You should strive to master the skills and knowledge gathered at each stage before moving on to the next. There is one caveat, and this relates to double-entry bookkeeping. Many accountants talk of a 'eureka' or a 'light bulb' moment. What they mean is that one day they woke up and found that double-entry bookkeeping simply makes sense! Thinking logically always helps. Every time you engage in a financial transaction, imagine the double-entry bookkeeping system at work. For example, you buy a newspaper from the shop. You have exchanged your money for an asset of (deemed) equivalent worth.

WORKED EXAMPLE 2.1 Mobius (1)

Let us suppose that you wish to start your own business, Mobius Inc. The following transactions shown in examples Mobius (1) to Mobius (3) represent the first week of trading for the entity.

On day 1, you opt to put financial distance between you and the trading entity and transfer $1,000 from your personal bank account to a bank account you hold in the name of the new enterprise – Mobius Inc.

Assuming that the new business is a separate legal entity, how does this affect the accounting equation?

Assets	–	Liabilities	=	Shareholders' funds (ie your injection of capital)
$1,000	–	$0	=	$1,000

NOTE As you can see, the accounting equation captures both sides of the transaction and only by making the entry twice does the equation (and, by extension, the statement of financial position) balance.

Continuing this exercise...

On day 2, you borrow $500 from a friend to provide further financial help to your business. How does this impact on the accounting equation?

$$\text{Assets} \quad - \quad \text{Liabilities} \quad = \quad \text{Capital}$$
$$\$1,500 \quad - \quad \$500 \quad\quad = \quad \$1,000$$

NOTE The effect of the financial transaction is to increase assets by $500 as the amount borrowed from your friend would be deposited in the current account of the business. The liabilities would increase by $500. This represents the new loan the business has taken on. The capital that you invested has neither increased nor diminished in the process of this transaction and therefore remains at $1,000. This, of course, means that your accounting equation continues to balance.

The transactions above illustrate that if an adjustment is made to one side of the equation, you **must** make an identical adjustment **either** to the other side of the equation **or** to the same side.

Exercise 2.2: Accounting equation adjustments

Continuing the worked example above, make the necessary adjustments for the following transactions:

(a) On day 3, Mobius Inc invests $500 of cash by acquiring a new computer.

(b) On day 4, Mobius Inc buys some raw materials worth $400 and holds them as inventories. The cash required to settle the invoices related to these purchases does not need to be found for 10 days as these are the credit terms offered by the supplier.

The transactions above relate exclusively to the statement of financial position. They only require us to make changes to assets, liabilities and equity with no profit implications. This is overly simplistic, therefore these next worked-through adjustments provide the opportunity to see how the accounting equation changes as an entity trades.

WORKED EXAMPLE 2.2 Mobius (2) – trading activities

On day 5, Mobius Inc uses the raw materials purchased the previous day to produce 30 units of finished goods stock.

On day 6, half of these are sold for $50 per unit. Cash is received immediately for five of those sold. The remainder were sold to customers on 10-day credit terms.

Solution

The transfer between raw materials and finished goods inventories has no impact on the accounting equation (in reality it is difficult to imagine that no value is added to the product [eg extra materials, direct labour], but for simplicity's sake, let us assume that this is the case). We would simply transfer $400 from one category of current assets to another – raw materials inventory to finished goods inventory. Therefore, at this stage, the accounting equation remains unchanged, as follows:

$$\text{Assets} \quad - \quad \text{Liabilities} \quad = \quad \text{Shareholders' funds}$$
$$\$1,900 \quad - \quad \$900 \quad = \quad \$1,000$$

However, the sale of the product does generate a change in the entity's net worth. Ultimately, most organizations hold as their corporate objective the maximization of shareholder wealth and it is unsurprising that goods are bought and subsequently every effort is made to sell them for a profit. In this case, the goods cost $400 and were transformed into 30 saleable units of inventory, of which half were sold for $50 per unit. Five were paid for immediately while 10 have been sold under 10-day credit terms. Therefore, the changes to the accounting equation that we will record are as follows (see Table 2.1):

(i) Revenue generated: 15 units * $50 = $750

(ii) Of which, cash collected was 5 * $50 = $250 and amounts owed by customers was 10 units * $50 = $500

(iii) The cost of the inventory used to generate these sales was $200.

Table 2.1

Assets	$	Liabilities	$	Capital	$
Opening balance	1,900	Opening balance	900	Opening balance	1,000
				Contribution to retained earnings:	
ii) Cash collected	250			i) Revenue	750
ii) Owed by customers	500				
iii) Inventories consumed	(200)			iii) Cost of sales	(200)
Closing balance	**2,450**		**900**		**1,550**

The effect on assets and liabilities is straightforward. Assets increase due to the extra amount of cash held and the amount of money owed by customers. Liabilities remain unchanged.

But why has the level of shareholders' funds changed? The business has generated $550 of profit ($750 of revenue less $200 of inventories consumed). These retained earnings are added to the shareholders' funds and remain there until such time as they are distributed.

WORKED EXAMPLE 2.3 Mobius (3) – the financial statements [week 1]

Preparing complex financial statements at this stage of your accounting learning is neither necessary nor desirable. However, it is possible to translate the information we have into a basic set of summarized financial statements:

Mobius Inc	
Summarized Statement of Financial Position	
As at the end of week 1	**$**
Assets	
Non-current assets	
Computer (500 [3])	500
Current assets	
Cash at bank (1,000 [1] + 500 [2] – 500 [3] + 250 [5c])	1,250
Inventories	
Raw materials (400 [4] – 400 [5a])	0
Finished goods (400 [5a] – 200 [5b])	200
Trade receivables – amounts due from customers (500 [5c])	500
Liabilities	
Loan from friend (500 [2])	(500)
Trade payables – amounts owed to supplier (400 [4])	(400)
Net assets	**1,550**
Shareholders' funds (capital and reserves)	
Capital (1,000 [1])	1,000
Retained profits (550 [transferred from income statement])	550
Shareholders' funds	**1,550**

Mobius Inc	
Summarized Income Statement	
For the period ended DD/MM/YYYY (week 1)	**$**
Revenue (750 [5c])	750
Cost of sales (200 [5b])	(200)
Profit	**550***
* Transfer to statement of financial position at the end of the period of account	

NOTE transaction numbers are shown in square brackets to help identify the matching accounting entry. You will notice that after each transaction is entered, the statement of financial position could be closed off and would balance, ie the top half would equal the bottom half.

Expert view 2.5: Revenue and expenses

The IASB would prefer we thought of gains and losses arising as a result of assets
and liabilities increasing and decreasing. However, it is probably more common
for non-accountants to think of profits as being generated when revenue exceeds
expenses.

Revenue typically relates to the income an organization generates by selling
goods and services.

Expenses (costs) are incurred in the process of generating revenue.

At the end of the period of account, an income statement is reset to zero because this
statement reports **'for the period ended'**, whereas the statement of financial position
shows the position of the entity **'as at the period ended'**.

Therefore, let us assume that the above transactions represent Mobius Inc's position
as at the end of the first week of trading and the business is about to begin the second
week. The income statement balances would be reset to zero and the profit of $550 taken
to the statement of financial position where it will be retained until it is used (consumed by
losses or distributed).

The income statement: cost of sales working

The cost of sales working applies the accruals concept to match the expense to the
period in which it is incurred. The cost of sales is sometimes referred to as 'the cost of
goods sold'. In other words, we are matching the units of product sold to the direct
cost of purchasing (producing) those units. The basic working is as follows:

Cost of sales	
Opening inventories	x
Purchases	x
(Closing inventories)	(x)
	x

Exercises: now attempt Exercise 2.3 on page 84

WORKED EXAMPLE 2.4   Mobius (4) – the financial statements
continued

Now that we have a statement of financial position as at the end of week 1, we can adjust straight to the face of the statements and thus monitor how the business's net worth and profitability levels change during the second week of trading, as shown in Table 2.2.

Remember: bookkeeping is a dual-aspect method and you will need to post every transaction twice for the statement of financial position to balance.

Table 2.2

Day of trading	
8	• The business acquired raw materials valued at $800.
	• Invoices need to be paid within 10 days.
9	• All the raw materials were converted into 60 units of finished goods inventories.
10	• The company received a utilities bill for $200 which it paid immediately out of cash. *Note: assume this charge relates exclusively to this period of account.*
11	• Mobius Inc sold 35 units of inventories for $60 per unit. Cash was received for 20 of these units and the remainder were offered to customers on 10-day credit terms.
12	• Mobius Inc bought a printer/scanner for $100.
	• Mobius Inc bought some stationery including paper and envelopes for $50.
13	• Mobius Inc received $500 from customers who had bought goods on credit terms.
14	• Amounts invoiced by suppliers during week 1 of $400 were paid.
	• Mobius Inc paid a web designer $750 to develop an online presence for the business.

Solution

The exercise has been completed in order of appearance in the text above. All transactions have been double-entered. In the solution below, each journal entry (adjustment) has been separately numbered so that you can trace each one through. For example, journal entry 1 increases raw materials by $800 and increases trade suppliers by $800. Note also that the opening balances from week 1 have simply been brought forward and therefore have no transaction number.

Mobius Inc
Summarized Statement of Financial Position
As at the end of week 2

Assets
Non-current assets

Computer (500)	500.00
Printer/scanner (100 [5])	100.00

Current assets

Cash at bank (1,250 – 200 [3] + 1,200 [4] – 100 [5] – 50 [6] + 500 [7] – 400 [8] – 750 [9])	1,450.00
Inventories	
Raw materials (0 + 800 [1] – 800 [2])	0.00
Finished goods (200 + 800 [2] – 466.67 [4])	533.33
Trade receivables – amounts owed by customers (500 + 900 [4] – 500 [7])	900.00

Liabilities

Loan from friend (500)	(500.00)
Trade payables – amounts owed to suppliers (400 + 800 [1] – 400 [8])	(800.00)
Net assets	2,183.33

Shareholders' funds (capital and reserves)

Capital (1,000)	1,000.00
Retained profits	
Brought forward	550.00
Profit generated during week 2	633.33
Shareholders' funds	2,183.33

Mobius Inc
Summarized Income Statement
For the period ended DD/MM/YYYY (week 2)

Revenue (2,100 [4])	2,100.00
Cost of sales (466.67 [4])	(466.67)
Gross profit	1,633.33
Expenses:	
Utilities (200 [3])	(200.00)
Printing, postage and stationery (50 [6])	(50.00)
Web development costs (750 [9])	(750.00)
Profit	633.33

Exercises: now attempt Exercise 2.4 on page 85

Underlying concepts: measurement rules and fundamental accounting concepts

Let's take a short break from these preparation exercises and turn our attention to some measurement rules and underlying concepts. You'll appreciate that not everything is as easy to account for as, say, exchanging cash for a newspaper. The above exercises develop a series of simple transactions during which we have deliberately minimized your exposure to recognition, measurement and presentation problems. The following section outlines some financial reporting complexity and the guidelines that have developed to deal with them.

Following this, we will pick up the case of Mobius Inc again and work through some more preparation exercises to illustrate how these concepts might be dealt with through numbers rather than text.

Measurement rules

There are some basic measurement rules which are applied in financial accounting. These rules explain *how* balances are recorded in the financial statements. Owing to the importance of the measurement basis used for the values recorded in the financial statements, it is unsurprising that few areas have attracted so much academic and professional commentary. The following are considered to be key:

- historical cost accounting;
- current cost accounting;
- mixed measurement model;
- money measurement concept;
- business entity concept.

Online content

More information is provided about these measurement rules online at: **www.koganpage.com/afm3**

Fundamental accounting concepts

There are a number of fundamental accounting concepts which are enforced through regulation. The following concepts are relevant:

- accruals concept;

- going concern;

- prudence;

- disaggregation;

- materiality.

A brief review of each follows.

Accruals concept

The accruals concept is often referred to as the matching concept or matching rule. Indeed, the reference to 'matching' is a simpler way to envisage its operation (even if it does not strictly hold in some domestic generally accepted accounting principles [GAAP]). The accruals concept states that revenues, profits and the associated costs should be matched to the same period's income statement.

,There are many everyday instances where a transaction would be recorded in different accounting periods dependent upon whether you employed an accruals accounting system or a cash accounting one. For example, electricity bills are commonly issued and paid in arrears. Imagine that you have 11 monthly invoices related to your electricity costs for the year ending 31 December and are awaiting the 12th and final invoice. You will need to accrue for the expense because the electricity was being consumed during the period of account. You will have to bring the cost into this period's income statement and provide for it by setting up a corresponding liability in the statement of financial position.

Extending this example, it is possible that you might need to estimate the level of consumption for the 12th month because the electricity company hasn't issued their invoice before your accounts finalization date. It is easy to see how accruals accounting can lead to increased subjectivity because sometimes it is necessary to estimate the value of future transactions.

Expert view 2.6: Do not confuse accruals and the accruals concept

Though the terms are clearly related, you should be careful not to define an accrual in the same way as you define the accruals concept. An entity would need to accrue for the electricity cost (ie bring the cost into this period's income statement) by setting up an accrual (ie set up a current liability in the statement of financial position) because of the accruals concept (ie matching concept). The accruals concept is also responsible for giving rise to assets (ie prepayments) and associated gains.

Going concern

Entities are required to prepare accounts on the basis that they are a going concern. To do so demonstrates to users that the business is commercially viable, able to pay its obligations as they fall due, and whose owners (or other controllers) intend it to continue in operation for the foreseeable future. In particular, when an entity provides assurances over its going concern status, one should be able to assume that the entity will not go into liquidation or scale down its operations in a material way within a period of 12 months or more.

Despite standard-setters and professional bodies assuring investors that they should not panic if an entity records a statement declaring that they are not a going concern, one should note that it is extremely difficult to find an annual report containing this statement. Providing a statement that an entity is not a going concern, some might argue, should be interpreted as a signal of transparency and openness. Instead of presenting an explicit negative statement about their going concern status, companies facing an uncertain future tend to refer to *doubts* over their foreseeable future.

The key financial accounting complication of not maintaining a going concern status is that the assets and liabilities should be valued and shown at their 'break-up' value ie the amount they would sell for if they were sold off piecemeal and the business were broken up. For example, non-current assets would need to be presented as current assets. Their previously recorded value (ie cost less accumulated depreciation) would need to be adjusted to their 'forced sale' value. The forced sale value is likely to be far lower than the carrying value.

Expert view 2.7: Going concern (extracts of going concern disclosures)

Though there are some jurisdictions (eg the United States) where a statement of an entity's going concern status is not expressly required, the directors of most companies include some reference to the likelihood of continuing to trade as normal into the foreseeable future. Indeed, such a statement is roundly encouraged by stakeholders even where not required (as shown by Gallagher and Paul, 2012). Examples from two companies follow: first, Whitbread plc, a major retail brand conglomerate; and second, Oxford Instruments plc, a leading provider of high-technology tools and systems for research and industry.

i) Whitbread plc

Annual report and accounts 2018

Available from Whitbread plc's download centre: **www.whitbread.co.uk/global/download-centre/reports-and-presentations.html**.

The directors' report (see page 91 of that document) reports as follows:

'Going concern

The Group's business activities, together with the factors likely to affect its future development, performance and position, are set out in the strategic report on pages 4 to 55. The financial position of the Company, its cash flows, net debt and borrowing facilities and the maturity of those facilities are set out in the Group Finance Director's review on pages 44 to 49.

In addition, there are further details in the financial statements on the Group's financial risk management, objectives and policies (Note 22) and on financial instruments (Note 23).

A combination of the strong operating cash flows generated by the business and the significant headroom on its credit facilities supports the directors' view that the Group has sufficient funds available for it to meet its foreseeable working capital requirements. The directors have concluded that the going concern basis remains appropriate.'

The auditor's report echoes the going concern sentiment, and on page 94, Deloitte LLP write:

'We have reviewed the directors' statement on page 91 about whether they considered it appropriate to adopt the going concern basis of accounting in preparing them and their identification of any material uncertainties to the group's and company's ability to continue to do so over a period of at least twelve months from the date of approval of the financial statements. '

We are required to state whether we have anything material to add or draw attention to in relation to that statement required by Listing Rule 9.8.6R(3) and report if the statement is materially inconsistent with our knowledge obtained in the audit.

We confirm that we have nothing material to report, add or draw attention to in respect of these matters.'

ii) Oxford Instruments plc

Annual report and financial statements 2018

Available from Oxford Instrument plc's download centre: **www.oxford-instruments.com/ investors**.

From the directors' report on page 34:

'Going concern

The Group's business activities, together with the factors likely to affect its future development, performance and position, are set out in the Performance, Strategy and Operations sections. The financial position of the Group, its cash flows, liquidity position and borrowing facilities are described in this Finance Review. The diverse nature of the Group, combined with its financial strength, provides a solid foundation for a sustainable business.

The Directors have reviewed the Group's forecasts and flexed them to incorporate a number of potential scenarios relating to changes in trading performance. The Directors believe that the Group will be able to operate within its existing debt facilities.

This review also considered hedging arrangements in place. The Directors believe that the Group is well placed to manage its business risks successfully

The Financial Statements have been prepared on a going concern basis, based on the Directors' opinion, after making reasonable enquiries, that the Group has adequate resources to continue in operational existence for the foreseeable future.'

Neutrality (and/or) prudence

Accounting transactions and other events are sometimes uncertain and yet, in order for the information to be useful for decision making and fulfil the fundamental qualitative characteristics, they still have to be reported in a timely manner (to correspond to the appropriate period of account). Thus, it is often necessary for management to make estimates that counteract the uncertainty. Historically, it has been preferable to err towards prudence. This is not to say that accuracy is not important to accountants and the information which they produce but there are times where erring on the side of caution mitigates related reporting risks.

The European Financial Reporting Advisory Group (EFRAG), alongside the national standard-setting bodies of France, Germany, Italy and the UK, published a joint bulletin in April 2013 outlining their position on the prudence convention. Within this bulletin they drew attention to the history of prudence and its usefulness. The Fourth EU Directive on Company Law of 1978 requires that 'valuation must be made on a prudent basis' and that, in particular, only profits made at the balance sheet date may be included, whereas account must be taken of all losses related to the financial year or to a previous one. The origins of prudence, however, date much further back.

Accounting regulators have preferred to write requirements that drive a conservative approach to recording transactions, ie in simple terms, a 'plan for the worst' approach. The tendency has been for losses to be recognized at the point at which management are aware of their probable realization, whereas gains are recognized only when they are certain to be received. So, while some see prudence as the opposite of imprudence – a clearly undesirable feature of any financial reporting system – others see prudence as introducing bias into the financial statements.

There appears to have been a shift in attitudes during recent years. The idea that prudence should be the dominant desirable attribute has passed and in its place the IASB have woven the concept of *neutrality*. It is not entirely certain what this means though. Certainly, the deletion of the term prudence from the section concerning the qualitative characteristics – which is part of the Conceptual Framework for Financial

Reporting document – was seen by some as a turning point. At the same time, the previously fundamental qualitative characteristic 'reliability' was replaced by 'faithful representation'. The Conceptual Framework's basis for conclusions states that faithful representation 'encompasses the main characteristics that the previous frameworks included as aspects of reliability'. The section continues by stating that 'substance over form, prudence (conservatism) and verifiability, which were aspects of reliability in the previous framework are not considered aspects of faithful representation'.

The IASB have been careful to design their Conceptual Framework to distinguish between the following:

i   the deliberate understatement of assets and profits, or overstatement of liabilities and expenses; and

ii   the adoption of a cautious approach in making the judgements necessitated by uncertainty so that assets and income are not overstated and liabilities and expenses are not understated.

See supporting online content **www.koganpage.com/afm3** for a brief article which draws attention to some practical drawbacks of (over-)prudence.

Expert view 2.8: Conditional versus unconditional conservatism

Academic literature also distinguishes conditional conservatism that results in asymmetric timeliness in the recognition of good and bad news (the latter recognized earlier) and unconditional conservatism, which results in systematic understatement of net assets. According to some academic literature, users find early recognition of losses useful, as they are less frequently anticipated by the market than gains. There is a general agreement on the usefulness of conditional conservatism, while unconditional conservatism is more contentious.

Disaggregation

To disaggregate means to separate into component parts. This principle is applied in accounting whereby material assets and liabilities should normally be disclosed separately at their gross amounts, rather than being netted off against each other. For example, netting off short-term borrowings from a positive cash balance is not permitted. In some circumstances, netting off can have a material impact on decision making.

Materiality

We have already discussed this concept, which might in its own way reinforce how fundamental it is to financial reporting and accounting more generally. We introduced materiality as the threshold quality. In other words, information is deemed to be material – by size or nature – where its exclusion would impair an assessment of an entity's position or performance. This rule is advantageous in many ways, not least because it allows accountants to focus their attention on the balances which are significant and, by default, to avoid absurd situations where immaterial balances are being investigated at great cost by companies' accountants.

WORKED EXAMPLE 2.5 Mobius (5)

Until this point, Mobius Inc's transactions have been relatively straightforward and uncontentious. You're now ready to move to the next level, and the following worked example shows how tangible non-current assets are accounted for. Though there are many standards that deal with accounting estimates, IAS 16 *Property, Plant and Equipment* is a good vehicle to allow us to discuss in more detail the prudence and accruals conventions.

We concluded the previous exercise when it was the end of week 2. Therefore, let us pick up the exercise at the start of week 3. When we left the example, the closing position looked like this (ie this will be the opening statement of financial position as of first day of week 3):

Mobius Inc
Summarized Statement of Financial Position
As at the start of week 3

Assets
Non-current assets

Computer	500.00
Printer/scanner	100.00

Current assets

Cash at bank	1,450.00
Inventories	
Raw materials	0.00
Finished goods	533.33
Trade receivables – amounts owed by customers	900.00

Liabilities

Loan from friend	(500.00)
Trade payables – amounts owed to suppliers	(800.00)
Net assets	2,183.33

Shareholders' funds (capital and reserves)

Capital	1,000.00
Retained profits (weeks 1 & 2)	1,183.33
Shareholders' funds	2,183.33

The following information is relevant to weeks 3 and 4:

Tangible non-current assets

(a) By the end of week 4, which marks the conclusion to your first full month's trading, you have noticed signs of wear and tear appearing on both of your tangible non-current assets – the printer/scanner and the computer. You believe that the printer will continue to function effectively for 20 months, but after this it will need to be scrapped. The computer is unlikely to be usable for business purposes after 40 months but you know a friend will buy it off you at that time for $100.

(b) On the first day of week 3 you decide to buy a new motor vehicle which will be used exclusively for business purposes. The useful economic life of the motor vehicle is estimated to be five years, at which stage the terminal value would be $0. The invoice from the supplier showed the following costs:

	$
Motor vehicle	19,500
Delivery charge	500
Additional extras:	
Non-standard black matt paint job	1,000
Convertible roof function	2,000
Tank of petrol	150
Road tax (for the year)	200
Total	23,350

You take out a loan with a coupon rate of 10 per cent for the full amount from your bank to finance the purchase. The interest is paid quarterly in arrears. The principal (ie capital amount borrowed) is due to be repaid in full in five years' time.

Solution and explanation

The depreciation expense which appeared in Figure 2.1 now deserves separate attention.

Depreciation is an accounting estimate. The cash to acquire these assets has been paid on the day of acquisition. We know that assets devalue over time and therefore it would be inappropriate to hold them on the face of our statement of financial position at their purchase price until the day they are sold or otherwise disposed of. Instead we spread the cost over the useful economic life of the asset (according to the *accruals convention*). Depreciation is the measure of wearing out, consumption or other reduction in the useful economic life of a non-current asset whether arising from use, effluxion of time or obsolescence through technical or market changes.

Printer/scanner

You have estimated that the economic life of the printer/scanner is 20 months. Therefore, at the end of the month, you should show the asset as being reduced by one-twentieth of its value, ie $100 / 20 years = $5 depreciation.

This depreciation charge gets netted off the carrying value (purchase price) of the non-current asset (ie $100 – $5 = $95) while the cost is taken to the income statement as an expense (reducing profit by $5). The amount which is shown on the face of the statement of financial position is called the net book value (NBV).

This process would continue each month until the asset reaches the end of its useful economic life. In other words, in each of the next 20 months you would charge $5 per month against the asset until all $100 has been consumed (Table 2.3).

Table 2.3

	Cost	Depreciation	Accumulated depreciation	Net book value
Month 1	100	5	5	95
Month 2	100	5	10	90
Month 3	100	5	15	85
Month 4	100	5	20	80
Month 5	100	5	25	75
Month 6	100	5	30	70
Month 7	100	5	35	65
Month 8	100	5	40	60
Month 9	100	5	45	55
Month 10	100	5	50	50
Month 11	100	5	55	45
Month 12	100	5	60	40
Month 13	100	5	65	35
Month 14	100	5	70	30
Month 15	100	5	75	25
Month 16	100	5	80	20
Month 17	100	5	85	15
Month 18	100	5	90	10
Month 19	100	5	95	5
Month 20	100	5	100	0

The depreciation charge shown in Table 2.3 is taken to the income statement every month. The NBV (the final column) appears on the face of the statement of financial position.

Computer

The treatment of the computer is similar. The only difference is that the asset has an estimated terminal (residual) value.

You have estimated that the computer will last for 40 months, at which point it will be sold for $100. Therefore, now we need only depreciate the asset down to its expected terminal value, as follows:

$$\frac{\text{Cost} - \text{residual value}}{\text{Useful life}} = \text{Depreciation charge}$$

$$\frac{\$500 - \$100}{40 \text{ months}} = \$10 \text{ per month}$$

Therefore, at the end of the first month, the computer would be worth $490 ($500 – $10) and the depreciation charge for this month (and every month until the end of the asset's useful life) would be $10.

Discussion point

Accounting standards allow managers to choose depreciation rates. Why do you think this is? And what are the advantages/disadvantages of this kind of accounting choice?

Acquisition of motor vehicle

IAS 16 *Property, Plant and Equipment* states that the cost of an asset will include all costs in bringing the asset to its required location and condition. As you can see, this is a subjective exercise. Is the convertible-roof function a necessary improvement or adjustment to the asset to ensure it is suitable for the purpose?

Remember that the capitalized balance goes to the statement of financial position and will be written off over the useful economic life of the asset. Any costs which you deem to be inappropriate to capitalize should be taken straight to the income statement. We suggest the following treatment:

	Capital $	Expense $
Motor vehicle	19,500	
Delivery charge	500	
Additional extras:		
Non-standard black matt paint job		1,000
Convertible roof function		2,000
Tank of petrol		150
Road tax (for the year)		200
Total	20,000	3,350

The carrying value of the asset would be recorded in the statement of financial position at a cost of $20,000 and would be depreciated over five years. There is no terminal (residual) value. However, if depreciation is calculated on a pro-rata basis, remember that you have owned this asset for only two weeks. Therefore:

Cost		20,000
Depreciation	20,000 / 5 years	
	= $4,000 per year	
	= $333.33 per month	
	= approx. $77 per week assuming 52 weeks a year	(154)
Net book value		19,846

Bank loan to finance the purchase of the vehicle

The total loan required was $23,350. The loan is repayable in full in approximately five years' time and therefore would be classified as a **non-current liability**.

The interest payments (at 10 per cent per annum) are due quarterly in arrears. The annual interest charge would be $2,335 ($23,350 * 10%). The quarterly charge would be $583.75. As we are accounting for only two weeks' worth of unpaid interest, the amount we need to accrue is $90 (calculated as: $2,335 / 52 weeks = (approx.) $45 per week).

As we owe the interest at the end of the first month of trading, it needs to be classified as a liability. Whereas the loan balance is repayable in several years' time, the interest is due within the next few months. Therefore this balance should be classified as a current liability. A corresponding charge against profit needs to be made for the period to ensure that we have matched the appropriate expense to the period.

The accounting entries would be as follows:

- Increase the cost of tangible non-current assets in the statement of financial position by $20,000.

- Charge $3,350 immediately to the income statement for the 'additional extras'.

- Increase the level of non-current liabilities by the same amount, ie $23,350. *Remember, you needed a loan to pay the motor vehicle supplier!*

- Charge $154 to the income statement related to the depreciation charge. The other side of the double entry needs to be posted to the accumulated depreciation account. The net effect of this entry is to reduce profit by $154 and reduce the carrying value of the motor vehicle by $154.

- Finally, you need to accrue for the interest which is unpaid at the month end. $90 needs to be charged against profit for the year and a current liability for unpaid interest needs to be shown in the statement of financial position.

Extracts from statement of financial position and income statement for the period ended week 4 (month 1)

NOTE In the following extracts we have simply highlighted the balances that have changed as a result of the above transactions.

Mobius Inc
Adjustments to be made to the Statement of Financial Position
Regarding week 4

	Adjustments	Notes
	$	
Assets		
Non-current assets		
Computer	(10)	2
Printer / scanner	(5)	1
Motor vehicle ($20,000 [cost] – $154 [accumulated depreciation])	19,846	3, 4
Current liabilities		
Loan interest accrual	(90)	5
Non-current liabilities		
Bank loan (10%; repayable in 5 years' time)	(23,350)	3
Shareholders' funds (capital and reserves)		
Loss	(3,609)	6

Mobius Inc
Adjustments to be made to the Income Statement
Regarding week 4

Expenses		
Depreciation – printer/scanner	(5)	1
Depreciation – computer	(10)	2
Motor vehicle costs (additional extras)	(3,350)	3
Depreciation – motor vehicle	(154)	4
Finance costs	(90)	5
Profit/(loss)	(3,609)	6

Notes:

1 Depreciation charge on printer/scanner for the period of account.

2 Depreciation charge on computer for the period of account.

3 Motor vehicle 'additional extras' acquisition costs.

4 Depreciation charge on motor vehicle for period of account.

5 Interest paid on loan.

6 Transfer profit (loss) to statement of financial position (this transfer has been made purely for illustration purposes and assumes that no other transactions took place during the period and we are closing off our ledgers).

Three further property, plant and equipment issues

Let us take this opportunity to discuss briefly three further issues which you should be aware of when accounting for tangible non-current assets:

- recognition and subsequent measurement;
- disposal of non-current assets;
- alternative depreciation methods.

Recognition and subsequent re-measurement

We have simplified the example by assuming that all non-current assets are tangible and that the assets are included at cost. The reality is that some non-current assets are intangible – thus making the carrying value more difficult to quantify – and an entity has the choice whether to revalue assets to their open market value (fair value) at the end of each accounting period. If management choose to adopt a revaluation policy then this must be maintained and certain assets should not be cherry-picked because of their value over other assets. In other words, if you have some property that you believe has increased in value and other property that hasn't, you cannot choose to revalue only those assets which you believe it would be beneficial to revalue from a financial position perspective.

Disposal of non-current assets

We have dealt with the acquisition of non-current assets but this is only a part of the story. These assets can be disposed of or sold. If we take the example of the computer in the example above, we are depreciating the asset down to a value of $100 over 40 months. That means that at the end of the second (complete) year the asset would be held in the statement of financial position at an NBV of $260 (ie $500 – $10*24 months). If you decide to sell the asset and find someone willing to pay you $300, you would make a profit of $40. If you sell the asset for $100, you would make a loss of $160.

At the point of disposal, the asset and its accumulated depreciation is completely written off (leaving no trace of the asset in your statement of financial position) and the gain (loss) on the difference between the sales proceeds and the NBV is credited (debited) to the income statement.

In a perfect world, there would be no difference between the sales proceeds and the NBV. This would mean that your depreciation estimations were accurate. However, it is unusual not to see gains or losses on disposal. These are simply a reflection of the level of under- or over-depreciation over the ownership period. In other words, a gain means that you were overly prudent in your estimation of the devaluation of the asset; a loss means that you were not prudent enough. The final entry to reconcile proceeds and the NBV is a correcting entry.

Alternative depreciation methods

There are many commonly accepted methods for calculating depreciation. The reason that the rules are flexible is because depreciation is an accounting estimate. Subjectivity is permitted but the underlying ethos is that balances should be a true and fair reflection and that the costs of ownership should be matched against the economic benefits which the asset provides. Organizations should record their assets and liabilities, gains and losses as appropriately and accurately as possible. Given that management are presumed to know more than other stakeholders, it is only right that they should be responsible for choosing the depreciation policy.

In the case of depreciation we are deriving a measure to establish the level of wear and tear on an asset, ie the consumption or other reduction in the useful economic life of a non-current asset whether arising from use, effluxion of time or obsolescence through technical or market changes. Therefore, it is easy to see why different methods of depreciation have evolved.

The two most commonly used methods to calculate depreciation are the straight-line basis and reducing-balance basis. It is simplest to illustrate the differences between these methods through a worked example.

WORKED EXAMPLE 2.6 Depreciation methods

You purchase an asset for $500 and expect the residual value to be $0. In the first instance, you depreciate the asset on a straight-line basis and in the second, you depreciate the asset on a reducing-balance basis:

1 The **straight-line basis** seeks to depreciate assets evenly over a period of time. You believe that the tangible non-current asset has a five-year useful economic life. Therefore, each year you will charge $100 depreciation against the asset ($500 / 5 years). Figure 2.3 shows the NBV of the asset over the time period.

Figure 2.3   An illustration of the impact of straight-line basis depreciation

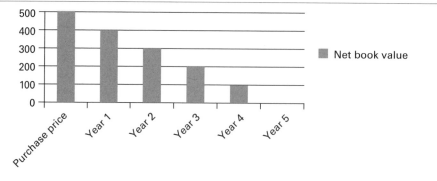

2 The **reducing-balance basis** is commonly used for assets which lose value early in their economic lives and less later. Examples of assets which you might choose to depreciate on a reducing-balance basis are motor vehicles, high-tech goods and so forth.

To calculate the reducing-balance basis depreciation charge you need to know an appropriate percentage to apply. Let us presume that the asset needs to be depreciated at 20 per cent on a reducing-balance basis (note: the above example shows the asset being depreciated at 20 per cent on a straight-line basis). In the first year, the depreciation charge is the same as under the previous depreciation basis because it is simply 20 per cent of the purchase price. However, the second year, and all subsequent years, calculates depreciation based upon the net book value (ie year 2 depreciation is $400 [NBV] * 20% = $80). The workings below and Figure 2.4 illustrate the difference.

	$	NBV $
Purchase price	500.00	
Year 1 depreciation charge (20%)	(100.00)	
Net book value at end of year 1		400.00
Year 2 depreciation charge (20%)	(80.00)	
Net book value at end of year 2		320.00
Year 3 depreciation charge (20%)	(64.00)	
Net book value at end of year 3		256.00
Year 4 depreciation charge (20%)	(51.20)	
Net book value at end of year 4		204.80
Year 5 depreciation charge (20%)	(40.96)	
Net book value at end of year 5		163.84
Year 6 depreciation charge (20%)	(32.77)	
Net book value at end of year 6		131.07
... And so forth		

Figure 2.4 An illustration of the impact of reducing-balance basis depreciation

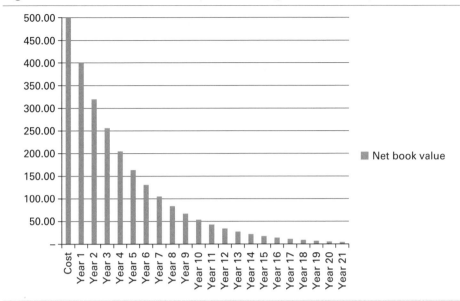

Recording accounting information

As we draw towards the conclusion of this chapter, you might like to have a visual representation of the way accounting books and records are maintained. We have simplified the record-keeping process as far as possible mainly because the advent of computerized bookkeeping packages means that many of these processes happen behind the scenes. At the press of a button these systems allow one to print exception reports, a trial balance at a certain date, draft financial statements and so forth. Systems also allow you to drill down to customer or supplier accounts, locating single invoices if required; this would have been a long and exhaustive process not so long ago! Of course, manual systems allow you to do the same; it is just that it is more time-consuming. The flow chart in Figure 2.5 shows how information is collated and transferred between ledgers, how it is subsequently summarized into a trial balance and then rephrased into a set of financial statements.

Figure 2.5   Accounting books and records

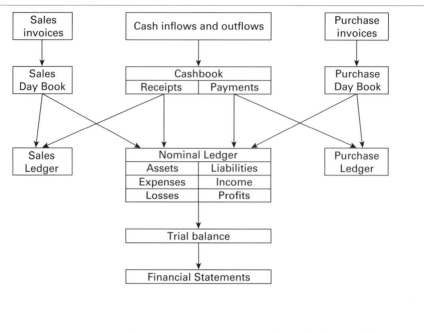

Exercises: now attempt Exercise 2.5 on page 85

WORKED EXAMPLE 2.7   Mobius (6)

Period-end adjustments

At the end of every accounting period, it is highly likely that a company will need to make a series of period-end adjustments. The depreciation of non-current assets is an example of one of these. Frequently the adjustments are correcting entries, accounting for estimates or adjusting the figures to an accruals basis. Let us once again consider the statements of financial position and income for Mobius Inc as at the end of week 4.

The following information is relevant:

(i)   Mobius Inc had a telephone line installed along with a broadband connection during the third week of trading. The phone company invoices quarterly in arrears and you have not yet received your first invoice. This transaction has not been recorded in your accounting records and therefore is not included within the financial statements above. You have estimated that the usage during this first period of account will cost approximately $100.

(ii)   On the last day of week 4, you found a suitable location to base the business. The monthly rental cost is $1,000 and the landlord required you to pay in advance. You paid in cash.

(iii) Mobius Inc sold $20,000 of product on credit terms. The total amount owed by customers (from all transactions) at the end of the period was $4,900.

(iv)   Mobius Inc bought a further $9,000 of raw materials on credit during weeks 3 and 4 of trading. Exactly $8,000 worth was converted into finished goods, of which three-quarters were sold. The remainder were held as inventories at the end of the period. These were the only goods held at the end of the period as those finished goods brought forward from weeks 1 and 2 were sold during week 3. Suppliers were owed $2,000 in total at the end of the accounting period.

Solutions

(i)   Mobius Inc reports on an accruals basis (not a cash basis). This convention asks that revenues, profits and the associated costs incurred while earning them should be matched to the same period's income statement. Therefore, we need to charge the relevant proportion of the telephone cost against this period's profit or loss. To operationalize this accounting entry, we need a corresponding entry in the statement of financial position. In other words, we need to charge the $100 telephone expense to the income statement and set up a current liability for the same amount in the statement of financial position.

(ii)   The $1,000 rental expense needs to be carried forward to the next period as this is the period in which it is incurred. Let us break down this transaction into two parts. The first part is the cash transaction. When the cash leaves the bank account, the corresponding entry would be to set up the rental expense in the income statement. However, as we know, the expense should be carried forward to the next period of account and therefore we have a charge of $1,000 against profit which should not be there. We need a period-end correcting entry as the second part of the accounting transaction.

   As the cash has been physically paid out, the 'cash at bank' balance cannot, and should not, be adjusted. Instead, we need to include a current asset of a different type; in this case, a prepayment. By increasing assets by $1,000 this leaves us with the other side of the entry to post to the income statement. All we need do is set this off against the $1,000 charge which we had included as part of the cash transaction. This reduces the rental cost in the income statement to $0 and sets off the prepayment gain against the cash loss, leaving the current asset position at a net $0 position.

NOTE The third part of the transaction is not dealt with here because it relates to the release of the prepayment. At the end of the next accounting period, the rental cost will need to be charged against profits and the prepayment removed from the statement of financial position (and possibly another set up in its place).

(iii) Revenue should be increased by $20,000. Trade receivables should be moved to $4,900. The cash balance should be corrected appropriately to reflect the amounts received from these sales and the amounts invoiced but not collected from prior periods.

(iv) The company has purchased $9,000 of raw materials, of which $8,000 was converted into finished goods stock and three-quarters sold. Therefore, there are inventories left over at the end of the period. The closing balance of raw materials should be shown as a current asset worth $1,000 and the closing finished goods inventories should be included at $2,000.

Closing trade payables (current liabilities) should be shown in the statement of financial position at $2,000. We must assume that all other balances have been paid.

The closing financial statements for the first four weeks of trading would be as follows:

Mobius Inc Summarized Statement of Financial Position As at the end of week 4	$	$
Assets		
Non-current assets		
Computer		490
Printer / scanner		95
Motor vehicle		19,846
		20,431
Current assets		
Cash at bank (1,450 [b/fwd] – 1,000 [2a] + 16,000 [3b] – 800 [4a] – 7,000 [4e])	8,650	
Inventories		
Raw materials (1,000 [4d])	1,000	
Finished goods (533.33 [b/fwd] – 533.33 [4b] + 2,000 [4d])	2,000	
Trade receivables – amounts owed by customers (900 + 20,000 [3a] – 16,000 [3b])	4,900	
Prepayments (1,000 [2b])	1,000	
	17,550	
Current liabilities		
Trade payables – amounts owed to suppliers (800 [b/fwd] – 800 [4a] + 9,000 [4c] – 7,000 [4e])	(2,000)	
Loan interest accrual	(90)	
Accruals (100 [1])	(100)	
	(2,190)	
Net current assets		15,360
Non-current liabilities		
Loan from friend		(500)
Bank loan		(23,350)
Net assets		11,941
Shareholders' funds (capital and reserves)		
Capital		1,000
Retained earnings (weeks 1–4)		10,941
Shareholders' funds		11,941

Mobius Inc
Summarized Income Statement
For the period ended DD/MM/YYYY (week 4)

	$	$
Revenue (2,850 [b/fwd] + 20,000 [3a])		22,850
Cost of sales		
Opening inventories	0	
Purchases (666.67 [b/fwd] + 533.33 [4b] + 9,000 [4c])	10,200	
Closing inventories (1,000 [4d] + 2,000 [4d])	(3,000)	
		(7,200)
Gross profit		15,650
Expenses:		
Utilities		(200)
Printing, postage and stationery		(50)
Web development costs		(750)
Depreciation (5+10+154)		(169)
Motor vehicle costs		(3,350)
Telephone services (100 [1])		(100)
Rental costs (+1,000 [2a] − 1,000 [2b])		0
Profit before interest and tax		11,031
Finance costs		(90)
Profit		10,941

WORKED EXAMPLE 2.8 Mobius (7)

Statement of cash flows

Mobius Inc is a simple business with no complex transactions and therefore converting the accruals-based financial information to reveal the cash flows is quick and straightforward. Of course, being at the end of the first period of trading also simplifies the preparation process. Note the format, in particular the categorization into three distinct sections: operating activities; investing activities; and financing activities. This is designed to facilitate the interpretation and analysis of the cash position.

Mobius Inc
Statement of Cash Flows
For the period ended DD/MM/YYYY (month 1) $

Cash generated from operating activities:

Cash generated from operations **(note 1)**	4,490
Interest paid (include either here or financing activities below)	(90)
Dividends paid (include either here or under financing activities below)	0
Net cash flow from operating activities	4,400

Cash flows from investing activities:

Assets purchased	(20,600)	
Assets sold	0	
Net cash flow from investing activities		(20,600)

Cash flow from financing activities:

Issue of shares	1,000	
Receipt of loan	23,850	
Repayment of loan	0	
Net cash flows from financing activities		24,850
Net cash inflow/(outflow) from activities		8,650
Opening net cash		0
Closing net cash		8,650

Note 1: Reconciliation of net cash from operating activities
Cash generated from operations

Profit for period	10,941
Interest paid	90
Depreciation	169
Increase in trade receivables (including prepayments)	(5,900)
Increase in trade payables (including accruals)	2,190
Increase in inventories	(3,000)
	4,490

Exercises: now attempt Exercise 2.6 on page 86

Expert view 2.9: Statement of cash flows

The advantage of being asked to prepare a statement of cash flows (over the preparation of the other financial statements) is that you are given the balancing figure – the closing balance of cash and cash equivalents. Sometimes this might be a combination of balances (eg petty cash, bank overdraft, short-term cash and cash equivalents) but ultimately, this makes the exercise easier to complete. Interestingly, you might like to note that when completing this exercise in real life, computerized bookkeeping packages often struggle to produce an accurate statement of cash flows unless the person responsible for inputting the data clearly labels items 'cash' and 'not cash'.

COMPREHENSION QUESTIONS

1 Outline the content and purpose of the statement of financial position.
2 Outline the content and purpose of the statement of comprehensive income.
3 Outline the content and purpose of the statement of cash flows.
4 What is the accruals concept? Provide one example to show you understand this.
5 If an entity's accounts are prepared on a break-up basis, what does this mean?
6 List and describe two methods of depreciation. For each, provide an example of an asset where it might be appropriate to use that method.

Answers available at **www.koganpage.com/afm3**

Exercises

Answers available at **www.koganpage.com/afm3**

Exercise 2.1: The components of financial statements

(a)   The income statement shows:

Income − Expenditure = Profit

Can you provide examples for each of these categories?

Examples of income	Examples of expenditure

(b)   The statement of financial position shows:

Assets − Liabilities = Shareholders' funds (net worth)

Can you provide examples of both assets and liabilities?

Examples of assets	Examples of liabilities

Exercise 2.2 can be found on page 56

Exercise 2.3: Climb On!

Worked Example 1.1 in Chapter 1 provided the following information:

For a long time, you have been wondering how to convert your passion for rock climbing into a business opportunity. During a recent climbing trip you met Chris, a climbing-gear designer. He agreed to give you 100 chalk bags and 100 climb-oriented t-shirts for $4 and $5 respectively. You came to an agreement with him that you'd make payments on an ad-hoc basis as the goods were sold. As soon as you arrived home you listed the first 30 chalk bags and 50 t-shirts on an internet-based auction site. These sold within 3 days of listing them for $8 and $10 respectively. Half of these customers paid immediately. You offered 20 day terms on the sales and your past experiences tell you that customers tend to take full advantage of this policy.

Required:

Based on this information, prepare a statement of financial position and an income statement.

Exercise 2.4: Goblin Combe plc

State which of the following items could appear as an asset on the statement of financial position of Goblin Combe plc, a leading premium drinks business:

- $150,000 of product sold during the year to Troillus Direct Inc under 40-day credit terms. The amount remained outstanding at the end of the year and management believe that the amount will never be paid.

- Goblin Combe plc holds $22 million of finished goods inventories as at the year-end. Of this amount, $500,000 relates to a product which was banned from sale during the year. The directors have ascertained that this particular product is highly effective as paint remover. A buyer has been found for this and they are willing to pay $100,000 for the full quantity of this otherwise unsaleable stock.

- A competing company produced a popular whisky called 'Arbol'. Goblin Combe plc acquired the company (and by default the 'Arbol' brand) at the start of the year for $30 million. The fair value of the assets less liabilities, at that time, was estimated to be $10 million.

- Goblin Combe plc hired a new corporate communication team. It is confidently expected that their services will lead to an increase in profits by over $12 million per annum.

- A product was developed by a rival company, Old Down Quarry Inc. The directors of Goblin Combe plc decided to buy the exclusive rights to manufacture and distribute this product for the next four years at a cost of $2 million. The new drink has already proved successful and sales have exceeded expectations.

Exercise 2.5: Climb On! (continued)

Trading continues apace for your new business Climb On! The products have proved to be popular and, seeing this as your opportunity to seize the day, you decide to expand and grow the business.

Here follows a summary of your **cash book**, ie all cash transactions during the year to 31 December 2019:

Cash In Description	$	Cash Out Description	$
Cash sales	32,000	Payments to suppliers	49,000
Receipts in respect of credit sales	106,000	Purchase of machinery	55,000
Capital invested (transfer from private bank account)	30,000	Rent and rates	7,800
Bank loan	45,000	Utilities	3,500
Interest received	200	Insurance	1,200
Sale of machinery	2,500	Telephone	300
		Postage and packaging	200
		Website development costs	1,500
		Travel/climbing trips	10,500
		General expenses	6,300
		Wages (staff)	12,000
		Drawings (your remuneration)	8,000
		Interest paid	2,300
		Balance carried forward	58,100
	215,700		215,700

The following information is also available:

(a) The machinery was purchased on 1 April 2019. The estimated useful economic life of these assets is four years. The residual value is estimated to be $nil. You may assume a full year's depreciation in the year of purchase but none in the year of sale.

(b) Some of the machinery quickly proved to be unnecessary and was sold during the year for $2,500. The original cost was $5,000.

(c) Utilities bills of £400 were still owed as at 31 December 2019.

(d) Closing inventories as at 31 December 2019 were $14,000.

(e) Trade receivables as at 31 December 2019 were $10,500.

(f) Trade payables as at 31 December 2019 were $18,000.

(g) You need to provide for $1,500 of accounting fees as at 31 December 2019.

Exercise 2.6: Climb On! (continued)

Based upon your solution to Exercise 2.5, prepare a statement of cash flows for Climb On! for the period ended 31 December 2019.

Reference

Gallagher, M and Paul, B (2012) Assessing Going Concern: Stakeholders would benefit from clarity in US disclosure requirements, *Point of view*, PricewaterhouseCooper LLP Publications, December

Supplementary reading

Bakar, N B A and Said, J M (2007) Historical cost versus current cost accounting, *Accountants Today*, January

Elliott, B and Elliott, J (2011) *Financial Accounting and Reporting*, 15th edn, Pearson Education, Harlow

Fahnestock, R T and Bostwick, E D (2011) An analysis of the fair value controversy, *Proceedings of The American Society of Business and Behavioral Sciences at Las Vegas*, 18 (1), pp 910–21

Hendriksen, E F and Van Breda, M F (1992) *Accounting Theory*, 5th edn, Irwin Professional Publishing, Burr Ridge, IL

Institute of Chartered Accountants in England and Wales (2009) Going concern: don't panic, *Accountancy*, January

Laux, C and Leuz, C (2009) The crisis of fair-value accounting: making sense of the recent debate, *Accounting, Organizations and Society*, 34 (6), pp 826–34

Power, M (2010) Fair value accounting, financial economics and the transformation of reliability, *Accounting and Business Research*, 40 (3), pp 197–220

Financial analysis: Part I   03

OBJECTIVE

The objective of this chapter is to help develop and refine financial accounting information analysis and interpretation skills. The emphasis of this first financial analysis chapter will be on undertaking appropriate forms of analysis, including calculating key management ratios. This chapter will show how the results of the various techniques described can be employed to help assess the position and performance of an entity.

LEARNING OUTCOMES

After studying this chapter, the reader will be able to:

- Identify the main aspects of performance which can be evaluated through financial statements.

- Apply horizontal, trend, vertical and ratio analysis to the financial statements contained within an organization's annual report.

- Evaluate a company from the viewpoint of current and potential investors as well as other stakeholders.

KEY TOPICS COVERED

- Aspects of financial analysis: profitability, liquidity, efficiency, solvency and investors' returns.

- The use of ratios and other techniques to analyse and appraise full sets of company accounts.

- This chapter will contain mini case study exercises in which students must evaluate a company from varying viewpoints.

MANAGEMENT ISSUES

Although it is useful that managers be able to compute ratios, it is more important that they are able to develop the analytical skills through interpretation and analysis of financial statements.

Introduction

This chapter considers various forms of financial statement analysis, including:

- horizontal analysis;
- trend analysis;
- vertical analysis;
- ratio analysis.

We will combine these approaches in the chapter that follows. We will assume that undertaking these forms of analysis is (relatively) new to you. When used appropriately, ratio analysis can be a highly effective way of manipulating data into meaningful information. The key to undertaking ratio analysis is to focus on the audience and their question(s). A current (or potential) investor, for example, might want to know about the position, performance and financial strategy of the organization. A lender might want to gauge the short-term liquidity – to gauge whether the firm can make their obligatory interest payments – and the long-term solvency – to identify whether there could be problems meeting repayment plans. On the other end of the continuum, an environmental campaigner would probably have very different motivations for investigating the annual report and financial statements. When calculating and interpreting key ratios they are likely to be judging the firm from a social, environmental or ethical perspective. Therefore, the ability to calculate a long series of financial ratios is good knowledge to have but a more useful skill-set to develop is being able to identify the most appropriate ratios and then having the capacity to interpret them.

The usefulness of financial ratios has long been established. Chen and Shimerda (1981) in their paper 'An empirical analysis of useful financial ratios' have this to say:

> Financial ratios have played an important part in evaluating the performance and financial condition of an entity. Over the years, empirical studies have repeatedly demonstrated the usefulness of financial ratios. For example, financially-distressed firms can be separated from the non-failed firms in the year before the declaration of bankruptcy at an accuracy rate of better than 90% by examining financial ratios. In determining bond ratings, when financial ratios were the only variables used, the resulting ratings were virtually identical with institutional ratings. There is one recurring question with the use of financial ratios: which ratios, among the hundreds that can be computed easily from the available financial data, should be analysed to obtain the information for the task at hand? (pp 51–60).

During this chapter we provide a list of financial ratios which we believe are the most useful for you to know and understand. Alongside each ratio we show how it can be calculated and a guide to help you develop your analysis and interpretation skills. In an attempt to make this more real to you and to bring the content alive, we have worked through the ratios of an airline.

We subdivide the chapter into five broad categories:

- profitability;
- liquidity;
- efficiency;
- solvency; and
- investors' returns.

Financial statement analysis for investment purposes

Investment-led financial statement analysis – buy, hold or sell – is predicated on the assumption that investors are rational, risk averse and seek to maximize their returns in terms of the present value of future cash flows. In other words, we presume that investors have an efficient frontier where returns are traded off against risks, and investments will be rejected where the rewards fail to meet established benchmarks.

However, before an investment should be made in an entity, there are two fundamental assumptions:

1 Buying shares on a stock exchange is not just an investment on paper, it is an investment in a business.

2 You should know the business before you make an investment in it.

Therefore, do not limit your assessment of position and performance to a numeric exercise. If you are going to undertake an analysis exercise for a business in which you are either an investor or considering making an investment, it is essential that you understand the industry and the firm's position in it. Among the issues which you should consider are:

- the objectives of the organization;
- the business strategy;
- knowledge of the products sold/services offered;
- knowledge of the products being developed;
- your level of trust in the senior management team, and their vision;
- the competitiveness of the industry and the position of the business within it;
- the reputational capital of the business;

- the political, legal, regulatory, social and ethical environment in which the business operates;
- the technology required to bring the product to market;
- the reliance on skilled and unskilled employees and the competitiveness of the job markets;
- and so on...

Discussion point

You already know a great deal about many companies and have access to a massive amount of information, including their annual reports and financial statements. What do you think institutional investors and their financial intermediaries know that you don't?

Other users and their needs

As stated earlier, investors are not the only user group who have financial information needs. They are also not the only group who are interested in an entity's financial statements. Table 3.1 sets out some broad motivations that these various user groups might have, alongside the type of information that would satisfy their needs.

Table 3.1 User groups' information needs

User group	Potential motivations to consult the annual report	Example financial information requirements
Investors	Concerned with the stewardship of the entity. The key issues are growth (historic and potential), performance (past, present and future), position, risk and returns.	What is the return on the investment (dividend and capital growth) versus the level of risk taken?
Employees	Employees would want to know whether the firm was stable and solvent.	Is the company financially stable and will it continue into the foreseeable future? Levels of borrowing and maturity would be useful information. How profitable is the business and the segment I work in?
Customers	Might be a motivation to investigate based upon fairness of prices, or maybe an over-reliance on one supplier.	Is the company profitable? If so, is there an issue of over-profitability? How do prices compare to competitors? Is the company (who is your supplier) solvent or should you be looking for an alternative?

(continued)

Table 3.1 (Continued)

User group	Potential motivations to consult the annual report	Example financial information requirements
Lenders	Is the firm solvent and does it have the short-term resources to meet interest payments?	Consider issues such as interest cover ratios, return on capital employed, debt to equity ratios.
Suppliers and other creditors	Suppliers would be primarily concerned with whether they will be paid what they are owed. They might also have dependency issues, ie whether the company who is their customer will continue to operate into the foreseeable future or whether they should be looking for new customers.	Consider issues such as liquidity (short-term financial position), working capital position and requirements, and solvency issues (medium- to long-term financial position).
Public	Is the firm operating in a manner that is environmentally, socially and ethically responsible?	For large entities, the annual report either includes or is accompanied by a corporate social responsibility report. This is, of course, highly useful to decision making about non-financial matters. The public, particularly communities within which big businesses operate, will also be concerned with community matters, eg how does the company treat employees in terms of remuneration; will the company continue to exist and invest in the local community; is it growing or contracting? Therefore, standard measures of profitability and performance will also be important to this user group.
Government and their agencies	The government and their agencies will be concerned with a range of issues such as taxation, directors' remuneration, employment details, governance and so forth. The annual report is often the nominated repository for such disclosure requirements.	The questions being asked will depend upon the nature of the enquiry. Levels of revenue are important to sales tax (value added tax [VAT]) concerns. Levels of operating profit will be relevant to corporation tax. The solvency of the entity might be interesting when establishing the broader macroeconomic environment.

Horizontal analysis and trend analysis

Technique outline

Horizontal analysis invites you to make horizontal comparisons on a line-by-line basis. The objective is to gauge relative levels of performance (or position) for a firm over a given period of time. It is possible, of course, to undertake this analysis on raw numbers (horizontal analysis), but more often than not, it is better to use the first period of account as your base position and set to '100' (trend analysis). You would then analyse future periods' percentage growth against this base position. Therefore, if revenue moved from $100 million in year 1 to $110 million in year 2, revenue growth could be expressed as either $10 million (horizontal analysis) or 1.1 (or 110 per cent of base; trend analysis) (ie $110m – $100m / $100m). Alternatively, if revenue fell during year 2 to $75 million, this would be recorded as 0.75 (or 75 per cent of base), indicating a 25 per cent decrease from the opening position.

Though carrying out this exercise can be time-consuming, it can also be rewarding in terms of its ability to reveal patterns and trends, as well as irregularities and anomalies. It is not uncommon for this analysis to be the first step for audit firms when they receive a new set of annual financial information. It is a straightforward analytical review. Comparing figures on a line-by-line basis can form the basis of discussions with the financial controller about the performance for the period. This technique also offers the opportunity to identify any exceptional movements in balances from previous years' accounts, and thus those balances that are higher risk (because of the possibility of misstatement). This can help to focus decision-makers on areas of potential material error or misstatement. Extrapolation of current trends to predict future growth (forecasting) is often employed as a credibility and/or robustness check and it is not uncommon for people to talk about the (field) hockey-curve effect, ie a graph depicting revenues increasing in the shape of a hockey stick are likely to be 'too good to be true'.

We have chosen to adopt Ryanair Holdings plc (hereafter, 'Ryanair') as a case study to showcase these techniques. Over the past decade or more the firm has become a household name across Europe and earned a reputation as a successful low-cost airline. By way of introduction, their corporate website states the following:

Ryanair Holdings plc, Europe's largest airline group, is the parent company of Buzz, Lauda, Malta Air & Ryanair DAC.

Carrying 154m guests pa on more than 2,400 daily flights from 82 bases, the group connects over 200 destinations in 40 countries on a fleet of over 470 aircraft, with a further 210 Boeing 737s on order, which will enable the Ryanair Group to lower fares and grow traffic to 200m pa by FY25.

Ryanair has a team of over 19,000 highly skilled aviation professionals delivering Europe's No 1 on-time performance, and an industry leading 34-year safety record.

Ryanair is Europe's greenest cleanest airline group and customers switching to fly Ryanair can reduce their CO_2 emissions by up to 50% compared to the other Big 4 EU major airlines.

(**www.ryanair.com** [February 2020])

Worked Example 3.1 provides 10 years' worth of selected financial information – 2010 through to 2019. Horizontal analysis reveals a strong growth profile.

Issues

The major issues with this kind of analysis are:

- Presuming that balances are comparable between years:

    - There are likely to have been changes in accounting policies, accounting require-ments, financial strategy and so forth that make direct like-for-like comparisons impossible.
- Deciding which period to set as the baseline year:

    - For example in 2009 Ryanair made a sizeable loss and therefore using this as the baseline year would generate substantially less useful results.

A note on financial analysis exercises

Remember that the simplest aspect of these exercises is completing the data collec-tion exercise and performing the mechanical calculations. The focus of any financial analysis should fall on the '*analysis*'. Ensure that you do not simply ask yourself questions such as 'how much' or 'how little' has balance X changed, but also 'why' and 'so what'. Some preliminary questions you might like to ask yourself are:

- What does this information tell me about the company's performance?
- Has the company done well compared with other financial periods?
- Has the company exceeded its own targets?
- How does it compare with other companies in the same industry?
- What are the future prospects of: i) the firm; ii) the local economy; iii) the global economy; iv) customers and suppliers; v) political reform; vi) social, environmen-tal and ethical circumstances etc?

Vertical analysis

What is vertical analysis?

While horizontal analysis identifies trends across time periods setting a specific year as the base, vertical analysis seeks patterns in the data on a year-by-year basis. In an

WORKED EXAMPLE 3.1 Horizontal analysis and trend analysis for Ryanair Holdings plc

Table 3.2

	2010 €'000s	2011 €'000s	2012 €'000s	2013 €'000s	2014 €'000s	2015 €'000s	2016 €'000s	2017 €'000s	2018 €'000s	2019 €'000s
Revenue	2,988,100	3,629,500	4,390,200	4,884,000	5,036,700	5,654,000	6,535,800	6,647,800	7,151,000	7,697,400
Operating expenses	2,586,000	3,141,300	3,707,000	4,165,800	4,378,100	4,611,100	5,075,700	5,113,800	5,483,700	6,680,600
Profit before interest and tax	402,100	488,200	683,200	718,200	658,600	1,042,900	1,460,100	1,534,000	1,667,300	1,016,800
Profit after tax	305,300	374,600	560,400	569,300	522,800	866,700	1,559,100	1,315,900	1,450,200	885,000
Dividends	0	500,000	0	0	0	520,000	0	0	0	0
Share repurchase	0	0	124,600	0	481,700	112,000	706,100	1,017,900	829,100	531,600
Interest payable (finance costs)	72,100	93,900	109,200	99,300	83,200	74,200	71,100	67,200	60,100	59,100
Basic earnings per share	20.68	25.21	38.03	39.45	36.96	62.59	116.26	105.30	1.22	0.77
Current assets	3,063,400	3,477,600	3,876,000	3,763,900	3,444,300	5,742,000	4,821,500	4,706,100	4,189,000	3,804,000
Trade receivables	44,300	50,600	51,500	56,100	58,100	60,100	66,100	54,300	57,600	59,500
Trade payables	154,000	150,800	181,200	138,300	150,000	196,500	230,600	294,100	249,600	573,800
Inventories	2,500	2,700	2,800	2,700	2,500	2,100	3,300	3,100	3,700	2,900

	2010	2011	2012	2013	2014	2015	2016	2017	2018	2019
Current liabilities	1,549,600	1,837,200	1,815,000	1,911,700	2,274,500	3,346,000	3,369,500	3,011,800	3,412,900	4,096,600
Non-current liabilities	3,165,200	3,804,900	3,879,300	3,758,700	3,251,800	4,804,300	4,252,000	4,554,900	4,480,000	3,939,200
Shareholders' equity	2,848,600	2,953,900	3,306,700	3,272,600	3,285,500	4,035,100	3,596,800	4,423,000	4,468,900	5,214,900
Capital employed	6,013,800	6,758,800	7,186,000	7,031,300	6,537,300	8,839,400	7,848,800	8,977,900	8,948,900	9,154,100

	2010 Base (100)	2011	2012	2013	2014	2015	2016	2017	2018	2019
Sales	2,988,100	121	147	163	169	189	219	222	239	258
Operating profit	402,100	121	170	179	164	259	363	381	415	253
Profit after tax	305,300	123	184	186	171	284	511	431	475	290
Interest payable	72,100	130	151	138	115	103	99	93	83	82
Basic EPS	21	122	184	191	179	303	562	509	6	4
Current assets	3,063,400	114	127	123	112	187	157	154	137	124
Current liabilities	1,549,600	119	117	123	147	216	217	194	220	264
Trade receivables	44,300	114	116	127	131	136	149	123	130	134
Trade payables	154,000	98	118	90	97	128	150	191	162	373
Inventories	2,500	108	112	108	100	84	132	124	148	116
Shareholders' equity	2,848,600	104	116	115	115	142	126	155	157	183
Non-current liabilities	3,165,200	120	123	119	103	152	134	144	142	124
Capital employed	6,013,800	112	119	117	109	147	131	149	149	152

income statement, the revenue should be restated as '100' and all subsequent figures are measured according to this baseline. In the statement of financial position, use your (net) assets figure as the baseline. This will mean, of course, you have two totals both adding up to '100'. This exercise will highlight those balances which are significant (in terms of size) from those which are less so. Again, auditors use this technique to identify material balances and areas of higher than average potential risk.

Worked Example 3.2 shows Ryanair's statement of financial position as at 31 March 2019 and income statement for the year ended 31 March 2019 plus one comparative period.

WORKED EXAMPLE 3.2 Vertical analysis for Ryanair Holdings plc

Table 3.3

Income statements				
For the year ended 31 March	**2019**		**2018**	
	€ m	**%**	**€ m**	**%**
Revenue	7,697.4	100.0%	7,151.0	100.0%
Operating expenses:				
Fuel and oil	(2,427.3)	−31.5%	(1,902.8)	−26.6%
Airport and handling charges	(1,061.5)	−13.8%	(938.6)	−13.1%
Staff costs	(984.0)	−12.8%	(738.5)	−10.3%
Route charges	(745.2)	−9.7%	(701.8)	−9.8%
Depreciation	(640.5)	−8.3%	(561.0)	−7.8%
Marketing, distribution and other	(547.3)	−7.1%	(410.4)	−5.7%
Maintenance, materials and repairs	(190.9)	−2.5%	(148.3)	−2.1%
Aircraft rentals	(83.9)	−1.1%	(82.3)	−1.2%
Operating profit	1,016.8		1,667.3	
Other income/(expense):				
Finance income	3.7	0.0%	2.0	0.0%
Finance expense	(59.1)	−0.8%	(60.1)	−0.8%
Foreign exchange gain/(loss)	(3.5)	0.0%	2.1	0.0%
Share of associate losses	(15.8)	−0.2%	0.0	0.0%
Gain on disposal of available for sale asset	6.0	0.1%	0.0	0.0%
Profit before tax	948.1		1,611.3	
Tax expense on profit on ordinary activities	(63.1)	−0.8%	(161.1)	−2.3%
Profit for the year	885.0		1,450.2	

Expert view 3.1: Reflections of other stakeholders

Ryanair is a successful airline. However, it has to satisfy a range of stakeholders and not just its current and potential shareholders. One of the problems airlines have is whether environmentalists will be as happy to see increased numbers of passengers and high levels of profitability.

Table 3.4

Statements of financial position				
As at year ended 31 March	**2019**		**2018**	
	€m	**%**	**€m**	**%**
Non-current assets				
Property, plant and equipment	9,026.9	68.1%	8,123.4	65.7%
Intangible assets	146.4	1.1%	46.8	0.4%
Available for sale assets	227.5	1.7%	2.6	0.0%
Derivative financial instruments	43.2	0.3%	0	0.0%
Total non-current assets	9,444.0	71.3%	8,172.8	66.1%
Current assets				
Inventories	2.9	0.0%	3.7	0.0%
Other assets	238.0	1.8%	235.5	1.9%
Trade receivables	59.5	0.4%	57.6	0.5%
Derivative financial instruments	308.7	2.3%	212.1	1.7%
Restricted cash	34.9	0.3%	34.6	0.3%
Financial assets: cash > 3 months	1,484.4	11.2%	2,130.5	17.2%
Cash and cash equivalents	1,675.6	12.6%	1,515.0	12.3%
Total current assets	3,804.0	28.7%	4,189.0	33.9%
Total assets	13,248.0	100.0%	12,361.8	100.0%
Current liabilities				
Trade payables	573.8	4.3%	249.6	2.0%
Accrued expenses and other liabilities	2,992.1	22.6%	2,502.2	20.2%
Current maturities of debt	309.4	2.3%	434.6	3.5%
Current tax	31.6	0.2%	36.0	0.3%
Derivative financial instruments	189.7	w1.4%	190.5	1.5%
Total current liabilities	4,096.6	30.9%	3,412.9	27.6%

(continued)

Table 3.4   *(Continued)*

Non-current liabilities				
Provisions	135.6	1.0%	138.1	1.1%
Derivative financial instruments	8.0	0.1%	415.5	3.4%
Deferred tax	460.6	3.5%	395.2	3.2%
Other creditors	0.0	0.0%	2.8	0.0%
Non-current maturities of debt	3,335.0	25.2%	3,528.4	28.5%
Total non-current liabilities	3,939.2	29.7%	4,480.0	36.2%
Equity and reserves				
Issued share capital	6.8	0.1%	7.0	0.1%
Share premium account	719.4	5.4%	719.4	5.8%
Other undenominated capital	3.2	0.0%	3.0	0.0%
Retained earnings	4,181.9	31.6%	4,077.9	33.0%
Other reserves	303.6	2.3%	(338.4)	−2.7%
Equity and reserves	5,214.9	39.4%	4,468.9	36.2%
	13,250.7	100.0%	12,361.8	100.0%

Interpreting vertical analysis information

It should be straightforward to appreciate why this mode of analysis is both appealing and informative. An analyst's focus will be immediately drawn to the most significant balances. By comparing with prior years' vertical analysis, it can also be used as a form of horizontal analysis. In the case of Ryanair, the key drivers of profitability are revenue, staff costs, depreciation, fuel and oil, route charges, and airport and handling costs. Fuel and oil costs equate to approximately one-third of total revenue (2019: 31.5%; 2018: 26.6%) and are therefore of prime importance to the end result. Thus, changes in the wholesale price of fuel – which is typically a volatile commodity – or a shift in the way the cost of fuel and oil is managed (hedging programme) can have far-reaching (positive or negative) consequences for an airline such as Ryanair.

The asset balances which stand out as important on face of the statement of financial position are the non-current assets (ie the aircraft) and the level of cash and cash equivalents. The horizontal analysis reveals that Ryanair does not maintain an annual dividend payment policy, although they do sporadically buy back their own stock. This is a way for the company to distribute some of its accumulated cash reserves. Nonetheless, some cash is required by the company as a buffer to protect itself during lean periods. Profits in the airline industry are notoriously unpredictable (a high reliance on fixed costs such as wages and depreciation means that the business is subject to relatively more volatile profits) and there are, unfortunately, many instances over the past decade of airlines – as well as a wide range of other companies – that have not survived. Trade payables have risen in 2019, and the cause of this is unclear. Only limited information is provided in the annual report, and therefore the reasons for this increase would require further investigation. The liability that is most prominent relates to long-term debt, which is required to purchase the non-current assets (aircraft).

Please note that there are many other useful and insightful observations one could make based upon the vertical analysis above. This is a method, however, which should be used in conjunction with other techniques as it simply allows an analyst to undertake a quick appraisal of key figures. The strength of the technique lies in its simplicity to perform and interpret. Its weaknesses stem from the same roots.

Ratio analysis

Introduction to ratio analysis

Undertaking ratio analysis, at least in theory, is a straightforward process. One simply needs to carefully select a relevant numerator and divide it by an equally relevant denominator to produce a calculation that has the potential to be meaningful in relation to appraising the performance, position and/or strategy of the entity. Once the result has been found, an interpretation and further analysis should follow where applicable. Your calculation will often provide a ratio (eg current ratio), a percentage (eg gross profit margin), but there are other ratios that show a number of times (eg interest cover) or a number of days (eg trade receivables collection period).

You should note at this stage the important consideration that attempting to interpret one ratio in isolation – even as a time-series – is, at best, unhelpful and at worst, misleading. The purpose of the exercise is to draw an opinion about relative levels of position and performance. The question we should be asking is, 'relative to whom or what'? In short, ratio analysis is most commonly used in order to:

- evaluate current year performance and position;
- compare performance and position across time periods (time-series analysis);
- assess whether target ratios have been met;
- review firm-specific performance against a peer or the industry as a whole (cross-sectional analysis).

Expert view 3.2: Ratio analysis interpretation skills development

Practise, practise and practise! Read, read and read!

We are surrounded by financial information and news. Though we can set out ratios to learn and give you some hints and advice on how to interpret the results, nobody is able to develop interpretation skills without practice and without reading what others have written:

> Ratios are tools, and their value is limited when used alone. The more tools used, the better the analysis. For example, you can't use the same golf club for every shot and expect to be a good golfer. The more you practise with each club, however, the better able you will be to gauge which club to use on one shot. So too, we need to be skilled with the financial tools we use. (Diane Morrison, CEO REC Inc)

As a word of caution and advice, we have found that it is common for students to learn a long list of ratios without meaningfully engaging with the material which they are being asked to examine. This is completely understandable, especially for those who have not been required to perform this type of analysis before but a more in-depth approach to understanding the ratio and then analysing the output of the ratio is more fulfilling. The problem is accentuated for those who are not actively engaging on a daily basis with current affairs, particularly the business news. We strongly advocate that you pursue a broader contextual understanding. Over time, this deeper engagement will make you a better analyst and lead to better decision making.

Key ratios

Profitability ratios

Profitability ratios are intended to measure the performance of the entity. As stated above, the two main ways to undertake ratio analysis such as this is by calculating and analysing changes over time (time-series analysis) or by comparing the results to a competitor or the industry (cross-sectional analysis).

Newcomers to profitability analysis might be drawn towards the bottom line of the income statement (ie profit for the year) and compare with the previous year's number. Indeed, as Extract 3.1 shows, profitability is a *headline grabber*. Higher than expected profits are interpreted as good news, while heavy losses and/or profit warnings are bad news that can have serious consequences for a firm's share (stock) price. The first press release identifies how Balfour Beatty plc returned to profit during 2016. This has attracted attention because it is seen as an encouraging sign. Equally, however, the two extracts in 3.1 show that these business reporters have dug deeper into the information to understand why the levels of profitability have changed; and, in the case of Bristol-Myers Squibb, whether there is a potential upside in a profit warning. Thus, though year-on-year profits are important, relying on them as an assessment of annual (or ongoing) performance is somewhat naive. Also, comparing actual profits between entities is not an especially useful measure given the importance of relative size to levels of return. We present the three core profitability ratios below alongside interpretation hints. These are:

- return on capital employed;
- gross profit margin; and
- net profit margin.

Of course, we strongly advise that you drill down into the results and undertake further analysis where appropriate. This can be done using other financial and non-financial performance-related information as well as by employing other analysis techniques, eg horizontal analysis, trend analysis or vertical analysis.

Extract 3.1: Profitability as a headline grabber

a) Profitability: The importance of the bottom line

Balfour Beatty returns to profit

BBC (16 March 2017)

The company behind Crossrail and the transformation of the former Olympic Stadium into West Ham's ground made an £8m profit, after a £199m loss in 2015. Balfour said… by 2014, it had become overly complex following more than a decade of acquisition-led growth. It added there had been an overall lack of leadership and strategic direction, and that its businesses had a tendency to compete with each other. However, Balfour says its business has now been simplified… Analysts have been encouraged by the company's progress. 'The self-help phase of the turnaround plan has restored the group to reasonable foundations, with the all-important construction division back in profit in the second half,' said Nicholas Hyett, equity analyst at Hargreaves Lansdown. 'The strategy now calls for the group to rebuild margins towards something close to industry standard – at around 2% it's not an overly ambitious target on the face of it, but something Balfour have failed to achieve for some time,' he said.

b) Profit warning

Bristol-Myers Squibb making lemonade from lemons
The Wall Street Journal (27 January 2017)
By Charley Grant

Bristol-Myers Squibb hasn't put its recent woes behind it just yet, but the moment of opportunity for value investors is getting closer. The company reported fourth-quarter sales of $5.2 billion, which topped analyst expectations, and adjusted earnings of 63 cents a share, which missed. It also cut its 2017 profit forecast. Shares slipped once again Thursday and have shed nearly 20% so far this year. The profit warning comes despite sales of the company's best-selling drug, the cancer treatment Opdivo, topping analyst expectations. A series of bad developments starting last August have weighed on the shares. Bristol-Myers has lost its leadership status in the race to conquer the lucrative lung cancer market with new immunotherapies. A key clinical trial testing Opdivo failed over the summer and rivals have gained ground... The good news is that much of this is already baked in and the stock has become much cheaper as a result.

(a) Return on capital employed (ROCE)

It is common for investors to view the return on capital employed (ROCE), or some closely related derivation of this ratio (eg return on equity, return on common equity, return on shareholders' funds, accounting rate of return), as the most important measure of performance. Below, we present the formula for the most commonly used version.
ROCE is calculated as:

$$\frac{\text{Profit}}{\text{Capital}} \times 100\% \text{ or, more precisely: } \frac{\text{Profit before interest and tax}}{\text{Capital employed}} \times 100\%$$

But when undertaking this analysis, please always try to remain unbiased and analytical. There are not just many variations of the ROCE, but also many of the other key management ratios that we will present over the next few pages. We strongly urge you to always perform your own calculations. Not only will this give you the comfort of knowing what has been included/excluded, it will help you understand the nature of the ratio, its purpose and meaning, and it will also aid more meaningful comparisons when undertaking cross-sectional analysis. Throughout this exercise, there is one fundamental but largely unspoken ratio that you should always bear in mind: garbage in = garbage out!

What does this ratio reveal? The ROCE weighs up the level of return generated during a period of account relative to the amount of capital that has been provided. Sometimes the ROCE is used as a threshold measure by management when deciding whether to accept or reject future proposed projects. It is also commonly used when appraising historic performance. In other words, looking at this relationship through the eyes of the capital provider, investors are attempting to gauge how well their money has been spent and how well the resources have been managed. In extreme cases, one could argue that an entity that returns less than the risk-free rate of return might be better off liquidating the assets and investing the cash proceeds in 10-year US government treasury bonds.

It is not true to simply state that the higher the ROCE the better. This oversimplifies the problem by ignoring context. A high ROCE does not necessarily mean that an entity is a *good* investment. Remember that investors weigh up returns against risk. For example, an entity with an average ROCE of, say, 10 per cent in the oil and gas extraction industry would be seen as a relatively poor performer, whereas the same ROCE achieved by a property trust company, for instance, would be seen as a healthy investment.

One could rightly suggest, however, that if the ROCE fell below the company's investors' expected weighted required rates of return, the investment would be deemed a poor one. Corporate entities are looking to invest in projects that generate wealth. If the ROCE falls below these required rates of return, the projects which are being undertaken are destroying wealth. Occasionally the decision to take on lower-yielding projects is necessary, but to do so on a regular and long-term basis increases the risk of capital extraction which would be detrimental to the position of the firm.

Drilling down to interpret the changes in the ratio A ratio provides a result about which one can make broad, descriptive and somewhat meaningless statements. For example, as Worked Example 3.3 shows, the ROCE has decreased from 18.6 per cent in 2018 to 11.1 per cent in 2019. When trying to interpret this ratio, one should not be limited to statements such as: 'This change points towards a bad year for Ryanair in terms of returns to investors and their performance.' Frankly, we don't know whether this actually indicates a bad (or a good) year for the company, whether this is a function of managerial decision-making, strategy, or an exogeneity (eg recession, commodity prices). Before we could make this assessment we would need to ask a number of follow-up questions, for example:

- Were the results in line with targets?
- How do the results compare to those from previous years?
- Does this ROCE meet or beat market expectations?
- How did competitors perform during the same period of account?

- How has this percentage decrease happened and what are the plans to improve (if any)?
- Is this ROCE sustainable or should we expect it to fall further?

If all you have to work with is the financial information itself, your analysis will be limited. Nevertheless, you will be able to make some strides towards identifying trends, patterns, strengths, weaknesses and potential areas of upside and downside risk. For accounting non-specialists it can be difficult to see how the balances in the primary statements interlink, but it is extremely helpful if you are able to engage with this idea. You might now have a better appreciation of why it is necessary to go through a series of financial accounting exercises – such as those set out in Chapters 1 and 2. This knowledge allows you to see and better understand the interrelationship between assets and liabilities, gains and losses.

There are two variables that determine an entity's ROCE: profit; and capital employed. For the ratio to move downwards like this (from 18.6 per cent to 11.1 per cent), one of the following must have occurred:

- Profit has decreased and capital employed has increased.
- Profit has decreased proportionately more than capital employed.
- Capital employed has increased proportionately more than profit.
- Profit has stayed the same and capital employed increased.
- Capital employed has stayed the same and profit has decreased.

In this example, operating profit dropped by approximately 40 per cent whilst capital employed increased by 2 per cent. The weight in the formula is leant to the denominator (because of the volume of capital employed) but these movements have a magnifying effect on the result. Further analysis shows that, whilst revenue increased by 7 per cent in 2019 (traffic growth of 9 per cent), during the same time period operating costs rose by 22 per cent. The company has an incredible industry-leading track record of being able to achieve revenue growth whilst at the same time cutting costs, but there were a number of events during fiscal year 2019 which put this out of reach. Indeed, summer 2018 was a very difficult period for airlines and package holiday firms. This contributed to the failure of at least one major name in the industry (Thomas Cook). There was a heat wave across Northern Europe and the football World Cup in Russia meant more people simply stayed at home. In addition, there were strikes and staff shortages that led to thousands of flight delays and cancellations. In response, Ryanair closed certain bases (Bremen and Eindhoven) and made capacity cuts elsewhere. The capacity was reallocated to growth markets, such as Turkey. Finally, there was the shadow of Brexit hanging over the UK throughout this period. That brought with it uncertainty and slowing economic growth.

The opening paragraph of the Chief Executive's report on the period reads as follows: 'We are pleased to present Ryanair's 2019 Annual Report, which covers a year of significant challenges. Overcapacity in Europe and our continuing growth saw average fares fall 6 per cent but this stimulated traffic growth of 9 per cent to 142m guests. Ancillaries performed well with spend up 11 per cent per guest. We faced a number of cost challenges including higher oil prices, a step up in payroll costs under new 5 year pay deals for pilots and cabin crew, and an extraordinary jump in our EU261 costs due to repeated ATC strikes and staff shortages through summer 2018. As a direct result of these lower air fares, our full year profits fell 39 per cent to €885m (€1.02bn excl. Laudamotion start-up losses). This was a reasonable performance by a robust business model in difficult trading circumstances. Despite these headwinds, we delivered an industry leading 96 per cent load factor, concluded union agreements with pilots and cabin crew in most of our major markets, and returned a further €560m to shareholders via share buy-backs' (Ryanair annual report, 2019, p 6).

There were no major movements in capital employed, but if there had been, we would need to drill down into those balances. For example, it might be that non-current liabilities could have increased, in which case you might want to see whether this was the result of borrowing to finance new long-term assets (loans for aircraft). If it was used to buy aeroplanes or other revenue-generating property, plant and equipment (PPE), we would expect to see an increase in non-current assets in the statement of financial position as well. This would then impact on ratios such as asset turnover. More importantly, we would expect to see increases in revenue as a result of asset purchases, assuming the assets were put to use. Related to this, it may be worth noting that there may be a lag because it is difficult to bring assets into immediate use. You will see that a shift in one ratio will typically have consequences for others, and hence your interpretation of performance and position shifts depending on the questions you are asking and/or the concerns you have.

Given this information, you should now have a whole host of further questions which you would want to investigate, for example:

- How did the company manage to increase revenue by 7 per cent but their non-current liabilities fell by 9 per cent?

- The reported load factor per aircraft is around 96 per cent (ie how full the average plane was), but does this include all aircraft? How does that compare with the break-even load factor past results, and can this result be repeated?

- Customer demand seems to be growing every year, but there seem to be capacity concerns amongst management and investors, particularly in Europe where there are many rival low-cost airlines.

- Were planes bought in previous years which have been brought into operational usage this year?

- What are the ownership arrangements for the aircraft? Does the company own them or are they held on operating leases?

- The average seat decreased in price during the period, but is this forecast into the future? Is this sustainable?

- And so forth...

Complications in the calculation

i) How should profit be defined?

When we refer to profit in the calculation of ROCE, it is usual to consider *operating profit* as the most useful indicator of performance rather than the profit for the year or retained profits. This is also referred to as profit before interest and tax (or 'PBIT'). The rationale for using this figure over others is that it provides a clearer message about current performance, and just as importantly, current stewardship. Using this figure also aids greater comparability between entities which are often subject to different financing requirements and taxation regimes.

Why exclude taxation costs?

Assuming that taxation regimes are fair and well-managed, then paying a bigger tax bill while maintaining the same effective tax rate could be interpreted as a reflection of better performance and, by extension, all things being equal, good stewardship. Therefore judging performance based upon profits after tax risks levelling out the playing field by inappropriately recognizing those companies with lower tax bills based upon lower pre-tax profits. Of course, we acknowledge that tax is controllable to a certain degree and sound financial planning alongside flexible accounting policies and practices can reduce the effective tax rate.

Why exclude finance costs?

First and foremost, because we are trying to match like with like. In other words, we are reporting capital employed as equity plus non-current liabilities, therefore we want to know what the profits due to both equity and debt finance providers are (ie before deductions for interest paid).

There is also a second, albeit lesser, reason for excluding interest paid. Interest expenditure normally dominates the finance costs category (although other costs are included, eg gains and losses on derivative financial instruments held for trading). Loans are normally matched to the term over which the assets are held. For example, an aeroplane is thought to continue to generate revenues for approximately 23 years and loans are negotiated on this basis. If the senior management team turnover rate is, say, one every five years or so, we must ask whether it is fair and appropriate to judge new management against old loans.

There is also some debate over whether profit before interest and tax actually means profit before interest *payable* and tax. Indeed, it is common for finance income to be added to the operating profit number while finance costs are excluded from operating profit.

ii) What does capital employed mean?

Those responsible for providing capital to a corporate entity have the expectation that the management will select and undertake value-generating activities which adequately and appropriately reward the risks which they have chosen to bear. Capital provision, or project financing, is considered to arise from one or both of these sources: equity and/or debt.

- Equity can be provided through internal financing, such as accumulated reserves or shortening the working capital cycle. However, it is far more common that the term equity is used in reference to the raising of funds through the sale of share capital.

- Debt is a term which is used to refer to all forms of borrowing – of which there are many. Companies might, for example, apply for loans from banks or other lenders, take out mortgages to help them buy land and buildings, long-term hire purchase agreements to acquire plant, vehicles and machinery, sell loan stock to finance an expansion plan, and so forth.

  - Note that we have drawn your attention only to long-term debt financing, thereby ignoring other forms of short-term debt such as a bank overdraft. In short, there are no rules for inclusion or exclusion of short-term borrowings. We suggest that if a bank overdraft is used as a long-term financing option, it should be included as debt under capital provided.

Capital provided can therefore be summarized as:

Equity + Debt

In relation to the statement of financial position, we suggest you use as a proxy for these two categories:

Shareholders' funds + Non-current liabilities

Occasionally you will see businesses average out the capital employed. We suggest that this is practical when appraising single one-off investments (as the opening and closing capital required will be easily to hand), but when your focus is on calculating the ROCE for the entity as a whole, it is simpler to extract the closing (period-end) positions and use these.

Extract 3.2: Profitability explained

Samsung forecast beats estimates despite scandals and fires

BBC online (7 April 2017)
Karishma Vaswani

Samsung Electronics is on track to report record annual earnings, despite its defacto boss going on trial in a political corruption scandal.

It is forecasting a 48% rise in profits in the January-to-March period, thanks to strong memory chip sales. That would be its best quarterly profit in almost four years and shows a recovery from the Galaxy Note 7 fiasco.

The estimates are not too shabby given the corruption allegations and the embarrassment of exploding phones.

The forecast $8.8bn (£7bn) profits don't include what the company is hoping to make from its new phone, the new and improved Galaxy 8, which hits the shelves later this month. Analysts are saying Samsung's second quarter results should even be better than the first quarter, because of the hype surrounding the Galaxy 8 and the artificial intelligence technology, called Bixby, embedded in it.

Google parent Alphabet's stock falls, but big earnings miss doesn't sway upbeat Wall Street analysts

Market Watch (30 October 2019)

Tomi Kilgore

Alphabet shares bounce off worst post-earnings levels as at least 18 analysts surveyed by FactSet raise price targets.
Alphabet Inc reported a big third-quarter earnings miss, but the Google parent's shares bounced sharply off their worst levels, as a gaggle of Wall Street analysts raised their price targets on the revenue beat and massive stock repurchases.

The internet giant's stock GOOGL, +0.36% GOOG, +0.46% fell 2.2% to $1,260.66 on Tuesday, a day after it reached an all-time intraday high of $1,299.24. The stock pared losses of as much as 4.5% seen in Monday's after-hours session, according to FactSet data, after Alphabet reported earnings per share that fell to $10.12 from $13.06 a year ago and missed the FactSet consensus of $12.28.

While profit disappointed, revenue rose 20% to $40.5 billion, above the FactSet consensus of $40.3 billion, and the company said it stepped up quarterly share repurchases by nearly 60% to $5.7 billion.

Of the 46 analysts surveyed by FactSet, no less than 19 have raised their stock price targets. The average target has increased to $1,455.88, which was 15.5% above Tuesday's closing price, from $1,415.54 as of the end of September.

The average rating remained at the equivalent of buy, as 39 analysts had bullish ratings and just 7 were at the equivalent of neutral. There are no sell ratings.

(b) Gross profit margin

The gross profit margin is a key ratio which enables the analyst to assess trading performance before deducting operating expenses. Or, in other words, the direct profit earned in relation to the sales made. The ratio is calculated as:

$$\frac{\text{Gross profit}}{\text{Revenue}} \times 100\%$$

It is rare that there are definitional problems like those shown in the calculation of the ROCE above. The gross profit is calculated as:

	Revenue
Minus	Cost of sales

We introduced cost of sales as being:

	Opening inventories
Plus	Purchases
Minus	Closing inventories

And, in many cases – specifically for merchandisers (ie, companies that sell product in an unrefined/unmodified way, like a supermarket) – this recording of cost of sales makes sense. However, for manufacturers the cost of sales is more appropriately referred to as the cost of goods sold. The revised inference is that you are expected to include the direct costs of production in this figure, which includes manufacturing overhead. Thus, the cost of goods sold includes not only direct materials purchase costs, but direct labour costs, production-related factory costs, and similar. Inclusion or exclusion of costs 'above the line' (ie within cost of sales or above the gross profit line) between entities can create difficulties when performing analysis. If you are undertaking sector (or industry) analysis and you identify significant differences from one company to the next, we suggest you calculate the net profit margin and ensure that this isn't the result of an expense classification difference.

Most companies will disclose their gross profit figure. Airlines, however, cluster all of their costs into operating expenses. This is unusual. It does mean that we are not able to calculate a gross profit margin for Ryanair. Nevertheless, when analysing a change in this ratio, your first challenge will be to work out why. There are only two variables:

- Has revenue increased, decreased or stayed the same?
- Has the cost of sales increased, decreased or stayed the same?

To help target your investigations, you might consider the following possible explanations as to why the variation could have arisen:

- Changes in the sales mix, eg:

  - Were new products launched during the year?
  - Were old products withdrawn from sale?
  - Were high-margin/low-margin products more/less popular this year than in prior years?

- Changes in sales price.
- An increase/decrease in discounts offered to customers.
- A change in inventories sourcing procedures or/and supplier(s).
- Changes to the products and the associated raw materials requirements.
- An increase/decrease in production process efficiency.
- An increase/decrease in discounts being offered by suppliers.
- Changes to cost classifications, from or to operating expenses.
- An increase/decrease in inventory value write-offs due to obsolescence or other factors.
- And so forth...

(c) Net profit margin

The net profit margin is a key ratio which enables the analyst to assess trading performance after the deduction of operating expenses. It is a measure of operating profit in relation to revenue and provides a guide as to how well the company has performed during the year. The ratio is calculated as:

$$\frac{\text{Operating profit}}{\text{Revenue}} \times 100\%$$

As discussed above (in relation to the ROCE), the calculation of the net profit margin can also be adapted to take different measures of profitability. Most commonly, the net profit margin uses operating profit (PBIT). This facilitates comparability and takes into account the costs which are controllable by management.

Levels of profitability are inherently difficult to compare between entities and between years, let alone between companies operating in different industries. Results will be dependent upon managerial stewardship and firm performance, but will also relate to external events such as the prevailing economic conditions and the degree of competition.

Ryanair's net profit margin has increased from 18.4 per cent in 2015 to 22.3 per cent in 2016. As with previous ratios, this observation requires further analysis and explanation. A naive observer would be keen to make the point that this is an improvement on the prior year and indeed, it might be. However, this statement is not verifiable without reference to other information. You might like to consider the following questions:

- What does your horizontal, trend and vertical analysis show you about the cost structure and year-on-year line item comparisons?
- Have costs risen in line with, above or below inflation?
- To what extent is the movement in the profit margin a reflection of commodity price movements which are less (or sometimes even un-)controllable, eg fuel costs?
- How have other companies responded to the economic climate and have their costs moved comparably to the entity under review?
- Have there been any recognition or measurement accounting policy changes, eg changes to depreciation rates?

Though each entity's cost structure and strategy will be different, the level of change in certain costs is generally worthy of separate enquiry when you are undertaking this form of analysis:

- research and development;
- depreciation and amortization;
- pension costs;
- employee costs, including staff training and development spend (if separately disclosed);
- directors' remuneration;
- government grants.

The following extract provides a brief business overview (Ryanair Annual Report, 2019: page 98):

Since Ryanair pioneered its low cost operating model in Europe in the early 1990s, its passenger volumes and scheduled passenger revenues have increased significantly because the Company has substantially increased capacity and demand has been sufficient to match the increased capacity. Ryanair's annual booked passenger volume has grown from approximately 0.9m passengers in the calendar year 1992 to approximately 142.1m passengers in fiscal year 2019.

Ryanair's revenue passenger miles ('RPMs') increased approximately 9% from 101,022m in fiscal year 2018 to 109,976m in fiscal year 2019 due to an increase of approximately 9% in scheduled available seat miles ('ASMs') from 105,735m in fiscal year 2018 to 115,524m in fiscal year 2019. Scheduled passenger revenues increased from €5,134.0m in fiscal year 2018 to €5,261.1m in fiscal year 2019. Average booked passenger fare decreased from €39.40 in fiscal year 2018 to €37.03 in fiscal year 2019.

Expanding passenger volumes and capacity, high load factors and aggressive cost containment have enabled Ryanair to continue to generate operating profits despite increasing price competition and increases in certain costs. Ryanair's total break-even load factor was 73% in fiscal year 2018 and 83% in fiscal year 2019. Cost per passenger was €42.08 in fiscal year 2018 and €47.02 in fiscal year 2019, with the higher fuel cost per passenger of €17.08 in fiscal year 2019 as compared to €14.60 in fiscal year 2018 being the most significant factor behind this increase. Ryanair recorded operating profits of €1,667.3m in fiscal year 2018 and €1,016.8m in fiscal year 2019. The Company recorded a profit after taxation of €1,450.2m in fiscal year 2018 and €885.0m in fiscal year 2019. Ryanair took delivery of 29 Boeing 737-800 aircraft in fiscal year 2019. The Company is planning on the basis of taking delivery of approximately 30 Boeing 737-MAX-200 aircraft in advance of summer 2020 and expects that these deliveries, net of lease handbacks and aircraft sales, will allow for an approximately 3% increase in fiscal year 2020 traffic.

However, past results are not necessarily indicative of future performance. To this end, it is worth noting the following extract (from Ryanair Annual Report, 2016: pp 98–99):

The historical results of operations discussed herein may not be indicative of Ryanair's future operating performance. Ryanair's future results of operations will be affected by, among other things, overall passenger traffic volume; the availability of new airports for expansion; fuel prices; the airline pricing environment in a period of increased competition; the ability of Ryanair to finance its planned acquisition of aircraft and to discharge the resulting debt service obligations; economic and political conditions in Ireland, the UK and the EU; the ability of the Company to generate profits for new acquisitions; terrorist threats or attacks within the EU; seasonal variations in travel; developments in government regulations, litigation and labor relations; foreign currency fluctuations, the impact of the banking crisis and potential break-up of the Eurozone; Brexit; the availability of aircraft; competition and the public's perception regarding the safety of low-fares airlines; changes in aircraft acquisition, leasing, and other operating costs; flight interruptions caused by extreme weather events or other atmospheric disruptions; aircraft safety concerns; flight disruptions caused by periodic and prolonged ATC strikes in Europe; the rates of income and corporate taxes paid, and the impact of the financial and Eurozone crisis. Ryanair expects its depreciation, staff and fuel charges to increase as additional aircraft and related flight equipment are acquired. Future fuel costs may also increase as a result of the depletion of petroleum reserves, the shortage of fuel production capacity and/or production restrictions imposed by fuel oil producers. Maintenance expenses may also increase as a result of Ryanair's fleet expansion and replacement program. In addition, the financing of new Boeing 737-800 and Boeing 737-MAX-200 aircraft will increase the total amount of the Company's outstanding debt and the payments it is obliged to make to service such debt. The cost of insurance coverage for certain third-party liabilities arising from 'acts of war' or terrorism increased dramatically following the September 11, 2001 terrorist attacks.

WORKED EXAMPLE 3.3 Ryanair's profitability ratios

Return On Capital Employed:

	2019	2018
	€m	€m
Operating profit (PBIT) (excluding finance income and costs)	1,016.8	1,667.3
Shareholders' funds	5,214.9	4,468.9
+	+	+
Non-current liabilities (including *all* non-current liabilities)	3,939.2	4,480.0
	$\dfrac{1,016.8 \times 100\%}{9,154.1}$	$\dfrac{1,667.3 \times 100\%}{8,948.9}$
	$= 11.1\%$	$= 18.6\%$

Gross profit margin:

$$\frac{\text{Gross profit} \times 100\%}{\text{Revenue}}$$

	2019	2018
Gross profit	N/A	N/A
Revenue	7,697.4	7,151.0
	$= \text{N/A}$	$= \text{N/A}$

(continued)

Return On Capital Employed:

	2019	2018
	€m	€m
Net profit margin:		
$\dfrac{\text{Operating profit (PBIT)}}{\text{Revenue}} \times 100\%$		
Operating profit (PBIT) (excluding finance income and costs)	1,016.8	1,667.3
Revenue	7,697.4	7,151.0

<table>
<tr><td></td><td>$\dfrac{1,016.8 \times 100\%}{7,697.4}$</td><td>$\dfrac{1,667.3 \times 100\%}{7,151.0}$</td></tr>
<tr><td></td><td>$= 13.2\%$</td><td>$= 23.3\%$</td></tr>
</table>

Extract 3.3: Ryanair Holdings plc: Chairman's report, 2019

CHAIRMAN'S REPORT

Dear Shareholders,

Last year we made significant progress in growing Ryanair as Europe's largest airline group. We aim to carry 200m guests per annum over the next 5 years. Highlights of the year include:

- Traffic grew 9% to over 142m guests
- Avg. air fares were cut 6% to €37
- Revenue rose 6% to €7.6bn as ancillary revenue increased by 11% per guest
- Ryanair Sun ('Buzz') was launched and traded profitably in its first year
- We acquired 100% of Lauda, and transformed its fleet and operations
- We negotiated union agreements in most of our key markets
- We took delivery of 29 B737s and 16 A320s while investing in our business for future growth
- We took decisive actions to improve on-time-performance (despite record ATC disruptions)

- We continued to deliver our environmental targets and now publish CO2 data monthly

- Over €560m was returned to shareholders via share buy-backs

At a time of excess capacity in the European short-haul market, Ryanair's cost leadership, and strong balance sheet, means that we are well placed to take advantage of the growth opportunities that will arise as airlines consolidate and/or exit the market. In May, your Board approved a further €700m share buy-back program which will, depending on market conditions, run for 9 to 12 months. Following this latest distribution, Ryanair will have returned €7bn to shareholders since 2008.

The Board, in conjunction with management, are closely monitoring delivery delays to the Boeing 737-MAX-200 aircraft. Subject to FAA and EASA regulatory approval, we hope to receive our first 'gamechanger' aircraft sometime between January and February 2020. Ryanair is therefore planning summer 2020 capacity on the basis of having 30 MAX aircraft, rather than the 58 originally scheduled, which will slow down growth from approximately 7% to approximately 3% in fiscal year 2021 where we will now carry 157m guests instead of the 162m previously expected.

As already announced, Michael O'Leary has agreed a new 5-year contract as Group CEO, which secures his services for the Group until at least July 2024. We welcome his agreement to commit for a further 5-year period, which gives certainty to our shareholders. Both Kyran McLaughlin and I have agreed to lead the Board until summer 2020, but we do not wish to be considered for re-election at the September 2020 AGM. In order to ensure a smooth succession, Stan McCarthy (who joined the Board in May 2017) agreed to become Deputy Chairman from April 2019 and will transition to Chairman of the Board next year. Stan brings enormous international experience (as a former CEO of Kerry Group plc) and leadership skills to the development of Ryanair over the coming years. Louise Phelan (who joined the Board in December 2012) has agreed to become Senior Independent Director when Kyran McLaughlin retires from the Board in summer 2020.

I wish to thank the 16,800 highly skilled aviation professionals across the Ryanair Group who strive, on behalf of our 142m guests, each year, to deliver the lowest fares, the best on-time performance and the greenest, cleanest air travel with an ever-improving customer experience for the benefit of our customers, our people and our shareholders.

Yours sincerely,
David Bonderman
Chairman

> **Expert view 3.3: Financial analysis provided by the senior management team**
>
> One of the benefits of modern corporate reporting is the provision of a large amount of self-analysis and reflection from the senior management team. Extract 3.3 shows how Ryanair's Chairman interprets the 2019 results. Of course, this text might be intended for self-promotion purposes and there are signs of impression management. Nevertheless, what is written by these company representatives is required to be consistent with the financial information which is reported elsewhere in the annual report. It is a fantastic learning tool for those who are new to corporate reporting and financial analysis.

Liquidity ratios

Liquidity ratios are intended to provide users with an understanding of the short-term position of an entity – where short-term means the next 12 months – and whether the firm has used these short-term assets (liabilities) efficiently. A change in levels of short-term assets and liabilities can also provide some assurances over solvency and the sustainability of current levels of performance, but at the same time, excessively high levels of current liabilities would be a red-flag issue for investors. However, excessively high levels of current assets might be interpreted as a poor use of resources. Achieving the correct working capital position balance (ratio of current assets versus current liabilities) is as much an art as a science. Note that these measures can be manipulated by window dressing, ie creating or holding assets, which you otherwise would not have, at the end of an accounting period. For example, Brüggen, Krishnan and Sedatole's (2011) article in *Contemporary Accounting Research* examines inventory levels and accounting practices before the 2008 financial crisis of the Big 3 North American car manufacturers (ie General Motors Co, Ford Motor Co, and Chrysler Group LLC). It seems that these companies felt pressured to generate short-term returns and managers reported feeling tempted to deliver these results by increasing inventory. Due to their absorption costing-based inventory recording and reporting system, increasing the volume of finished goods inventories can artificially distort profits upwards despite no corresponding increase in sales. Therefore, monitoring numbers such as inventory holding period is important to understanding the business you are analysing.

There are many liquidity ratios which could be produced; however, two key ratios which you should start with are the current ratio and the acid test ratio (otherwise known as the quick ratio).

(a) Current ratio

The current ratio is calculated as follows:

$$\frac{\text{Current assets}}{\text{Current liabilities}}$$

The result is expressed as a ratio, but can also be seen as a level of coverage. You might see references to target ratios. More specifically, in the past a current ratio of 2:1 and a quick ratio of 1:1 were seen as being ideal. The presumption is that an entity can remain liquid if it has the ability to cover its immediate bills two times over if called upon to do so. Times, however, have changed and the perceptions of over/under-resourcing have also shifted. Management are frequently appraised on their ability to extract the maximum value out of their short-term liquid resources.

Commentators who hold to the belief that there is an optimum ratio of current assets to current liabilities often neglect to mention the pay-off between liquidity and profitability. If one has finite inventory production capabilities and makes the conscious decision during a period of account to stockpile inventories, then (assuming all other things are equal) the following would occur:

- current assets will be higher at the end of the period;
- thus, the current and quick ratios will increase;
- but the amount of inventory sold will be lower;
- and therefore profits will be lower.

As Worked Example 3.4 shows, the proportion of current assets held versus current liabilities in 2019 by Ryanair was 0.93; or, current liabilities were covered by current assets less than one time (0.93 times). It is common for an increase in the ratio to be interpreted as an indicator of a *better* position. As with the profitability ratios, however, liquidity ratios need to be treated with more care. We need to try to interpret the changes in the light of the drivers of the change and the broader context in which the change has occurred.

In the case of Ryanair, the ratio has moved because current liabilities have increased substantially. Trade payables more than doubled, increasing by €324 million from 2018. This is almost certainly a function of the poor trading conditions and the timing of the year end, as opposed to a deliberate creditor payment policy. Moreover, accrued expenses and other liabilities increased by almost €490 million. This was partially offset by a lower level of debt maturing in 2020. Increased current liabilities were also matched with decreased current assets, which again push the ratio downwards. The value of financial assets declined by €646 million, whilst cash and cash equivalents increased by €160 million. There was also a notable increase in value of derivative financial instruments accounts. Taken together, these movements account for the majority of the €385 million decrease in current assets. These changes are mostly explained by the pressure exerted on the firm by tougher than expected trading conditions. It is also normal for a company with a large cash reserve to buy back shares (or pay dividends) in these circumstances.

Whilst Ryanair's liquidity position – as measured by the current ratio – appears to have worsened, the result should not be over-exaggerated. It is important to look at results and the related ratios in a broader context. This was a period of economic uncertainty and trading conditions were – and continue to be – difficult for the industry. Thus a key question when analysing Ryanair's position and performance is the relative performance of the firm during this period vis-à-vis competitors, including but not limited to other low cost airlines.

(b) Acid test (quick) ratio

The acid test ratio is similar to the current ratio. The denominator remains the same (ie current liabilities) but the numerator, current assets, is adjusted for inventories. The acid test ratio is calculated as follows:

$$\frac{\text{Current assets minus inventories}}{\text{Current liabilities}}$$

The rationale for removing inventories from current assets is that they are the least liquid of assets within the class. When businesses are faced with an immediate need for cash and face genuine bankruptcy risk, their inventories are worth very little. When an entity sells inventories as a going concern, they are almost always worth more than their cost. When an entity is being wound up, the inventories held are normally worth significantly less than cost as buyers perceive the opportunity to buy at a bargain price, plus they are aware that continued spare-parts production will likely cease and maintenance will not be as readily available if the company does not survive. This phenomenon has been shown to affect companies across a wide range of industries and size does not mean you get treated differently, for example MG Rover (motor vehicles) and Lehman Brothers (financial services).

Inventories held for airlines are typically low, especially airlines like Ryanair which specialize in low-cost short-haul journeys. Ryanair carry a small amount of on-board food and duty-free goods which are intended to be sold in-flight. Therefore it could be deemed that liquidity is less relevant. It might be interesting to note that when airlines are faced with bankruptcy concerns, it is more common for competitors or new entrants to attempt to take advantage of their position by buying the struggling firm's non-current assets – planes and landing slots – at heavily discounted prices (rather than their inventories).

While you might be shocked by the huge balances of cash and cash equivalents at Ryanair, it is far from the only company to have accumulated large cash reserves over the past decade. There are several reasons for this, including: a lack of positive net present value projects to invest in, high tax rates in the United States making remittance over the border costly, a reluctance to return cash to investors during a period of uncertainty. Therefore, an adaptation of the quick ratio might be more informative:

$$\frac{\text{Cash flows from Operating Activities}^*}{\text{Current liabilities}}$$

* This balance comes from the statement of cash flows.

WORKED EXAMPLE 3.4 Ryanair's liquidity ratios

Current ratio:

$$\frac{\text{Current assets}}{\text{Current liabilities}}$$

	2019 €m	2018 €m
Current assets	3,804.0	4,189.0
Current liabilities	4,096.6	3,412.9

$\dfrac{3,804.0}{4,096.6}$	$\dfrac{4,189.0}{3,412.9}$
=0.93 : 1	=1.23 : 1
(or 0.93 times)	(or 1.23 times)

Quick ratio:

$$\frac{\text{Current assets} - \text{inventories}}{\text{Current liabilities}}$$

	2019 €m	2018 €m
Current assets	3,804.0	4,189.0
Less	−2.9	−
Inventories		3.7
	= 3,801.1	= 4,185.3
Current liabilities	4,096.6	3,412.9

$\dfrac{3,801.1}{4,096.6}$	$\dfrac{4,185.3}{3,412.9}$

	=0.93 : 1	=1.23 : 1
	(or 0.93 times)	(or 1.23 times)

Adapted quick ratio:

$$\frac{\text{Cash flow from operating activities}}{\text{Current liabilities}}$$

	2019	2018
	€m	€m
Cash flow from operating activities	2,017.5	2,233.2
Current liabilities	4,096.6	3,412.9
	$\dfrac{2,017.5}{4,096.6}$	$\dfrac{2,233.2}{3,412.9}$
	=0.49 : 1	=0.65 : 1
	(or 0.49 times)	(or 0.65 times)

Efficiency ratios

Efficiency ratios are calculated to provide analysts with information about the utilization of (short-term) resources. This broad definition means that there are many ratios which could be calculated and many relationships which might be worthy of detailed attention. We would urge you to start with three basic working capital ratios and investigate further if required. These are as follows:

- trade receivables collection period;
- inventories holding period;
- trade payables payment period.

The aim of the exercise is to gauge whether the entity under consideration has managed their resources more or less efficiently than i) in previous years and ii) their competitors. As with other ratio categories, however, the interpretation of the results will depend upon context, eg:

- the industry the firm operates in;
- the working capital management strategy (aggressive or defensive) adopted by the entity;
- the state of the economy;
- competitors' approaches to working capital management;
- credit rating and availability of short-term credit;
- and so forth...

The application of the prudence concept in financial accounting means that results remain broadly comparable year on year. The inventories are valued at the lower of cost and net realizable value, the trade receivables figure is shown net of balances owed but which are not likely to be received, while trade payables includes amounts owed to suppliers which are obligated liabilities of the entity.

Other ratios you might consider that could be used to explore efficiency include:

• inventory turnover ratio (Cost of Sales / (Closing) Inventories);

• average inventories turnover ratio (Cost of Sales / Average Inventories [opening inventories plus closing inventories divided by 2]);

• non-current assets turnover ratio (Revenue / Non-current assets);

• revenue per employee (or any other non-financial cost driver);

• revenue per aeroplane (or any other major asset class).

Extract 3.4: Liquidity issues in the news

AlpenRoute Asset Management seeks to sell stakes in Market Kurly for liquidity

Pulse News, 19 February 2020

AlpenRoute Asset Management seeks to sell stakes in Market Kurly for liquidity

South Korea's AlpenRoute Asset Management that recently suspended redemption of 230 billion won ($193 million) worth of funds is readying to sell its stake in Market Kurly, a fast-rising local online grocery store.

The private equity fund reportedly is preparing to sell its stake in Market Kurly to resolve a liquidity problem caused by recent withdrawal requests from investors who became increasingly wary after losing big from Lime Asset Management's massive suspension of fund repayments, according to industry sources on Tuesday.

Kent & Lime calls it quits

Power Retail 12 April 2017

By Prinitha Govender

Over four years ago menswear online retailer Kent & Lime started out because it wanted to make shopping for men easy, but sadly this week the company made a decision to call it quits following issues with cash flow. 'We are closing because time and money was against us. We explored every avenue, every possible scenario but the emotional and realistic decision to end Kent & Lime was the right thing to do,' said Kent & Lime in a compelling statement on its homepage (which is no longer operational), thanking its customers, brand partners and all those who supported the business… Will Rogers, co-founder of Kent & Lime said: 'In late 2016 we decided to change from a stock holding model in favour of working with brands and retailers supplying us stock based on drop ship. This was a more fluid and commercial set up that had the very real potential to decrease working capital pressures. Whilst we were actively raising capital we also needed results, unfortunately the encouraging results we did create were not enough to secure investment in time. We made the decision to close as the time and working capital to complete the model change was eating our runway.'

Forever 21 takeover group plans to keep struggling retailer open

TRD National, 4 February 2020
By Mary Diduch

Simon Property's CEO made that pledge during the mall owner's Q4 earnings call

The Simon Property Group-led partnership now poised to take over Forever 21 intends to keep the ailing retail chain open. The bid has to succeed in an auction, but should it go through, the group would buy most of Forever 21's assets for $81 million, plus the retailer's operating liabilities. Simon's stake in the investment group is just under 50 percent, the Chief Executive said. He added that Forever 21 is a well-known brand – with $2 billion in global sales – that the company will keep operating should the offer go through.

[…] In a bankruptcy court filing last week, Forever 21 said it has shuttered over 100 stores and reduced its annual rent payments by $91 million. But the retailer said it still had liquidity problems, prompting the need for an auction.

(a) Trade receivables collection period

The trade receivables collection period is calculated as follows:

$$\frac{\text{Trade receivables}}{\text{Credit sales}} \times 365 \text{ days}$$

A note on the calculation of trade receivables collection period

Note that the credit sales figure is rarely disclosed in an annual report. The headline figure, revenue, however, is almost always shown separately and can be used as a proxy for credit sales. Sometimes this is disaggregated into categories, which might be helpful for your analysis (for example, BMW Group plc divide revenue between motor vehicle sales and financial services revenue [interest received on loans offered to purchase BMWs by BMW Group plc]). You should be aware that substituting revenue for credit sales might distort your analysis. Though the majority of companies trade exclusively through short-term credit agreements (eg invoices demanding payment is received within 28 days), this is not always the case. If you are investigating the ratios of a supermarket, for example, the majority of customers pay in cash at the checkout/till. These businesses permit only a handful of customers to buy 'on account'. If, in this case, you use revenue to calculate the trade receivables collection period, the result produced will drastically shorten the *real* collection period.

Some argue that it is more appropriate to use average trade receivables than closing trade receivables. They suggest that this tells you how long the average customer takes to pay. Both closing and averaging have weaknesses. If it is obvious that they produce significantly different results, a reconciliation alongside an explanation would be required.

Interpreting the trade receivables collection period

Though there are benefits to both buyer and seller, analysts tend to view trade receivables as short-term interest-free loans to customers. The longer you allow your customers to pay, the longer your working capital cycle. In turn, this means that you must be without cash for a longer amount of time. In this regard, there is an opportunity cost attached to trade receivables, ie an entity could be doing something more valuable with their cash, for example investing it profitably in operations.

In short, the trade receivables collection period is designed to indicate the length of time (in days) it takes for credit customers to pay for the products or services they purchased. Commonly a shorter collection period compared to prior years and industry averages is better. This means that you are recycling your cash quicker. Assuming that the entity is profitable, this also means that you are contributing to the generation of cash more effectively. In other words, you are using your resources more efficiently. A shorter(or shortening) trade receivables collection period could indicate improved credit collection management, eg careful selection of creditworthy customers, chasing late payments more vigorously, and so forth.

There are, however, several problems with this naive interpretation:

- The nature of the calculation means that weight is added to larger customers. Thus, if one large customer pays faster (slower), it will skew the result.

- If several smaller customers are not paying, it would be difficult to pick up from this simple ratio calculation; and yet this might be information important to your analysis and to the business more generally.

- One might be suspicious of the policies and processes of a company with a shorter than average trade receivables collection period.

- A business that maintains a demanding (pushy?!) cash collection department/ strategy runs the risk of alienating customers, especially if the operational area is competitive and customers could go elsewhere for similar products or services.
  - Offering large discounts might speed up collection but there would be an offsetting impact on profitability.
- A shorter than average number of collection days might be due to an underlying weakness in the calculation, eg the inclusion of cash sales in the revenue figure.

Unfortunately, Ryanair's trade receivables collection period provides an almost meaningless result (see Worked Example 3.5). On the face of it, the calculation shows that the number of outstanding days is low (around three days). This would ordinarily be interpreted as an extremely efficient use of short-term resources. When this is analysed in context, however, this interpretation doesn't tell us a lot. The majority of Ryanair's customers are not offered a credit settlement period. Instead, customers pay when they book their flights, ie by cash in advance. As we do not have the disaggregated revenue figure, it is impossible to say what proportion of customers is allowed credit terms, and how long those credit terms are. What we can learn, however, is that the risk of customer default is immaterial. The company does separately disclose that: `No individual customer accounted for more than 10% of our accounts receivable at March 31, 2019, at March 31, 2018 or at March 31, 2017' (Ryanair Holdings plc, Annual Report 2019, p 168) and less than 0.2 per cent of this balance was deemed to be impaired, or irrecoverable.

On a side note, a bigger problem for analysts when interpreting an airline's financial numbers is how to interpret the current liabilities figure. Airlines take payment for flights in advance (hence no trade receivables), and therefore they are required to disclose these amounts as short-term liabilities in the balance sheet. When the flight takes off – often months after the payment date – is the point at which the service is deemed to be delivered and the accounting rules allow the revenue to be recognized.

(b) Inventories holding period

The inventories holding period is calculated as follows:

$$\frac{\text{Inventories}}{\text{Cost of sales}} \times 365 \text{ days}$$

Inventories are frequently a significant asset class for businesses and represent a large amount of short-term resource being tied up. The inventories holding period tells the analyst how many days the business is keeping their average item of stock. Given that any holding of inventories represents tied-up cash – and by extension the lost opportunity to use that cash for value-creating activities – then the shorter the inventories holding period, the better.

Interpreting yearly differences should be straightforward. The following might explain movements:

- a variation in sales mix;
- a change in products or services offered;
- commodity price movements;
- supply chain changes;
- a growth (decline) in demand;
- improved (worsened) inventories control management;
- high (low) levels of obsolete stock;
- a change in buying strategy, eg bulk purchasing (to take advantage of discounts), or more cautious buying policies;
- a period of firm-specific growth;
- and so forth.

There are two issues that prevent comparability between entities:

1 There are different inventory demands between industries and this will lead to large differences in the result of the inventories holding period calculation. For example, supermarkets stock short-life products by and large and therefore their inventory days will be relatively low, whereas house-building companies might have long inventory days given the nature of their business.

2 Not all business inventory management strategies are alike, either within or between industries. Some companies will adopt sophisticated inventory management practices while others will lag behind. Every entity will weigh up the costs versus the benefits of introducing advanced inventory control systems innovations and make their choice accordingly. For example, just-in-time (JIT) systems are popular in the motor vehicle production industry. This involves having high-quality raw materials delivered by the supplier, as the name suggests, *just in time* for production! Note that this system is not for everybody, though, as there are many potential problems that could arise, for example a breakdown in the relationship with supplier(s), unexpected production discrepancies, quality issues, late changes to orders, priority orders and so forth.

If we look more closely at Ryanair's inventory holding period, the first thing to note is that we are forced to derive a cost of sales figure to use in the calculation. Most companies disclose this figure, but airlines classify all expenses as operating expenses. Of course, dealing with real-world information is messy and so we can't always expect to get exactly what we want from a set of financial statements. Every major company is likely to have idiosyncratic reporting characteristics. Indeed, one of the reasons why financial analysis is so much fun is because it tests our abilities to collect and then interpret data. In the case of Ryanair, there is a strong temptation to use only maintenance, materials and repairs, but a more balanced view might be to use operating expenses as a whole. Both calculations are shown below. The differences are sizeable but whichever way we look at them, inventories holding is not a material risk for Ryanair, at least in terms of the 'size' of the balance. The numerator, ie the inventories balance, represents less than a third of 1 per cent of the entity's total assets and less than half of 1 per cent of profit after tax.

This was not always the case, however. Inventories held by the company were reduced significantly during 2005. The inventory holding period (using 'Maintenance, materials and repairs') at that time moved from over 12 days in 2004 to below one day in 2005. The figure now stands at 0.16 days. This is because Ryanair only holds essentials in stock, for example a limited amount of food available for on-board snacks and a small selection of gift-type products which are intended to be sold mid-flight. This was part of the company's cost-cutting strategy and it is amazing that the things which appear common sense to us today, were financially innovative ideas at the time. As Extract 3.5 shows, on-board food is not a trivial matter for airlines. Bean counting is an oft-used derogatory term for accountants, but this article brings the expression to life (well, 'berry counting') as well as the importance of the function to a successful business. The report highlights one airline, Delta, who saved $210,000 per annum simply by cutting one strawberry from their salads.

Extract 3.5: Airlines' on-board food

Beyond Mile-High Grub: Can Airline Food Be Tasty?

Published March 10, 2012 in *The New York Times*
By Jad Mouawad

Last year, Delta hired Michael Chiarello, a celebrity chef from Napa Valley, to come up with new menus for business-class passengers flying on transcontinental routes – New York to Los Angeles and New York to San Francisco. It was not the first time that Delta had worked with a renowned chef. The airline has served meals created by Michelle Bernstein, a Miami chef, since 2006 in its international business class.

'Our chefs are like portrait painters,' Mr Wilander says. 'They can get pretty creative. But we need to translate that into painting by numbers.' That process began last May, when Mr Chiarello met with executives and catering chefs from Delta at a boxy industrial kitchen on the edge of the San Francisco airport to demonstrate some of his recipes. Among the dozens of dishes he tried were an artichoke and white-bean spread, short ribs with polenta, and a small lasagna of eggplant and goat cheese.

'I am known for making good food, and airlines generally are not,' says Mr Chiarello, who is also the author of a half-dozen cookbooks, the host for a show on the Food Network, and a former contestant on 'Top Chef Masters' and 'The Next Iron Chef.' 'I probably have a lot more to lose than to gain doing this.'

Huddled around him, white-toqued chefs from Delta and its catering partners weighed each ingredient on a small electronic scale, took scrupulous notes and pictures and tried to calculate how much it would cost to recreate each dish a thousand times a day.

It took Mr Chiarello six months to come up with the menu. He tested recipes, picked seasonal ingredients, considered textures and colors and looked at ways to present his meals on a small airline tray. Then Delta's corporate chefs had to learn his way of cooking and serving. Bean counters – the financial kind – priced each item. Executives and frequent fliers were drafted to taste his creations.

There were a lot of questions. How should cherry tomatoes be sliced? (The answer: Leave them whole.) What side should a chicken fillet be grilled on? (Skin first.) How many slices of prosciutto can be used as appetizers? (Two large ones, rather than three, struck the balance between taste and price.)

For airlines like Delta, these are not trivial matters. A decision a few years ago to shave one ounce from its steaks, for example, saved the airline $250,000 a year. And every step of kitchen labor increases costs when so many meals are prepared daily. An entrée accounts for about 60 per cent of a meal's cost, according to Delta, while appetizers account for 17 per cent, salads 10 per cent and desserts 7 per cent.

Delta also calculated that by removing a single strawberry from salads served in first class on domestic routes, it would save $210,000 a year. The company hands out 61 million bags of peanuts every year, and about the same number of pretzels. A one-cent increase in peanut prices increases Delta's costs by $610,000 a year.

Others are catching on. United Airlines said in February that it would upgrade its service to first- and business-class passengers and would change the way it prepares meals 'to improve the quality and taste.' It also said it would start offering a new ice cream sundae option with a choice of six toppings on international flights. On domestic flights, premium passengers will get new snacks, including warm cookies.

(c) Trade payables payment period

The trade payables payment period is calculated as follows:

$$\frac{\text{Trade payables}}{\text{Credit purchases}} \times 365 \text{ days}$$

A note on the calculation of trade payables payment period

The trade receivables collection period, as discussed above, demands that revenue is divided by credit sales and multiplied by 365 days. However, the credit sales figure is rarely provided and therefore we need to find a substitute. Though revenue is not a perfect replacement, it is normally a satisfactory proxy. The same problem exists for credit purchases. This figure is rarely publicly disclosed. Therefore we need to find a substitute. Commonly, one would use the cost of sales figure. This is because (i) in its simplified state, the cost of sales is the product of opening inventories plus purchases minus closing inventories; and (ii) it is unusual for a large business not to make purchases on credit terms.

The complications for analysing Ryanair's efficiency ratios (see Worked Example 3.5) are that: firstly, expenses are classified as operating expenses; and secondly, trade payables could relate to any of these operating expenses presented. Therefore, we have used operating expenses as a substitute for cost of sales. Note that this is unusual outside the airline industry.

Interpreting the trade payables payment period results

If one views holdings of current assets, such as trade receivables and inventories, as reducing an entity's cash resource, then current liabilities such as trade payables can be seen as an offset to these effects. While trade receivables are essentially an entity making interest-free loans to customers, trade payables are the reverse, ie suppliers granting interest-free loans to the business. Therefore, it is common to believe that a higher trade payables payment period is preferable.

However, when the number of days a company takes to pay their suppliers increases beyond a certain level, significant additional risks could arise, mainly resulting from behavioural issues and the loss of supplier goodwill. A relationship breakdown could bring serious problems; for example, a supplier who is made to wait disproportionately long before payment could penalize the slow-paying entity by providing poor-quality product. In a worst-case scenario, they might simply stop supplying products or services at all and poison the market against the slow payer.

In the case of Ryanair (see Worked Example 3.5), the trade payables payment period increased in 2019 to 31 days. This is unusually high for the company, whose payment period has hovered between 15 and 20 days for the past decade. The high figure in 2019 is probably due to the timing and circumstances, as opposed to a shift in policy. It should be noted that in 2003 the number of days was as high as 41! This is the kind of area where further inquiry would be recommended, first to identify if there is a shift in internal policy, and second to identify the causes and consequences (if any).

WORKED EXAMPLE 3.5 Ryanair's efficiency ratios

Trade receivables collection period:

Trade receivables x 365 days
Credit sales[a]

[a] *We have had to substitute revenue for credit sales.*

	2019	2018
	€m	€m
Trade receivables	59.5	57.6
Revenue	7,697.4	7,151.0

$$\frac{59.5 \times 365}{7,697.4} \qquad\qquad \frac{57.6 \times 365}{7,151}$$

$$= 2.8 \text{ days} \qquad\qquad = 2.9 \text{ days}$$

Inventory holding period:

Inventories x 365 days
Cost of sales[b]

[b] *We have had to find an appropriate substitute for cost of sales given that airlines do not classify items as direct costs, rather only as operating expenses. A possible expense relating to inventories is 'maintenance, materials and repairs' but we have calculated the inventory holding period based on this figure and the total operating expenses figure. Note therefore that these calculations are for illustration purposes only.*

	2019	2018
	€m	€m
Inventories	2.9	3.7
Maintenance, materials and repairs	(i) 190.9	(i) 148.3
Operating expenses (see note above; substituted for cost of sales)	(ii) 6,680.6	(ii) 5,483.7

$$\text{(i) } \frac{2.9 \times 365}{190.9} \qquad\qquad \text{(i) } \frac{3.7 \times 365}{148.3}$$

$$= 5.5 \text{ days} \qquad\qquad = 9.1 \text{ days}$$

(ii) $\dfrac{2.9 \times 365}{6,680.6}$

= 0.16 days

(ii) $\dfrac{3.7 \times 365}{5,483.7}$

= 0.25 days

Trade payables payment period:

$\dfrac{\text{Trade payables} \times 365 \text{ days}}{\text{Credit purchases}^c}$

^c In the same way as one would substitute revenue for credit sales in the calculation of trade receivables collection period, one would normally substitute cost of sales for credit purchases in the calculation of trade payables payment period. However, because airlines do not disclose a cost of sales, we need to find an appropriate substitute for this figure. As with the inventory holding period, we have opted to use operating expenses, but stress again that this is for illustration purposes only.

	2019	2018
	€m	**€m**
Trade payables	573.8	249.6
Operating expenses (see note above)	6,680.6	5,483.7

$\dfrac{573.8 \times 365}{6,680.6}$

= 31.4 days

$\dfrac{249.6 \times 365}{5.483.7}$

= 16.6 days

Solvency ratios

We explained in the previous sections that liquidity ratios are intended to provide users with an understanding of the short-term financial position of an entity. Solvency ratios allow users to evaluate how the entity is positioned for the medium and long term. It would be very difficult for a company to invest in projects that generate value without some form of financing. The question the executive team have to ask themselves is where does that money come from? Essentially there are two choices: debt or equity. Increased debt financing increases the risk of bankruptcy, also known as finance risk.

Figure 3.1 Financing a new project

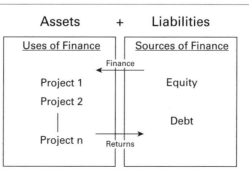

Expert view 3.4: Debt – the company's perspective versus the shareholders' perspective

From a company's perspective: Debt is a preferable financing option because, by and large, it is cheaper to service than equity and because of the tax relief allowed on interest payments but not allowed on dividend payments (if you wish to prove this to yourself, just think about the order of the income statement and note that the tax charge occurs *after* the interest charge).

From a shareholder's perspective: Debt financing increases the (perceived) risk as it normally has all, or some, of the following characteristics:

- Interest payments are an obligation. (Dividends are discretionary.)

- Debt is secured. For example, non-repayment of mortgage payments on a building can lead to the asset(s) being repossessed by the lender and sold to settle the liability. (Shares are rarely secured over assets.)

- Debt has a finite life, ie there is a redemption date. (Equity is a permanent investment.)

- Equity providers rank last in a winding up.

See Chapter 10 for a more detailed discussion of gearing and financial risk.

The primary solvency ratio considers relative levels of debt versus equity. This is called a 'gearing ratio'. It sheds light on the way the business is financed and draws attention to the levels of financing risk. It is argued that as an entity's levels of debt rise, equity finance providers (ie shareholders) require a greater return to offset the rising financing risk. The graph shown in Figure 3.2 highlights the relationship between the cost of debt and the cost of equity as financing risk (ie proportionately higher borrowings) is introduced into the business. The cost of debt is the weighted average required return of providers of debt finance. The cost of equity is the required return of investors with an equity stake in the business. Note that at extreme levels of financing risk, the required returns of both debt providers and equity providers increase drastically. This reaction builds in the compensation required for the exposure to bankruptcy risk.

As you can imagine, it is difficult for an analyst to compare the level of financing from one company to the next, or one period to the next. Judging the optimum level of debt in the capital structure is part science and part art. Thus, solvency ratios are hard to interpret, and even harder for outsiders like us. As a general rule, a careful balance between debt and equity needs to be achieved. A *high* gearing ratio (the proportion of debt to equity) would suggest a greater exposure to financing risk.

Figure 3.2   The costs of financing a new project

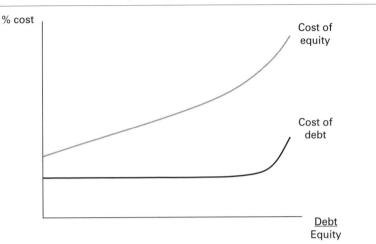

However, the critical question is: 'what is high?' Also, a low gearing ratio would suggest that the comparative cost advantage that debt offers has not been appropriately taken advantage of. Again, this does not provide any insight into the question: 'what is low?' Compounding our interpretation issue is the problem that there will be inherent differences at the firm level, industry level and global level which will need to be explored and explained.

At the firm level, differences may arise because:

- Access to debt and equity markets vary.
- The availability of debt at a firm level will differ between entities and between time periods.
- The riskiness of the investment and proposed projects will need to be considered by providers of finance in context.
- There may be varying managerial preferences towards debt or equity and, when management change, these preferences are likely to change also.
- And so forth.

At the industry level, differences may arise because:

- The types of projects being funded vary and therefore so do their financing requirements. For example, a company investing in large assets for continuing revenue generation (eg house building, large construction projects, aeroplanes etc) will have greater and more regular financing requirements. Both real and relative debt levels will normally be higher in these industries as a result.
- Market perceptions of the industry's capital requirements will vary.
- And so forth.

At the global level, differences may arise because:

- There will be varying levels of availability for different forms of financing owing to the economic scenario.

- Global market sentiment towards future investment and financing arrangements changes over time.

- There may be government or regulatory interventions. For example, legislation over financing levels (financial institutions being required to maintain tier 1 capital ratios, for example) or restrictions on credit lines to small, medium or large businesses within certain geographies.

- Global and domestic money markets demand and supply levels will vary.

- It might be less beneficial given (expected) rates of inflation and the opportunity costs of other investments.

- And so forth.

There are three core ratios which are most frequently undertaken which shed light on an entity's exposure to financing risk:

1 capital gearing ratio;

2 interest cover;

3 dividend cover.

(a) Capital gearing ratio

There are several acceptable ways to calculate a company's level of gearing. All things being equal, we would like to use the following definition:

$$\frac{\text{Market value of Debt}}{\text{Market value of Equity}} \times 100\%$$

Or alternatively:

$$\frac{\text{Market value of Debt}}{\text{Market value of Equity} + \text{Market value of Debt}} \times 100\%$$

However, if we only have the financial statements available, a practical and straightforward alternative is:

$$\frac{\text{Non-current liabilities}}{\text{Shareholders' funds}} \times 100\%$$

Or alternatively:

$$\frac{\text{Non-current liabilities}}{\text{Capital Employed}} \times 100\%$$

Calculation difficulties

- Financing risk measures market value against market value rather than book value against book value. These figures will be markedly different, especially for a mature and profitable company. It would be extremely rare for a company which has traded for several years to continue to sell their shares at book value; investors will be asked to pay a premium. Applying book values will probably add weight to debt. Prudence might tell you, however, that this is not an altogether bad thing. Nevertheless, it is worth noting that the gearing ratio as calculated using this method will be for guidance purposes only.

- Non-current liabilities will contain balances which are not debt instruments, for example provisions. Ideally, the only non-current liabilities you would capture would be those which related directly to long-term debt obligations.

- Current liabilities may contain some liabilities which are being used to finance the business, and which therefore should be included in the calculation of gearing. For example, a bank overdraft or other short-term bank loans might be plugging a financing gap. Their short repayment terms might contribute to a clearer understanding of financing risk if included in the calculation.

- The problems associated with the definition of shareholders' funds were covered above in the description of ROCE. These issues also exist here.

Interpreting the gearing ratio   As stated above, the larger the gearing ratio the greater the financing risk. Theoretically, investors do not mind how high financing risk rises provided that they are adequately and appropriately compensated for it. Various prompts on how to interpret an increase (decrease) in the ratio are provided above.

In the case of Ryanair, the gearing ratio hovered around 54 per cent for about a decade through to 2016 (minimum: 49.7 per cent [in 2014]; maximum: 56.3 per cent [in 2011]), but in recent years it has dropped. In 2019 it was 43 per cent. Aircraft are expensive, and Ryanair maintains a relatively young fleet. Therefore we would expect to see high levels of debt in the capital structure. Maintaining a high gearing ratio is built into the company's operational strategies and business model. Furthermore, investors expect it. It would be poor financial management to finance long-lived assets through short-term loan obligations or cash.

Making comparisons with other airlines is difficult, and it might not take us mean-ingfully towards an understanding of the optimum debt: equity ratio for Ryanair. An airline that has a strong purchase and early replacement policy regarding their fleet of planes would have proportionately higher financing requirements than other airlines.

Nonetheless, maintaining a gearing ratio of around 50 per cent might appear high to some observers. Should we be concerned? In response, it is worth noting that the company maintains high levels of liquidity and the amount of cash retained as a buffer suggests that any short-term problems could be dealt with. A key problem when interpreting solvency ratios is that we are asked to speculate about medium-to long-term performance, ie future profits and cash flows that will be generated by the business in order to continue operating at the same levels as today. Any inter-pretation that involves estimating future demand (or events) is subject to error. As with other ratios, therefore, an analyst would search for additional information to support their interpretation. For example, it would be interesting to see estimated future demand. This doesn't have to come solely from the airline; there are external agencies that also undertake forecasting analysis, and the regulatory body also coor-dinates a survey.

Extract 3.6: The chicken or the egg: solvency problems versus liquidity?

'Lack of solvency created bank's problems'

Management at the Co-operative Bank 'took its eye off the ball' leading to significant internal management issues, a banking analyst has claimed.

By Kevin White | Published May 15, 2013 | FTadviser (Financial Times online)

Speaking after the mutual plunged into crisis last week, Ian Gordon, a banking analyst for Investec, said the Co-operative Bank's problems were rooted around a lack of solvency.

Last week ratings agency Moody's downgraded the bank's creditworthiness on concerns it could need a government bailout...The size of the hole in the balance sheet could be as high as £1.8bn, according to an analyst note from Barclays this week. The note said Co-op bond holders may be targeted, as the mutual cannot issue equity. The subsequent downgrade in its credit rating led to an almost immediate resignation of the bank's chief executive Barry Tootell, and the announcement of a strategic review of the entire business by new group chief executive Euan Sutherland.

Mr Gordon said: 'Unlike the liquidity problems faced by the likes of HBoS, Northern Rock, and Bradford & Bingley in 2008, the Co-operative Bank's problems lie in solvency, or a lack of it.' The bank had a £113,300 fine in January from the FSA over failure to handle 1629 PPI complaints correctly. It also wrote down £150m on the Finacle IT project (to date). He added that the price action seen last Friday, which saw bond prices fall by 25 per cent, 'suggested that the market was pricing in the prospect of a default'. He added: 'The bank is less capitalized than some of its peers and as a mutual it has been allowed by the regulator to be run with less scrutiny. 'For the bank to be made as safe and secure as possible it needs a cash injection, but I don't think that will necessarily lead to a bailout. It's more likely the Co-operative Group itself will step in.'

When asked whether the bank had a lack of solvency, a spokesman for the Co-operative Bank said: 'We are aware of the solvency issues and the need to improve capital ratios.' When asked about Mr Gordon's comments that the bank had been run with less regulatory scrutiny, the spokesman added: 'It is true that the bank is not a plc but we regularly publish our accounts and engage with investors, the press and regulators, and are subject to considerable scrutiny.'

According to its results for 2012, the banking division contributed 17.6 per cent of revenue to the group, with its revenue of £2.21bn for 2012 dwarfed by the food retail division's revenue of £7.44bn. It repeated an overall operating loss of £280.5m for 2012 (compared to 2011 profit of £141.1m) and a loss before tax of £673.7m (compared to 2011 profit of £54.2m).

What happened between 2013 and 2017? An update on the Co-op Bank story

The Co-op Bank is the new Bradford & Bingley

The Guardian Online (13 February 2017)

By Patrick Collinson

The proposed sale means the prospect of an independent, ethically based challenger bank to the major high street player is dead. Co-op Bank, now that it has announced its sale, is going the way of the Bradford & Bingley – to be broken up, run off and the name consigned to history. The good bits – its 1.4 million current account holders, and a now half-decent mortgage book – have value. The bad bits – the remaining toxic loans (much of them acquired from the disastrous merger with Britannia building society) – will have to be run off. But make no bones about what is happening here … The co-operative title, in any case a misnomer under hedge fund ownership, must surely die once Co-operative Group abandons its remaining 20% parcel of shares… In some ways it is a miracle that Co-op Bank survived after the £1.5bn black hole was discovered in 2013, irrespective of the antics of its 'crystal methodist' chairman exposed in the tabloids. Never forget that it was not bailed out by taxpayers like its bigger brothers … But the continued low-interest-rate environment is a painful cap on its ability to generate income. Co-op is a bank that has a fundamentally weak capital base, and few obvious ways to rebuild it organically. In the new world of app and online banking, where customers rarely visit branches, Co-op just can't be an independent 'challenger' either to its big ugly sisters in banking, or the nimble upstarts.

(b) Interest cover

The interest cover ratio shows the number of times a company (theoretically) could have paid their finance costs from their earnings. The ratio is calculated as follows:

$$\frac{\text{Operating profit}}{\text{Finance costs}}$$

This is therefore a guide to the solvency of the business. Again, as with other ratios, it is difficult to suggest that there is an optimum level of coverage. We would suggest, however, that if the interest cover ratio falls below 1, this is a strong signal that current debt levels are unaffordable, ie the company cannot afford to pay its obligations even once. If, in the following months or years, interest payments are not made, the lender might bring into effect claw-back clauses.

A high level of coverage is also not desirable. If a company could afford to pay its finance costs, say 10 times over, then investors might question whether the company is taking appropriate advantage of comparatively cheaper forms of financing, ie debt.

In the case of Ryanair, interest payments can be covered approximately 17 times, and in 2018 the coverage was more than 27 times! This helps allay any concerns about the affordability of the debt (solvency issues). There is a slight contradiction here in so much as the interest coverage might be deemed too high. In other words, should the company be looking to borrow more, especially given that debt is cheaper than equity as a form of finance?

(c) Dividend cover

This is another useful measure, especially for a company where shareholders are regularly rewarded by dividends (and not just capital growth). The dividend cover ratio shows an analyst how many times the company could have paid the dividend out of available profits. It is calculated as:

$$\frac{\text{Profit after tax}}{\text{Dividends}}$$

As with the interest cover ratio, there is no optimum position. Indeed, this is a particularly thorny issue, and one that regulators take seriously. Dividends are a way to keep investors happy, and therefore companies could pay them out even if they can't afford them. In this case, a ratio of less than 1 would indicate a lack of afford-ability and a reduced likelihood of the dividend remaining at that level. A high level of coverage might have shareholders questioning why the dividend payment wasn't larger, especially if there is no evidence that profits are being re-invested in positive profit/cash-generating activities.

Ryanair rarely pays dividends. Instead, shareholders are rewarded through a combination of capital growth (ie the share price increases) and capital being re-allo-cated to shareholders via share buy-backs.

WORKED EXAMPLE 3.6   Ryanair's solvency ratios

Gearing ratio:

$$\frac{\text{Non-current liabilities}}{\text{Capital employed}} \times 100\%$$

	2019		2018	
	€m		€m	
Non-current liabilities	3,939.2		4,480.0	
Capital employed	9,154.1		8,948.9	
		$\frac{3,939.2}{9,154.1} \times 100\%$		$\frac{4,804.3}{8,948.9} \times 100\%$
		= 43.0%		= 50.1%

Interest cover:

$$\frac{\text{Operating profit}}{\text{Finance costs}}$$

	2019		2018	
	€m		€m	
Operating profit	1,016.8		1,667.3	
Finance costs	59.1		60.1	
		$\frac{1,016.8}{59.1}$		$\frac{1,042.9}{60.1}$
		= 17.2 times		= 27.7 times

Dividend cover:

$$\frac{\text{Profit after tax}}{\text{Dividends}}$$

	2019	2018
	€m	€m
Profit after tax	885.0	1,450.2
Dividends	N/A	N/A
	= N/A	= N/A

Investor ratios

Current and potential investors are the intended primary users of financial statements. The ratios set out above would carry some interest to all stakeholders whereas
the set of ratios that follow are of the greatest value and interest to this primary user
group. Again, there are many ratios an investor might calculate to appraise their
stance in relation to the entity under consideration, but you will come across the
following most regularly as they are also the most useful:

- investor returns: dividend yield and capital yield;
- earnings per share;
- price to earnings ratio.

(a) Investor returns: dividend yield and capital yield

The dividend cover ratio allows analysts to interpret an entity's dividend payment in
book value terms, ie how many times a company could have paid the dividend from
available annual accounting profits. Of more interest to shareholders is the yield on
the investment they have made. There are two components to an annual return on
equity: dividends and capital growth. These are calculated as:

$$\frac{\text{Dividend (per share)}}{\text{Market price (per share)}} \times 100\%$$

PLUS

$$\frac{\text{Capital growth (per share)}}{\text{Market price (per share)}} \times 100\%$$

The dividend yield ratio reveals to an investor the rate of (dividend) return on their
investment. Given that Ryanair paid no dividends during 2018 or 2019, we provide
Worked Example 3.7 to illustrate how investors can measure their annual returns.

WORKED EXAMPLE 3.7

Table 3.5

	Share price at 1.1.X0	Share price at 31.12.X0	Dividend for the year
Mirage plc	160p	180p	12p
Lost Illusions plc	100p	105p	3p

The dividend yield for the two entities is as follows:

Mirage plc

$$\frac{12}{160} \times 100\% = 7.5\%$$

Lost Illusions plc

$$\frac{3}{100} \times 100\% = 3.0\%$$

Note, however, that there is also capital growth to factor into your returns analysis.
Mirage plc

$$\frac{20\,(180 - 160)}{160} \times 100\% = 12.5\%$$

Lost Illusions plc

$$\frac{5\,(105 - 100)}{100} \times 100\% = 5.0\%$$

Therefore, the total annual return on each of these two stocks can be measured as:

$$\text{Mirage plc} = 20.0\% \ (7.5\% + 12.5\%)$$
$$\text{Lost Illusions plc} = 8.0\% \ (3.0\% + 5.0\%)$$

(b) Earnings per share (EPS)

The EPS is normally shown on the face of the income statement, ie it is a publicly disclosed figure. To avoid manipulation of this figure, there are accounting regulations which govern the calculation of this figure (IAS 33 *Earnings Per Share*). In summary, the basic calculation is as follows:

$$\frac{\text{Profit attributable to shareholders}}{\text{Weighted average number of shares outstanding during the period}}$$

The standard interpretation of EPS is that as the figure increases, the better the position of the shareholder. Owing to the complexities of the underlying accounting and possible transactions, it is possible (although not straightforward) for management to play around with this ratio so that it tells investors what they want to hear. Note, however, that there is a high chance that accounting-based manipulation of earnings can only work for a finite period of time before the string unravels.

Expert view 3.5: IAS 33 definition of basic EPS

The lengthier explanation as set out in IAS 33 is: basic EPS is calculated by dividing profit or loss attributable to ordinary equity holders of the parent entity (the numerator) by the weighted average number of ordinary shares outstanding (the denominator) during the period. [IAS 33.10] The earnings numerators (profit or loss from continuing operations and net profit or loss) used for the calculation should be after deducting all expenses, including taxes, minority interests and preference dividends. [IAS 33.12] The denominator (number of shares) is calculated by adjusting the shares in issue at the beginning of the period by the number of shares bought back or issued during the period, multiplied by a time-weighting factor. IAS 33 includes guidance on appropriate recognition dates for shares issued in various circumstances. [IAS 33.20–21]

Given Ryanair's decreased profits in 2019, EPS has reduced to €0.7739 per ordinary share (2018: €1.2151). It is also worth noting that the denominator is decreasing due to the share buy-backs.

(c) Price to earnings (P/E) ratio

The P/E ratio is a common measure used to appraise an investment through the eyes of the equity provider (ie shareholder). Interpreting this ratio, however, is not straightforward. Applying an unsophisticated view, the underlying principle is that the result gives you a multiplier, ie how many times you would need to multiply current earnings before arriving at the price you would pay for the share on the open market. In turn, this allows you to appraise the value of your investment and any future investments the company intends to make, thus allowing you to price future projects and the entity as a whole. It also provides an indication of how quickly an investment in the stock of this entity might pay back. In other words, a P/E ratio of, say, 10 could be interpreted to mean that the current price is 10 times the value of current earnings; or it would take 10 consecutive earnings at that level to repay the investment at that price.

However, there are more detailed explanations. Essentially, the P/E ratio can be summarized as the Price to Book (P/B) ratio divided by Return on Equity (ROE); where the P/B ratio is a function of the magnitude of abnormal earnings (ie ROE minus the required rate of return of your equity provider), multiplied by the growth in book value of equity, taken into perpetuity, and then discounted to its present value using the cost of equity. But this is an introductory textbook, and therefore we will save this story for another time. Instead, for the time being, the P/E ratio can be calculated as follows:

$$\frac{\text{Market price (per share)}}{\text{Earnings (per share)}}$$

When investors see a profitable business carrying a high P/E ratio, the expectation is for future growth (in earnings) above inflation. The basic tenets of supply and demand intermixed with efficient markets presumptions lead rational investors to infer that a high P/E ratio driven by a change in the numerator, ie share price (market value per share), indicates stronger than average demand for the stock. Where there is demand, the share price rises and this precedes the realization of the amount paid by shareholders for this future growth. Demand is created by above average performance, or more commonly, the promise of future above average performance.

As you can imagine, the share price of a company can move for many reasons and accounting earnings might not be a genuine reflection of position and current or future performance. Therefore, not only would you need to undertake further investigation into the underlying data; ultimately, you would also need to appraise the P/E ratio in context. Comparing P/E ratios between companies in the same industry can be especially revealing (see online content at: www.koganpage.com/afm3).

Ryanair's P/E ratio on 31 December 2017 was 15.48, on 31 December 2018 was 12.36, and on 31 December 2019 was back up to 16.97. The P/E ratio is volatile, and between 31 December 2017 and 31 December 2019 has ranged between 10.25 and 19.76. However, the P/E and EPS ratios of an airline are always likely to be somewhat volatile compared to other industries because of the idiosyncrasies of the airline business, exposure to certain systematic risks which are beyond the control of the management (eg commodity prices, weather, local and global politics, environmental regulations, etc), and more volatile profits due to a high reliance on fixed costs (which makes underlying operating profits more volatile than companies with high levels of variable costs). Nonetheless, Ryanair maintains a relatively high P/E ratio compared to its peers, which is an indicator that the market believes that the company will continue to be profitable over and above costs and inflation.

Weaknesses and limitations

As we have progressed through this chapter, the major weaknesses and limitations of the various financial analysis techniques might have been obvious to you. Some of the questions you might have been asking yourself are the following:

1 Is true comparability possible?

Sub-questions include:

- What entities are we comparing, and why have we chosen to compare them?
- What are the differences between these entities strategically, economically, politically, culturally?
- Do these entities have similar accounting policies? In other words, do the financial statements capture comparable information?
  - Though accountants are required to choose policies that ensure financial information is presented in a representation that is 'true and fair', managerial judgement is still required. For example, the difference between two identical companies estimating the useful economic lives of identical assets differently can have a serious impact on profits. If one airline chooses to depreciate planes over 25 years while another believes they will last for only 10 years, this will have a significant impact on accounting profit from year to year, with the latter entity recognizing the costs earlier than the former.
  - Annual results can be manipulated without needing to employ accounting flexibility. For example, cutting back on certain items of expenditure – such as staff training and development costs, advertising and marketing expenses – during the year will produce an immediate improvement in profits. The medium- to long-term impact on profits, however, will inevitably be detrimental.
  - There are complex accounting transactions which can be hidden, often by posting the movement through equity and holding back the realization of gains/losses to future periods.
- Is comparability between time periods possible?
  - Have there been one-off events during the year which have impacted positively/negatively on the profitability of the entity?
  - If so, should we (can we) adjust for these in our analysis?
  - Is the broader economic/political/social/cultural climate comparable?

2 Financial statements are backwards-looking and are composed from historic information. The preparation and audit of the annual report is a lengthy exercise and for public listed companies, the filing deadline is three months after the year-end. Therefore, by the time you are able to analyse the financial statements for the year ended 31 March 2019, for example, the first quarter of the following year will be nearly complete. Regardless of business, industry, geography or any other externality, three months can be a long time!

3 The financial statements do not tell the whole story (see Chapter 4). During the past couple of decades we have witnessed an exponential growth in the means and methods a company is able to use to communicate with investors and other stakeholders. The hunger from the public for news has also made companies more proactive in their communication strategies. Though the annual report continues to be important, its previous status as the cornerstone to an investor's under-standing of the entity's position and performance has been replaced. For analysts, working with live information at their fingertips, the annual report has taken on a more confirmatory role.

Discussion point

What is the difference between discretionary and voluntary disclosure? And what are the potential costs and benefits of providing additional information?

Conclusion

In this chapter, we have outlined four possible methods to analyse financial information:

- horizontal analysis;
- trend analysis;
- vertical analysis;
- ratio analysis (profitability; efficiency; liquidity; solvency; and investor ratios).

We have presented these in an accounting context and have applied each method to the annual report. We have argued that, to extract the greatest value from your analysis, you need to view the investment through the eyes of the interested party. For example, if you are undertaking analysis on behalf of a potential investor who is considering buying shares in a company, you need to understand that you are offering advice to someone who will be acquiring a stake in a business. This busi-ness is in competition with others and therefore they also need to be examined. The context – economic, social, political and technological – is also critically important as it will inform your analysis.

The mechanics of financial statement analysis are relatively simple. The subsequent interpretation of the results, however, is far more difficult. Let us presume that you are calculating the gross profit ratio and using this information to interpret performance; one approach you could take would be as follows:

- Perform calculations: period comparisons; inter-industry comparisons.
- Appraise relative performance in naive terms, ie:

  - Has the ratio increased or decreased; has the industry ratio increased or decreased?
  - State that an upward move would generally be considered positive, while downward would be negative.
  - State that a gross profit ratio higher than those of peers would be generally considered a positive sign.

- Try to explain why there has been a change:

  - Has anything changed related to the business or their accounting policies comparing this year to those previous (time-series analysis) OR between this entity and other entities in the industry (cross-sectional analysis) OR between the current political/economic/social/technological climate and that of prior periods?
  - Use horizontal analysis, trend analysis and vertical analysis to make sense of the accounting numbers that underpin this change (ie revenue and cost of sales).

- Try to find other supporting evidence to substantiate your reasons, eg press releases.
- Answer the question 'so what?':

  - What are the implications and consequences of this change?
  - Do you believe it is sustainable (or will be sustained)?
  - What are the implications for the investment?

- What are the limitations in the analysis you have performed?

  - What further information would you need before you were satisfied that your recommendation was appropriate and accurate?

Financial analysis is subjective. There is a wealth of data available, both quantitative and qualitative. Part of the skill in undertaking these exercises is knowing when and where to stop. You will need to apply judgement and this is fine-tuned through practice and experience.

COMPREHENSION QUESTIONS

1 List THREE profitability ratios and show how they should be calculated.

2 Discuss THREE possible reasons why an entity's gross profit margin might increase from one year to the next.

3 What is meant by 'liquidity' and why might a supplier want to assess the liquidity position of one of their customer companies?

4 Show how you might appraise the solvency of an entity and state what you feel might be some red-flag issues.

5 What are the limitations of ratio analysis as a form of financial analysis?

Answers available at **www.koganpage.com/afm3**

Exercises

Answers available at **www.koganpage.com/afm3**

Exercise 3.1

Hawk Limited (Hawk) manufacture and distribute washing machines. The board of directors (BoD) have been concerned for some time that their share of the market has been in decline, mainly as a result of industry-wide competition. They are also aware that to a certain extent the industry has become the victim of its own success as washing machines have become more reliable and durable and therefore do not need replacing as regularly. Therefore, the BoD are considering making an investment in Sparrow Limited (Sparrow).

Sparrow manufacture dishwashers. The BoD believe that the synergistic gains will include advantages over competitors from shared technologies, a greater distribution network, an increase in skilled employees and management, and a shared clerical and manufacturing headquarters.

Table 3.6 shows the recently issued (summarized) financial statements of Hawk and Sparrow for the year ended 31 October.

Table 3.6

Statements of comprehensive income	Hawk		Sparrow	
	2019	2018	2019	2018
	£000s	£000s	£000s	£000s
Revenue	12,000	13,000	9,500	7,800
Cost of sales	(8,000)	(8,200)	(4,100)	(2,600)
Gross profit	4,000	4,800	5,400	5,200
Operating expenses	(2,500)	(2,550)	(2,600)	(2,700)
Finance costs	(550)	(500)	(900)	(300)
Profit before tax	950	1,750	1,900	2,200
Income tax expense	(300)	(600)	(800)	(900)
Profit for the period	650	1,150	1,100	1,300
Statements of financial position				
Non-current assets	13,075	12,000	11,000	6,000
Current assets	2,600	2,800	1,500	1,400
Current liabilities	(3,200)	(3,000)	(2,500)	(1,500)
Non-current liabilities	(275)	(250)	(4,500)	(1,500)
	12,200	11,550	5,500	4,400
Equity and reserves	12,200	11,550	5,500	4,400
Current assets include:				
Inventories	800	900	700	400
Trade receivables	1,000	1,800	750	600
Bank	800	100	50	400
Current liabilities include:				
Trade payables	1,550	1,300	650	400
Other payables	1,200	1,200	1,000	200
Current tax payable	450	500	850	900

Required:

(a) The BoD of Hawk Limited have asked you to analyse the position and performance of Sparrow Limited.

(b) As part of this analysis, the BoD have also asked that you use the information above to compare and contrast the position and performance of Hawk Limited with Sparrow Limited. They have asked you to conclude your analysis by stating, with reasons, whether you feel Hawk Limited should make a bid to acquire Sparrow Limited.

Exercise 3.2

Extracts from the (summarized) financial statements of Barksdale plc, a retail group, for the year ended 31 December 2019 are shown in Table 3.7 together with an extract from the chief executive's report that accompanied their issue.

Table 3.7

Statement of comprehensive income

	2019	2018
	£m	£m
Revenue	9,062	9,022
Cost of sales	(5,690)	(5,535)
Gross profit	3,372	3,487
Operating expenses	(2,501)	(2,276)
Operating profit	871	1,211
Finance income	50	65
Finance costs	(215)	(147)
Profit on ordinary activities before taxation	706	1,129
Income tax expense	(199)	(308)
Profit for the year	507	821

Statement of financial position

	2019	2018
	£m	£m
Non-current assets	5,868	5,979
Current assets		
Inventories	1,020	850
Trade receivables	45	47
Cash and cash equivalents	5	100
Other current assets	320	185
	1,390	1,182
Total assets	**7,258**	**7,161**
Share capital and reserves	2,100	1,964
Non-current liabilities	2,851	3,208
Current liabilities		
Trade payables	1,410	1,250
Other current liabilities	897	739
	7,258	**7,161**

Extract from the chief executive's report:

The year at a glance

During the year we acted decisively to meet the challenges of the global economic downturn, taking steps to manage costs tightly and respond quickly to the changing needs of our customers. Our adjusted profits are down on last year to £507m. This is due in part to conditions on the High Street as well as our conscious decision to improve our value, without compromising our quality. We have built unrivalled trust in the Barksdale brand over the last 125 years, and will not sacrifice our core principles when times get tough. Though we have a strong emphasis on food, furniture and general merchandise, it is clothing that is our customers' biggest discretionary purchase and as the UK's leading clothing retailer, with the largest market share, it was inevitable that demand would ease off as customers reined in their spending. Although value market share is marginally down from 11.0 to 10.7 per cent, we have held our volume market share at 11.2 per cent. We believe this is evidence that our team is in tune with our customer base. We paid a dividend of £300 million during 2019 compared to £350 million which was paid out in 2018.

Required:
Based solely on the information provided above, you have been asked by a potential investor to analyse the position and performance of Barksdale plc.

References

BBC (2013) [accessed 27 June 2017] Anglo American Boss says profits 'unacceptably poor', BBC News, 26/07 [Online] http://www.bbc.co.uk/news/business-23466885 (archived at https://perma.cc/8J6D-DWP4)

BBC (2013) [accessed 27 June 2017] Wet 'N' Wild waterpark enters administration, BBC News, 17/10 [Online] http://www.bbc.co.uk/news/uk-england-tyne-24561902 (archived at https://perma.cc/8UGR-QDW3)

BBC (2017) [accessed 27 June 2017] Balfour Beatty returns to profit, BBC News, 16/03 [Online] http://www.bbc.com/news/business-39289206 (archived at https://perma.cc/LXF5-Y8JB)

Brüggen, A, Krishnan, R and Sedatole, K L (2011) Drivers and Consequences of Short-Term Production Decisions: Evidence from the auto industry, Contemporary Accounting Research, **28** (1), pp 83–123

Chen, K H and Shimerda, T A (1981) An empirical analysis of useful financial ratios, *Financial Management*, pp 51–60

Collinson, P (2017) [accessed 27 June 2017] The Co-op Bank is the new Bradford & Bingley, The Guardian, 13/02 [Online] https://www.theguardian.com/business/2017/feb/13/the-co-op-bank-is-the-new-bradford-bingley (archived at https://perma.cc/74WF-P4EG)

Govender, P (2017) [accessed 27 June 2017] Kent & Lime calls it quits, Power Retail, 12/04 [Online] https://edm.powerretail.com.au/news/kent-lime-close-liquidation/ (archived at https://perma.cc/YP49-FLWL)

Grant, C (2017) [accessed 27 June 2017] Bristol-Myers Squibb: Make lemonade from lemons, The Wall Street Journal, 26/01 [Online] https://www.wsj.com/articles/bristol-myers-squibb-make-lemonade-from-lemons-1485449533 (archived at https://perma.cc/JV2P-QQJA)

Mouawad, J (2012) [accessed 27 June 2017] Beyond Mile-High Grub: Can airline food be tasty? The New York Times, 10/03 [Online] http://www.nytimes.com/2012/03/11/business/airlines-studying-the-science-of-better-in-flight-meals.html (archived at https://perma.cc/7D4W-PRNK)

Ryanair Annual Report (2019) [accessed 28 February 2020] Ryanair Investor Relations [Online] https://investor.ryanair.com/results/ (archived at https://perma.cc/T8M2-73LN)

Vaswani, K (2017) [accessed 27 June 2017] Samsung forecast beats estimates despite scandals and fires, BBC News, 07/04 [Online] http://www.bbc.co.uk/news/business-39523869 (archived at https://perma.cc/H854-FCJM)

White, K (2013) [accessed 27 June 2017] Lack of solvency created bank's problems, FT Adviser, 15/05 [Online] https://www.ftadviser.com/2013/05/15/regulation/regulators/lack-of-solvency-created-bank-s-problems-MHAKj6GyzpR48ThLDMytXI/article.html (archived at https://perma.cc/H854-FCJM)

Financial analysis: Part II   04

OBJECTIVE

The objective of this chapter is to further develop an understanding of financial analysis and interpretation skills. The first financial analysis chapter focused upon the interpretation of financial statements as presented in the annual report. This second chapter provides an overview of some other key forms of corporate financial communication and an introduction to some basic underlying theory.

LEARNING OUTCOMES

After studying this chapter, the reader will be:

- Able to understand that financial information is communicated through varying means and in different forms.
- Aware that corporate communication may be factually accurate but it might be presented, written or distributed in a way that sends out information signals.

KEY TOPICS COVERED

- Different forms of corporate communication.
- Examples and an overview of corporate communication use, misuse and abuse.

MANAGEMENT ISSUES

We continue to build on Chapter 3 which leads with the presumption that interpreting and analysing financial information is a key skill for managers and their decision making. We move away from the financial statements and look at other parts of the annual report as well as other forms of corporate communication.

Introduction

Equity investors (ie, shareholders) are not allowed access to a company's premises without pre-agreed authorization, let alone being granted access to the organization's books and records. Instead investors, as with all stakeholders, rely on the company to provide them with information. The financial statements – and more broadly the annual report – were considered in the previous chapter and are one means of communicating with stakeholders. These are not, however, the only way that financial information is disclosed by an entity. Instead there are many ways the firm communicates with its various audiences as it tries to translate complex managerial decisions into useful decision-making information for a wide range of users with varying levels of financial sophistication.

Within the annual report there are several sections which disclose information that could be important to your financial analysis. You might also like to consider reviewing the following when undertaking your analysis:

- reflections from members of the senior management team on position, performance and strategy;
- operating and financial review/management commentary/management discussion and analysis (title varies dependent upon jurisdiction);
- directors' remuneration report;
- corporate social responsibility report;
- corporate governance procedures, practices and policies;
- background information on company directors.

Furthermore, the annual report is not the only place where a company produces a set of financial statements. For large companies, interim reporting is required (quarterly or half-yearly). Companies also regularly release earnings statements which show the current performance and position; though these present adjusted numbers, they are driven by the IFRS-led financial statements. Whenever significant transactions or events occur – for example a sale of new shares, a proposed merger or acquisition – financial statements are released along with a set of forecasted financial numbers. To view financial information simply in terms of financial statements is to adopt too narrow a perspective.

Several studies from the 1980s and 1990s show that the annual report is either the most important or second most important source of information for users of financial statements. A more recent study by Abraham, Marston and Darby (2012) investigating the sources of information perceived to be most useful for risk analysis is presented in the following table:

Table 4.1   Sources of information perceived to be most useful for risk analysis (Abraham *et al*, 2012)

Information source	Mean score (out of 5)	Standard deviation
Meetings with management	4.5	0.7
Results announcements	4.2	0.9
Trading statements	4.1	0.8
Peer companies	4.0	0.5
Annual report & accounts	3.9	1.0
Industry experts	3.8	1.0
Analysts	3.6	1.1
Interim statements & quarterly reports	3.6	1.0
Interim reports and accounts	3.4	1.0
Market news	3.2	1.0
Newspapers	3.0	0.9
Financial news channels	2.8	0.9
Internet bulletins	2.3	1.1

Though it would be useful to discuss all of these forms of communication, there are constraints over time and space. Therefore, we propose to cover those which we think are most interesting and thought provoking. We will look at:

- corporate social responsibility reporting;
- earnings announcements, conference calls and investor presentations;
- media relations: press releases and newspaper coverage;
- social media and internet bulletins.

The drive for information

Not only has there been a major expansion in the forms and means of corporate communication in recent times, but there has also been a huge upsurge in demand for information from investors and other stakeholders. This combination of increased supply and demand has created a beast that seemingly cannot be sated. It has been said that every day individuals are exposed to around 13,000 separate corporate messages. When situations are out of the ordinary, the messages and responses multiply.

A further impact of this new era for communication is that media outlets have adopted a more sensationalist approach. This has been driven partly by the availability of material but also by the economic pressure on news outlets brought about by increased competition and the need to fill 24 hours of news, 7 days a week, 365 days a year.

If we take crisis events as extraordinary, it has been shown that the mass media's communication approaches, forms and strategies fundamentally differ from those which are adopted on an average news day. Often these will involve delivering greater volume, bolder immediacy and increasingly graphic portrayals of events; especially those moments of crisis or catastrophe. In turn, the response to crisis from the (perceived) responsible organization(s) has been shown to be moderated correspondingly. Crises elicit emotions from stakeholders and thus there is an attribution effect and responsibility needs to be either taken or denied.

It has been stated within crisis communication research that honesty, openness and candour are paramount, whilst the impact of poor and/or incomplete corporate communication contributes to negative perceptions and possible value destruction. In other words, we know that the messages coming out of companies can be deliberately – and sometimes appallingly – distorted in order to manage consumers' impressions. However, creative accounting is likely to impact on the reputations of individuals and companies where it is uncovered.

Stakeholder management

The primary purpose of corporate communication is managing relationships with stakeholders. These relationships are required to create, develop and foster reputational capital. It is necessary to acknowledge that many businesses have stepped back from the neo-classical economic theory of organization and accepted socio-economic theory in its stead. The word 'accounting' has as its root 'accountability'. Indeed, linguistically, these two words do not share a stem; they share meaning. Though we acknowledge that the primary corporate objective is the maximization

Figure 4.1   Stakeholder salience theory: the three core attributes

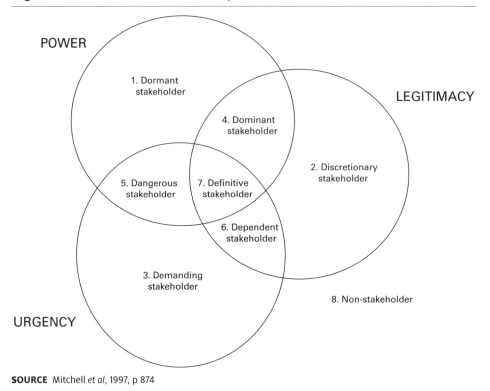

SOURCE Mitchell *et al*, 1997, p 874

of shareholder wealth, we also believe that businesses must also be accountable to stakeholders beyond this group.

Earlier we established that the users of financial information were varied. Their interests differ, their objectives are varied and the information they require from corporate disclosure might not always be the same. They are, however, important to the continuance of the organization as their acceptance sustains the reputational capital. Also related to this, it is necessary for organizations to open up to other stakeholder groups beyond current and potential investors because this develops checks and balances that help to protect the welfare of society. Though it might not be possible to correlate 'doing good' directly with returns, a combination of engagement, words and actions can foster intangible returns such as employee, customer and supplier goodwill.

Companies and their management teams are aware, however, that there are different needs and relative salience of stakeholders, ie those that drive value and with whom it is *essential* the firm communicates fully and transparently in order to protect reputational capital, and those where it is simply *desirable*. Note also that stakeholder salience is in flux, and it is possible to shift between categories dependent upon context. Thus, stakeholder theory allows us to better understand the needs of stakeholder groups, and it also gives us an indication of which one(s) to prioritize. While early theory subdivides stakeholders according to the form of their interest, ie economic or moral, a more detailed stakeholder salience model has been developed which categorizes stakeholders according to the existence of three attributes. This might not appear immediately relevant to you at first glance; however, you should note that it inevitably guides a company's communication strategy and therefore will also influence how you should approach the information that is presented.

Mitchell, Agle and Wood (1997) propose three underpinning attributes to salience:

- power (ability to levy power upon an organization);
- legitimacy (the legitimacy of the claim on the organization);
- urgency (the degree to which a stakeholder can call for immediate action).

The stakeholder's relative level(s) of power, legitimacy and urgency determines their level of prominence. It also defines the depth and breadth of stakeholder-targeted communication. The seven stakeholder categories (an eighth – non-stakeholder – is also recorded) are shown in Figure 4.1. These classifications are further analysed in Table 4.2. Note: this theory has been extensively explored and examined in recent years; as a result a fourth attribute consistently emerges as relevant – proximity.

Table 4.2   Stakeholder classifications

Latent stakeholders – possess one (of the three) attributes.
Owing to the limited time and resources available to managers, it is likely that they will do very little about stakeholders whom they believe possess only one of the three attributes. It is possible that their existence (ie the latent stakeholders) will not be acknowledged. Note that this relationship cuts both ways, and these stakeholders are unlikely to pay attention to the entity.

Category	Attribute(s)	Description
1. Dormant	Power	Possess power to impose their will on a firm, but by not having a legitimate relationship or an urgent claim, their power remains unused.
2. Discretionary	Legitimacy	Possess the attribute of legitimacy, but they have no power to influence the firm and no urgent claims.
3. Demanding	Urgency	Those with urgent claims but having neither power nor legitimacy are the 'mosquitoes buzzing in the ears' of managers: irksome but not dangerous, bothersome but not warranting more than passing management attention, if any at all.

(continued)

Table 4.2   *(Continued)*

Expectant stakeholders – possess two attributes.
Stakeholder salience will be moderate where two of the stakeholder attributes – power, legitimacy, and urgency – are perceived by managers to be present.

4. Dominant	Power and legitimacy	In the situation where stakeholders are both powerful and legitimate, their influence in the firm is assured, since by possessing power with legitimacy, they form the 'dominant coalition' in the enterprise (Cyert & March, 1963). The expectations of any stakeholders perceived by managers to have power and legitimacy will 'matter' to managers.
5. Dangerous	Power and urgency	When a stakeholder lacks legitimacy but has urgency and power, that stakeholder will be coercive and possibly violent, making the stakeholder 'dangerous', literally, to the firm. 'Coercion' is suggested as a descriptor because the use of coercive power often accompanies illegitimate status.
6. Dependent	Legitimacy and urgency	Dependent stakeholders lack power but have urgent legitimate claims; they depend upon others (other stakeholders or the firm's managers) for the power necessary to carry out their will. Because power in this relationship is not reciprocal, its exercise is governed either through the advocacy or guardianship of other stakeholders, or through the guidance of internal management values.

Definitive stakeholders – possess all three attributes.
Stakeholder salience will be high where all three of the stakeholder attributes are perceived by managers to be present.

7. Definitive	Power, legitimacy and urgency	By definition, a stakeholder already exhibiting both power and legitimacy will be a member of a firm's dominant coalition. When such a stakeholder's claim is urgent, managers have a clear and immediate mandate to attend to and give priority to that stakeholder's claim.

SOURCE Adapted from Mitchell *et al*, 1997: 874–79.

Given this, it is unsurprising that the IASB has arrived at the verdict that the primary user group of the annual report is current and potential investors. Other users typically do not have the (immediate) power to demand managerial action in response to their needs, such as the removal of board members or the halting of certain projects. In line with early stakeholder theory, the primary group's interests are mainly economic in nature, which is deemed important, and therefore there is an almost constant dialogue with them. However, most, if not all, large businesses recognize the importance of reputational capital and therefore also have a communication programme to engage with the secondary users and their (mainly) moral concerns.

> **Discussion point**
>
> Why do the IASB view current and potential investors as the primary user group?
> Can you explain your answer in terms of stakeholder salience theory?

Corporate social responsibility reporting

Corporate social responsibility (CSR) reporting is an area which has developed rapidly in recent years. Reports that were once willfully ignored are now state-of-the-art representations of the aims, goals, achievements and aspirations in the fields of ethical, social and environmental performance and position. The demand for organizations to behave responsibly has been consumer driven; ultimately, we all want to live in a better world. See, for example, the volume of 'fair-trade' products available on the shelves in the supermarkets or even the ethical banking alternatives now on hand.

Stakeholders whose salience was (and is) not high were asking companies to answer concerns of a moral nature. Their replies have become thorough. In turn, there has been a recent reported shift in perspective from definitive stakeholders – those with high salience – towards these disclosures, perceiving them to have economic as well as moral value.

During the past decade, there has been a dramatic growth in investment in funds with a social responsibility focus under professional management. This means that investors are deliberately choosing to buy stock in businesses that meet social responsibility targets. There has been commensurate demand for non-financial CSR information which cannot be obtained through the traditional path of analysing financial statements.

CSR reports place emphasis on issues such as:

- community matters;
- health and safety;
- diversity and human resources matters;
- environmental programmes.

Recent times have seen the emergence of Integrated Reporting. The Prince's Accounting for Sustainability Project (A4S) and the Global Reporting Initiative (GRI) combined to announce the establishment of the International Integrated Reporting Council in August 2010. The Council is guided by representatives from the accounting profession, the accounting academy, regulatory bodies and standard-setters, and in December 2013 the IIRC released the International <IR> Framework ('the Framework'). Under this Framework, organizations are encouraged to disclose information about their strategies, performance and results in various areas ranging from financial to social and environmental issues. Whilst this is still voluntary in almost all parts of the world, strong governance alongside consistency in the demand and format of disclosure must surely be beneficial.

Whilst CSR reporting shows some signs of manipulation and distortion, there are genuine grounds for hope and optimism. Researchers regularly highlight areas of good practice. It is the aim of the majority of those who work in this field: to encourage improvements to information and its communication; to promote fuller and more transparent disclosures; and to make suggestions to help bridge the information asymmetry gap between stakeholders and management. We simply urge the reader to be alert for signs of information management, whilst at the same time praising the steps forward that have been made (and are being made) in this field over a relatively short time frame.

Earnings announcements, conference calls and investor presentations

The annual report has recently come to be regarded as a confirmatory (or regulatory) document, mainly because large companies have regular (normally quarterly) results/earnings announcements, sometimes referred to as press releases. These announcements provide summarized (adjusted) IFRS numbers for the period under consideration. These announcements also include a summary of the material movements during the period plus an analysis of the position and performance. These range in complexity and in content but also commonly provide an outline of the company strategy and the possible impact this might have on future performance.

There has been a great deal of work undertaken investigating the use of *promotional language* in these releases and the impact that has on the investor community. Though results are mixed, it would appear that longer reports tend to quell the negative impact of unexpected earnings (probably because they close the information asymmetry gap); tone affects investors' reactions; and framing can influence investors' perceptions.

Whereas CSR information is principally aimed at secondary stakeholders, this information is intended for investors and their financial intermediaries. These are the definitive stakeholders in Mitchell *et al*'s (1997) framework. Both the earnings announcement documentation and the conference call or investor presentation that follow are publicly accessible (available through the corporate website and live broadcast over the internet), but the list of invitees is short. The communication is principally directed at financial analysts who act as financial intermediaries on behalf of investors.

In the UK, these events occasionally coincide with the release of the annual report. Normally, however, the annual report follows between a couple of days and a couple of weeks after the earnings announcement. Given that we operate in markets which interpret information almost instantaneously, this time lag means that, in many cases, the annual report is out of date before it is even sent to the printers.

There are those who argue that the conference call/investor presentation does not provide incremental information over and above the accompanying earnings announcement. However, analysts' time is a key limiting resource and, therefore, others state that their attendance at these events proves by default that they have some worth. All agree that improved timeliness is a genuine benefit to this communication event. There is an argument that the company-enforced limiting of stakeholder participation creates a two-tier system. This occurs even amongst the definitive stakeholders themselves, as not all analysts and investors are invited to attend. We are convinced by the conclusions of the seminal study by Frankel, Johnson and Skinner (1999, p 149) which stated: 'we find that conference calls provide information to market participants over and above the information contained in the corresponding press release [earnings announcement], as evidenced by elevated return variances and trading volumes.' While we feel that some of this value is social and political, rather than simply economic, we strongly urge you to consider these events when undertaking your financial analysis.

Discussion point

Have you ever listened in to a conference call or watched an investor presentation? If so, how influential did you find what was voiced, as opposed to the setting, the managers' tone, the body language, and so forth? If you've never watched (listened to) an investor presentation (conference call), why not take a look at one today? They are normally easy to find. Find the company's investor relations page and look for a heading 'webcasts', 'results' or 'presentations'. If you are willing to provide a few basic details (name, occupation, workplace) then you will be granted free access.

Media relations: press releases and newspaper coverage

Communicating with, and through, the mass media has become central to organizations and the investor relations role. There is evidence that links a favourable representation in the media with improved performance. To achieve success, however, companies need to get their message out and have it interpreted in the way they would like. Newspapers and news organizations are vital to generating publicity. They are also important to preserving and enhancing reputational capital and transmitting information to stakeholders who might otherwise be hard to reach (or influence). The mass media therefore essentially acts as a conduit.

As stated above, the public are bombarded with daily corporate slogans and messages. It is also worth remembering, however, that journalists are also bombarded with events and press releases. How does one message get picked up by the press whilst others are left behind? There are certain techniques and strategies that can be employed but often it is simply down to fads, fashions, extraordinary events or luck.

In most mainstream newspapers, business news used to be limited to a single page buried towards the middle of their publication. In recent times, there has been an upsurge in the demand for this information and coverage has increased proportionately. The way that news outlets interpret events impacts on corporate reputation. Companies have a new awareness that the way the media interprets their financial information can have an impact far beyond their definitive stakeholders. Some financial information can even provoke latent and expectant stakeholders into action. See, for example, the reporting of the tax affairs of Starbucks, Amazon and Google (Extract 4.1).

Extract 4.1: Media relations

Google, Amazon, Starbucks: The rise of 'tax shaming'

By Vanessa Barford & Gerry Holt

BBC News Magazine (4 December 2012) (an extract from the news release: full story available at: **http://www.bbc.co.uk/news/magazine-20560359**)

Global firms such as Starbucks, Google and Amazon have come under fire for avoiding paying tax on British profits. There seems to be a growing culture of naming and shaming companies. But what impact does it have?

Companies have long had complicated tax structures, but a recent spate of stories has highlighted a number of tax-avoiding firms that are not seen to be playing their part.

Starbucks, for example, had sales of £400m in the UK last year, but paid no corporation tax. It transferred some money to a Dutch sister company in royalty payments, bought coffee beans from Switzerland and paid high interest rates to borrow from other parts of the business. Amazon, which had sales in the UK of £3.35bn in 2011, only reported a 'tax expense' of £1.8m. And Google's UK unit paid just £6m to the Treasury in 2011 on UK turnover of £395m.

Everything these companies are doing is legal. It's avoidance and not evasion. But the tide of public opinion is visibly turning. Even 10 years ago news of a company minimizing its corporation tax would have been more likely to be inside the business pages than on the front page. What changed? And is 'shaming' of companies justifiable and effective?

Momentum has been growing for the last few years.

In September 2009, *The Observer* ran with the headline: 'Avoiding tax robs our public services, declares minister'. The paper reported that the government was planning to say tax is a 'moral issue' and that it was 'determined to end avoidance and evasion'.

October 2010 – and the Vodafone case – saw the *Daily Mail* report: 'Vodafone closes Oxford Street store at £6bn tax protest'.

...

Another impact of tax shaming is that some people, such as 45-year-old self-employed businessman Mike Buckhurst, from Manchester, boycott brands. 'I've uninstalled Google Chrome and changed my search engine on all my home computers. If I want a coffee I am now going to go to Costa, despite Starbucks being nearer to me, and even though I buy a lot of things online, I am not using Amazon. 'I'm sick of the "change the law" comments, I can vote with my feet. I feel very passionate about this because at one point in my life I was a top rate tax payer and I paid my tax in full,' he says.

Occasionally the BBC website opens up stories to comment and these are subsequently 'rated' by other users. There is some debate in the online community about the type of stories that are opened up and the parties concerned. Nevertheless, they provide a direct line into the minds of stakeholders. We note from the story cases of individuals opting out of products offered by these 'named and shamed' companies. One of the most interesting things about this story to the interested observer is the two most highly rated comments (see Extract 4.2). These individuals draw attention to another company which is also alleged to be involved in this form of tax management – Apple. Their comments suggest that there is media bias towards this organization.

Extract 4.2: Two most popular comments on the story: 'Google, Amazon, Starbucks: The rise of "tax shaming"'

Muesli3
4th December 2012–12:43

I am curious as to why in every single article it's the same three companies being mentioned. How is it that these companies are getting shamed much more than Apple with their 2% rate?!

> **production_malfunction**
> 4th December 2012–13:07
>
> I totally agree with the other comments on here regarding Apple. How these people are managing to get away with only paying 2%, while at the same time avoiding media scrutiny, is beyond me.
>
> BBC put down your iPhones and do your job please.

It has been found that companies participate in the framing of news items. Companies write press releases in the hope that journalists will pick them up. Journalists rely on companies to write press releases because they cannot be everywhere at once. This sometimes creates a peculiar dialogue between unrelated – and sometimes conflictingly motivated – parties being reflected outwards. Often the original press release is simply paraphrased and disseminated. With this in mind, you will frequently find that press releases written by companies and made available to journalists are written in the third person to make things simpler for the journalists to adopt.

Press releases tend to carry predominantly good news, ie news intended to create value, for example the launch of a new product, undertaking a successful tender. Despite journalists being told to eschew a positive linguistic turn and focus on facts, corporate communication via press releases continues to be inherently optimistic in tone and therefore it is common for the related news release to be influenced towards this position. Some have suggested they tend towards the *propagandaic*. Interestingly, it has been found that the tone is hardened when the communication addresses economic or financial matters. Nevertheless, it is interesting to see that almost every study of corporate communication has picked up strong signals linked to attribution theory. In other words, companies tend to attribute successes to 'I' or 'we' and failures to an externality.

Behind the scenes, it is common for companies to communicate formally and informally with news outlets. They do not simply issue press releases and cross their fingers. They also brief face-to-face through press conferences and meetings/interviews with company personnel. In addition, companies actively monitor the effectiveness of their communication strategies.

In summary, the media is a perfectly acceptable way to substantiate your financial analysis and to triangulate findings. Newspapers need to sell copy and therefore you should expect a level of sensationalism, therefore in turn you should employ a healthy level of scepticism. However, this can only go so far. If the information is inaccurate and leads to a significant level of value destruction, it is likely that they will be held to account. Normally, newspapers will provide information which has come from a reputable source (often the company itself) which extends your analysis, lending weight to some arguments whilst rejecting the validity of others.

Social media and internet bulletins

As yet, little is known about how social media and internet bulletins will impact on corporate communication and the transmission/translation of financial information. In the meantime, we can only comment on what has happened. The majority of the world's corporate household names maintain social media accounts, such as *Facebook*, *YouTube*, *Weibo* and *Twitter*. Their audiences are different, not just in terms of the demographic but also the information needs. There are all sorts of other internet-based means that allow companies to transmit information in a more accessible way to stakeholders, eg blogs, bulletin boards and so forth.

We have observed three major changes as a result of this new media technology (although there are bound to be many more): the immediacy of information availability; the reach of this information; and the ability for users to comment on content. The advantages are that companies can be first to *frame* an event and set the news agenda. However, the immediacy means that an inappropriate lead, a lack of thoughtfulness in the communiqué or an inaccurate reflection of the events can have serious effects.

As the technology and the behaviour of the actors develop, it will be possible to work out if this new media is fad or fashion and here to stay. At the same time, an ethical framework will surely emerge to govern the authors and the audience. This is essential for the long-term sustainability of this form of communication. In the meantime, the digital landscape is a potential goldmine of untapped information that will bolster your financial analysis with previously hard-to-reach evidence. Equally, note that this might also be a swamp of managed corporate stories which you'd be better off ignoring.

Discussion point

Do you use Twitter, Facebook and/or some other form of social media? Do you follow any companies? Why do you think companies have a social media presence?

Conclusion

In summary, information resources have never been so accessible and up to date. Though there is still a gap in the communication levels between those deemed definitive stakeholders (current and potential investors) and others, the gap is closing and the richness and value of the extra information to which they have access are diminishing and eroding.

Having undertaken your financial analysis based upon the annual report and financial statements of an entity, you will undoubtedly be left with more questions than you have answers. Turning to these additional sources – earnings statements, investor presentations, conference calls, CSR reports, newspapers, corporate websites, social media – will provide you with an almost inexhaustible secondary data set which can be used to support (or contradict) your initial observations.

COMPREHENSION QUESTIONS

1 Discuss what is meant by the term 'stakeholder salience' and why it might be important to incorporate this theory into a business's communication strategy.

2 In terms of the accounting standard-setting process, provide examples of who might be classified into each of the following categories and explain why you believe this to be the case:

   a dormant stakeholders;

   b demanding stakeholders;

   c definitive stakeholders.

3 Can you explain why analysts might view meetings with management as more important than the annual report?

4 Can you explain why analysts might view conference calls/investor presentations as more important than the annual report?

5 Can you explain why the annual report continues to be a useful document?

6 Describe one occasion where you have been influenced to buy a product or engage in an activity as a direct result of an item of corporate communication, eg social media update; and explain what that was, how it happened and outline why you think it happened this way.

Answers available at **www.koganpage.com/afm3**

References

Abraham, S, Marston, C and Darby, P (2012) Risk Reporting: Clarity, relevance and location, Institute of Chartered Accountants of Scotland, Research Report, ISBN 978-1-904574-87-3

Cyert, R M and March, J G (1963) *A Behavioral Theory of the Firm*, Prentice-Hall, Englewood Cliffs, NJ

Frankel, R, Johnson, M and Skinner, D J (1999) An empirical examination of conference calls as a voluntary disclosure medium, *Journal of Accounting Research*, **37** (1), pp 133–50

Mitchell, R K, Agle, B R and Wood, D J (1997) Toward a theory of stakeholder identification and salience: defining the principle of who and what really counts, *Academy of Management Review*, **22** (4), pp 853–86

Supplementary reading

Barker, R G (1998) The market for information – evidence from finance directors, analysts and fund managers, *Accounting and Business Research*, **29** (1), pp 3–20

Barker, R, Hendry, J, Roberts, J, *et al* (2012) Can company-fund manager meetings convey informational benefits? Exploring the rationalisation of equity investment decision making by UK fund managers, *Accounting, Organizations and Society*, **37** (4), pp 207–22

Brown, S, Hillegeist, S A and Lo, K (2004) Conference calls and information asymmetry, *Journal of Accounting and Economics*, **37** (3), pp 343–66

Cornelissen, J (2011) *Corporate Communication: A guide to theory and practice*, 3rd edn, Sage, London

Frankel, R, Johnson, M and Skinner, D J (1999) An empirical examination of conference calls as a voluntary disclosure medium, *Journal of Accounting Research*, **37** (1), pp 133–50

Mayew, W and Venkatachalam, M (2012) The power of voice: managerial affective states and future firm performance, *Journal of Finance*, **67** (1), pp 1–44

Mayew, W J, Sharp, N Y and Venkatachalam, M (2013) Using earnings conference calls to identify analysts with superior private information, *Review of Accounting Studies*, **18**, pp 386–413

Business planning 05

OBJECTIVE

To provide an understanding of how budgeting fits into the business planning process, and the different approaches which may be taken to budgeting.

LEARNING OUTCOMES

After studying this chapter, the reader will be able to:

- Understand the role of budgeting within the business planning process.
- Distinguish and evaluate different approaches to budgeting.

KEY TOPICS COVERED

- Business planning and the role of budgets in that process.
- The function and uses of budgets.
- The budget-setting process – different approaches.
- Practical budget-setting.
- Flexible budgeting.
- Zero-based budgeting.
- Activity-based budgeting.

MANAGEMENT ISSUES

Managers should be aware of how budgeting contributes to the overall business planning process and be familiar with the range of budgeting approaches available to them.

Introduction

In this chapter we will look at how budgeting fits into the overall framework of decision making, planning and control within an organization. We will also look at some of the range of approaches to budgeting and explore how different approaches are more appropriate to different types of organization.

What is a budget? A budget can be defined as the plans of an organization expressed in quantitative terms. It is usually detailed and sets out the planned income and expenditure of a future period of time. Although budgets are primarily seen as being monetary, operational budgets may also set out non-monetary elements such as stock levels and staffing requirements.

Typically a budget will be broken down into several levels, so that there will be a master budget for the organization and then budgets for different divisions, functions or areas of the business, all of which feed into the master budget.

The budget period will depend upon the needs of the organization. Most organizations prepare detailed budgets for a 12-month period which corresponds with their fiscal year. They may also prepare less detailed budgets for longer periods such as five years or ten years. Equally, many organizations break their annual budget down into shorter periods such as quarterly or monthly. In some cases weekly or even daily budgets may be used if that proves to be a useful management tool.

Why budget?

Budgeting is an important part of the management process – the way in which an organization sets goals and plans actions, allocates resources, controls and measures performance and rewards people. Budgeting plays a central role in all of these activities. It therefore needs to be understood and recognized as something broader than simply a set of numbers for income and expenditure over the next 12 months.

However, despite its widespread use, budgeting is far from perfect as a management tool. Indeed, there is debate within some circles as to how beneficial budgeting is. Some commentators argue that in today's uncertain and complex markets meaningful budgeting is not possible. At the end of this chapter we explore some of the arguments against budgeting and some of the alternatives which have been put forward.

Discussion point

What is budgeting information used for?

Business planning and control: the role of budgets

A budget needs to be understood as a tool to help managers achieve organizational objectives. First and foremost it is an important element of the planning and control functions within an organization. Figure 5.1 illustrates how budgeting fits into this planning and control process.

A major advantage of budgeting is that it forces an organization to be explicit about setting long-term objectives and short-term goals and planning to achieve these. Without budgeting there is a danger that managers concentrate purely on the day-to-day running of the business. A budget helps identify the resources that are needed, and when they will be needed, so that the right resources are in place at the right time.

The budgeting process, if implemented well, can integrate the many areas of an organization, coordinating activities, communicating strategies, motivating staff, providing accountability and transparency.

Budgets form an important mechanism for *coordinating* actions across different parts of an organization. Each department or division within an organization, by working to their part of the budget, will ensure *goal congruence* in terms of achieving overall organizational objectives.

Budgets form an important part of *communication* within organizations. When a budget is set and communicated throughout the organization, this provides

Figure 5.1   The planning and control process

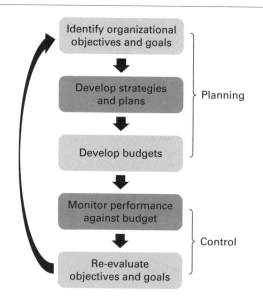

'top-down' communication by sending clear messages to employees within different divisions as to what is expected of them over the next period. In turn, as budgets are monitored and performance is evaluated against budgets, there is 'bottom-up' communication as this monitoring feeds back important information to senior management as to how actual activities are unfolding in relation to the original business plans.

Budgets can be an important *motivational tool*, particularly if incentives such as financial bonuses are derived from performance against budgets. The effectiveness of budgets as a motivational tool is dependent upon the degree to which employees 'buy into' the budget. This is more likely to occur if they have a meaningful participation in the preparation of the budget. These behavioural issues are explored in more detail later in this chapter.

Budgets also provide *accountability* from managers in terms of the objectives they pursue and the results they achieve. Managers will be responsible for achieving budget targets and reporting on their results.

A communicated budget also provides *transparency* about the allocation of resources within the organization.

Although budgets are primarily forward-looking in terms of planning for the future, managers can also use them to *evaluate* past performance. In the next chapter we will look at this evaluation process in more detail.

Extract 5.1: The use of budgets in practice

A survey of 558 medium and large firms in the United States and Canada in 2010 found that 79 per cent used budgets for control purposes (Libby and Lindsay, 2010). A similar survey in 1987 found a comparable figure of 83 per cent of firms used budgets for control.

The budget-setting process

The budget-setting process within most organizations follows certain clear steps. There may be some variation between organizations according to their exact budgeting approach, but Figure 5.2 sets out what is a typical budgeting process for most organizations.

Large organizations will have a budget committee which has overall responsibility for the preparation of the budget. The budget committee is usually made up of managers from all levels and divisions of the organization in order to achieve good

Figure 5.2   The budget-setting process

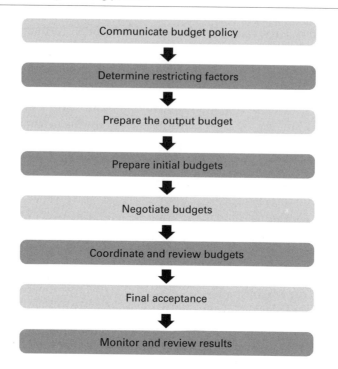

cooperation and coordination. The budget committee will oversee the following steps during the budget-setting process:

1 *Communicate budget policy.* The first step in budgeting is to communicate the budgeting policy to all those involved in the budget-setting process. This is to ensure that everybody fully understands the policy and to try to ensure that contributions to the budget are in line with that policy. For example, the budgeting policy may be to increase sales by 5 per cent over the next 12 months while at the same time increasing profit margins by 2 per cent. This policy will form the basis of the individual elements of the budget and will inform the process.

2 *Determine restricting factors.* Before the process of establishing the figures for the different areas of the budget can start, the organization must consider what factors will restrict performance over the budgetary period. There will always be some restricting factors. These may, for example, be the production capacity of a factory, the amount of skilled labour available in certain areas of activity, the quantity of raw materials available, or the size and capacity of the market. If these restricting factors are not identified and taken into consideration, there is a serious risk that an unachievable budget will be set.

Extract 5.2: Restricting factors

Restrictions on performance that shape budgets can come in many forms. In 2017 Japan suffered its worst potato harvest in 34 years. As a consequence Japanese potato crisp maker Calbee found itself facing a restriction in production levels and higher raw material costs.

3 *Prepare the output budget.* For most organizations the logical place to start the budget is with the level of output. This is because it is usually the output which determines the resources required throughout the organization. Output can be determined in terms of sales or level of service provided. For organizations that produce multiple products or services, this budget needs to be broken down into more detail to determine the relative mix of each output element.

  Some organizations, such as those in the public sector, may have fixed levels of resources that constrain output according to funding available. However, even in such situations, it is good practice to start with the desired level of output. Even with fixed resources, different levels and mixes of outputs of sales or services can be achieved by allocating resources in different ways.

4 *Prepare initial budgets.* Once the level of output has been determined, initial budgets for the other areas of activity can be established. These budgets will include those for production, purchasing, staffing, advertising and support services. Who is responsible for producing each of these budgets will vary across different organizations and depends upon the budgeting philosophy of the organization. The different approaches are discussed in the section below on practical budget setting.

5 *Negotiate budgets.* This is not a step which is included within the budgeting process of all organizations. However, when an organization is structured in such a way as to give divisional managers a high degree of autonomy, this is a necessary step. It is particularly important if divisional managers hold budgets for which they become responsible at the monitoring stage and those budgets include costs of services provided by other divisions. The budget-holding manager should be given the opportunity to negotiate the level of service and cost from the service provider. If this step is omitted, budget-holding managers may be disincentivized by budgets they feel unable to work to.

6 *Coordinate and review budgets.* If individual budgets have been produced by the budget-holding manager, and particularly if there has been a negotiation process as set out in step 5 above, it will be essential to coordinate and review individual budgets to ensure that they fit together. One problem with delegation of budget

setting to individual managers is that self-interest may interfere such that indi-vidual budgets do not fit together to produce a coordinated overall budget. It is essential that there is goal congruence between individual budgets, that is to say, that they all fit together towards achieving the overall goal of the organization as set out in the budget policy in step 1. One role of the budget committees is to oversee and mediate any negotiation process and to coordinate and review the overall budget before final acceptance.

7 *Final acceptance.* Once individual budgets have been prepared, negotiated and coordinated, there needs to be a final acceptance of the budget as a whole. At this stage the budget can be finalized and will be ready for implementation.

8 *Monitor and review results.* The final stage in the budgeting process takes place once the budget is being implemented. During implementation, actual perfor-mance should be measured against budget at regular intervals. Any significant variances from budget should be recorded and investigated, as they represent a deviation from the business plan. If necessary, management action should be taken either to modify activities to bring them back in line with the budget, or to modify the budget to reflect changes which may have occurred since the budget was produced and which were not anticipated during the budgeting process. Different organizations have different approaches towards dealing with budget variances and these are explored in the next chapter which looks in more detail at performance management.

Discussion point

Who should be involved in the budget-setting process? Why is the negotiation stage so important?

Practical budget setting

So far in this chapter we have considered the benefits of producing a budget and looked at the overall budget-setting process. In this section we will look at some of the more detailed practical aspects of budgeting.

Levels of budgeting

Large organizations will have several levels of budget which feed into a master budget as illustrated in Figure 5.3.

Figure 5.3   Levels of budgeting

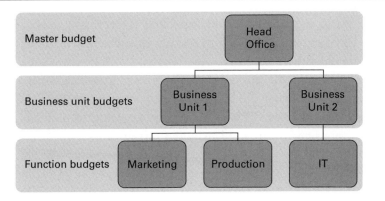

The master budget integrates all the budgets from the different business units of the organization. It will be made up of both the operational budget and the financial budget.

The operational budget comprises those budgets which make up the details of the operations of the business. These will include the sales budget, the production budget, direct labour and purchasing and the overhead budget. These budgets feed into the budgeted income statement.

The financial budget includes the cash budget, the capital budget and the budgeted balance sheet.

Different approaches to budget preparation

Budgeting is sometimes mistakenly seen as a purely accounting function. Although accountants are typically involved in the coordination of the budget-setting process, and in the production of budget-monitoring reports, the budget-setting process should involve employees at all levels within the organization. If line managers as well as senior management are involved in setting budgets, this will ensure greater ownership of the finalized budgets throughout the organization. It will also enable the organization to take advantage of localized and specialist knowledge to ensure a more accurate budget.

The sequence in which budgetary decisions are made is important, as this can have a significant impact on the budget which emerges from the process. The budget-setting process can be classified into two main approaches: a top-down approach or a bottom-up approach.

The top-down approach to budgeting

The top-down approach, as the name implies, involves senior management producing a master budget and then devolving activity targets and expenditure limits down throughout the organization. Once this overarching framework for the budget has been established, the details of the budget, in terms of allocations to individual divisions or activities, can be discussed and negotiated. Under this approach, any budget negotiation becomes one of how best to allocate individual activity budgets in order to best achieve organizational goals.

The main advantage of the top-down approach to budgeting is that senior management are able to set the budget in line with their strategic vision for the future of the organization. This improves policy prioritization and coordination. Senior management can set demanding targets which will strengthen fiscal discipline within the organization. Those organizations which use the top-down approach to budgeting use the budgeting process as part of the communication from senior management as to the strategic vision of the organization and how that is to be implemented.

A disadvantage of the top-down approach is that it can lead to low commitment from employees. If low-tier managers have had no involvement in the design of the budget, they are less likely to take ownership of the budget and to show commitment towards achieving it. However, a top-down approach does not necessarily mean that employees have no input into the budgeting process. The allocation of resources to individual projects and activities can be left open to discussion and line managers can still be given substantial freedom to negotiate detailed spending within their overall budget allocation.

The bottom-up approach to budgeting

When a bottom-up budgeting approach is adopted, budget proposals are produced within each division or section of the organization and then fed upwards. They are then compiled, coordinated and integrated into a master budget.

A characteristic of this approach is that total expenditure tends to be determined through a process of negotiating the details of the budget with each function manager. Because of this, the bottom-up approach often works best in an unconstrained budgeting environment: an environment in which individual line managers are free to put forward expenditure proposals if these can be justified in terms of revenue generation. The approach is less suited to organizations which have fixed expenditure limits; although it can be used in such situations, this will involve substantially more negotiation and adjustment.

The rationale behind the bottom-up approach is greater involvement of divisional managers and employees. If employees are involved in setting the budget they are more likely to be committed to achieving budget targets.

Extract 5.3: Circle bring bottom-up management to the NHS

When Circle became the first private company to take control of a full-service hospital in the UK, it introduced a new management philosophy which moved away from the traditional top-down approach found in the National Health Service. The chief executive of Circle, Ali Parsa, whose background was in the banking industry, believes in incentivizing staff to do things better and more efficiently and delegating power down so that they are able to do so. Staff hold a 49.9 per cent stake in the business, and shares are awarded based on performance. Employees are divided into clinical teams of between 50 and 100, each led by a doctor, a nurse and an administrator. Each team has responsibility for its own budget, financial performance, and how well patients do. Teams meet regularly to monitor performance and have the power to do things differently if they believe they can improve the operation of the hospital. The ideology behind the model is that staff, if given both a financial interest and the power to act, are better at identifying improvements and efficiency changes than managers who are divorced from the day-to-day activities.

This approach also enables senior management to take advantage of the local knowledge and specialist expertise of divisional managers who are 'closer to the ground'. This avoids the situation of senior management setting unrealistic budgets because they don't have a detailed knowledge of the activities and costs involved in achieving objectives within individual functions.

Despite the advantages outlined above, the bottom-up approach does present a number of challenges:

- It can be an extremely time-consuming and costly process to involve a greater number of people throughout the organization.

- It makes it more difficult to ensure congruence towards organizational goals. Individual line managers are likely to put forward budget proposals based upon local needs and wants rather than those which contribute towards those of the organization as a whole.

- It makes it much more difficult for senior management to maintain tight fiscal control. Budget proposals from individual line managers will inevitably argue for increases in expenditure.

There is also a risk that line managers who are allowed to set their own budgets will set themselves undemanding targets, or that they will create 'slack' for themselves to avoid criticism for not achieving targets. Within individual divisions, line managers have little incentive to identify and propose savings that could be used to increase profitability or to finance new initiatives. In a bottom-up budgeting system the budget negotiation process can become an exercise in preserving existing levels of funding and attempting to obtain additional resources.

Another feature of the bottom-up approach is that it is inherently incremental in nature. This makes significant reallocations between sectors or large restructuring of the budget unlikely.

Incremental budgeting

Incremental budgeting involves taking the previous year's figures and adjusting them for any known changes such as inflation, wages increases or changes in level of activity. The major advantage of this approach to budgeting is that the budget-setter has a clear starting point based upon previous actual performance. The disadvantage of incremental budgeting is that any inefficiencies or wastage in budgets may be rolled forward year after year.

Incremental budgeting has had much bad press, particularly from those advocating alternative approaches. Much of this criticism arises out of poor implementation of incremental budgeting rather than the approach itself, and one should not be too hasty in dismissing many of the benefits of this approach. The problem is that many organizations in practice simply take last year's budget and add a percentage to it to allow for inflation. This approach can justifiably be criticized. However, incremental budgeting can still be an extremely good approach if done well. If there are no major changes in the way a business operates, looking at last year's figures as a starting point for the next year makes a great deal of sense. However, these figures must be scrutinized in detail to ensure that any necessary adjustments are made to remove unused budgets and/or inefficiencies and to reflect known changes for the coming year.

Are the top-down and bottom-up approaches mutually exclusive?

In practice, all budget preparation processes will have both a top-down and a bottom-up element. Although there is a clear conceptual difference between the two approaches, all good budget-setting will involve elements of both.

Top-down budgeting should not be seen as a tool for limiting the discretionary powers of line managers. Nor does it eliminate the process of negotiating budgets and choosing between competing programmes and activities. However, some top-down element is essential to provide clarity during the process of prioritization through the focus on organizational-level goals. At the same time, it is not feasible to impose detailed function budgets from above without having some assurance that these will achieve their goals.

The two approaches of top-down and bottom-up do not therefore represent absolutes, but rather differing emphasis of balance during budget-setting. The challenge is to find the right balance which achieves all of the aims of the budget-setting process.

Discussion point

Given that both the top-down and bottom-up approaches to budgeting have strengths and weaknesses, how do you think the two approaches might be combined to take advantage of their relative strengths and overcome their weaknesses?

The basic steps of preparing a budget

In the previous section we explained that the overall master budget is made up of an operational budget and a financial budget, each of which is composed of several functional budgets. There may be functional budgets for several business units across the organization. This can mean a lot of individual budgets to coordinate. In order to facilitate this coordination there is a logical sequence to the preparation of a master budget. For commercial organizations the first step will be to forecast sales and to prepare a sales budget. Other operational budgets will then follow from this. Figure 5.4 illustrates a typical budget preparation sequence.

The following example illustrates the budget preparation steps set out in Figure 5.4. The example is kept simple as it is intended to demonstrate clearly the main steps of budget preparation rather than the detailed practical issues which may be involved during each stage.

Figure 5.4   The budget preparation sequence

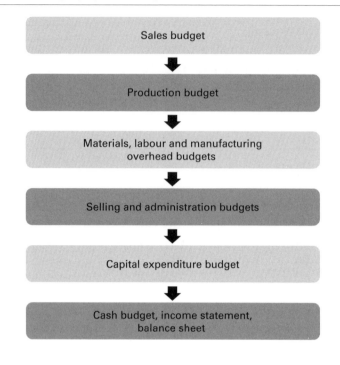

WORKED EXAMPLE 5.1 Preparing a budget

Rad Co manufactures one model of vehicle radiator which is sold to just one customer, a major car manufacturer. The radiators are incorporated into several different models of vehicle.

The following information has been compiled for the preparation of the budget for the next financial year:

1 Expected sales of radiators for the year are 180,000 units. The expected selling price per unit is $20. All sales are made on credit.

2 The manufacture of each radiator requires 8 metres of tubing and $0.7m^2$ of sheet metal. Over the coming year, tubing is expected to cost $0.50 per metre and sheet metal is expected to cost $1.50 per square metre.

3 The manufacture of each radiator requires three stages, all of which are performed by computerized machines:

	Time (hours)	Cost per hour ($)
Cutting	0.10	12.00
Forming	0.13	20.00
Welding	0.15	15.00

4 The production process has the following overhead costs:

	$
Production staff salaries	240,000
Other factory operating costs	320,000

5 The customer demands a very short supply time on radiators and order levels can fluctuate at short notice. Rad Co therefore maintains an inventory of finished units. At the start of the year 8,000 units are expected to be held in inventory. However, in order to ensure a greater buffer against fluctuations in demand, the production director wants to increase inventory of finished radiators to 12,000 units by the end of the year.

6 Inventory of raw materials at the start of the year is expected to be as follows:

Tubing	100,000m
Sheet metal	10,000m²

The production director plans to increase these inventory levels by 5 per cent during the year.

7 Administration and selling overheads are expected to be $500,000.

8 The balance sheet at the start of the year is expected to include the following figures:

	$	$
Share capital		800,000
Retained profits		720,270
Non-current assets: cost	1,400,000	
Less: accumulated depreciation	460,000	940,000
Trade receivables		433,700
Trade payables		69,230
Cash at bank		62,000

9 The customer has been demanding greater credit terms and after some negotiation these will be increased over the coming year such that closing trade receivables are expected to be 20 per cent of the total sales for the year.

10 Closing trade payables are expected to be 8 per cent of the purchases for the year.

11 Planned capital expenditure for the year is $80,000.

12 Non-current assets are depreciated on a straight-line basis at a rate of 15 per cent on cost.

Using this information we will now illustrate how the budget is put together, following the steps set out in Figure 5.4.

The sales budget

The first step will be to produce the sales budget. This will detail both the physical quantity of sales and their financial value. In the example this is a relatively straightforward task as these figures are given:

$$180,000 \text{ units} \times \$20 = \$3,600,000$$

In practice a variety of means will be used in order to establish the physical quantity of sales. These figures may be based upon market research, they may be based upon known contracts or they may be aspirational in terms of increased sales targets. A variety of statistical and mathematical techniques may be used in forecasting sales.

Establishing the sales price is a complex topic in its own right. Chapter 8 of this text examines pricing in detail.

The production budget

The level of production will be derived from the level of sales. Production must be budgeted at a level which meets sales requirements and planned inventory levels. This can be derived as follows:

	Units
Sales	180,000
Less: opening inventory	8,000
	172,000
Add: planned closing inventory	12,000
Production required	184,000

Direct material usage budget

Material usage will be derived from the level of production established above. We have the number of units of production needed and from the information in the example we know how much material is required for each unit. The material usage budget will therefore be as follows:

Tubing	(8 m × 184,000 units)	=	1,472,000 m
Sheet metal	(0.7 m² × 184,000 units)	=	128,800 m²

Direct material purchases budget

Material purchasing must be sufficient to meet production needs and planned levels of inventory. In this example there are only two direct materials to purchase (tubing and sheet metal). Once purchase quantities have been established, these can be costed to establish a purchasing budget:

	Tubing (m)	Sheet metal (m²)
Production usage	1,472,000	128,800
Less: opening inventory	100,000	10,000
	1,372,000	118,800
Add: closing inventory (Opening +5%)	105,000	10,500
Purchase quantity	1,477,000	129,300
Cost per unit	$.50	$1.50
Purchase cost	$738,500	$193,950

Machine usage budget

The machine usage budget will detail the number of hours of running time required for each machine together with the total cost of that operation. In this example (Table 5.1) we can assume that production is within capacity, but in practice it will be necessary to ensure that sufficient machine time is available to meet budgeted production levels.

	Time (hours)	Cost per hour ($)	Total cost ($)
Cutting	$0.10 \times 184,000 = 18,400$	12.00	220,800
Forming	$0.13 \times 184,000 = 23,920$	20.00	478,400
Welding	$0.15 \times 184,000 = 27,600$	15.00	414,000
			1,113,200

Fixed production overhead budget

The figures for production overheads are given in the example:

	$
Production staff salaries	240,000
Other factory operating costs	320,000
Total production overhead	560,000

Administration and selling budget

The figure is provided in the example:

Administration and selling overheads	$500,000

Capital expenditure budget

Capital expenditure must be budgeted to meet both the short-term and long-term capital needs of the organization. Chapter 9 of this textbook looks at the capital expenditure decision in detail. In this example the figure is provided:

Planned capital expenditure $80,000

Workings for preparation of financial budgets

Before we can complete the cash budget, the income statement and the balance sheet, we need to calculate values for closing inventory of both finished goods and raw materials and for closing trade receivables and trade payables. From these we can derive a cost of goods sold. We also need to calculate the depreciation charge for the year.

Working 1: Raw materials closing inventory

From the production information we can calculate the value of the closing inventory:
Closing inventory of raw materials:

Tubing	105,000 m × $0.50	=	$52,500
Sheet metal	10,500 m^2 × $1.50	=	$15,750
			$68,250

Working 2: Finished goods closing inventory

In order to calculate the value of the closing finished goods inventory we need to first calculate the direct cost per unit:

Finished goods cost per unit:	$	$
Direct materials:		
tubing (8 × $0.50)	4.00	
sheet metal (0.7 × $1.50)	1.05	5.05
Machining:		
cutting (0.10 × $12.00)	1.20	
forming (0.13 × $20.00)	2.60	
welding (0.15 × $15.00)	2.25	6.05
Total direct cost per unit		11.10
Units in stock		× 12,000
Closing stock value		$133,200

Working 3: Cost of goods sold

	$
Opening inventory	88,800
Production cost (184,000 × $11.10)	2,042,400
	2,131,200
Less: closing inventory	133,200
Cost of goods sold	1,998,000

Working 4: Depreciation

Depreciation is charged at 15 per cent on cost:

Cost: $1,400,000 (opening balance) + $80,000 (expenditure) = $1,480,000

Depreciation charge for the year: $1,480,000 × 15% = $222,000

Accumulated depreciation: $460,000 (opening balance) + $222,000 = $682,000

Working 5: Closing trade receivables

Closing trade receivables are expected to be 20 per cent of total sales for the year:

$$\$3,600,000 \times 20\% = \$720,000$$

Working 6: Closing trade payables

Closing trade payables are expected to be 8 per cent of total purchases for the year:

Purchases from the direct material purchasing budget = $738,500 + $193,950 = $932,450 ×

$$8\% = \$74,596$$

Cash budget

The cash budget sets out expected cash receipts and payments throughout the budget period and the impact on the cash balance. This is an outline cash budget and most organizations will prepare a much more detailed forecast of cash flows and cash requirements. This cash-flow planning is looked at in more detail in Chapter 7 of this text.

	$
Receipts	
Cash from trade receivables	3,313,700
(433,700+3,600,000–720,000)	
(opening balance + sales – closing balance)	
Payments	
Payments to trade payables	
(69,230+932,450–74,596)	927,084
(opening balance + sales – closing balance)	
Machine costs (from machine usage budget)	1,113,200

Fixed production overheads	560,000
Administration and selling costs	500,000
Capital expenditure	80,000
	3,180,284
Net receipts (receipts – payments)	133,416
Add: opening cash balance	62,000
Budgeted closing cash balance	195,416

Budgeted income statement

	$
Sales	3,600,000
Less: cost of sales (see working 3)	1,998,000
Gross profit	1,602,000
Fixed production overheads	560,000
Depreciation (see working 4)	222,000
Production profit	820,000
Administration and selling costs	500,000
Budgeted net profit	320,000

Budgeted balance sheets

	$	$
Non-current assets		
Cost (working 4)		1,480,000
Less: accumulated depreciation (working 4)		682,000
		798,000
Current assets		
Raw materials (working 1)	68,250	
Finished inventory (working 2)	133,200	
Trade receivables (working 5)	720,000	
Cash at bank (from cash budget)	195,416	1,116,866
Current liabilities		
Trade payables (working 6)		74,596
Total net assets		1,840,270
Financed by:		
Ordinary share capital		800,000
Retained earnings (720,270+320,000)		1,040,270
		1,840,270

Budgeting in different types of organization

The previous section outlined the basic budget-setting process. This is a generic process which is relevant to most types of organization. However, there will be some variation and significant differences between different types of organization. Some of these special considerations are set out below.

Production businesses

The budget set out in Worked Example 5.1, although simple, is typical of that for a production business. Many production businesses use a standard cost system to establish their production budgets. A standard cost is the business's estimated cost of producing a product based upon previous experience of material usage and time taken together with up-to-date material costs, direct labour costs and factory over-head costs. Standard costing is examined in more detail in Chapter 6.

Service businesses

Organizations that provide services have a number of characteristics which make the budget-setting process different from production businesses. Service-based businesses include professionals and others who primarily sell their time and skills rather than a tangible product. Service providers usually have a higher proportion of fixed costs than manufacturing businesses. A very large part of those fixed costs will be employee costs, as services are provided by people rather than manufacturing plants. Also, services cannot be stored in the same way as physical inventory. This means that if the sale of a service is missed, that opportunity can be gone for ever. Service businesses therefore tend to focus their budget-setting process around employee costs and ensuring high utilization of employees.

Public-sector and not-for-profit organizations

Public-sector organizations include government and local government and public services such as health services, police, fire service and the army. Other not-for-profit organizations will include charities.

The aim of budgeting for a not-for-profit organization is to maximize the benefits from expenditure given the resources available. Budget allocations should reflect current organizational priorities and spending should be contained within sustainable levels.

A comparison of private- and public-sector budgeting is provided in Table 5.1.

Table 5.1   A comparison of private- and public-sector budgeting

Private sector	Public sector
Market driven	Resource constrained (ie funded by taxation)
Resources influenced by market demand	Resources controlled by government through grant settlements
Reliance upon external sales	Activity politically determined
Need for flexibility	Fixed budgets
Profit oriented	Service oriented
Single or limited number of objective(s)	Multi (and often conflicting) objectives
Outputs identifiable and measurable	Outputs subjective and qualitative

Not-for-profit organizations sometimes approach budgeting in a different sequence by preparing expenditure budgets first. However, levels of expenditure should be derived from planned levels of activities, which are 'outputs' in the same way as sales are for commercial organizations.

Merchandising businesses

If an organization is a merchandiser it buys in products to sell on, either wholesale or retail, and undertakes no direct production itself. In this case there will be no production budget. Rather, such organizations will have a merchandise purchasing budget.

Limitations and problems with budgeting

At the beginning of this chapter we mentioned that some commentators have criticized budgeting as a management tool. In this final section we will conclude the examination of business planning by discussing some of the perceived limitations and problems of the budgeting techniques we have covered and looking at the alternatives which have emerged in recent years.

Extract 5.4: Frustrations with budgeting

A survey conducted in 2000 which questioned financial executives about their current experience with their organizations' budgeting revealed that 84 per cent of participants were frustrated with their organizations' budgeting processes. (Comshare, 2000)

The dissatisfaction with current budgeting practices has resulted in practice-led developments in two directions: some practitioners are seeking to improve the budgeting process and make it more relevant, whereas others claim that budgeting should be abandoned altogether.

Should organizations budget?

Budgeting has been criticized by both practitioners and academics as being outdated and unsuitable for the uncertainty involved in the rapidly changing post-industrial business environment: budgeting is seen as consuming too much managerial time and the benefits are not worth the cost; budgets inhibit firms from adapting to changes in a timely manner owing to their fixed nature; budgeting is disconnected from strategy, thereby putting it out of kilter with the competitive demands facing firms; and the use of budgets as a performance measure leads to unreliable performance evaluation and promotes dysfunctional behaviour in employees. The Beyond Budgeting Round Table (BBRT) is an international network of organizations that seek to find business planning and control tools that could replace budgeting and help organizations become more adaptive to change. The BBRT website contains a list of 10 specific criticisms of budgeting.

Extract 5.5: The Beyond Budgeting Round Table

The Beyond Budgeting Round Table (www.bbrt.org) sets out 10 explicit criticisms of budgeting:

1 Budgeting prevents rapid response.

2 Budgeting is too detailed and expensive.

3 Budgeting is out of date within a few months.

4 Budgeting is out of kilter with the competitive environment.

5 Budgeting is divorced from strategy.

6 Budgeting stifles initiative and innovation.

7 Budgeting protects non-value-adding costs.

8 Budgeting reinforces command and control.

9 Budgeting demotivates people.

10 Budgeting encourages unethical behaviour and increases reputational risk.

We will examine some of these criticisms and other issues with budgeting in more detail below. However, it should be understood that this criticism from the BBRT is not an attack directed at business planning *per se*, but rather the management model which it perceives as lying behind traditional budgeting approaches. It calls this the 'command and control' management model – one which involves senior executives commanding and controlling the organization from a corporate centre. Budgeting is perceived as a symptom of this management model which restricts and constrains organizations that need to be more flexible and able to respond quickly to the business environment.

We would like to examine three particular problems of budgeting in more detail. These are the cost of budgeting, some negative behavioural aspects of budgeting and the problems of budgeting in a volatile business environment.

Cost

Budgeting requires a considerable amount of time and effort which can use up and divert valuable resources. As with any other 'expenditure' within a business, benefits should outweigh the costs. If an organization feels that it is not getting value for money from its budgeting, it needs to look at how it can increase the value of the budgets produced or how it can cut the cost of budgeting.

The value of budgets can be increased by using them more effectively as tools for controlling operational costs and for ensuring that organizational goals are met. Good budgets can be particularly effective in controlling cash flow and thereby reducing the need for bank borrowing.

There are several ways in which the costs of budgeting can be reduced. One way is to use a rolling budget (see below for details). Another way is through the effective use of computerization which can both increase the efficiency and speed of budget preparation and increase the usefulness of budgets by incorporating strategic tools such as sensitivity analysis and scenario-building.

Defenders of traditional budgeting point out that although budgeting can be time-consuming and costly, it is not as resource hungry as some of the alternatives proposed by its critics.

Behavioural aspects of budgeting

Budgeting is, at its core, a human activity and as such it is subject to all the behavioural problems found in any area of human endeavour. The behavioural side of budgeting is a vast topic which cannot be covered comprehensively within a textbook such as this. However, this section aims to set out some of the key issues and arguments around the human dimension of budgeting that can limit the accuracy and usefulness of budgets.

The first issue is commonly referred to as **bounded rationality**. This can be explained as the fact that, when budgeting, we are looking to the future and cannot possibly know what will happen. The accuracy of budgets will therefore be limited by the boundaries of our abilities to predict the future. This problem is often compounded by the fact that budgets tend to be built on the assumption that the future will resemble the past. A second and related problem is the fact that budgeting often involves dealing with vast amounts of data. Even with the use of computers to help assemble and process these data, there will be a human element in interpreting and analysing them. Often the amount of data available is too much for people to be able to use effectively as part of their decision making.

Another human problem with budgeting is that people often stick with trusted strategies, particularly if the incremental approach to budgeting is used. The usefulness of budgets is therefore limited by users' inability to break out of habitual patterns of behaviour. Related to this problem is a similar issue which is sometimes called **satisficing** behaviour. This refers to the fact that managers will choose workable solutions to problems rather than optimal solutions. Typically, if a solution to a problem is being sought, once a workable solution is found it will be operationalized. It is not human nature to continue to seek alternative solutions once a workable solution has been found.

Budget preparation can often involve dealing with conflicting objectives. The budget negotiation process can be viewed as a **game** played between senior management and line managers. Line managers, if given freedom to set their own budgets, may follow personal objectives which conflict with those of the organization as a whole. In particular, managers will exaggerate their need for resources and will set themselves targets which they know they can meet. At the same time, senior management, aware of these tendencies, will attempt to restrict resource allocation to that which is necessary to maintain anticipated activity levels. Research has shown that where managers are able to put forward their own spending proposals, resource requirements can be over-estimated by up to 30 per cent.

There is another gaming problem which relates to managerial behaviour once budgets have been allocated. **The hockey-stick effect** refers to the tendency for budget holders to make sure that all of their budgeted funds are spent by the end of the budget period, irrespective of whether such spending is necessary. This is often done out of fear that an underspent budget will be cut in the future – managers seek to 'use' their budget before they lose it. Managers may hold back on spending during the year and then suddenly increase spending just before the end of the budget period in order to bring spending up to the budget limit. This behaviour manifests itself in a spending pattern which, if graphed, looks like a hockey stick, hence the name.

Budgeting in a volatile business environment

Opponents of budgeting argue that budgets are only useful tools in a stable business environment in which future events can be predicted with reasonable accuracy. However, the modern post-industrial business environment has proved to be anything but stable, being characterized by constant change, innovation and technological development. This means, it is argued, that budgets are often out of date and irrelevant even before they are implemented.

Defenders of budgeting point out that even in a volatile business environment there is still a need for forecasting and planning. It could be argued that cashflow planning becomes even more important as business volatility increases. The beyond budgeting approach advocated by the Beyond Budgeting Round Table and its supporters still includes cash-flow forecasts and rolling cost forecasts. Many academics and management consultants therefore argue that the need is not to move beyond budgeting but rather to improve budgeting.

Extract 5.6: Beyond budgeting at Statoil

Statoil, the Norwegian oil company, has eliminated traditional budgeting from the company's management and reporting processes. The company's management saw budgeting as a barrier to what they wanted to achieve as a global oil exploration company in a turbulent, dynamic and demanding business environment. The problem with traditional budgeting, as they saw it, is that it tries to achieve too many things with one set of figures. Traditional budgeting is used to control costs, allocate resources and set targets. By trying to achieve all three of these objectives, traditional budgeting falls prey to manipulation and gaming from employees: managers will set themselves undemanding targets in order to achieve bonuses; a requirement to spend within budget stifles innovation and change in response to the business environment.

Statoil no longer uses budgets for oil exploration. Rather, under the new 'Ambition to Action' regime the business aims to get the optimum cost level to maximize value. There is a differentiation between good and bad costs. Good costs generate more income than you put in. The new approach aims to give more freedom and responsibility to managers. There is still planning, forecasting and monitoring, and the business uses KPIs (key performance indicators). However, the performance regime used attempts to move the management mindset from a mechanical adherence to milestones and triggers to a holistic understanding of business performance.

Improving business planning and budgeting

Not all critics of budgeting suggest that the process should be abandoned. There has been strong interest in recent years, both among academics and practitioners, in improving budgets to make them more useful for the current business environment. Key elements which have been identified for improving the process are better communication and collaboration. In particular, rather than budget negotiation being a process of arguing for and justifying budget allocations, it should be a process of sharing and exploring views of the future operating environment.

Although there is an advocacy for going 'beyond budgeting', the mainstream of current thinking on budgeting focuses on improving the budgeting process. This includes better integration between strategic planning and budgeting, better feeding of business intelligence into the budgeting process, greater inclusion and teamwork and less bureaucracy. These measures will reduce the cost of budgeting and improve its effectiveness.

Four developments in budgeting that are being more widely adopted are rolling budgets, zero-based budgets, activity-based budgets and kaizen budgets. We will therefore look at these developments in a little more detail.

Rolling budgets

A rolling budget is sometimes also called a continuous budget. This approach involves always having a 12-month ongoing budget. Rather than set a budget for a fixed 12-month period, the organization at the end of every month will add another month to their budget so that there is always a 12-month budget in place. The advantage of this approach is that managers' attention is continuously placed on what will be happening over the next 12 months, rather than the remaining months of a fixed-period budget. The process often also involves revising the 11-month budget that was already set.

The rolling budget is extremely useful for organizations that have uncertain levels of activities and need to respond by adjusting their capacity and operating levels. For example, a building contractor may operate a rolling budget in order to ensure that labour and equipment are in place during busy periods but that they are not idle when work is not available. This approach enables both greater flexibility and tighter control through its frequent revision and updating. However, the process can be resource-intensive and time-consuming as the organization is effectively continuously producing a budget. It also requires a more flexible management approach, as managers may find themselves working to constantly changing budgets. If not implemented and managed well, this can lead to confusion and frustration.

Zero-based budgeting

Zero-based budgeting (ZBB) involves building the budget without reference to what happened in the past. The idea behind ZBB is to avoid some of the pitfalls of incremental budgeting. These include continuing existing inefficiencies and failure to re-evaluate how things are done. The ZBB approach starts each budget afresh, rather than basing the budget on historical data from previous periods. Managers must make a case for resources and their budget will be zero unless they can justify the budget allocation they require. The advantage of this approach is that every activity is questioned and has to be justified in terms of costs involved and benefits accrued. Resources are therefore allocated according to results and needs and wasteful budget 'slack' is eliminated. The approach also encourages managers to question the way resources are being allocated and to look for alternatives.

Many organizations and particularly the health sector have seen substantial benefits from using ZBB. It can result in an organization radically changing its cost structures, cutting substantial amounts from overhead and support costs whilst increasing efficiency and competitiveness. It encourages managers to be forward thinking in terms of identifying what activities and resources will be needed to compete in future market conditions. Because this is done on a ground-up basis rather than an incremental approach of targeting areas where costs can be cut, managers must justify what to keep rather than what to remove. This can produce far more substantial changes in cost and performance.

The ZBB process is therefore particularly useful for organizations which have recently experienced substantial structural change such as an acquisition or a merger which may have left a legacy of unnecessary overhead costs. Also, changes in the competitive environment may create increasing pressures on costs such that an organization needs to re-examine the way it delivers its goods or services.

The ZBB process is both complex and time-consuming. This can also make it costly such that ultimately there has to be a payoff in terms of the costs and benefits. The process can also create internal conflict within organizations as managers are forced to compete annually for budget allocation. ZBB has also been criticized for focusing on short-term benefits to the detriment of longer-term strategic development.

Although ZBB is a good idea in principle, many organizations have found that in practice it is best combined with incremental budgeting. It can be useful to prepare a zero-based budget periodically; to do so continually year after year offers little benefit, particularly if there are no major changes to the way the organization is operating. Some organizations have therefore incorporated ZBB by using it only every few years or when a major change occurs within the organization. Between the ZBB sessions they revert to an incremental approach.

The ZBB approach became very popular in the 1970s, having originally been developed at Texas Instruments in Dallas (Pyhrr, 1973). However, due largely to the practical problems outlined above, many companies implemented the approach in some form and found that it did not work for them. It has fallen out of popularity in recent years. It is, however, still used in many areas of the public sector.

> ### Extract 5.7: ZBB at InBev
>
> InBev, the Belgium-based brewing company, has successfully used zero-based budgeting as a tool for cutting unnecessary costs after acquisitions, enabling it to become the largest brewer in the world. The management team at InBev have a reputation for ruthless efficiency in cost-cutting in new acquisitions to ensure that they create value. They have achieved this by extending their ZBB practices to newly acquired subsidiaries, requiring businesses to justify every expense each year.

Activity-based budgeting

One approach to improving the budgeting process which has gained popularity over the past decade is activity-based budgeting (ABB).

The most comprehensive model of ABB has been developed by the Consortium of Advanced Management, International (CAM-I), published in a book entitled *The Closed Loop* in 2004. This model is illustrated in Figure 5.5.

Figure 5.5   Activity-based budgeting

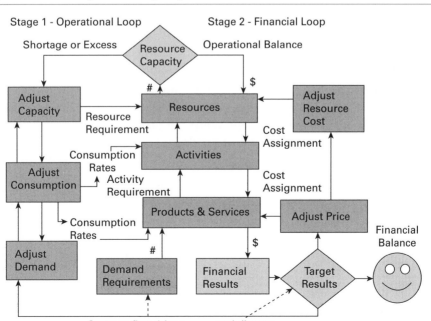

ABB focuses on the activities of an organization rather than its departments or products. The approach is based upon the concept that costs are driven by activities. It focuses on how activities add value within the organization and expresses budgets in terms of activity costs. This is in contrast to the traditional approach to budgeting which involves focusing on the input of resources and identifying those in terms of functional areas.

The advantage of ABB is that the cost of activities within the organization are clearly highlighted in a way that does not happen in the traditional budgeting approach. These activities can then be linked back to the mission and strategic goals of the organization.

ABB has developed many of the ideas of ZBB and can be linked with activity-based costing as part of a more general activity-based management approach.

This approach has been popular with many public-sector organizations such as law enforcement and health care, as it enables such organizations to identify the costs of the individual services they provide.

Kaizen budgeting

Kaizen is a Japanese term that refers to the philosophy of continuous improvement. We will look at this concept again in more detail in Chapter 8 when we examine pricing and costing strategies. The concept of kaizen focuses on gradual and continuous improvement over time, rather than the large changes and fast improvements sought through approaches such as zero-based budgeting. The focus of a kaizen approach is on finding small areas that can be improved. By making continuous small improvements in several areas over a long period of time, large cost savings can be achieved.

Kaizen budgeting can require a great deal of management time, resources and planning, as this approach involves considering all parts of the business, pinpointing possible improvement and implementing them. Building kaizen improvements into budgets can be difficult in practice, as it is often not possible to predict the levels of costs savings that will be achieved. For this reason, many companies budget for cost reductions based upon historic kaizen savings, or aspirational savings based upon specific kaizen projects.

One of the benefits of kaizen budgeting is that it can be used to measure the performance of managers in terms of the cost savings that they achieve over time. It is therefore often an approach that is linked to incentive schemes. However, a problem with kaizen budgeting is that cost reductions are difficult to sustain in the longer term. It is easier to find cost savings in the first few years, after which the opportunity for further savings will decrease. If kaizen cost-saving targets are set too high this will result in extensive unfavourable budget variances and under-performance, which can be demotivating for managers and counter-productive.

Conclusion

This chapter has explored how budgeting is an important part of the management process. We have seen how corporate strategies can be deployed across business activities and departments through the use of budgets. We have examined different approaches to the budget-setting process and looked at the details of how a budget is prepared. We have also looked at budgeting within its wider managerial context and examined some of the criticisms of budgeting practices, together with some recent developments. This prepares the ground for the next chapter (Chapter 6) which looks at how budgets, once set, can be integrated into organizational performance management.

COMPREHENSION QUESTIONS

1 What is the difference between strategic planning and business planning?

2 How can budgeting contribute to strategic planning?

3 What benefits may an organization derive from a formal budgeting process?

4 What are the elements of a master budget?

5 Explain the difference between incremental budgeting and zero-based budgeting.

6 What are the advantages and disadvantages of a 'bottom-up' approach to budgeting?

7 How would the budget-setting philosophy of a service provider differ from that of a manufacturing business?

8 Discuss the potential conflict between using a budget as a motivational device and as a means of control.

9 Identify and comment on three behavioural problems that might be experienced in a system of budgetary control.

Answers available at **www.koganpage.com/afm3**

Exercises

Answers available at **www.koganpage.com/afm3**

Exercise 5.1: Selecting a suitable budget-setting approach

You have been elected onto the budget committee of a hospital and have been tasked with reviewing the approach taken by the hospital towards budget-setting. The hospital has a relatively stable level of income which comes from government allocations. At the same time it has a very high proportion of fixed costs which are largely made up of salary and wage costs. The hospital engages in a wide and diverse range of activities.

Required:
Identify and discuss the factors which should be considered when selecting a suitable budget-setting approach for the hospital.

Exercise 5.2: The objectives of budgeting

Ingram Co is a small engineering company. The company does not have a computerized accounting or budgeting system, but rather the chief accountant manually produces a budget each year in conjunction with the senior management team.

   The managing director has expressed concern at the time and cost of producing the budget each year, and has asked whether any short cuts could be taken.

Required:

(a) Write a memo to the managing director which:

(b) explains the objectives of budgetary planning and control systems;

(c) identifies and explains the stages involved in the preparation of budgets;

(d) identifies ways in which the budget-setting process could be improved for Ingram Co.

Exercise 5.3: Budgetary information

Khan Co is a publishing business. The budget committee is scheduled to meet very soon to discuss plans for next year's budget-setting process. One item on the agenda is the sources of information that will be needed in order to set next year's budget.

Required:
Write a short briefing document for the budget committee which sets out the main sources of information that should be used in setting next year's budget.

Exercise 5.4: Budgetary style

Chin Co, an architectural services firm, uses a top-down budgeting approach. The budget is prepared by Michael Chin, the CEO, and once finalized it is distributed to departmental managers for implementation. Michael Chin sees the budget as an important means of improving company performance and he therefore sets extremely demanding sales targets. Employees receive wage bonuses based upon their performance against the budget.

Required:
Discuss the likely impact that Michael Chin's budgeting style will have upon employee and business performance at Chin Co.

References

Comshare, Inc (2000) Comshare Survey of Top Financial Executives: Planning and budgeting today [Online] www.comshare.com (archived at https://perma.cc/CDL4-N58L)

Libby, T and Lindsay, R M (2010) Beyond budgeting or budgeting reconsidered? A survey of North-American budgeting practice, *Management Accounting Research*, **21** (1), pp 56–75

Pyhrr, P (1973) *Zero-base Budgeting: A practical management tool for evaluating expenses*, John Wiley & Sons, Inc, New York

Supplementary reading

Hansen, S C (2004) *The Closed Loop: Implementing activity-based planning and budgeting*, Bookman, Indianapolis, IN

Hansen, S C, Otley, D T and Van der Stede, W A (2003) Practice developments in budgeting: an overview and research perspective, *Journal of Management Accounting Research*, **15**, pp 95–116

Budgets and performance management

06

OBJECTIVE

To provide an understanding of the role of budgets, standards and variance analysis in performance evaluation.

LEARNING OUTCOMES

After studying this chapter, the reader will be able to:

- Interpret a variance report and assess its implications for management intervention.
- Identify behavioural aspects of budget management.
- Recommend strategies to prevent or remedy adverse behavioural aspects of budget management and to harness positive aspects.
- Evaluate alternative views on performance management.

KEY TOPICS COVERED

- Standard costing and variance analysis.
- Profit-related performance measures.
- Performance measurement in not-for-profit organizations.
- Behavioural aspects of performance management: gaming; achievement motive; creative accounting.
- Alternative views on performance management: activity-based costing (ABC); balanced scorecards (BSC); just-in-time (JIT); and total quality management (TQM).

MANAGEMENT ISSUES

The primary concern of managers is not the calculation and production of performance management data, but rather their interpretation and analysis.

Introduction

In this chapter we will build upon your knowledge from Chapter 5 by looking at the way feedback on actual performance is compared against financial plans to enable appropriate management decisions and action.

In its broadest sense, performance management is about ensuring that the goals of the organization are consistently met in an effective and efficient manner. It is a multidisciplinary activity that includes aspects of human resource management, financial management, operations, marketing and systems management and management accounting as well as strategic planning and analysis. There are therefore many perspectives on performance management.

In order to better understand how this chapter fits into the wide-ranging activity of performance management, it is useful to sub-categorize performance management into two broad areas – strategic and operational – although in practice these often overlap.

Strategic performance management is concerned with implementing the strategy of the organization and, if necessary, challenging the validity of that strategy as a means of achieving organizational goals.

Operational performance management is concerned with managing operations to ensure that they stay in line with the corporate strategy. An operational performance management system can therefore be understood as a set of metrics used to quantify and measure the activities of the organization to give feedback to managers on their actions.

It is this latter area of performance management that is the primary focus of this chapter, although we will touch on some broader strategic issues. We will look at the sources of management information for goal-setting and performance management and the different performance measures which can be used, both financial and non-financial. We will also look at practical aspects of performance management both in the private sector and in the not-for-profit and public sectors.

The calculation of costing information for performance management can be a complex arithmetic exercise. This information is usually produced by accountants and presented to managers in the form of performance management reports. This chapter therefore focuses on the interpretation and analysis of performance data rather than their production.

Attempts to measure organizational performance are only meaningful with reference to some benchmark against which efficiency and effectiveness can be judged. It is therefore essential that the right frame of reference is chosen. Much of the development in academic thinking and business practice over the past few decades has been focused around establishing an appropriate framework of reference against which performance should be measured. In this chapter we will look at some of the arguments behind recent developments and consider multidimensional sets of performance measures which include both internal and external measures of performance together with financial and non-financial measures.

No matter what the approach towards performance management, there are some important principles which must always be followed. These relate to how responsibility for managing the budget is broken down within the organization and how individual managers are held accountable for the way they manage performance.

Responsibility centres

The first general principle of performance management is clear delineation of responsibility. Within large organizations, responsibility for managing the master budget is broken down into different areas and delegated to line managers. The different budget sub-units are usually referred to as **responsibility centres**. A responsibility centre is the organizational unit (division, section, branch or geographic region) that is headed by a manager who is responsible for its activities and results. There are four main types of responsibility centre: a cost centre; a revenue centre; a profit centre; and an investment centre.

Cost centre

In a cost centre the manager is responsible for managing costs only. The budget is allocated to cost centres for those areas of the business which generate costs but not income. For example, a production manager in a factory producing shoes will be responsible for managing the cost of production but not for any revenues earned from selling the shoes.

Revenue centre

In a revenue centre the manager will be accountable for the level of revenue earned. For example, a book retailer with a chain of 20 bookstores will have a manager responsible for the sales revenue generated by each store. The manager may also have responsibility for some selling expenses, but this responsibility will be limited, as the main costs of running the store such as property costs and staffing costs will be managed by the central office.

Profit centre

In a profit centre the manager will be responsible for both costs and revenues and therefore also profit. The manager of a profit centre usually has more autonomy than the manager of a cost or revenue centre, as increased costs can be incurred and justified if they result in higher profits.

Investment centre

In an investment centre the manager will be responsible not just for costs and revenues but also for managing the level of investment required to earn the revenues. Performance will therefore be measured not just in terms of profitability but also in terms of asset turnover or return on capital employed (ROCE). The performance measures for investment centres are examined in more detail later in this chapter.

The controllability principle

The second general principle of performance management is controllability. A manager should only be held responsible for the things over which he or she has control. If line managers are to be given responsibility for budget areas and held accountable for the performance against budget, it is important that delegated budgets are separated into two elements: controllable and non-controllable. Controllable elements are those which are influenced by factors over which the manager has control, whereas non-controllable elements are those which are beyond the manager's control. This level of segregation is not always easy and will depend upon the structure and systems of the organization.

For example, material prices will normally be regarded as non-controllable by a production manager if price increases are due to external market forces. On the other hand, material prices will be regarded as controllable if the manager has control over the timing and source of material purchases. Material costs may exceed budget because the manager failed to purchase sufficient materials on time and had to source extra at short notice from an alternative supplier at a higher cost.

> ### Discussion point
>
> If the responsibility and controllability principles are not followed, what are the potential negative consequences for an organization?

Profit-related performance measurement

In this section we will look at how financial performance can be measured and evaluated for cost centres, revenue centres and profit centres. Worked Example 6.1 provides a simple illustration of a monthly budget for a manufacturing business. We will look at how actual performance is reported against this budget and examine some of the techniques used by managers to better understand why actual performance has differed from budget.

WORKED EXAMPLE 6.1 Woodburn Co – performance against budget

Woodburn Co makes and sells wood-burning stoves. It has only one model – the 'Optiburner'. The budget for November predicts sales of 200 stoves, giving a profit for the month of $9,000. The budget is made up as follows:

Table 6.1

		$
Sales revenue	($180 per unit × 200 units)	36,000
Direct materials	($10 per m² × 3.5 m² × 200 units)	7,000
Direct labour	($12 per hour × 1 1/4 hrs per stove × 200 units)	3,000
Variable overheads	($8 per hour × 1 1/4 hrs per stove × 200 units)	2,000
Fixed overheads	($180,000 per year ÷ 12 months)	15,000
Total expenses		27,000
Operating profit	(Sales revenue – Total expenses)	9,000

At the end of November the accountant of Woodburn Co prepares the report set out in Worked Example 6.2. This report shows the actual results against the original budget. The original budget was for sales of 200 units whereas actual sales have been 230 units.

WORKED EXAMPLE 6.2 Fixed budget variance report for Woodburn Co

Table 6.2

	Actual results	Variance		Original budget
	$	$		$
Sales revenue	40,250	4,250	F	36,000
Direct materials	8,349	1,349	A	7,000
Direct labour	3,105	105	A	3,000
Variable overheads	2,760	760	A	2,000
Fixed overheads	16,000	1,000	A	15,000
Total expenses	30,214	3,214	A	27,000
Operating profit	10,036	1,036	F	9,000

The difference between the budgeted figure and the actual figure is reported in the middle column and is called a **variance**. Where actual results are better than budget the variance is reported as 'favourable' (F), as is the case with sales revenue which exceeds budget by $4,250. Where actual results are worse than budget the variance is reported as 'adverse' (A), as is the case with direct material costs which exceeds budget by $1,349.

The report shows actual results against the original budget. It is therefore not surprising to find that the actual profit differs from the budget, as actual sales were 230 units against a budget of 200 units. A budget that remains unchanged even if the organization deviates significantly from the originally planned level of activities is called a **fixed budget**.

A problem with comparing actual outcomes with the original fixed budget is that this gives limited information. If managers are to be able to identify problems and decide on appropriate action, they must understand *why* actual costs differ from the budget.

In Worked Example 6.2 actual sales have exceeded the budget by 30 units (or 15 per cent). It would therefore be reasonable to expect costs also to be greater than budget. From the variance report we can see that this is indeed the case. However, what we are not able to ascertain is whether these costs are still reasonable for the level of sales actually achieved. In order to obtain this level of detail we need to be able to 'flex' the budget to reflect the actual level of activity.

A **flexed budget** is one which has been adjusted in order to take account of any differences between actual levels of activity and the original budgeted level of activity. For most organizations this approach has many advantages over fixed budgeting. Accurate estimation of actual levels of activity can be difficult and flexing the budget allows for improvement and refinement of original estimations. It can also help reveal problem areas in the original budget and provide management with the opportunity to correct them.

Flexing the budget is particularly important if actual levels of activity become significantly different from the original budget owing to external factors. Monitoring against a budget which is no longer relevant can produce meaningless budget performance reports. It is far more useful to be able to compare wage costs and material costs against what they are expected to be for actual levels of sales rather than original and no longer relevant levels of sales.

In order to flex the budget, the original (fixed) budget figures are adjusted to what they would have been for the actual level of sales. Worked Example 6.3 shows a budget variance report after the budget has been flexed. In this example the original (fixed) budget would have been calculated before the start of the accounting period. The flexed budget, on the other hand, is not produced until after the accounting period, as it is only then that the actual level of activity is known.

WORKED EXAMPLE 6.3   A flexed budget variance report for Woodburn Co

Table 6.3

	Actual results $	Flexed budget variance $		Flexed budget $	Fixed budget variance $		Original (fixed) budget $
Sales revenue	40,250	1,150	A	41,400	5,400	F	36,000
Direct materials	8,349	299	A	8,050	1,050	A	7,000
Direct labour	3,105	−345	F	3,450	450	A	3,000
Variable overheads	2,760	460	A	2,300	300	A	2,000
Fixed overheads	16,000	1,000	A	15,000	0		15,000
Total expenses	30,214	1,414	A	28,800	1,800	A	27,000
Operating profit	10,036	2,564	A	12,600	3,600	F	9,000

With the use of a flexed budget it is possible to analyse the total variance into two columns:

The **fixed budget variance** is the difference between the original fixed budget and the flexed budget. This variance reflects the change in costs that would be expected due to the changed level of activity.

The **flexed budget variance** is the difference between the actual results and the flexed budget. This shows the variance between actual costs and the costs that would be expected for the actual level of activity.

The calculation of the variances shown in Worked Example 6.3 enables managers to obtain a more detailed analysis of the difference between actual profit and budgeted profit for a given period of activity. When total variance is divided between a fixed budget variance and a flexed budget variance, it is usually the flexed budget variance which is most useful to managers in assessing organizational performance, as this variance shows the difference between actual costs and what costs should have been for the actual level of activity.

However, even with total variance broken down into fixed budget and flexed budget variance, there is still a limited amount of information available to managers. The usefulness of variance analysis is greatly enhanced if the organization uses standard costing. This enables the analysis of variances in much greater detail.

Extract 6.1: CIMA guidance on performance reporting

CIMA (the Chartered Institute of Management Accountants) produced the following guidance on performance reporting. The ideal monthly management pack for reporting to the board should be between 10 and 20 pages and contain the following elements:

- Executive summary with a synopsis of KPIs and identifying all key issues.

- Action plan specifying corrective actions and contingencies with best/worst-case scenarios.

- P&L account showing period and cumulative positions with highlighted variances against budget – and major variances. Trend analysis shown graphically.

- Projected outturn recalculated on the basis of actual performance and action plans.

- Profiled cash flow summarizing actual and projected receipts, payments and balances on a regular basis to year-end.

- Capital programme – analysis of progress of major capital schemes showing percentage completion, current and projected expenditure, completion cost and timescale.

- Balance sheet showing working capital position in tabular form or using performance indicators, eg debtor and creditor days.

SOURCE CIMA (2003)

Standard costing

A standard cost is the planned cost of producing one unit of a product or service, or in some cases the planned cost of a process. This standard is usually based upon a reasonable expectation of the time and materials involved that allows for idle time and material wastage which would be a normal part of the way a business operates.

Budgeting and standard costing are not the same thing and it is possible to budget without the use of standard costs. However, there is an interrelationship between the two activities in that a budget can be seen as being made up of standard costs multiplied by the expected level of activity. For example, if the standard labour cost of producing one unit of a product is $6 and the budgeted level of production is 5,000 units, then the budget for production labour will be $30,000 (5,000 × $6). Standard costs are therefore a useful tool in budget-setting and if the business wishes to undertake a detailed analysis of actual performance against budget, it is helpful to have standard costing information underpinning the budget.

In practice there are a number of different ways of setting standards and different organizations use different types of standard. Standards are usually classified as being either basic, ideal or attainable:

- A **basic standard** is one which represents a constant standard that will not change over time.

  - This type of standard is not widely used. It is found in some manufacturing industries that have products with long life cycles and processes which remain unchanged over many years of production.

  - By keeping the same standard over a long period the company is able to assess the efficiency of performance across several years.

  - This type of standard is not appropriate for businesses that have changing processes and practices or fluctuating prices, as it would not give a meaningful measure of actual performance. Also, it would be an impractical measure for a business producing non-standardized products or services which are made to customer specifications.

- An **ideal standard** represents the cost of producing a product in perfect conditions, with maximum efficiency and no wastage.

  - The rationale for the use of an ideal standard is to set the highest target possible and to strive towards this, rather than being satisfied with less than optimum performance.

- – In practice an ideal standard will never be achieved and therefore actual performance will always be below standard.
- – This may be demotivating for employees and would be an inappropriate standard to use if bonuses were attached to performance evaluation.
- A currently **attainable standard** makes allowances for normal levels of wastage and lost time and represents the cost under normal but efficient levels of activity.
  - – Such a standard represents an achievable target and is therefore more appropriate for performance measurement.
  - – The concept of being 'attainable' is not fixed and therefore an attainable standard can be set at a relatively easy or difficult level for performance management purposes.
  - – In practice such standards need to be demanding enough to provide sufficient incentive for employees to improve beyond current levels of efficiency, but not so demanding as to prove to be a disincentive.

Whichever approach is adopted towards standard-setting, it is important that the standards used are accurate. The method of deriving standards is therefore extremely important and will vary across different types of organization. Some businesses use what is known as the **engineering approach** which involves industry engineers and operation managers defining processes, routines and exact material usages and costing these. This approach is likely to be used if an ideal standard or a highly demanding attainable standard is desired. It will also be used for a new product or process for which the company has no past actual performance data. A second approach involves analysing actual past costs, removing unwanted inefficiencies and setting a standard based upon this. Businesses operating in a competitive industry will often attempt to **benchmark** their costs against those of competitors. They will obtain information on the actual performance of their competitors and set standards to match or undercut these. Many organizations use a combination of the above approaches.

Discussion point

How might a heating engineer who installs house heating boilers establish a standard cost for an installation?

Extract 6.2: Benchmarking and performance at Samsung

Samsung, the South Korean-based multinational conglomerate, arrived at its current world-leading position through a process of benchmarking and refinement. When he succeeded his father as Samsung Group chairman in 1987, Lee Kun-Hee set about transforming the conglomerate from a Korean competitor to a global leader. Mr Lee insisted that the Group's subsidiaries should measure their performance against global leaders in their field, rather than benchmark against other Korean companies. Business units that did not measure up to global performance, such as sugar and paper processing, were divested even though they were profitable, because they were not capable of achieving leadership in global markets. Investment was concentrated on a handful of businesses deemed capable of competing globally. Mr Lee also increased the autonomy of successful businesses by eliminating cross-business subsidies and below-market transfer prices, thereby freeing the businesses to compete more effectively in global markets.

Standard costing and variance analysis

The use of standards enables a more detailed level of variance analysis than that which we saw in Worked Example 6.3. This is illustrated in Figure 6.1. In particular, the use of standards enables flexed budget variances to be analysed into two key elements. These are generally referred to as a volume variance and a rate variance.

A **volume variance** measures the efficiency with which resources are used by showing the difference between actual usage and standard usage. This can refer to the volume of sales (sales volume variance), usage of materials (material usage variance) or the time taken by direct labour to complete a process (labour efficiency variance). This volume difference is multiplied by the standard cost to show the impact upon profit.

A **rate variance** (which may also be called a price variance or a cost variance) measures the difference between the actual price paid for something (eg materials or labour) and the expected (standard) price. This difference in price is multiplied by the actual quantity used to show the total impact upon profit. In some cases it is possible to break this rate variance down into even more detail through the calculation of **mix and yield variances**.

Figure 6.1 Analysis of profit variance

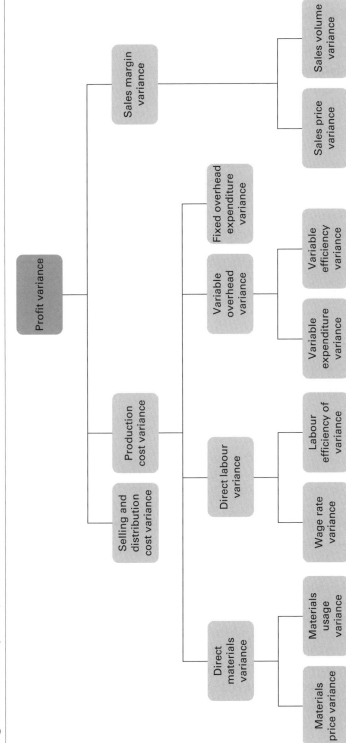

Variance analysis

When variance analysis is performed using standard costing, it is usual to present that analysis in the form of an operating statement or budget reconciliation report. There is no standard format for this information. Different organizations use different styles of report and give them different names.

Worked Example 6.4 presents a budget reconciliation report for Woodburn Co, based upon the information given in Worked Example 6.1. This report reconciles the actual profit for the period back to the original budgeted profit and analyses this difference in terms of the variances set out in Figure 6.1.

WORKED EXAMPLE 6.4 Budget reconciliation for Woodburn Co

Table 6.4

	$		$		$
Budgeted net profit					9,000
Sales variances:					
Sales margin price	−1,150	A			
Sales margin volume	3,600	F	2,450	F	
Direct cost of variances:					
Material price	−759	A			
Material usage	460	F	−299	A	
Labour rate	1,035	F			
Labour efficiency	−690	A	345	F	
Production overhead variances:					
Fixed overhead expenditure	−1,000	A			
Variable overhead expenditure	0				
Variable overhead efficiency	−460	A	−1,460	A	1,036
Actual profit					10,036

The reconciliation report in Worked Example 6.4 provides a reconciliation between the original budgeted profit of $9,000 and the actual profit of $10,036. The following analysis examines the variances set out in that budget reconciliation in more detail.

Sales variance

The sales variance is expressed not in terms of sales price but rather sales margin, that is to say, the profit margin from sales. The reason for this is that managers will be primarily interested in the impact which changes in sales have upon profitability. The total sales variance is broken down into two elements, the price variance and the volume variance.

From the sales margin price variance, the manager can see the impact upon profitability of any changes from the budgeted price. In the Woodburn Co example the sales margin price variance is adverse ($1,150A), which means that the actual sales price was less than the budgeted sales price. As this is a simple example we can calculate the actual sales price: $40,250 (actual sales revenue) ÷ 230 (actual units sold) = $175. The budgeted sales price was $180, therefore the sales department discounted the stoves sold by $5 each. This reduction in sales price has cost the company $1,150 in lost profit.

However, this is not the full story. If we look at the sales margin volume variance we can see that the reduction in price has generated an increase in volume of sales with a favourable variance of $3,600. The importance of breaking the total sales variance down into a price and volume variance is that it enables the manager to evaluate whether the reduction in sales price was beneficial to the company. In this case we can see that it was. The reduction in sales price adversely affected profit by $1,150 but the resultant increase in volume increased profits by $3,600. Therefore, the net impact was to increase profit for the month by $2,450.

Materials variance

The total materials variance is broken down into a price variance and a usage variance. The price variance measures the cost of materials against budget and the usage variance measures the amount of material used in comparison to what was expected for the actual level of production.

In the Woodburn Co example the material price variance is adverse ($1,150A), which means that materials cost more than was expected, but material usage variance is favourable ($460F), which means that fewer materials were used than would be expected for the volume of production. In practice these two variances are often interrelated and the reason for one may lie with the other. For example, it could be that the material price variance is adverse because better-quality materials which cost more were purchased. In turn, this increase in quality may have resulted in less wastage and therefore a favourable usage variance. If this was a strategy employed by Woodburn Co, management can assess its overall success by looking at the total materials variance. This is adverse ($299A), which would suggest that buying more expensive materials and using less has not been beneficial to the business because this has reduced profit for the period by $299. This is of course an over-simplification and material usage variances can arise for other reasons, such as labour inefficiencies, faulty production or mistakes that require products to be scrapped. Managers always need to investigate variances carefully to understand why they have occurred.

If multiple materials are used in a manufacturing process and it is possible to vary their mix, for example by substituting one material for another, then the material usage variance can be further analysed into mix and yield variances. The material mix variance measures the financial impact of varying the mix of materials. If a more expensive material has been used rather than a cheaper one, or the mix between the two has changed, then the overall cost of materials will be higher. The material yield variance measures the efficiency of turning inputs into outputs. A certain quantity of materials input should produce a certain quantity of outputs. If the mix of materials is changed, the quantity of output may be adversely affected and this will show an adverse material yield variance, even if the change in mix shows a favourable variance.

Extract 6.3: Is variance analysis still relevant?

Despite the rising popularity of Beyond Budgeting, a 2017 survey (Conine *et al*, 2017) of 154 senior finance executives at USA Fortune 500 companies found that 100 per cent still use budgets and variance analysis to assess actual results. The study concluded that using variance analysis to inform decision-making has several positive impacts, including promoting consistent good performance, establishing trust in senior management, assisting in risk management and safeguarding shareholder value.

Labour variance

The total labour variance is divided into a rate variance and an efficiency variance. The rate variance provides information about the hourly cost of the labour (ie the rate at which labour was paid) and the efficiency variance assesses how efficient labour was in comparison to the standard time it should take to build a stove. In this case the labour rate variance is favourable ($1,035F) and the labour efficiency budget is adverse ($690A). This may suggest that lower-paid and perhaps less experienced labour was employed and because of their lack of experience they have been less efficient. The overall labour variance is $345 favourable, which indicates that this change in labour strategy has been financially beneficial to the business.

A phenomenon which should be taken account of when assessing labour variances is the **learning curve**. If employees are involved in a new task, they will become more efficient as they learn how to do this more effectively. The learning curve is also seen with increases in volume of production. As production increases, staff usually become more efficient so that the cost per unit decreases. However, this increase in efficiency comes at a declining rate and will top out at some point.

Two other important factors are **idle time** and **wastage**. Idle time will relate to the labour efficiency variance and wastage will normally relate to the material usage variance but can be connected to labour variances because less experienced employees are more likely to increase wastage of materials. Levels of idle time and wastage can be categorized into 'normal' and 'abnormal' and it is important that a performance management system is able to differentiate between the two.

Normal idle time or wastage will be due to the way a production process operates and so will be expected and should be built into efficiency measures. For example, employees may be idle during the recalibration or refitting of machinery. This does not mean that managers should not be concerned about reducing 'normal' idle time or wastage, but this is a matter of improving or re-engineering systems and procedures, rather than one of employee performance management. Abnormal idle time or wastage, on the other hand, is not expected as part of a normal production process and should be investigated as a matter of employee performance management.

Discussion point

An engineering company has just installed a new highly accurate high-speed laser cutting machine. What impact might this have on material and labour variances?

Fixed overhead expenditure variance

Fixed overheads, by definition, are not expected to change with levels of activity. Therefore, any variance in fixed overhead costs will be due entirely to changes in level of expenditure which should not have occurred just because of changes in production volume. In the Woodburn Co example there is an adverse fixed overhead variance of $1,000. This should be investigated as there is no reason for fixed overhead costs to increase just because of the higher level of sales.

Variable overhead expenditure variance

It is normal to allocate variable overhead costs based upon labour hours. As a result, any variances in direct labour efficiency (as seen in the direct labour efficiency variance) will also impact upon variable overhead costs. Because of this, the total variance is broken down into an efficiency variance and an expenditure variance. In the example it can be seen that the variable overhead variance of $460A is entirely due to the adverse labour efficiency already identified and not to any change in actual expenditure.

Summary

This analysis illustrates how variances on their own do not provide answers for managers, but rather they direct managers towards asking the right questions. Variance analysis can be seen as an example of **management by exception.** That is to say, by focusing on variances, management's attention is directed to those areas of the business that are not performing according to plan. Many regard this as an efficient management approach.

Extract 6.4: Standard costing in practice

KPMG, the international accountancy firm, in association with CIMA (the Chartered Institute of Management Accountants), carried out a global survey into the use of standard costing in 2010. Their report found widespread use of standard costing but highlighted serious shortcomings in the standard costing information used in many large manufacturing organizations. Some businesses were using outdated standards and standards which contained uncontrollable costs in their performance management.

It was found that the best companies use more than one type of standard to support different areas of decision making. Effective performance management focused on variance analysis and remedial action in controllable areas of performance. In addition, in order to deal with economic volatility these businesses undertook frequent updates of their standards to keep them relevant and useful for performance management.

Exercises: now attempt Exercise 6.1 on page 234

Performance management in investment centres

The manager of an investment centre is not just responsible for the costs, revenues and profits of that centre, but also for the investments made in order to earn those profits.

Investment centres therefore need performance measures which address the efficiency of investments, that is to say they address both income and assets. In this section we will look at the most commonly used investment centre performance indicators.

Return on investment (ROI)

The return on investment (ROI), which is synonymous with ROCE, is the most commonly used performance measure for evaluating investment centre financial performance. The ROI measures the level of income earned in relation to the assets employed to earn that income. This is usually expressed in the following formula:

$$\text{ROI} = \frac{\text{Operating income}}{\text{Total assets}} \times 100\%$$

Expert view 6.1: ROI

ROI is also used to evaluate potential investments in the form of accounting rate of return (ARR) and so is discussed in more detail in Chapter 9. The difference is that in investment appraisal the technique is applied to estimates of future income, but for performance measurement it is applied to historic income, ie that which has already been earned.

The popularity and widespread usage of ROI can be attributed to the fact that, because it gives a measure as a percentage, it allows for easy comparison of performance between different businesses, business divisions and the same business division over time.

A second and related measure sometimes used in investment centres is the capital turnover. This measures sales revenue in relation to assets and shows how efficiently the centre is using its assets to generate sales:

$$\text{Capital turnover} = \frac{\text{Sales revenue}}{\text{Total assets}} \times 100\%$$

This measure may be more appropriate for a division that is primarily responsible for income generation and has little or no control over costs.

Residual income (RI) and economic value added (EVA)

Residual income presents an alternative means of measuring income against assets of an investment centre. Whereas ROI measures performance in percentage terms, RI measures it in absolute terms. RI is calculated with the following formula:

$$RI = \text{After-tax operating income} - (\text{Cost of capital} \times \text{Invested assets})$$

The cost of capital charge deducted from operating income is the company's weighted average cost of capital (WACC) multiplied by the total assets invested in the division. It represents the cost of financing the assets of the division and hence the minimum acceptable level of income for the division. RI is therefore a measure of the surplus or residual which the division earns over and above the minimum required by the company's investors.

In the early 1990s Stern Steward & Co consultants made some refinements to residual income and termed their new measure **economic value added (EVA)**. This measure has been widely adopted over the past 20 years and research suggests that up to 25 per cent of businesses now use it to evaluate divisional performance.

$$EVA = \text{Adjusted after-tax operating income} -$$
$$(\text{Cost of capital} \times \text{Adjusted average invested capital})$$

For EVA the operating income and capital invested are both adjusted to bring them closer to approximation of equivalent cash figures. This is to remove distortions which occurred owing to the way income and capital have to be reported for financial accounting purposes.

WORKED EXAMPLE 6.5 Investment centre performance

The following information relates to the performance of an investment centre:

Total assets of division	$500,000
Sales revenue of division	$770,000
After-tax operating income	$65,000
Adjusted after-tax operating income	$70,000
Adjusted total capital of division	$560,000
Cost of capital	12%

Using these figures we can calculate the performance of the investment centre:

Return on investment:

$$ROI = \frac{\text{Operating income}}{\text{Total assets}} = \frac{\$65,000}{\$500,000} = 13\%$$

Capital turnover:

$$\text{Capital turnover} = \frac{\text{Sales revenue}}{\text{Total assets}} = \frac{\$770,000}{\$500,000} = 154\%$$

Residual income:

RI = Operating income − Cost of capital charge
= $65,000 − ($500,000 × 12%) = $5,000

Economic value added:

EVA = Adjusted after-tax operating income −
      Cost of invested capital × Adjusted average invested capital
= $70,000 − ($560,000 × 12%) = $2,800

Which is the best measure: ROI or EVA?

As ROI and EVA represent two very different measures of divisional performance, the question naturally arises as to which is the better. In practice each of the two measures has both advantages and disadvantages:

- The advantage of ROI is that it enables easy comparison between divisions and different companies, particularly if they are of different sizes. Also, managers are usually more comfortable dealing with percentages.

- The disadvantage of ROI is that it can encourage divisional behaviour which is not in the interest of the business as a whole. For example, if a division has a current ROI of 20 per cent it will be reluctant to invest in a new project which offers a return of only 15 per cent, as this new project would reduce the average ROI for the division. But if the overall ROI of the company is 12 per cent, the new project with a return of 15 per cent represents a good investment because it will increase the company ROI. When using the ROI measure it is possible for the interests of the division and the business as a whole to conflict.

EVA overcomes this problem by moving focus away from percentages, but in doing so it suffers from the disadvantage of being an absolute measure and therefore being less useful for comparison with other divisions or businesses of a different size. A major advantage of EVA is that because it makes a charge for the capital used, it raises managers' awareness that capital has a cost and that the balance sheet needs to be managed just as carefully as the income statement. The EVA enables managers to assess a proper trade-off between the two.

Non-financial performance indicators

The usefulness of financial measures and variance analysis as a management control and performance measurement system has been challenged by some commentators. One criticism is that currently used financial measures arose in manufacturing businesses operating in a relatively stable business environment and as such they offer insufficient focus on quality for modern service-oriented businesses. They are also focused on the short term, which means that management decisions will be directed towards short-term financial gains at the potential cost to long-term sustainability and development. Another criticism is that the speed of change in the modern business environment is a barrier to effective standard-setting and variance analysis. Some commentators have gone as far as to claim that standard costing is now obsolete. Others have suggested that it can be updated to incorporate qualitative considerations to make it more suitable for modern businesses.

In *Relevance Lost*, an influential book published in 1987, the authors Johnson and Kaplan outlined the limitations of short-term financial measures of performance and argued for the use of more non-financial measures. Johnson and Kaplan claimed that short-term financial measures have become less relevant in a modern business environment characterized by rapid change, innovation and shorter product life cycles. They proposed that a range of non-financial performance measures should be used, covering not just operations, but also marketing and research and development.

Johnson and Kaplan encouraged the use of performance indicators that will better predict an organization's long-term goals rather than just short-term financial performance. This should, for example, include measures of efficient product design, flexible production capability, quality, delivery time and customer feedback. One result of these criticisms has been the development of what has come to be known as the **balanced scorecard**.

The balanced scorecard

The balanced scorecard (BSC) was developed in the early 1990s as a performance management tool which addresses some of the criticisms of traditional finance-focused measures discussed above. Its best-known proponents are Kaplan and Norton who published an article in the *Harvard Business Review* in 1992 followed by a book, *The Balanced Scorecard*, in 1996. Since then it has become the most widely adopted performance management framework.

The principle of the balanced scorecard is that it presents a mix of financial and non-financial performance measures which are derived from corporate strategy and which focus on the main activities required to implement that strategy. Kaplan and Norton proposed three non-financial areas and one financial area to provide four 'perspectives' on performance (see Figure 6.2). A company should choose a small number of performance

Figure 6.2 The balanced scorecard

measures (typically five or six) to reflect performance from each of these perspectives and attach targets to each measure which indicate expected levels of performance.

Financial perspective

The financial perspective considers the organization's performance from the point of view of the shareholders. The primary concern is how well the organization is creating value for its owners. Kaplan and Norton suggested three core areas that should drive the business strategy: revenue (growth and mix); cost reduction; and asset utilization.

Customer perspective

This perspective considers the organization's performance from the point of view of customers. The organization should understand its customer profile and the market segments in which it competes.

Internal perspective

This perspective is concerned with the internal workings of the organization and what must be done well in order to satisfy customers. It involves identifying critical business processes. Kaplan and Norton identified three key areas of added value: the innovation process; the operations process; and the post-sales process.

Learning and growth perspective

This perspective focuses on continual improvement and innovation within the organization. It involves a recognition that markets, products and processes are continually changing and that in order to continue satisfying customers and making good financial returns the organization must keep learning and developing. An emphasis of this perspective is continued investment in infrastructure – systems, organizational procedures and people, in order to provide the capability to perform and improve in the other three perspectives.

Using a balanced scorecard

The four perspectives detailed above are those initially put forward by Kaplan and Norton. In practice, each organization should choose perspectives which it feels are most appropriate to its corporate mission and strategic vision. It should then select performance measures and set targets in line with these perspectives. Extract 6.5 shows an extract from the balanced scorecard of a major electricity utility supply company.

Extract 6.5: Balanced scorecard for an electricity utility supplier

Objectives	Performance measures	Targets
Financial perspective		
Maximize returns	● ROCE	15%
Profitable growth	● Revenue growth	12%
Leveraged asset base	● Asset utilization rate	90%
Manage operating costs	● Operating costs per customer	$125
Customer perspective		
Industry-leading customer loyalty	● Customer satisfaction rating	90%
Internal perspective		
Business growth	● Percentage of revenue from deregulated products or services	10%
Continued public support	● Customer satisfaction (5-point scale)	4.5
Customer service excellence	● Promised delivery percentage	97%
Optimize core business	● Percentage rated capacity attained	90%
Learning and growth perspective		
Market-driven skill	● Strategic skill coverage ratio	85%
Employee satisfaction	● Employee satisfaction rating (5-point scale)	4.5
World-class leadership	● Leadership effectiveness rating (5-point scale)	4.5

Development of the BSC

Since its introduction in the early 1990s the balanced scorecard has attracted some criticism. One early criticism was that the model developed by Kaplan and Norton focused primarily on the needs of US-based SMEs and as such was not very useful to other types of organization. This has led to a number of variant models (with alternative perspectives or different numbers of perspectives) aimed at being more appropriate to a broader range of organizations. A further criticism has been the focus on shareholders to the detriment of other stakeholders. Current thinking on business strategy emphasizes the importance of well-rounded stakeholder management. There is also little empirical evidence to support the claim that the use of the balanced scorecard produces better financial performance. Despite this, the balanced scorecard and its various derivatives are still extremely popular and widely applied by commercial businesses, non-profit organizations, schools, colleges, government bodies and the military.

Kaplan and Norton have gone on to develop their ideas since the initial introduction of the balanced scorecard. In their latest book *The Execution Premium*, published in 2008, they incorporate the balanced scorecard into a broader **execution premium process (XPP)**, a broader holistic system of implementing and monitoring strategy.

Exercises: now attempt Exercise 6.3 on page 235

Performance measurement in not-for-profit organizations

A not-for-profit organization (NPO) is one which does not aim to earn profits for the owners. Rather, revenues allocated, earned or donated are used in pursuit of the organization's goals. NPOs typically refer to charities and public service organizations such as education, health, police, fire service and social welfare. However, NPOs can also include museums, churches, religious organizations, sports organizations and political organizations. Not-for-profit status is a legal status which will vary from country to country.

NPOs face unique challenges in assessing their performance as the performance measures used by commercial organizations are in many cases not relevant.

For example, the variance analysis examined in Worked Example 6.4 above was concerned with the impact upon profitability of actual performance against budget. As generating profits is not a goal for NPOs, this approach to performance measurement is not appropriate. The challenge for NPOs therefore is to find alternative performance measures which better suit their organizational goals and aims.

Not only are NPOs different from commercial organizations in not being unified by a profit motive (Table 6.5), they are also a heterogeneous category, having a wide range of goals which lead to a wide range of activities. These activities and goals are often seen as intangible and difficult to quantify. This increases the challenge of finding appropriate performance measures.

However, there are some points of commonality that allow for a general framework of performance management. The activities of NPOs can in most cases be categorized into three key areas: fundraising, management and programme implementation. Adequate performance management therefore needs to include measurement of performance in each of these areas.

One performance measure which is common to most NPOs is the proportion of resources spent on management and fundraising as opposed to carrying out programme activities. A smaller proportion of resources spent on management and fundraising is seen as a positive performance indicator, and this measure is frequently used by tax authorities and watchdog organizations when rating NPO performance.

Although the proportion of total resources spent on programme activities is important, it is not in itself an adequate performance measure. Good performance is not just about spending money. It is possible for an NPO to spend a high proportion of its total resources on programme activities but for it to be ineffectual in reaching its goals. Performance measurement for NPOs must therefore focus on output and outcomes as well as inputs. It is therefore useful to clarify these three important concepts of inputs, outputs and outcomes:

Table 6.5   The features which typically make NPOs different from commercial businesses

- There are no shareholders to whom management have a primary responsibility to provide a financial return.
- Generating profits is not a goal of the organization.
- NPOs often provide services or goods free of charge.
- Income is received from individuals or organizations that are different from those receiving the benefits of the organization's work.
- Those providing resources to the NPO often do not expect a financial return in the same way as private-sector investors.

Inputs can be defined as all the resources used to carry out the organization's mission and implement projects and programmes. This will include financial resources (earned, allocated or donated) and also staff and volunteer time.

Outputs are the level of services provided by the NPO. Outputs will usually be measured in non-financial terms and will depend upon the goals of the organization. For example, an anti-malaria charity may report the number of mosquito nets distributed; a hospital heart surgery department may report the number of operations performed; a college may measure the number of people attending workshops or training classes; a humanitarian charity may report the number of people provided with shelter, food and water following a disaster.

Outcomes are the effects which services provided (outputs) have on the organization's stated mission. Outcome measures should focus on how well outputs are achieving organizational goals. These measures attempt to gauge how effective the organization is being. For example, the anti-malaria charity may report the number of cases of malaria in the area in which it is working; the college may report the number of students entering new jobs.

There are many approaches to performance measurement in NPOs, but all are based around three important factors often referred to as the '3Es': economy, effectiveness and efficiency. This framework provides a focus for NPO performance measures which cover inputs, outputs and outcomes:

Economy is concerned with achieving goals within given levels of resource input. Most NPOs operate with restricted resources and must therefore be able to achieve their goals effectively with a limited budget. For example, a hospital with a fixed level of funding must be able to operate within its fixed budget, without overspending, regardless of how effective or efficient it is.

Effectiveness is concerned with achievement of outcomes and focuses upon the organization's goals. For example, a drug rehabilitation clinic may have a corporate mission of reducing the number of people dependent upon illegal drugs. That clinic may treat a large number of patients at a low cost and thereby be deemed efficient. However, if a high proportion of those patients relapse, the clinic may be deemed to have low effectiveness in achieving its goals.

Efficiency is concerned with the relationship between inputs and outputs. Efficiency measures look at the amount of resources used to achieve outputs.

For example, two care homes may both provide similar levels of care for the same number of residents, but if one does so at a considerably lower cost than the other, it can be considered to be more efficient.

NPO efficiency can be measured in each of the three key areas of activity: fundraising, management and programme implementation. There may be external benchmarks for efficiency, or it may be possible for an organization to track its efficiency performance over time with reference to past data. For example, a hospital heart surgery department could calculate the cost per operation performed. This could then be compared to similar data from other hospitals or tracked over several years to measure the efficiency of the department.

Value for money (VFM) as a public-sector objective

In many public sector organizations the principle of the 3Es is implemented under the term **value for money** (**VFM**). VFM can be defined as the optimal use of resources to achieve the intended outcomes. An organization is said to be achieving high VFM when there is an optimum balance between the 3Es: relatively low costs (economy), high productivity (efficiency) and successful outcomes (effectiveness).

NPO performance measurement: an example

Extract 6.6 presents a balanced scorecard developed by the Kenya Red Cross Society. The mission of the society is 'to work with vigour and compassion through our networks and with communities to prevent and alleviate human suffering and save lives of the most vulnerable'. The society's strategic vision is 'to be the most effective, trusted and self-sustaining humanitarian organization in Kenya'.

From this mission statement and strategic vision the society has derived the following four perspectives: beneficiary/stakeholder; financial stewardship; business processes; and organization capacity. Each of these perspectives has been given a small number of objectives against which performance measures and targets have been set. These are set out below.

Extract 6.6: NPO Balanced scorecard

Objective	Performance measure	Target
Perspective: beneficiary/stakeholder		
Improve livelihoods	• Households that meet minimum standards	50%
	• Reduction on relief aid in target communities	20%
	• Lives saved during emergencies	100%
Increase contribution to national policy	• Activities supported by legal framework	100%
	• Appropriate national policies contributed to	75%
	• Projects aligned to appropriate national policy	100%
Enhance community ownership	• Average age of projects running after completion	10 yrs
	• Contribution to project budget by community	20%
	• Projects replicated by community and partners	TBD
Increase access to services	• Services within the standard distance	95%
	• Beneficiaries reached	TBD
	• Information available to stakeholders	75%
Perspective: financial stewardship		
Optimize resource utilization	• Percentage of core cost to total cost	30%
	• Cost per beneficiary	TBD
Perspective: business processes		
Improve service delivery	• Increase in integrated programme	80%
	• Programme success	95%
	• Programme standards compliance	100%
Strengthen partnerships	• Active partnerships	95%
	• Formal partnerships	95%
	• Partner confidence score	80%

Objective	Performance measure	Target
Strengthen disaster risk management (DRM) processes	• Incidences responded to on time	100%
	• Compliance to DRM process standards	100%
	• People assisted	20%
Perspective: organization capacity		
Strengthen branch network and infrastructure	• Branches meeting minimum standards	100%
	• Participation in membership activities	60%
	• Income raised locally	TBD
Internalize the economic engine	• Core costs paid from own funds	50%
	• Funding gap	100%
	• Growth in disaster fund	20%
Improve human resource alignment	• Job satisfaction index	95%
	• Staff retention	TBD
	• Appropriate skills and competencies	TBD
	• Percentage of hours spent on projects	80%
Improve health and safety	• Emblem awareness index	TBD
	• Reduce incidences to staff	ZERO
	• Safety compliance score	100%
Improve knowledge management	• Evidence-based decision making	100%
	• Documentation and dissemination of lessons	95%
	• Employee information awareness	TBD

Behavioural aspects of performance management: gaming and creative accounting

Performance measurement has an impact on the environment in which it operates and will influence the behaviour of those whose performance is being measured. Deciding what to measure, how to measure it and what targets to set will all influence employee behaviour. Sometimes this can have unintended negative consequences.

One important consequence of the increased emphasis on performance measures is the pressure that performance measurement puts on employees. Research shows that the increasing demands of performance measurement systems can increase tension, frustration, resentment, suspicion, fear and mistrust in employees. This in turn reduces employee job satisfaction, increases absenteeism and has been shown to result in a reduction in long-term performance.

Other research has identified how employees respond to performance measures. One consequence is that 'what gets measured gets done'. If employees know that their performance is being measured, they will inevitably focus on achieving those targets against which they know they will be assessed. This may be to the detriment of other areas of performance. A further problem is that multiple and diverse performance measures may generate tension and conflict between performance targets. This can cause confusion and distrust of performance measures and can prove to be demotivating.

Another behavioural risk of setting performance measures is that managers will take actions to improve their measured scores through 'creative accounting' without improving underlying performance. Many examples of such practices can be found across a wide range of industries. For example, hospitals that are assessed on the length of waiting lists have redefined and delayed the point at which a patient enters the waiting list. Repair and maintenance departments that are assessed on how quickly they respond to repair requests similarly redefine and delay the point at which a request is formally recognized and therefore when the 'clock starts ticking'. In many cases these changes, which are effectively a manipulation of the definition of waiting time, mean that there is no actual improvement in performance.

A further problem can arise with benchmarking, which is a process intended to assess and improve performance. Sometimes managers will use benchmarking to defend rather than improve poor performance. The manager will focus on explaining why their department or organization performed poorly against the benchmark, citing factors that make their situation different from those against which it is being assessed. In such cases, the benchmarking exercise leads to little or no improvement in performance.

Exercises: now attempt Exercise 6.4 on page 236

External influences on performance

All organizations, whether they be profit-seeking or not-for-profit, are experiencing increased external scrutiny and pressure to meet the expectations of external stakeholders. Current academic work on external financial reporting is greatly concerned with impression management and measures of corporate social responsibility. As a consequence, performance management is increasingly being used to assess the impact of organizational actions on stakeholders outside the organization.

These developments are reflected in the widespread use of the balanced scorecard and other similar models of performance management which include measures of the impact of the organization's performance on customer satisfaction, employee satisfaction or local community satisfaction. This in turn has shaped the way in which performance management systems are developed and the kind of performance

Figure 6.3   PEST analysis: a framework for focusing managers' attention on those external factors (political, economic, social and technological) that may impact upon organizational performance

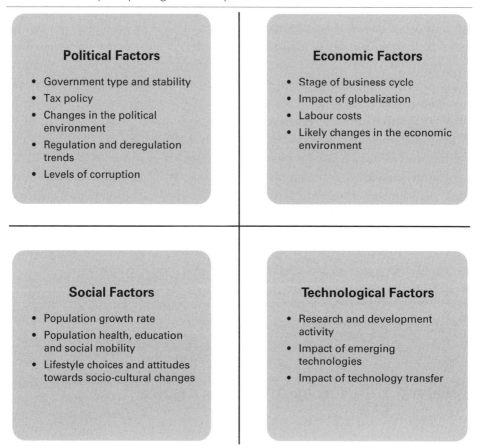

Political Factors

- Government type and stability
- Tax policy
- Changes in the political environment
- Regulation and deregulation trends
- Levels of corruption

Economic Factors

- Stage of business cycle
- Impact of globalization
- Labour costs
- Likely changes in the economic environment

Social Factors

- Population growth rate
- Population health, education and social mobility
- Lifestyle choices and attitudes towards socio-cultural changes

Technological Factors

- Research and development activity
- Impact of emerging technologies
- Impact of technology transfer

measures that are used. Techniques are now widely used to assist management in identifying and assessing those external factors which can impact on organizational performance and which therefore need to be taken into consideration in performance management. These include tools such as PEST analysis (Figure 6.3) and Porter's five forces model.

There has also been an increased need to interpret performance in the light of external considerations and, in particular, societal ethical issues that may impact on business performance. Performance measurement is now turning to factors such as carbon footprinting, sustainable use of resources, ethical sourcing of materials, employee welfare, pollution and recycling.

Performance management in modern business systems

Recent developments in management accounting such as target costing, life-cycle costing, just-in-time (JIT), throughput accounting and total quality management (TQM) have changed the nature and use of performance measures within many organizations. This raises the question of whether traditional performance measurement accounting techniques such as standard costing still have a place in modern business systems.

One of the common features of the techniques mentioned above is a move towards viewing the organization more holistically as a system or flow of processes rather than a collection of individual activities. Management attention is therefore directed towards improving overall performance rather than optimizing the performance of individual areas in isolation. This can lead to some conclusions about performance that are counter-intuitive to those focused on traditional measures.

For example, throughput accounting is concerned with improving the overall efficiency of total production processes. There is a focus on identifying and removing bottlenecks in production systems. Businesses employing the principles of throughput accounting have often found that overall performance is improved by allowing an increase in idle time in some areas of the system and by substantially reducing production batch sizes. Under traditional variance analysis idle time is seen as an evil which should be eradicated. Equally, it can be hard to grasp how overall financial performance can be improved by cutting batch sizes, as this means a greater number of smaller orders, more set-ups (with a resultant increase in idle time) and more deliveries. These factors all result in higher costs. However, because throughput accounting looks at the holistic picture, such changes can substantially reduce inventory levels which in turn reduces the amount of money the business has tied up in inventory, together with cutting costs of damaged, lost and obsolete inventory.

Also, smaller batch sizes can result in a more flexible approach to production which means meeting customer needs more closely and more quickly. This can give the business an important competitive advantage. As a result of these changes, sales volumes and production throughput can be significantly increased. This can create economies of scale which can lower operating costs to offset the higher costs associated with smaller batch sizes.

So these new accounting techniques together with new approaches to manufacturing have brought new challenges for control and performance measurement. There is a change in emphasis towards performance measures that encompass both financial and non-financial aspects, such as measures of on-time deliveries, reduction in inventory, cooperation with suppliers, process cost reduction, quality improvement, reduced cycle time and product complexity.

Furthermore, these new techniques bring with them the aims of continuous innovation, change and development. For example, a JIT approach involves continuous improvement and a commitment to constant change. Performance measurement systems are required that encourage employees to focus on the critical elements of efficient operations and to provide effective links across the value chain. Continuous improvement and innovation are also important aspects of TQM. This approach needs performance measurement systems that incorporate benchmarking against industry competitors and the integration of quality and strategic information. Within this context, traditional management accounting performance measures can be regarded as an impediment. Focus has moved from recording and reporting costs and cost variances against budget, to understanding and controlling the causes of costs. Organizations need organic and flexible performance management systems.

However, these new developments do not totally negate the usefulness of standards and standard costing. In many organizations they have been integrated into these new techniques. For example, target costing, with its emphasis on continuous improvement, requires a review of resources used in the past to identify where fewer resources might be used in the future. This can involve reviewing old standards and setting new standards for improvement.

Extract 6.7: Performance management at Toyota

Toyota, the Japanese manufacturing giant, employs the philosophy of just in time as part of its performance management and production control systems. The company calls its approach the Toyota Production System (TPS). The company's philosophy is to 'make only what is needed, when it is needed, and in the amount needed'. This approach means that the focus of performance management is upon the flow of parts into production and the flow of items through the production process. Parts should be available just when they are needed within the production process and they should be available in the right place at that time. Toyota concentrates its performance management on measuring and fine-tuning work cycle times, workflow, optimum movement of products and reducing waste time, materials and capacity.

Exercises: now attempt Exercise 6.2 on page 235

Conclusion

We started this chapter by describing how performance management is a multidisciplinary activity which extends beyond accounting to virtually every area of organizational management. We have described some of the basic principles of performance management and looked in some detail at traditional techniques. We have also looked at recent developments in performance management and how tools and techniques have responded to changes in modern management practices. In particular, this chapter has emphasized how performance management has moved away from purely financial measures to a broader perspective which encompasses non-financial aspects of performance and the considerations of external stakeholders.

COMPREHENSION QUESTIONS

1 What are the four main ways of delegating responsibility for budget management?

2 What are the advantages and disadvantages of using flexible budgets?

3 What type of standard costing system would be most appropriate for a manufacturing business that uses budget targets as part of its employee motivation and reward package?

4 Compare the relative advantages of ROI and EVA as divisional performance measures.

5 What are the four perspectives of the balanced scorecard as originally recommended by Kaplan and Norton?

6 Explain how the concept of VFM can be used to measure performance in a public-sector organization.

7 Explain how performance measures may have unintended behavioural consequences.

Answers available at **www.koganpage.com/afm3**

Exercises

Answers available at **www.koganpage.com/afm3**

Exercise 6.1: Evaluating cost variances

Walkon Co manufactures wooden flooring. The company buys timber which it cuts to standard-length boards, sands and polishes to sell on to builders. The variance analysis shown in Table 6.6 has been produced for the production department for the last accounting period.

Table 6.6

	$
Material price variance	20,000 (F)
Material usage variance	25,000 (A)
Labour rate of variance	14,000 (A)
Labour efficiency variance	18,000 (F)
Variable overhead expenditure variance	13,000 (A)
Variable overhead efficiency variance	8,000 (F)
Fixed overhead expenditure variance	10,000 (F)

F = favourable variance; A = adverse variance

In response to the variance analysis the production manager has made the following comments:

1 We were experiencing poor staff morale and a high staff turnover so I increased wage rates during the period. I believe that this has improved staff morale and produced a positive benefit to the company. I was able to source an alternative supplier of raw materials. I negotiated a very good price which I believe has saved the company a considerable amount of money.

2 We had a large sanding machine which I felt was not being sufficiently used and was therefore costing the business too much money. I sold this machine and hired a sander only when we needed one.

Required:

Comment on the performance of the production department based upon the variance analysis and the comments from the production manager provided above.

Exercise 6.2: Total quality management

Coat Co manufactures men's clothing. The company has for many years operated a traditional standard costing and variance analysis approach to performance management. The marketing director has recently been on a training course about quality improvement and has suggested that the company moves to a TQM approach to performance management. His recommendation will be considered at the next meeting of the board of directors.

Required:

Write a brief report which considers some of the practical issues that Coat Co would face should the company decide to change from a standard costing to a TQM approach to performance management.

Exercise 6.3: Non-financial performance indicators

Jake Designs is a small firm which specializes as a consultant in product packaging and marketing within the cosmetics industry. The company recently appointed a new finance director, Katie Williams. In her first meeting with the CEO of Jake Designs, Jake McLeod, Katie expressed concerns at the limited focus of the current performance management system. Katie explained that, although the current system provided good details of the financial performance of the business, it is also important to include non-financial performance indicators, particularly those which will provide a better indication of the future performance of the business. She has suggested that the following performance measures should be reported to the board of directors:

- number of customers;
- average fees per customer;
- average job completion time;
- employee turnover rate;
- employee job satisfaction;
- level of customer satisfaction;
- percentage of revenue from new customers.

Jake McLeod is sceptical about Katie's suggestion. He is concerned that these additional performance measures will just cause more work for the accounting department and may act as a distraction from more important tasks such as ensuring that invoices go out promptly and customers pay on time.

Required:

Explain why the inclusion within the performance management system of the non-financial information suggested by Katie will provide a better indication of potential future success of the business.

Exercise 6.4: Negative behavioural consequences

Tools4U Co operates a chain of tool hire stores across the country. Tool purchases and store staffing levels are managed centrally, so each store is treated as a revenue centre, with the store manager being responsible for the level of sales revenue earned, but not the costs. Store managers earn a bonus of 10 per cent of their salary if the outlet exceeds sales revenue targets for the year.

Required:

Identify how a store manager may be able to manipulate results in order to gain more frequent bonuses.

References

Conine, TC and McDonald, M (2017) The application of variance analysis in FP&A organizations: Survey evidence and recommendations for enhancement, *Journal of Accounting and Finance*, **17** (8)

Johnson, H T and Kaplan, R S (1987) *Relevance Lost: The rise and fall of management accounting*, Harvard Business School Press, Boston, MA

Kaplan, R S and Norton, D P (1992) The balanced scorecard – measures that drive performance, *Harvard Business Review*, **70** (1), pp 71–79

Kaplan, R S and Norton, D P (1996) *The Balanced Scorecard: Translating strategy into action*, Harvard Business School Press, Boston, MA

Kaplan, R S and Norton, D P (2008) *The Execution Premium: Linking strategy to operations for competitive advantage*, Harvard Business School Press, Boston, MA

Supplementary reading

Starovic, D (2003) *Performance Reporting to Boards: A guide to good practice*, CIMA, London

Cash and working capital management 07

OBJECTIVE

To provide an understanding of the importance of cash management to a business and the impact of working capital management strategies on cash flow and liquidity.

LEARNING OUTCOMES

After studying this chapter, the reader will be able to:

- Discuss the importance of cash management to a business.
- Interpret a cash budget and identify potential problems.
- Formulate strategies for improving cash flow and liquidity.

KEY TOPICS COVERED

- The cash-flow cycle.
- Information which a cash budget provides, and why this is important.
- The format and construction of a cash-flow forecast.
- The evaluation of different decisions which impact on cash requirements (financing of asset purchases, credit terms to customers).
- Strategies for improving cash flow.

> **MANAGEMENT ISSUES**
>
> Managers need the ability to evaluate the impact of managerial decisions and strategies on cash requirements. They also need to be able to analyse cash budgets and use them to make appropriate managerial decisions.

Introduction

Planning and managing cash flows lies at the centre of business success. We hear many aphorisms which confirm how important this is: 'cash is king' and 'cash is the lifeblood of the business' are two commonly used expressions. Why is this the case? Quite simply, a business cannot survive without cash. It is possible for a business to function for several years without making a profit provided that it still has cash. But once the cash runs out the business will very quickly fail. This was the fate of many so-called 'dot-com' businesses in the 1990s.

Extract 7.1: Cash flow and small business failure

Dun and Bradstreet, one of the world's leading credit rating agencies, report that 90 per cent of small business failures are caused by poor cash flow.

Why does a business need cash?

Cash is needed in a business for a number of reasons: to purchase inventory and to pay wages, rent, utility bills etc. A business also needs cash to purchase assets such as machinery, equipment, vehicles and premises. In addition, cash is needed to pay dividends to investors, pay interest on loans and pay any taxes due. On top of this, at any one time a business may have cash tied up in current assets such as inventory and accounts receivable. This will be a normal part of operating the business, but the more money that is tied up in assets the greater the cash requirement for the business. For example, if a business offers credit to its customers, this will delay the receipt of cash from sales and will in turn increase the amount of cash the business needs because it still needs to pay wages and other bills. In a similar fashion, if a business increases its levels of inventory it will also increase its need for cash.

What is cash flow?

Cash flow refers to the ways in which cash moves in and out of a business through receipts and payments and also how it circulates within the business to be tied up in various assets such as inventory of accounts receivable. This flow of cash is represented in Figure 7.1. How quickly that cash flows and how much cash is tied up in assets will dictate the cash requirements of the business.

Cash flow within a business is usually categorized into three different aspects:

- **Operating cash flow**: cash flowing in and out of the business from normal day-to-day operations such as receipts from sales and payments for wages, purchases of inventory, utility bills and rent.

- **Investment cash flow**: the flow of cash in and out of the business relating to the purchase and sale of non-current assets.

- **Financing cash flow**: cash inflows from new financing such as new equity or loans and cash outflows from repayment of financing and payment of interest and dividends.

These three aspects of cash flow are all included within Figure 7.1.

Figure 7.1 Cash flows in a typical business

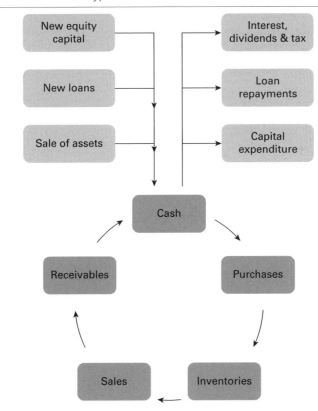

The **cash-flow cycle** (sometimes known as the **cash conversion cycle**) refers to the circular flow of cash shown at the bottom of Figure 7.1. During the normal operations of a business, cash gets tied up in working capital: cash is used to pay for purchases and becomes tied up in inventory. This inventory must be sold and the sales revenue collected from customers before it is converted back into cash. The cash-flow cycle measures the length of time in days that it takes for a business to convert purchases into cash. This is an important metric as it can provide the foundation for establishing how much cash the business needs. The faster cash flows around this cycle, the less is tied up in working capital and therefore the less cash the business needs. Figure 7.2 shows this cycle for a typical business.

Figure 7.2   The cash conversion cycle

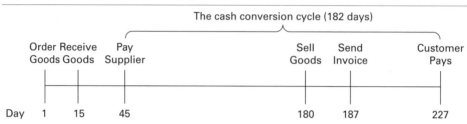

Figure 7.2 shows a timeline of what typically happens within the business from ordering goods in to eventually receiving payment for the sale of those goods to a customer. The goods are ordered in on day 1 but they are not received until day 15. This time lapse between ordering the goods (day 1) and receiving the goods (day 15) is known as **lead time**.

If the business has bought the goods on credit, there will be another time lag between receiving the goods and paying for the supply of them. In Figure 7.2 there is a time lag of 30 days (45 – 15) which is a typical credit period for a supplier. At this point the clock starts ticking on the cash conversion cycle. The business has paid out money for goods which will not be converted back into cash until they are sold and the customer has paid. The cash conversion cycle is therefore the time lapse between paying a supplier and receiving payment from the customer. In Figure 7.2 the supplier is paid on day 45 and the customer pays on day 227. The cash conversion cycle is therefore 182 days (227 – 45).

How much cash does a business need?

The amount of cash which a business chooses to hold will always be a trade-off between costs and benefits. Both holding too much cash and holding too little cash can have a cost to the business. On the one hand, there is a cost to holding cash and so the more cash the business holds the greater the cost. This is usually measured as an **opportunity cost,** that is to say, the return that could have been earned by investing the cash in other assets. On the other hand, there is also a cost to raising cash if it is not available when needed. So if a business holds too little cash, this will also create costs. This will be either the cost of converting assets into cash (by selling them) or the cost of arranging loans.

Cash, unless it is held in a high-interest investment account, represents shareholders' capital that is not being put to work earning a return for the investors. There will therefore be a pressure to reduce the amount of cash the business holds. The lower the cash balances, the lower the amount of capital the business uses to operate. Reducing cash will improve the return on capital employed (ROCE), as demonstrated in Worked Example 7.1.

WORKED EXAMPLE 7.1 Cash balance and ROCE

Quint Co earns a profit before interest and tax of $280,000. The company has total capital of $1,850,000. The current ROCE is therefore:

$$ROCE = \frac{\$280,000}{\$1,850,000} = 15.14\%$$

Included within the capital of $1,850,000 is a cash balance of $300,000. The finance director decides that the company does not need to hold this cash and therefore uses it to repay a loan.

This action will reduce the capital of the business to $1,550,000. This in turn increases the ROCE:

$$ROCE = \frac{\$280,000}{\$1,550,000} = 18.06\%$$

The company is therefore able to increase its financial performance (as indicated by ROCE) without any change in the level of profit simply by reducing its cash balance.

Although Worked Example 7.1 demonstrates that holding too much cash can have a negative impact on the business's financial performance, if the business does not hold sufficient cash it can experience trading problems (such as **overtrading; see Expert view 7.1**) which will also have a negative impact on profitability and shareholder returns. This means that a business is constantly seeking to hold just enough cash to meet its needs, but no more than is necessary. Managing cash is a constant balancing act between having too much cash and not enough.

Extract 7.2: Cash mountain at Microsoft

Microsoft, the US software giant, generates over US $20bn in excess cash every year and consequently is sitting on a mountain of cash. You might think that this is an enviable position to be in, but in fact it is a major headache for the company. This is an unutilized asset that is substantially lowering the ROCE. How does Microsoft deal with this? Large cash balances require large investments to use them up and the most expensive investments are usually acquisitions – buying up other companies. This is why we see Microsoft making a series of high-cost takeovers – Hotmail, Skype, Firefly, CompareNet, Yammer... the list is long. Microsoft has recorded over 150 corporate acquisitions since 1987. They need to in order to use up all that cash.

Expert view 7.1: Cash flow and overtrading

Overtrading is a problem which hits many businesses. It occurs when the business tries to grow too quickly and has insufficient funds to pay the increasing costs which accompany an increase in sales. A growing order book may seem like good news, but it also creates a demand for more cash within the business. Meeting growing levels of sales also requires increases in working capital: more inventory and more money tied up in trade receivables. Extra orders may also mean overtime payments to employees and the purchase of more equipment. A business therefore needs to manage its growth carefully to ensure that it can be funded.

The amount of cash which an individual business needs to hold will depend upon the nature of its operations and the attitudes of its managers. Financial theory categorizes the reasons for holding cash into four 'motives':

- the transaction motive;
- the precautionary motive;
- the speculative motive; and
- the compensating balances motive.

The transaction motive

Any business will need to hold a certain amount of cash in order to pay the day-to-day bills. For most businesses, there will be a gap between receiving cash from sales and needing cash to make payments to employees and for purchases, utilities and equipment. The greater this gap, the more cash the business will need to hold. This cash may be held directly by the business (in cash registers and secure safes) or may be held in non-interest-bearing bank accounts. Some businesses hold a balance of cash in deposit accounts which earns some interest. Because such accounts provide easy access to cash, interest rates are usually low; better returns will be available elsewhere.

The precautionary motive

Most businesses will wish to hold a certain reserve of cash in case of emergencies. This will include unforeseen and unexpected expenses and may be referred to as 'financial slack'. If a business does not have a certain amount of slack in its cash balances, it may have to raise money quickly and in the short term if an unexpected need arises. This could prove to be very costly. Research has shown that although holding precautionary cash balances has a cost, this is less than the cost of having to raise cash at short notice when an emergency arises.

Extract 7.3: Cash holdings and the rise of the precautionary motive

You might expect that the improvements in information and financial systems over recent years have enabled businesses to reduce their cash holdings. In fact, the opposite is true. The average cash to assets ratio of industrial companies in the United States has more than doubled since 1980. Research has identified that this trend correlates with industry risk – ie businesses are holding more cash to protect themselves against riskier cash flows: the precautionary motive. The situation is amplified by the fact that new manufacturing technologies have reduced inventories and receivables, thus tying up less cash in other assets.

The speculative motive

Businesses will also hold cash in order to be able to take advantage of unexpected opportunities such as new investments, changes in interest rates and favourable fluctuations in exchange rates. Good investments may be missed if the business does not have funding readily available. If interest rates are low, businesses will typically maintain higher speculative balances of cash; if interest rates are high, businesses will commit these balances to high-yield investments.

Extract 7.4: ING Direct and Emirates – speculative gains

Businesses that have sufficient cash funds available at the right time are able to benefit from unexpected opportunities. The benefit is often greater if competitors are not in a similar position to take up the opportunity:

At the time of the Icelandic banking crisis, ING Direct snapped up the deposits being offloaded by failing Icelandic banks.

Emirates bought up the new Airbus A380 at a time when other airlines had insufficient funds due to the industry downturn after 11 September 2001. This gave Emirates a competitive advantage as the A380 had greater range, passenger capacity and fuel economy than the planes being used by competitors.

The compensating balances motive

Most businesses that maintain current accounts with commercial banks are required to maintain a minimum balance in their account. This minimum balance, referred to as the compensating balance, is to compensate the bank for the services they provide and essentially provides the bank with free use of the business's money. If such a balance is not maintained, higher fees are normally imposed by the bank.

Methods of establishing cash balances

A number of models have been developed to assist managers in establishing appropriate cash levels. In this chapter we will look at the two most popular and widely used models: the Baumol–Tobin model and the Miller–Orr model. Each model takes a very different approach to establishing the cash balance that a business should hold.

The Baumol–Tobin model of cash management

The Baumol–Tobin model is a transaction-based model which assumes that a business's demand for cash is consistent over time and can be predicted with certainty. As a business uses its available cash it will need to convert investments into cash by selling them. This will incur transaction costs and therefore there is an incentive to minimize the number of such sales. However, if large quantities of cash are converted

Figure 7.3 The cost of holding cash

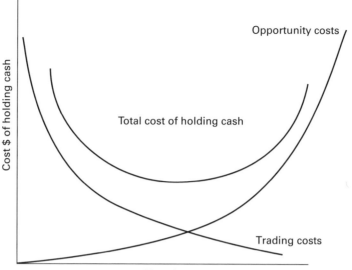

each time, there will be a high opportunity cost of lost interest because of holding cash balances rather than investments. The model therefore attempts to establish optimum cash balances by determining the amount of cash that should be converted from investments each time cash is required.

The Baumol–Tobin model therefore attempts to establish optimum cash balances by quantifying the trade-off between the opportunity costs of holding too much cash and the transaction costs involved in holding too little cash. This trade-off can be represented diagrammatically as shown in Figure 7.3.

The opportunity costs represent the interest forgone by holding funds as cash rather than placing them in an investment. These costs rise with the size of the cash balance.

The trading costs represent the costs of having to raise cash in the short term either by liquidating assets or by taking out a loan. The lower the size of the cash balance, the higher these trading costs will be.

If frequent small conversions to cash are made, average cash balances will be low and opportunity costs minimized, but trading costs will be high owing to the high frequency of transactions. See Figure 7.4.

On the other hand, if large quantities of investments are converted to cash, trading costs will be minimized but average cash balances and therefore opportunity costs will be high. See Figure 7.5.

Using the Baumol–Tobin model, the business attempts to minimize the total costs of holding cash, which will be made up of both trading costs and opportunity costs. Thus, the optimal cash balance (ie that which has the lowest total cost to the business) is found where the opportunity cost equals the trading cost (see Figure 7.3).

Figure 7.4   Frequent cash conversions

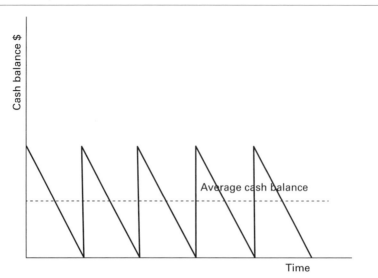

Figure 7.5   Infrequent cash conversions

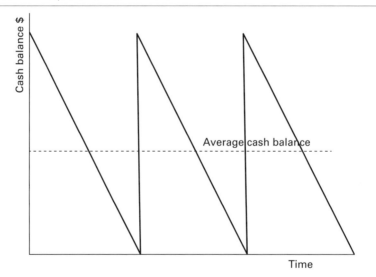

The Baumol–Tobin model determines the optimum quantity of cash to convert each time cash is required. This quantity is represented mathematically by the expression:

$$C = \sqrt{\frac{2TF}{K}}$$

Where: C = the optimal cash order quantity
T = the total amount of cash needed in a period
F = the cost of selling assets to raise cash
K = the opportunity cost of holding cash (the interest rate)

WORKED EXAMPLE 7.2 The Baumol–Tobin model

The following information relates to Ergin Co: the fixed cost of selling assets to raise cash is $500; cash outflows exceed cash inflows by $9,000 per week; the interest rate earned on marketable securities is 5 per cent.
    What is the optimum cash balance for Ergin Co?

Answer
Using the Baumol–Tobin model:

$$C = \sqrt{\frac{2TF}{K}} = \sqrt{\frac{2 \times \$9,000 \times \$500}{5\%}} = \$13,416$$

So when the Ergin Co requires cash, it should convert $13,416. This means that the average cash balance carried by the business will be approximately $6,708 (13,416 ÷ 2).

The Baumol–Tobin model suggests that when interest rates are high, cash balances should be kept to a minimum. However, the model is based upon a number of assumptions, which reduces its usefulness in complex real-world situations. The model assumes that:

- Cash outflows are predictable and even over time.
- Cash inflows are predictable and regular.
- Day-to-day cash needs are funded from a bank current account.
- A 'buffer' of short-term investments is held which can be liquidated to provide cash when needed.

In practice these assumptions do not hold true for most businesses. In particular, cash inflows and outflows are not even and regular and can be difficult to predict. Therefore a more useful model for cash management is one which allows for irregularity and fluctuations in cash flows. One such model is the Miller–Orr model.

The Miller–Orr model of cash management

The Miller–Orr model provides a method of cash management for businesses that do not have uniform cash flow and therefore find it difficult to predict levels and timing of cash inflows and outflows. The model allows for daily variations in the cash balance within prescribed control limits known as the **upper limit** and the **lower limit**.

The model is applied by firstly deciding upon a minimum acceptable cash balance (the lower limit). This is set by management and will be used to establish a buffer of cash for emergencies. The lower limit will depend upon how much risk of a cash shortfall management are willing to accept. This in turn will depend upon the consequences (and costs) of experiencing a cash shortfall together with how quickly and easily the business can access additional funds.

Having established this minimum cash balance, the Miller–Orr model can be used to establish a maximum cash balance (the upper limit) and a **return point**. The return point represents the optimum cash balance. Cash is then managed as follows:

> If cash levels reach the upper limit, an amount is transferred into investments in order to bring the cash balance back down to the return point.

> If cash levels drop to the minimum level, an amount is converted from investments into cash to bring the cash balance back up to the return point.

This principle is demonstrated in the diagram in Figure 7.6. The difference between the upper limit and the lower limit is known as the **spread**. This is calculated using the formula shown in Figure 7.7.

Figure 7.6   Cash limits

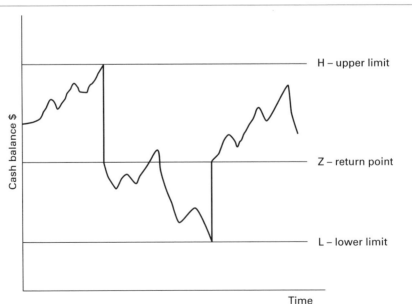

Figure 7.7   The spread formula

$$\text{Spread} = 3 \left[\frac{\frac{3}{4} \times \text{transaction costs} \times \text{variance of cash flows}}{\text{Interest rate}} \right]^{1/3}$$

In the figure:

- The transaction costs represent the cost of converting short-term investments into cash or vice versa.

- The variance of cash flows is a measure of the fluctuation in the cash flows and therefore cash balances. The assumption underlying the Miller–Orr model is that although cash balances can fluctuate randomly, these fluctuations are normally distributed. It is therefore possible to calculate a mean balance and standard deviation of cash balances based upon past data (Variance = Standard deviation^2).

- The interest rate represents the return that can be earned by converting cash into marketable securities or other similar investments.

Both the variance and interest rates should be expressed in daily terms.

Once the spread is calculated, the return point can be found using the following formula:

$$\text{Return point} = \text{Lower limit} + (1/3 \times \text{spread})$$

We will now see how this model is applied using a simple illustration in Worked Example 7.3.

WORKED EXAMPLE 7.3   The Miller–Orr model

Zetoc Co sets its minimum cash balance at $5,000 and estimates the following:

- Transaction costs = $500 per sale or purchase of short-term investment.

- Standard deviation of cash flows = $1,200 per day (therefore variance = $1.44m per day).

- Interest rate = 7.3 per cent per year (= 0.02 per cent per day).

Given the lower limit of $5,000, what upper limit and return point should Zetoc Co set for its cash management?

Answer
Using the formulae above:

$$\text{Spread} = 3[(3/4 \times \$500 \times \$1.44m) \div 0.02\%]^{1/3} = \$41,774$$

Therefore the upper limit = $5,000 + $41,774 = $46,774
And the return point = $5,000 + (1/3 × $41,774) = $18,925

This means that Zetoc Co should try to maintain its cash balance at around $18,925 (in practice this will probably be rounded to $19,000 or even $20,000 for convenience).

If the cash balance rises as high as $46,774, the company should transfer $27,849 ($46,774 – $18,925) from the bank account into short-term investments in order to bring the balance back down to $18,925. On the other hand, if the cash balance falls as low as $5,000, the company should convert $13,925 ($18,925 – $5,000) of short-term investments back into cash to bring the balance up to $18,925.

Discussion point

Create a list of businesses that you know and decide which cash management model would be the most appropriate for each (ie, is the business's cash flow predictable or unpredictable?).

Exercises: now attempt Exercise 7.1 on page 277

Cash forecasting: the cash budget

A business needs to produce a cash budget alongside the budgeted income statement and balance sheet in order to ensure that the business holds sufficient cash to achieve the targets set within the operational budget. A cash budget (sometimes referred to as a **cash-flow forecast**) shows the amount and timing of cash receipts and cash payments. In doing so, it also predicts the amount of cash the business will need.

A cash budget may be produced on a daily, weekly or monthly basis dependent upon the volatility of cash flows of the business and the need for level of detail. In this section we will show you how the cash budget is a useful tool for planning the business's future cash needs and how it can be used to inform management strategies.

The format and construction of a cash budget

Cash-flow planning is central to good cash management. It is therefore important that managers are able to produce and understand cash budgets. The following example demonstrates how to produce a simple cash budget for a business.

WORKED EXAMPLE 7.4 A simple cash budget

Pascal starts a furniture-making business. Budgeted sales and purchases for the first six months of his business are:

	Jan $	Feb $	Mar $	Apr $	May $	Jun $
Sales	5,000	6,000	6,500	7,000	6,000	7,000
Purchases	4,000	6,000	4,000	4,000	3,500	4,000

1 Pascal anticipates that 50 per cent of his sales will be for cash and 50 per cent on credit terms of one month.

2 Inventory will be kept very low and bought in the month it is sold. Inventory is paid for with cash as it is bought.

3 Workshop rent is $1,200 per month, paid on the first day of each month.

4 Pascal has a van. This costs $400 per month. Pascal pays all van costs in cash.

5 Pascal starts the business with an opening bank balance of $5,000.

Required:
Prepare a cash budget for the first six months of Pascal's business.

Answer:
There are a number of logical steps in producing a cash budget:

• Forecast sales.

• Forecast cash receipts from sales.

• Forecast cash payments.

• Estimate end-of-period cash balances.

In this simple example we will show you how to carry out each of the steps and to compile the information into a cash budget.

Forecast sales

When preparing a cash budget it is necessary to determine cash receipts in two steps. Firstly, a budget must be established for sales. In the second step this sales forecast is translated into a cash receipts forecast. The reason for these two steps is that the cash budget is concerned with the timing of cash receipts and sales do not necessarily translate directly into cash, particularly if sales are made on credit.

Worked Example 7.4 is relatively straightforward and we are given predicted sales figures. In practice, these would have to be established based upon market research, known contracts or past trends. A variety of statistical and mathematical techniques may be used in forecasting sales.

	Jan	Feb	Mar	Apr	May	Jun
	$	$	$	$	$	$
Sales	5,000	6,000	6,500	7,000	6,000	7,000

For many businesses the pattern of sales is not even throughout the year, but rather is seasonal. For example, 40 per cent of toy sales occur in the six weeks before Christmas. Accurately establishing this pattern can be extremely important for cash-flow planning.

Discussion point

List six business types that you think will have seasonal fluctuations in their sales. Explain why their sales will fluctuate.

Forecast cash receipts from sales

Once a sales forecast has been prepared, it is necessary to determine when those sales will be collected as cash receipts. If sales are made on credit, there will be a delay between the point of sale and the point of cash receipt.

In Worked Example 7.4 Pascal predicts that 50 per cent of his sales will be for cash and 50 per cent on one month's credit. Based upon this prediction we can establish when cash from sales will be received. For the purposes of this exercise we will assume that cash from cash sales is received immediately and that cash from credit sales is received in the following month. In practice, all customers may not pay on time and some cash receipts may be even later. However, we will keep it simple for this example.

In the table below, the forecast sales for each month are split so that 50 per cent of the money is received in that month (the cash sales) and 50 per cent is received in the following month (the credit sales). For example, January's forecast sales of $5,000 will be received in cash as $2,500 in January and $2,500 in February.

	Jan	Feb	Mar	Apr	May	Jun
	$	$	$	$	$	$
Sales	5,000	6,000	6,500	7,000	6,000	7,000
Cash sales	2,500	3,000	3,250	3,500	3,000	3,500
Credit sales	0	2,500	3,000	3,250	3,500	3,000
Total receipts	2,500	5,500	6,250	6,750	6,500	6,500

Of course, 50 per cent of the cash from June's sales will be received in July, but as this lies outside our six-month budget period we can ignore this.

Forecast cash payments

Cash payments should be recorded when they are expected to be made. You should start with those payments that are fixed amounts due on known dates, such as loan repayments, interest charges, rent or any other standing payments. Payments to creditors should be scheduled based upon predicted purchase patterns and known credit periods.

In Worked Example 7.4 we are given a schedule of purchases and told that these purchases are made in cash. We are also given information about workshop rent and van running costs. This information can be used to produce a schedule of cash payments as set out below:

Payments:	Jan	Feb	Mar	Apr	May	Jun
	$	$	$	$	$	$
Inventory	4,000	6,000	4,000	4,000	3,500	4,000
Rent	1,200	1,200	1,200	1,200	1,200	1,200
Van	400	400	400	400	400	400
Total	5,600	7,600	5,600	5,600	5,100	5,600

Estimate end-of-period cash balances

Finally, we can combine our cash receipts and cash payments forecasts to establish the net increase or decrease in cash balance each month. This allows us to estimate end-of-period cash balances. In Worked Example 7.4 we are told that the opening cash balance will be $5,000. Using this information we can now create a full cash budget. This is set out in Table 7.1.

Table 7.1 shows the total expected cash receipts and cash payments in each month and the resultant increase or decrease in the cash balance. For example, in January total receipts are $2,500 whereas total payments are $5,600. This will result in a decrease in cash balance of $3,100. As the opening cash balance is $5,000, this means that the closing cash balance will be only $1,900. As $1,900 is the closing cash balance in January, it will also be the opening cash balance for February.

It can be seen from this cash budget that if the projected pattern of cash receipts and payments occurs, Pascal will run out of money by the end of February when the closing cash balance is predicted to be negative $200. This means that either he will have to put in place arrangements to borrow money in February or he will have to change his plans somehow to avoid this negative cash situation. However, we can see from the forecast that this situation is only temporary and by the end of March cash balances should be positive again until the end of the six-month period of the forecast (see the next section for a more detailed discussion of how to improve cash flows).

It is the fact that the cash budget allows us to identify potential problems such as this in advance that makes them so useful. In the next section we will look in more detail at how cash management can be improved by concentrating on the key areas that cause cash problems for businesses.

Table 7.1   Cash budget for Pascal

	Jan $	Feb $	Mar $	Apr $	May $	Jun $
Cash receipts						
Cash sales	2,500	3,000	3,250	3,500	3,000	3,500
Credit sales	0	2,500	3,000	3,250	3,500	3,000
Total receipts	2,500	5,500	6,250	6,750	6,500	6,500
Cash payments						
Inventory	4,000	6,000	4,000	4,000	3,500	4,000
Rent	1,200	1,200	1,200	1,200	1,200	1,200
Van	400	400	400	400	400	400
Total payments	5,600	7,600	5,600	5,600	5,100	5,600
Increase/(Decrease)	(3,100)	(2,100)	650	1,150	1,400	900
Opening balance	5,000	1,900	(200)	450	1,600	3,000
Closing balance	1,900	(200)	450	1,600	3,000	3,900

Exercises: now attempt Exercise 7.2 on page 278

Cash management: strategies for improving cash flow

There are certain key areas that always have the potential to cause cash problems for any organization. Good cash management therefore needs to focus on these four key areas:

- managing accounts receivable;
- managing accounts payable;
- managing inventory;
- strategic financing of assets.

The first three areas in this list are concerned with the amount of money tied up in working capital. Managing these three areas is therefore known as **working capital management**. Good working capital management can substantially reduce the amount of cash a business needs.

The fourth area of asset financing is equally important. Research has shown that one of the greatest growth barriers to businesses is an inability to finance new assets for growth. We will therefore examine different methods of financing assets and how these impact upon cash flows.

Managing accounts receivable

> ### Extract 7.5: The reality of offering credit
>
> Around 90 per cent of businesses that operate in industry or wholesale offer credit to their customers. In addition, around 40 per cent of retail sales are made on credit. This means that accounts receivable are a cash management issue for the vast majority of businesses.

Good management of accounts receivable can substantially reduce the cash needs of a business. On the other hand, poor management of accounts receivable is often a source of cash-flow problems, particularly in small businesses. Effective management of accounts receivable involves four key steps:

- formulating an appropriate credit policy;
- setting credit levels;
- credit control; and
- debt collection.

Credit policy

Cash flow can be improved by offering shorter credit periods to customers and thereby reducing the amount of cash tied up in accounts receivable. The best credit policy from a cash-flow point of view is to offer no credit and trade in cash sales only. That would mean that cash is received as soon as a sale is made. However, in many industries it is common practice to offer credit to customers and a business would not be able to trade if it did not offer credit terms similar to those of competitors.

Many businesses offer early settlement discounts on their invoices to encourage customers to pay earlier. Although this technique can be successful, it is not necessarily financially beneficial to the business. The discount offered must be weighed up against the cost of the outstanding debt, as illustrated in Worked Example 7.5.

WORKED EXAMPLE 7.5 Credit policy and early settlement discounts

Mahmoud Co trades in an industry in which it is usual practice to offer 30 days' credit
on all sales. Analysis of Mahmoud Co's sales ledger reveals that customers on average
actually take 38 days to pay.

The sales director has suggested that the company increase its credit period to
60 days, which he says will make Mahmoud Co more attractive to customers and will
increase sales by 5 per cent. The finance director has suggested that if the credit
period is extended, the company should also offer an early settlement discount of 2 per
cent for payments made within 14 days. He believes that 25 per cent of customers will
take advantage of the early settlement discounts and that this will counterbalance the
extended credit taken by other customers.

The company has annual sales revenue of $5 million and earns a contribution of 40 per
cent on sales. Accounts receivable are financed by an overdraft which has an annual
interest rate of 6 per cent.

Should the company change its credit policy in the way suggested by the sales director
and the finance director?

Answer

The current collection period on accounts receivable is 38 days. This means that the
average balance on accounts receivable is $520,548 ($5m sales × 38/365).

If the new credit policy is implemented, the average collection period will increase
to (25% × 14 days) + (75% × 60 days) = 49 days. Sales will also increase by 5 per cent to
$5.25 million per year. The level of accounts receivable will therefore increase to: $5.25m ×
49/365 = $704,795.

With this increase in outstanding accounts receivable, financing costs will increase
by ($704,795 – $520,548) × 6% = $11,055 per annum. The discount offered to early settlers
will cost $5.25m × 25% × 2% = $26,250. However, from the 5 per cent increase in sales the
company will earn additional contributions of $250,000 × 40% = $100,000.

Therefore, there will be a net financial benefit to the company of $62,695 ($100,000 –
$26,250 – $11,055) by changing the credit policy and offering an early settlement discount.
Mahmoud Co should implement the policy change.

Credit analysis

The second step in good credit management is to set appropriate credit levels for
customers. This involves assessing the creditworthiness of customers and deciding
how much credit you are going to extend to them.

Businesses should make use of credit references and other sources of information. There are a number of banks and other financial service businesses such as Experian or Equifax that provide credit checks and will report on both individual and corporate customers. Businesses should also do some credit checking themselves. They should analyse the accounts of potential new customers for signs of liquidity problems and potential bankruptcy problems.

Assessing creditworthiness is not just a one-off task for new customers. Credit levels should be constantly reviewed and checks frequently made on customers. Sales staff can be very helpful in obtaining information about customers, such as rumours and reputation within the industry. They are also in regular contact with customers and therefore are able to feed back their impressions from dealings with the customers and visits to their premises.

It is frequent practice to extend little or no credit to new customers and to gradually extend credit limits as customers prove their creditworthiness by prompt payment of invoices.

Credit control

Once credit limits have been set, they need to be constantly monitored and controlled. There are two aspects to this task. Firstly, the company must ensure that no customer exceeds their credit limit. Before any new order is accepted the current outstanding balance from the customer should be checked to make sure that the new order does not take the customer over their credit limit. For example, if a customer had a credit limit of $15,000 and currently had outstanding invoices of $12,000, an order worth $4,000 would not be processed until the customer had paid off at least $1,000 of the outstanding balance.

The second aspect of good credit control is ensuring that customers pay on time. One of the most frequently used tools for this task is the **aged debtors report**. This is a report generated from the sales ledger which shows the outstanding balance from each customer broken down by age of the debt. An extract from an aged debtors report is shown in Table 7.2.

Table 7.2 shows an extract from an aged debtors report for a company which offers 30 days' credit to customers. This report enables managers to identify if there are problems with any customers and to initiate action to chase outstanding debts. In the report it can be seen that the first account, Adam Co, has no amounts outstanding outside of the 30-day credit period. However, Benson Co and Cantor Co both have outstanding invoices which have not been paid within the credit period.

Benson Co has an outstanding balance of $27,613.59, all of which is more than 60 days old. This would suggest that there is a problem with this customer. No further credit sales should be made to the customer and action should be taken to recover the outstanding balance.

Extract 7.6: The cost of unpaid invoices

Analysis published in 2018 by Bacs (the company that transfers money between banks) suggests that late payment of invoices costs the world's economy almost £250 billion every year. This restricts business growth and leads to an estimated 50,000 small and medium-sized businesses closing each year. Although all businesses can suffer as a result of slow payment, smaller businesses are the hardest hit. Statistics reveal that 43% of small and medium-sized businesses suffer late payment, and the average cost of recovering overdue money is £9,000 per year.

Table 7.2   Aged debtors report

Customer	Total	<30 days	30–60 days	60–90 days	>90 days
	$	$	$	$	$
Adam Co	15,981.81	15,981.81	–	–	–
Benson Co	27,613.59	–	–	18,279.03	9,334.56
Cantor Co	18,516.37	17,935.70		580.67	–

Cantor Co appears to be paying invoices within the credit period, with the exception of one small invoice for $580.67. This might suggest that there is a dispute on the invoice. This needs to be investigated and resolved.

Debt collection

Even with a good credit policy in place and frequent credit checks on customers, it is necessary to ensure that debts are collected promptly. The longer a debt is outstanding, the greater the likelihood that the customer will never pay and the business will incur a **bad debt**.

To ensure prompt payment, invoices should be sent promptly. Ideally, invoices should be sent as soon as goods are shipped. If an account becomes overdue an action should be taken immediately. There is a series of escalating follow-up actions which can be taken if an invoice is not paid on time:

- Send the customer a statement of their account which highlights overdue balances and late payment penalties.
- Telephone the customer to ask for payment.
- Send a formal letter to the customer reminding them that payment is overdue and late payment penalties will be incurred.

- Visit the customer in person (this will usually be done by a member of the sales department) to discuss the outstanding balance and secure payment.
- Send a solicitor's letter threatening legal action if the balance is not paid.
- Hand the debt over to a debt collection agency that will enforce payment on behalf of the company.

If the customer is consistently failing to pay invoices on time, the business should restrict credit to that customer until all outstanding bills are cleared.

Invoice discounting and debt factoring

Even if a business follows all of the steps above for good credit management it may still find itself having a large amount of money tied up in accounts receivable. For example, if the business operates in an industry in which it is necessary to offer credit to customers, it may not be able to avoid having large balances of accounts receivable. If this is the case, there are some ways in which the business can free up this cash.

One such method is **invoice discounting**. This involves using accounts receivable as collateral against borrowing from a finance company. The finance company will typically lend up to 80 per cent of the value of outstanding sales invoices. As invoices are paid and new ones are issued, the amount of borrowing available will be adjusted to maintain that fixed percentage. Interest will be charged on the amount borrowed and usually the finance company also charges a monthly service fee.

In order for invoice discounting to work, the finance company must be confident of the creditworthiness of customers. Borrowing available is rarely greater than 80 per cent of total outstanding invoices as this provides the finance company with a margin for bad debts. Also, a finance company may refuse to lend against certain invoices if it feels that they represent a high risk. As security, the finance company providing the loan will take a **floating charge** over the accounts receivable of the business.

Expert view 7.2: Fixed and floating charges

Anyone lending money to a company will want some security against that loan. It is therefore usual to take a charge against an asset of the company. For example, a lender may take a charge against one of the business's buildings. In the event of default on the loan the lender has the legal right to seize the asset, sell it and recoup the amount they are owed. If this charge is against a clearly identified asset, it is known as a fixed charge. However, in the case of some assets such as accounts receivable it will be difficult to fix the charge against any one asset as individual invoices are constantly being raised and paid off. In this case the lender will raise a floating charge over the class of assets in general.

Invoice discounting can prove to be a very effective and flexible means of raising extra cash for a business that has no other options. The business will only pay interest on the amount it borrows, which will not necessarily be the full amount available. The system essentially works rather like an overdraft but it is usually more expensive than a bank loan or overdraft and therefore would only be used if these were not available.

Another method of releasing cash from the sales ledger is **debt factoring.** Unlike invoice discounting, which is borrowing against the value of accounts receivable, debt factoring involves actually selling sales invoices on to a third party called a factor. Some banks offer factoring services or the factor may be a specialist financial company. If an invoice is sold to a factor a cash advance (typically around 80 per cent of the invoice value) is made immediately. The balance of the invoice value less the factor's fee is then paid upon settlement of the invoice by the business's customer. The factor may or may not take on the risk of bad debts. Usually this is an optional extra which carries an increased fee.

The debt-factoring company may also take on responsibility for managing the sales ledger and chasing and collecting unpaid sales invoices. Although there is obviously an additional cost of this service, it can be beneficial as a form of outsourcing; as the factor has expertise in this task it can reduce bad debts, speed up debt collection and free management time to concentrate on core activities.

A related but less frequent method of raising cash against accounts receivable is **forfaiting.** This is sometimes used by exporting businesses and involves selling individual export sales invoices using a method similar to debt factoring.

Exercises: now attempt Exercise 7.3 on page 278

Managing accounts payable

Just as a business needs to collect its accounts receivable as soon as possible in order to improve its cash flow, it can also improve cash flow by paying creditors as late as possible. The ultimate cash-flow position for a business is to buy on credit and sell for cash, such that cash is received from customers before payments must be made to suppliers. In this way, sales finance purchases. Unfortunately, for most businesses this is not the case and so extra cash is needed to 'buffer' the timing difference between converting accounts receivable to cash and having to pay creditors.

The longer the cash conversion cycle (the time gap between collecting accounts receivable and paying creditors), the more cash the business will need. Therefore, good management of accounts payable can involve extending credit periods as far as possible. In the first instance, the business should seek to get favourable credit terms from its suppliers. It should then carefully manage its payments to stretch these credit terms as far as practicable. However, the business should always take care against stretching it too far as it could result in the supplier suspending the account. This could disrupt trading and also result in poor credit ratings which cause the business difficulty in setting up accounts with new suppliers.

If suppliers offer discounts for early payment, the business needs to balance the advantage of reduced purchase costs against the cost of having to make the payment earlier.

Good management of accounts payable also involves ensuring that only valid invoices are paid. It is therefore important that the business has in place a good system of **internal controls** to check physical receipts of inventory against invoices and to note any omissions or damage.

WORKED EXAMPLE 7.6 Should you take a cash discount?

Red Co purchases supplies at a cost of $5,000. The supplier's standard credit terms are 30 days, but the supplier offers a 2 per cent discount if the invoice is paid within 10 days. Red Co has an overdraft which incurs an interest charge of 0.05 per cent per day.

Should Red Co take the early payment discount?

Answer

If Red Co takes the early payment discount it will save $100 on its purchases. However, it will also incur higher interest charges on the overdraft as follows:

$$\$4{,}900 \times 20 \text{ days} \times 0.05\% = \$49$$

As the early payment discount outweighs the additional overdraft interest charges, Red Co should make the early payment. It will be $51 ($100 − $49) better off by doing so.

Managing inventory

Holding inventory can be very expensive, particularly if the goods held are of high value or large quantities are involved. This can mean a substantial amount of cash tied up in inventory. So why do businesses carry inventory? In practice, there are a number of reasons:

- Inventory of finished goods may be held as a buffer where there is fluctuation and uncertainty in patterns of demand. If it is difficult to predict patterns of demand, a high level of inventory will be necessary to ensure that inventory does not run out at those times when demand is high. Some businesses with seasonal sales (such as firework manufacturers) will carry high levels of inventory throughout much of the year because they will be producing throughout the year for sales over a very short period.

- Running out of inventory may carry a cost to the business. If no inventory is available customers will buy from a competitor. This could mean not only a lost sale but also a lost customer.

- Some businesses manufacture in batches, such that they will produce a large quantity of one item and then retool the production system to run a batch of another inventory item. This method of operating may be necessary to achieve economies of scale through large runs of production or it may be a requirement of the manufacturing process. In either case, it will result in the business carrying inventory to ensure that all items are available even when they are not being produced.

- A business may purchase large quantities of raw materials at a time in order to take advantage of bulk discounts. This will result in the business carrying inventory.

- Most retailing businesses need to carry sufficient inventory for the shop to look full in order to be attractive to customers.

The amount of inventory carried needs to be just right – not too much and not too little, as each carries a cost to the business.

The costs of carrying too much inventory include:

- the opportunity cost of having money tied up in inventory;
- higher storage costs;
- increased handling and insurance costs;
- increased costs of inventory deterioration, obsolescence and theft.

On the other hand, the costs of carrying too little inventory include:

- the cost of unfulfilled orders;
- the cost of lost customers;
- idle machines and employees if raw material inventory runs out.

Inventory management

Good inventory management is a matter of minimizing the costs associated with holding inventory, whether they be the costs of holding too much or the costs of holding too little inventory. There are many inventory control models which tell a business how much inventory to order and when to order it in order to minimize costs. In this chapter we will look at four approaches to inventory management:

- the inventory turnover ratio;

- inventory reorder levels;

- ABC inventory management;

- the economic order quantity model;

- just-in-time inventory management.

The inventory turnover ratio

The most common method of analysing and assessing inventory levels is to use the inventory turnover ratio. This ratio shows a business how many days' worth of inventory it is holding on average throughout the year. It is expressed by the following formula:

$$\text{Inventory holding (in days)} = \frac{\text{Average inventory}}{\text{Cost of sales}} \times 36.5$$

Inventory can be measured against sales turnover, but it is better to use cost of sales because inventory is recorded at cost and therefore you are comparing like with like. Also, it is possible to use the end-of-year inventory balance but if inventory levels change seasonally, using an average balance is a more accurate measure.

The inventory turnover ratio can be useful for benchmarking the level of inventory the business holds in two ways:

Firstly, inventory holdings can be analysed over time to see if the inventory levels are changing in relation to the level of sales (as reflected in cost of sales). If inventory days are increasing, this may suggest unnecessary stockpiling or it may reveal that the business is holding obsolete and unsaleable inventory. If inventory levels are falling over time, this may reflect more efficient inventory management or it could be a result of inefficient management which may result in stockouts and lost sales.

Secondly, the ratio enables comparison with industry rivals. If the business finds that it is holding inventory for longer than its competitors, it should be concerned that it is not operating as efficiently as it could in its inventory management. Too much cash is being tied up in inventory and this has a cost for the business.

WORKED EXAMPLE 7.7 Comparing inventory turnover

The following data are being extracted from the most recent financial statements of Ant Co and its two main competitors, Ben Co and Crab Co:

	Ant Co	Ben Co	Crab Co
	$m	$m	$m
Cost of sales	140.0	50.2	300.8
Opening inventory	17.5	4.2	21.8
Closing inventory	19.1	4.6	23.2

Using these data, the respective inventory turnover ratios can be calculated:

Ant Co:

Average inventory = (17.5 + 19.1)/2 = 18.3

Inventory turnover = (18.3 ÷ 140.0) × 365 = 48 days

Ben Co:

Average inventory = (4.2 + 4.6)/2 = 4.4

Inventory turnover = (4.4 ÷ 50.2) × 365 = 32 days

Crab Co:

Average inventory = (21.8 + 23.2)/2 = 22.5

Inventory turnover = (22.5 ÷ 300.8) × 365 = 27 days

This analysis shows that Ant Co is holding its inventory for considerably longer than its competitors. This would suggest that it is carrying too much inventory and needs to adjust its inventory management policy.

Lead time and buffer stock

If a business uses inventory in a fairly regular and consistent manner, its inventory levels will look like the graph in Figure 7.8.

Figure 7.8 Inventory reorder level

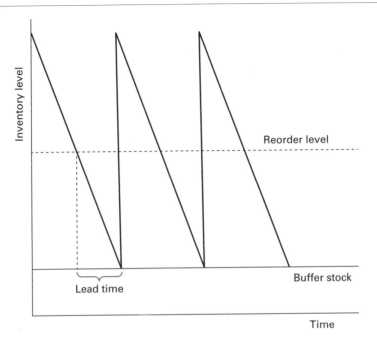

The business will manage its inventory level in the following manner:

- Firstly, it will establish a **buffer stock** (also known as safety stock or buffer inventory) which represents the minimum inventory it wishes to carry. This is an insurance against stockouts and the disruption which they would cause.

- Secondly, the business needs to calculate the **lead time** on receiving new inventory. This is the time delay between placing an order and actually receiving delivery of the inventory.

- Using this information, the business can work backwards from the buffer stock level, using the lead time, to establish the level of inventory at which a new order should be placed – the **reorder level**. As inventory falls to this level the inventory management system should trigger an order to the supplier.

Many businesses use a computerized inventory control system which is linked to the ordering system and in some cases also linked to the supplier's sales and stock dispatch systems so that the whole process is automated. This automation can substantially reduce the lead time on inventory delivery and consequentially reduce the quantity of inventory that the business needs to carry. When taken to the extreme, this results in just-in-time inventory management (see below).

Economic order quantity (EOQ) model

The EOQ model is an approach to inventory management which attempts to minimize the costs of holding inventory. The model recognizes that there are two opposing sets of costs which need to be balanced and attempts to do so by calculating the optimum quantity of inventory to order at any one time:

- If large quantities of inventory are ordered at a time, the business will incur higher costs in storage and handling; there will be a higher cost of inventory obsolescence, damage or loss; and the opportunity cost of having cash tied up in inventory will be greater.

- If small quantities of inventory are ordered each time, orders will need to be placed more frequently and levels monitored more closely. This will increase order costs.

Figure 7.9 illustrates how these opposing sets of costs lead to a total cost of stock-holding which has an optimum (ie minimum) cost when storage costs = order costs.

Figure 7.9   The economic order quantity

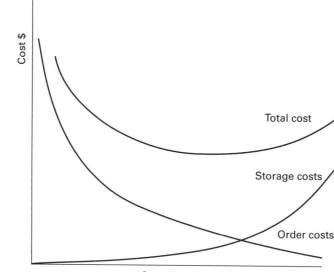

This relationship can be expressed with the following formula:

$$EOQ = \sqrt{\frac{2C_O D}{C_H}}$$

Where: C_H is the cost of holding one unit of stock for one year
C_O is the cost of ordering a consignment of stock
D is the annual demand

Therefore, when using the EOQ model, the amount of inventory held by the business will be dictated by the most economic quantity to order. This will be the quantity which minimizes the total cost of holding inventory. The method is illustrated in Worked Example 7.8.

WORKED EXAMPLE 7.8 Optimizing inventory order levels

The management of Pantar Co wishes to minimize the business's inventory costs. The company accountant has identified the following costs and figures in relation to inventory item P31:

- Annual demand for P31 is 80,000 units.
- P31 costs $3.00 per unit.
- Inventory management costs for P31 are:
  - Ordering cost: $15.00 per order
  - Holding cost: $2 per unit per year.

Required:
Calculate the total cost of inventory for P31 if Pantar Co applies the EOQ.

Answer
The EOQ for P31 will be:

$$= \sqrt{(2 \times 15 \times 80,000)/2} = 1,095 \text{ units}$$

Therefore, the number of orders placed in a year will be:

$$= 80,000/1,095 = 73 \text{ orders per year}$$

The annual ordering cost:

$$= 73 \times \$15 = \$1,095 \text{ per year}$$

The average inventory of P31 held by Pantar Co will be:

$$= 1,095/2 = 547.5 \text{ units}$$

The annual holding cost:

$$= 547.5 \times \$2 = \$1,095 \text{ per year}$$

(Note that the annual ordering cost = annual holding cost at the optimum level as illustrated in Figure 7.9.)

Inventory purchase cost:

$$= 80,000 \times \$3 = \$240,000$$

Total cost of inventory with EOQ policy:

$$= \$240,000 + \$1,095 + \$1,095 = \$242,190 \text{ per year}$$

ABC inventory management

ABC inventory analysis is a method of prioritizing different inventory lines in order to focus management attention on the most critical areas of inventory. It employs the **Pareto Principle** – the principle that 80 per cent of overall revenue is based upon only 20 per cent of inventory items. This means that not all inventory lines are equally important. Efficient management means focusing on the most important lines and less on other areas of inventory. For this reason the technique is also sometimes known as **selective inventory control**.

When applying the ABC approach all inventory is evaluated and divided into three categories – A, B or C – as illustrated in Table 7.3.

- Category A contains inventory that is most important to the business. The category usually contains items that are carried in relatively low quantities but have a high individual value. This inventory needs a high degree of attention. The business has a lot of money tied up in the inventory but it carries low quantities and so could easily run out. The usage of this category of inventory needs careful forecasting and the level should be closely monitored.

- Category B inventory needs less sophisticated management than category A. This is an intermediate category between A and C.

- Category C contains inventory that has low value but is carried in high volumes. This requires much less close management than category A. The business can apply the simplest control possible to this area of inventory.

Table 7.3 ABC inventory analysis

Category	Inventory quantity (%)	Inventory value (%)
A	12	72
B	28	18
C	60	10
Total	**100**	**100**

Expert view 7.3: ERP and ABC analysis

Many businesses operate enterprise resource planning (ERP) systems. These are integrated computer software modules which support the different process areas of the business. This can include financial accounting, management accounting, customer relationship management, project management, supply chain management, manufacturing processes and human resource management. **ABC inventory analysis** is usually built into these systems.

Just-in-time (JIT) inventory management

JIT is an approach to inventory management that has gained popularity in recent years as part of a broader **lean manufacturing** approach. It is usually integrated into a materials requirement planning (MRP) system.

Expert view 7.4: Lean manufacturing

Lean manufacturing is a management philosophy which was developed within the Japanese manufacturing company Toyota. The focus of lean manufacturing is to ensure that any expenditure results in the creation of value for the end customer. Any activity or expenditure which does not add value is seen as wasteful and therefore a target for elimination. The approach involves removing unnecessary processes and material movements, streamlining systems to remove idle time or unnecessary delays, and reducing inventory levels.

As with the other inventory management techniques we have already examined, the aim of JIT is to minimize inventory costs. However, the JIT approach focuses primarily on minimizing inventory holding costs through efficient monitoring of inventory usage and placing orders so that they arrive only when needed. The goal is to mini-mize the amount of cash tied up in inventory, thereby improving ROCE.

Successful operation of a JIT inventory system requires good forecasting of production requirements, short and predictable lead times, and good coordination with suppliers. Good communication both up and down the supply chain is criti-cal. Implementing JIT inventory management often involves integrating information systems with suppliers, and good communication is critical. Although many busi-nesses have successfully implemented JIT and have increased efficiency and cost savings as a result, it is important to recognize that the system also has drawbacks. By removing buffer stock the business has no emergency fallback in case of disrup-tion in the supply chain.

Advantages of JIT:

- A JIT system eliminates the cost of holding inventory.
- Inventory obsolescence is avoided.
- Cash is freed up for investment in other activities.
- Warehouse space can be freed up for other value-adding activities.
- Production can be more flexible and responsive to customer requirements.

Disadvantages of JIT:

- There is no 'buffer stock' so late delivery of inventory will cause disruption in production.
- The business becomes vulnerable to disruptions in the supply chain caused by labour strikes, transportation problems or information system problems.
- It is more difficult to respond to unexpected fluctuations in demand.

Extract 7.7: JIT at Dell Computers

Dell, a leading supplier of personal computers, revolutionized the industry by using JIT systems. Dell takes orders directly from a customer and builds computers to that customer's order, an approach to production which is known as a **pull system**. The company keeps only five days of inventory on hand, which compares with competitors who have up to 90 days of inventory.

This approach has given Dell a competitive advantage over its rivals which enabled it to become the market leader in personal computers. The reduced time to market enables Dell to keep up to date with technological advancements so that customers are always offered the latest-specification computers. Dell has achieved this by integrating the entire value chain from delivery and sales back to design and development.

Exercises: now attempt Exercise 7.4 on page 279

The financing of asset purchases

One of the greatest cash demands for businesses is the purchase of new assets such as machinery, equipment or vehicles. Research has shown that the inability to finance the purchase of new assets is one of the greatest barriers to growth for businesses.

If a business does not have the cash available to purchase new assets, it will need to raise more cash by issuing new shares or by taking on a new loan. However, if the business is not able to raise cash by these means, there are alternative methods of financing the purchase of new assets which reduce the demands on cash flow.

One alternative method of financing assets is to use a hire purchase (HP) agreement. This is a legal contract through which the purchases are made through a series of payments over time. In reality the purchaser is hiring the asset and making a series of (typically monthly) rental payments. Once these rental payments equal the cash purchase price plus an agreed interest charge, ownership of the asset passes to the purchaser. If the purchaser defaults on the rental instalments, the owner may repossess the asset. The main advantage of an HP agreement is that it removes the need to have the purchase price in cash up front. The purchaser is able to spread the cost of the asset over time through a series of payments.

Another method of financing the purchase of new assets is to lease those assets rather than purchase them. There are two types of lease which a business could enter into: a finance lease or an operating lease.

A lease is a contractual arrangement through which a party owning an asset (the lessor) gives use of that asset to a second party (the lessee) in return for a series of rental payments. Ownership of the asset remains with the lessor.

A finance lease is usually defined as one in which the risks and rewards of ownership of the leased asset are transferred to the lessee but not the actual ownership. The lease term is all or most of the life of the asset. The total rental payments throughout the lease period add up to the cash price of the asset plus a finance charge. Responsibility for repair and maintenance of the asset may remain with the lessor, but often this becomes the responsibility of the lessee. In many cases, ownership of the asset is transferred to the lessee at the end of the lease term.

An operating lease is one in which the lease term is short in comparison to the life of the asset. Operating leases are commonly used to acquire equipment or vehicles for short-term use. For example, if you went on holiday and leased a car for a week, that would be an operating lease. Under an operating lease the lessor remains responsible for maintenance and repair of the asset, which can be an advantage for the lessee. However, this will be reflected in the lease cost. If an asset is required infrequently for short periods, using an operating lease can be a smart way of easing cash flows, as it removes the need to tie up valuable cash in an infrequently used asset. On the other hand, it can be an expensive option if the asset is leased too frequently.

The decision of whether to enter into a finance lease or an operating lease will obviously depend upon an assessment of how long an asset is required and how frequently it will be used. A finance lease is essentially an alternative means of financing the acquisition of an asset. On the other hand, an operating lease is a means of acquiring the use of an asset for short periods of time without having to tie up cash in the purchase of that asset.

There are also tax and accounting disclosure implications for businesses deciding between hire purchase, finance leasing and operating leasing. These may have an impact on the finance method chosen.

Interpreting and analysing a cash-flow forecast

Now that you have learnt how to produce a simple cash-flow forecast, we will look at a more complex example and learn how to analyse and interpret it. Within larger organizations it will usually be the case that cash-flow forecasts are produced by the accounting department. As a manager you will be using that forecast to make both operational and strategic decisions.

Expert view 7.5: Cash-flow forecasting

Large organizations usually have a specialist division within the accounting department that is dedicated to cash planning and cash-flow forecasting. This is usually known as the **treasury department**.

Worked Example 7.9 sets out a cash-flow forecast for the start-up of a new business. We will take a detailed look at this forecast and identify any potential problems which may be looming for the business. We will also identify any changes to business plans that could be recommended in order to improve the business's cash flow and cash position.

WORKED EXAMPLE 7.9 Cash-flow analysis

Jill has recently been made redundant from her job as a designer. She has decided to use her redundancy money to realize her dream of starting a business which manufactures and sells high-quality greenhouses. In order to start the business Jill has applied for a business start-up loan from the bank. The bank requires a business plan, which includes a cash-flow forecast. Jill has prepared the cash budget for the first six months of the business (Table 7.4).

In relation to the cash budget, Jill has provided you with the following information:

1   The business will commence on 1 June with $55,000 in the bank. $30,000 of this will come from Jill's redundancy money. The remaining $25,000 will come from a business start-up loan.

2   Jill will rent a workshop unit on an industrial estate. This will cost $900 per month, payable at the start of each month.

3   A van will be bought in June at a cost of $12,000.

4   General workshop costs (light, heat, power etc) and the van's running costs are expected to be $400 per month.

Table 7.4

	June $	July $	Aug $	Sept $	Oct $	Nov
Receipts						
Sales	0	0	40,000	60,000	60,000	80,000
Payments		0				
Materials	0	30,000	20,000	20,000	35,000	50,000
Wages	3,500	3,500	3,500	4,200	4,200	4,200
Drawings	1,750	1,750	1,750	1,750	1,750	1,750
Workshop	900	900	900	900	900	900
Advertising	8,000	1,000	1,000			
General	400	400	400	400	400	400
Van	12,000					
Land Rover	450	450	450	450	450	450
Equipment	12,000		25,000			
Loan		1,200	1,200	1,200	1,200	1,200
	39,000	39,200	54,200	28,900	43,900	58,900
Increase/(Decrease)	(39,000)	(39,200)	(14,200)	31,100	16,100	21,100
Opening Balance	55,000	16,000	(23,200)	(37,400)	(6,300)	9,800
Closing Balance	16,000	(23,200)	(37,400)	(6,300)	9,800	30,900

5   Jill will also lease a Land Rover Discovery car starting in June. The monthly lease payments will be $450, payable on the 10th of each month.

6   The greenhouses will be sold to local garden centres. Sales are expected to be as follows:

	June	July	Aug	Sept	Oct	Nov
Number of greenhouses	10	15	15	20	25	30

The sales price of each greenhouse will be $4,000. In order to stimulate interest from customers, Jill has offered two months' credit.

7   Purchases of materials, which will be on one month's credit, are expected to be as follows:

June	July	Aug	Sept	Oct	Nov
$30,000	$20,000	$20,000	$35,000	$50,000	$60,000

8   Jill will initially employ a workshop manager at a cost of $1,500 per month and two further staff at a cost of $1,000 per month each, payable on the last day of the month. When sales reach 20 greenhouses per month, she will employ an additional person at a cost of $700 per month. Jill will herself draw $1,750 cash each month from the business.

9   Jill wishes to undertake a substantial advertising campaign to launch the business. This will cost $8,000 in the first month and $1,000 per month for a further two months, payable in the month incurred.

10 The machinery and equipment needed will be bought immediately at the start of June. Most can be bought second-hand for $12,000 cash. Other machinery, costing $25,000, will be bought new on two months' interest-free credit.

11 Repayments on the business loan, including the interest element, will be $1,200 per month. These will be payable on the 15th of the month, commencing in July.

Required:
Analyse Jill's cash budget and make any recommendations which you feel would improve her cash management.

Answer
The cash budget reveals that despite starting the business with an investment of $55,000, Jill will very quickly run out of cash. In both of the first two months of business there is a predicted fall in cash of nearly $40,000. This means that by the end of the second month of trading Jill will have to find another $23,200. By the end of the third month this amount will have increased to $37,400. These forecast figures would suggest that unless Jill secures a substantial additional source of finance (nearly $40,000), her business will fail within two months.

Alternatively, Jill can make changes to her business plans to reduce the cash requirements of the business. In this way Jill may be able to launch her business successfully without the need for an extra $40,000.

We would suggest that Jill makes the following changes to her business plans:

Inventory management

The forecast shows that Jill intends to buy a substantial amount of raw material inventory in the first month. This means that cash will be tied up in inventory that may not be realized as cash for several months. We recommend that Jill buys materials as they are needed and not create a large inventory. She should seek out suppliers who are able to supply quickly so that she can manage the business successfully with relatively low levels of inventory.

Management of accounts receivable

Jill is proposing to offer an extremely generous credit period to new customers. The impact of this is that there will be no cash receipts for the business for the first two months. The business cannot afford such a generous credit policy. Jill should therefore aim to gain orders from customers without the need for such a long credit period. If she can gain sufficient customers in the first few months offering only a one-month credit period, this will increase the cash inflow into the business by $40,000, substantially easing the cash-flow problem.

Jill should also consider using either invoice discounting or debt factoring to release some of the cash that will be tied up in debtors.

Expenditure plans

Excessive expenditure can be a drain upon the cash flow of a business. Jill therefore needs to look at areas of her business plan where she can cut expenditure to keep cash within the business.

One potential area is Jill's own planned drawings from the business. Jill plans to draw $1,750 from the business each month, right from the very start of the business. Jill should look at her own personal spending and reduce this amount to the absolute minimum that she can manage to live on for the first few months of the business. Then, once the business is well established and cash flows are eased, she will be able to draw more money in the future.

Another potential area for savings is the advertising plans. Jill plans to undertake a substantial advertising campaign to launch the business. This will cost $8,000 in the first month and $1,000 per month for a further two months. As Jill intends to deal with local garden centres she may be able to secure sufficient sales through personal contact and negotiation. This will reduce or totally remove the need for the advertising campaign. Alternatively, Jill can still advertise using cheaper methods.

Purchase and financing of assets

Substantial cash expenditure on new vehicles (the van and the Land Rover) and new equipment is planned. Jill should look both at her needs and at the planned method of financing the purchases.

Jill plans to buy a van in the first month of the business at a cost of $12,000. This cost could be spread if Jill purchased the van on a finance deal or lease. This would substantially ease the cash flow in the first few months of the business.

Jill should also consider whether the Land Rover is necessary and, if so, whether she needs to buy it so soon after the launch of the business. Jill may aspire to driving a Land Rover but a cheaper vehicle may be sufficient for her needs until the business is established and has more cash available.

Jill plans to buy a substantial amount of equipment ($37,000) within the first few months of the business. The cost of this would be spread if the equipment could be bought on a finance deal. This may prove more expensive if the equipment cannot be bought second-hand using a finance deal, but Jill needs to balance out the cash-flow benefits of a finance deal with the reduced cost of second-hand equipment.

Repayments on the business loan are $1,200 per month. Jill could try to negotiate a longer period for the loan so that the repayments could be spread over more months and thereby reduced in the critical first months. Alternatively, she could ask for a deferment in the repayments so that she does not need to make any payments in the first two or three months.

Management of accounts payable

Purchases will be made on one month's credit. Jill should try to negotiate a longer credit period with her suppliers or seek out alternative suppliers who are willing to offer more credit. In addition, she could seek early payment discounts with suppliers.

Conclusion

In this chapter we have looked at the importance of cash management. We have explored the reasons for holding cash and the different motives which determine the level of cash a business will hold. We have examined models which aim to assist managers in optimizing cash levels within the business. We have also explored how good management of different assets within the business, such as inventory, accounts receivable, accounts payable and non-current assets, can greatly improve the cash-flow requirements of the business. Lastly, we have explored the importance of cash-flow planning and how managers can use cash-flow budgets to inform planning decisions.

COMPREHENSION QUESTIONS

1 Explain the business problems that may be associated with holding insufficient cash balances. What are the problems of holding too much cash?

2 Distinguish between the transaction motive and the speculative motive for holding cash. How do these two motives differ in terms of their impact upon the level of cash held?

3 Explain how a business can benefit from a cash forecast, even if it already has an income and expenditure forecast and a balance sheet forecast.

4 Discuss the assumptions which underpin the Baumol–Tobin model of cash management and explain how they may limit the usefulness of the model for some businesses.

5 Explain the difference between a finance lease and an operating lease as a means of financing the purchase of an asset.

6 Discuss the ways in which factoring and invoice discounting can assist in the management of accounts receivable.

7 Explain what you understand by the terms 'buffer stock' and 'lead time' and briefly consider any stock policy that would minimize or eliminate such costs.

Answers available at **www.koganpage.com/afm3**

Exercises

Answers available at www.koganpage.com/afm3

Exercise 7.1: Managing the cash account

The management of Darum Co have set a minimum cash balance of $7,500. The average cost to the company of making deposits or selling investments is $24 per transaction. An analysis of cash flows over the last 12 months reveals a standard deviation of $2,000 per day. The average interest rate on investments is 4.6 per cent.

Calculate the spread, the upper limit and the return point for the cash account of Darum Co using the Miller–Orr model. Explain the relevance of these values for the cash management of the company.

Exercise 7.2: Cash-flow forecasting

Jade opens a sandwich shop. She sells sandwiches directly over the counter for cash, but also provides buffet lunches for local businesses. These customers are allowed one month's credit.

Budgeted sales for the first six months of the business are as follows:

	Jan	Feb	Mar	Apr	May	Jun
	$	$	$	$	$	$
Counter sales	4,000	3,500	3,500	4,000	4,000	5,000
Buffet sales	4,000	5,000	3,000	4,000	3,500	4,000

Purchases of bread and fillings are all made locally for cash. Expected purchases are:

	Jan	Feb	Mar	Apr	May	Jun
	$	$	$	$	$	$
Purchases	3,000	3,000	3,000	4,000	3,500	4,000

1 Jade employs two assistants in the shop. Each is paid a monthly salary of $1,000. This is payable on the 25th of the month.

2 Shop rent is $700 per month. This is paid on the first day of the month.

3 Shop heat and light costs are $300 per quarter, payable in arrears in March and June.

4 The bank balance on 1 January is $1,000.

Required:

(a) Prepare a cash-flow forecast for the first six months of Jade's business.

(b) Comment on changes which Jade might make in order to improve her cash flow.

Exercise 7.3: Managing accounts receivable

Andro Co makes all its sales on credit and allows its customers 30 days' credit. However, analysis of the financial statements shows that the average accounts receivable period in the last financial year was 70 days. This has increased from 50 days in the previous financial year. In addition, bad debts as a percentage of sales increased from 3 to 6 per cent. The CEO has expressed great concern at these figures and has asked for your assistance in improving the management of accounts receivable.

Required:

Write a report to the CEO of Andro Co which details ways in which the company could improve the management of its accounts receivable.

Exercise 7.4: Inventory management

Rio Co currently employs an inventory management policy of reordering inventory when levels fall to 3,500 units. This reorder level allows for the lead time of two weeks and maintains a buffer stock.

The company orders 10,000 units at a time. Forecast production demand during the next year is 70,000 units. The cost of placing and processing an order is $300, while the annual cost of holding a unit in the warehouse is $1.50. These costs are expected to be constant during the next year.

Required:

(a) Calculate the cost of the current ordering policy.

(b) Determine whether a saving could be made by using the EOQ model.

Reference

Bacs (2018) Cost of collecting late payments rockets [Online] www.bacs.co.uk/NewsCentre/ PressReleases/Pages/CostOfCollectingLatePaymentsRockets.aspx (archived at https:// perma.cc/KX5U-5LBS)

Supplementary reading

Baumol, W J (1952) The transactions demand for cash: an inventory theoretic approach, *Quarterly Journal of Economics*, **66**, pp 545–56
Miller, M H and Orr, D (1966) A model of the demand for money by firms, *Quarterly Journal of Economics*, **80** (3), pp 413–35
Tobin, J (1956) The interest elasticity of the transactions demand for cash, *Review of Economics and Statistics*, **38** (3), pp 241–47

Pricing decisions 08

OBJECTIVE

To provide an understanding of the factors, both internal and external to the business, that should guide the pricing decision.

LEARNING OUTCOMES

After studying this chapter, the reader will be able to:

- Recommend appropriate costing methods for pricing.
- Assess the potential impact of different competitive environments on pricing.
- Identify appropriate pricing strategies to fit different markets and products/services.

KEY TOPICS COVERED

- Costing and pricing – different approaches to costing.
- Consumer behaviour and pricing.
- Competitor behaviour and pricing.
- Pricing new products or services.
- Product life cycle and pricing.
- Special pricing strategies.

MANAGEMENT ISSUES

Pricing is not an exact science. Much of the detailed mathematics of the economics of pricing is impossible to apply in practice. Managers need an understanding of the broad principles which should guide them in the pricing decision.

Introduction

In this chapter we will examine the factors which a business needs to take into consideration when establishing the most appropriate price for its products or services. In practice, pricing strategies can be both short term and long term and businesses will employ a combination of pricing strategies to achieve their corporate goals. For example, a business may have a long-term goal of being a high-quality provider and will have a long-term strategy of setting prices high to reflect this. However, the business may reduce prices in the short term in order to improve cash flows, increase market share or deter competitors.

Some of the factors involved in pricing may appear obvious. For example, it is important to take into consideration the costs of delivering a product or service in order to ensure that profit is made or at least costs are covered. However, how those costs are established is not necessarily always obvious or simple. Also, a business needs to be mindful of its customers and competitors when establishing pricing strategy. How will customers and competitors react to your prices? In some circumstances this may be an extremely important question, because if you get it wrong you will lose all your customers to your competitors. The pricing decision can therefore be said to be made up of 3 C's: costs, customers and competitors (Figure 8.1).

Another way of looking at this is to say that there are three different perspectives which need to be considered when making a pricing decision:

The accountant's perspective: this perspective is concerned with the relationship between revenues and costs. The sales price must be set at such a level as to ensure that revenues exceed costs in order to generate a profit.

The economist's perspective: this perspective is concerned with the competitive environment in which the business operates. Different market types have an impact on the ability of a business to control its own pricing.

Figure 8.1 The pricing decision

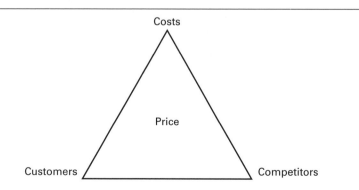

The marketer's perspective: this perspective is concerned with the way in which customers react to prices and how pricing should be integrated into the overall marketing mix.

The accountant's perspective can be said to be inward-looking in that it is concerned with the internal workings of the business and how these generate costs. The economist's perspective and the marketer's perspective are both outward-looking in that they are concerned with the business's external environment and how that impacts upon price.

In this chapter we will look at each of these perspectives in turn to establish a good understanding of the factors involved, and then we will see how all three perspectives can be combined into coherent pricing strategies.

The accountant's perspective – costing and pricing

Understanding the cost of delivering a product or service is important to all organizations. Profit-seeking organizations have at least to break even and not-for-profit organizations need to cover their costs.

The way in which a business will establish the cost of delivering its goods or services will depend upon the way that the business operates and the information that is available. In this section we will look at several well-established costing methods and the circumstances to which they are most suited:

- absorption costing and full-cost-plus pricing;
- marginal-cost-plus pricing;
- activity-based costing and pricing;
- life-cycle costing and pricing.

Absorption costing and full-cost-plus pricing

Absorption costing, which is aimed at establishing the full cost of production, originally arose in manufacturing businesses operating in a relatively stable environment. When using the absorption costing approach, sales price is determined by calculating the full cost of a product or service, including relevant overhead costs, and then adding a percentage mark-up to achieve the desired level of profit.

WORKED EXAMPLE 8.1 Pricing using absorption costing

Grogstore Co manufactures stainless-steel beer barrels. The manufacturing depot has two production departments: cutting and welding. The direct costs of producing each barrel are as follows:

Materials:	2m² of stainless steel @ $3 per m²
Labour – cutting:	15 minutes per barrel @ $14 per hour
Labour – welding:	20 minutes per barrel @ $18 per hour

Budgeted overhead costs for next year are:

	$
Property costs	92,000
Managers' salaries:	
Cutting department	25,000
Welding department	28,000
General administration costs	143,000
Machine power	28,000

The following information relates to each of the production departments:

	Cutting	Welding	Total
Floor space (sq. m)	35	25	60
Number of employees	6	10	16
Labour hours	9,000	17,000	26,000

What price should Grogstore charge for the barrels if it wishes to earn a profit mark-up on total costs of 30 per cent?

Solution

The first step in establishing a full-cost price is to identify all the direct costs of manufacturing a barrel. These will include the costs of materials and labour which go directly into the barrel:

	$
Materials: (2m² @ $3 per m²)	6.00
Labour: cutting (15 minutes @ $14 per hour)	3.50
Labour: welding (20 minutes @ $18 per hour)	6.00

Once total direct costs have been established, the relevant parts of overhead costs are incorporated into the product cost. This is done through a method known as the '3 A's' of absorption costing: **allocate**, **apportion** and **absorb**.

This method involves attributing overhead costs firstly to relevant production cost centres, and then from the cost centre to the individual product.

Expert view 8.1: Cost centre

A cost centre is a department or segment of the business to which costs are allocated or apportioned.

In the case of Grogstore Co we can identify two production cost centres: the cutting department and the welding department. This is, of course, a very simple example and in reality most organizations will have many cost centres.

All overhead costs which can be directly attributed to a given cost centre should be **allocated** to it. For example, as there is a manager responsible for the running of each department, his or her salary can be allocated to that department.

	Cutting	Welding
	$	$
Allocated costs:		
Managers' salaries	25,000	28,000

Overhead costs which do not relate directly to one cost centre but rather relate to the running of the business as a whole are then apportioned to each cost centre in the most appropriate and fair way. For example, the property costs can be **apportioned** based upon space occupied by each cost centre:

Cutting department share of property costs: $35/60m^2 \times \$92,000 = \$53,667$
Welding department share of property costs: $25/60m^2 \times \$92,000 = \$38,333$

In a similar manner, administration costs can be apportioned between the two production cost centres based upon the number of employees in each department, and the machine power cost can be apportioned based upon the number of hours worked in each department (labour hours). This will result in the total cost allocation and apportionment between the two production cost centres shown in Table 8.1.

Table 8.1

	Cutting $	Welding $	Total $
Allocated costs:			
Managers' salaries	25,000	28,000	53,000
Apportioned costs:			
Property costs (floor space)	53,667	38,333	92,000
Admin costs (no. of employees)	53,625	89,375	143,000
Machine power (hours worked)	9,692	18,308	28,000
Total	141,984	174,016	316,000

There is no fixed basis for apportionment of costs. The method used will depend upon perceptions of what is most appropriate and what information is available. The most important factor is fairness – the allocation and apportionment of costs must fairly reflect the extent to which the cost centre contributes to the generation of those costs.

Once all overhead costs have been allocated or apportioned to production departments and a total cost calculated for each department, that cost is 'absorbed' into individual products by calculating an **overhead absorption rate (OAR)**. This OAR is usually based upon the level of activity (or amount of time) contributed from each department in the making of a single product.

Therefore, for the cutting department of Grogstore Co the OAR can be calculated based upon labour hours as follows:

$$\text{OAR} = \frac{\text{Total overhead costs}}{\text{Labour hours worked}} = \frac{\$141,984}{9,000 \text{ hrs}} = \$15.78 \text{ per hour}$$

This means that for every hour of work done in the cutting department, $15.78 will be charged to the product. As each barrel requires 15 minutes of cutting department time, it will be charged $3.95 ($15.78 × 15/60 minutes) of cutting department costs.

The OAR for the welding department will be:

$$\text{OAR} = \frac{\text{Total overheads costs}}{\text{Labour hours worked}} = \frac{\$174,016}{17,000 \text{ hrs}} = \$10.24 \text{ per hour}$$

As each barrel requires 20 minutes of welding department time, it will be charged $3.41 ($10.24 × 20/60 minutes) of welding department costs.

We can now establish the total cost of producing each barrel, including the relevant overhead costs (Table 8.2).

Table 8.2

Direct costs:	$
Materials: (2m² @ $3 per m²)	6.00
Labour – cutting: (15 minutes @ $14 per hour)	3.50
Labour – welding: (20 minutes @ $18 per hour)	6.00
Overhead costs:	
Cutting department (15 minutes @ $15.78 per hour)	3.95
Welding department (20 minutes @ $10.24 per hour)	3.41
Total cost:	$22.86

An appropriate sales price can now be calculated by adding the required profit mark-up of 30 per cent:

$$\text{Sales price per barrel} = \$22.86 \times 130\% = \$29.72$$

Expert view 8.2: Mark-up and margin

Once a full cost has been established for a product, the price is calculated by adding mark-up to that full cost. This mark-up is usually a standard percentage which is established by management. For example, a company may decide to add a mark-up of 25 per cent to all its products. If product A has a full cost of production of £80, the sales price will be calculated as:

$$\text{Sales price of Product A} = £80 \times 1.25 = £100$$

At this point it is worth discussing the difference between mark-up and margin, as these are two terms which are frequently confused: mark-up is profit expressed as a percentage of costs; whereas margin is profit expressed as a percentage of sales price.

A simple illustration will show the significance of understanding the difference. Imagine a product that has a cost of £60 and a sales price of £80. This means that the profit will be £20.

$$\text{Mark-up} = \frac{\text{Profit}}{\text{Cost}} = \frac{£20}{£60} = 33\%$$

$$\text{Margin} = \frac{\text{Profit}}{\text{Price}} = \frac{£20}{£80} = 25\%$$

Problems with full-cost-plus pricing

Although full-cost pricing is in theory a method of always ensuring that all costs are covered and a known profit is earned, there are a number of problems with implementing this method in practice.

Firstly, the technique requires the estimation of some important figures, such as annual overhead costs and the volume of output. These figures will not be known for certain until an accounting period is complete, yet they are needed at the start of an accounting period if a price is to be established. Although the technique theoretically establishes the total cost of a product, in practice this is just an estimation and not the actual cost. There is therefore always a risk that estimates are inaccurate and the method does not establish an accurate cost for pricing.

Another problem is that the basis of apportioning and absorbing overheads may well be arbitrary and may result in an unfair or inappropriate apportionment of overhead costs between different products and services. This may result in some products or services being overpriced, which could make them uncompetitive. For example, one of the authors once worked in a business division which operated from the old premises of the business after the other divisions had moved into new premises. This building was far too big for the needs of the division and was half empty. Despite this, the division was charged for the full running cost of the premises.

A further disadvantage is that by simply calculating the full cost as it currently stands and adding a mark-up to this, there is no incentive within the system to reduce costs. When we look at pricing within the competitive environment later in this chapter, it will be seen that this can be a significant issue.

Marginal-cost-plus pricing

One way of overcoming some of the problems of full absorption cost pricing is to avoid the process of estimating and apportioning overhead costs. Also, for some businesses, the basic variable costs of production are easy to identify, but overheads are less easy to apportion and allocate. In this case, sales price is determined by adding a profit mark-up to the marginal (variable) cost. This method of costing is widely used in retailing and in professional services.

A retailer can easily identify the cost of products bought in for resale and can establish a consistent gross profit margin by applying a mark-up to this cost. Different retailing businesses have different levels of mark-up. In clothing retailing it is usual to have mark-up on purchase cost of 400–500 per cent. However, in food retailing where volumes of sales are higher, profit margins are much lower and mark-up on direct costs may be as little as 25 per cent.

The marginal-cost-plus pricing method is also frequently used by professional service firms such as solicitors and accountants. For such businesses the direct cost of delivering a service will be the salary of the solicitor or accountant working for the client. The price charged to the client will be based upon a multiple of that salary. This is illustrated in Worked Example 8.2.

WORKED EXAMPLE 8.2 Marginal-cost-plus pricing

A solicitor is paid a salary of £30 per hour. For every hour which she spends working for a given client, that client will be charged £30 × 300% = £90. This price will cover the direct cost of the solicitor's salary and any office overhead costs, and will leave a profit for the firm.

Exercises: now attempt Exercise 8.1 on page 312

Activity-based costing (ABC) pricing

Activity-based costing is a method of costing which was developed to address some of the criticisms of absorption costing discussed above. In a bid to identify and apportion costs more accurately, this approach attributes costs to different organizational activities, rather than departments. The method therefore uses the concept of **cost pools** – the collection of costs which relate to a given activity.

Under absorption costing, different overhead costs will be apportioned to a department which may undertake a range of activities. For example, the production department may accumulate costs for ordering, receiving and holding inventory, machining, assembly, packaging and dispatching. Under ABC these would be identified as separate activities with separate cost pools. The difference between the two approaches to costing is illustrated in Figure 8.2.

Once costs have been apportioned to activities, the **cost driver** for each activity is determined. The cost driver is the metric which best explains why resources are consumed by a particular activity and therefore why the activity incurs costs. The cost driver provides an explanation of the size of the cost pool. This system of activity-based costing is best illustrated with an example which compares the approach with that of traditional absorption costing.

Figure 8.2   Traditional absorption costing vs ABC. (a) Traditional absorption costing system; (b) activity-based costing system

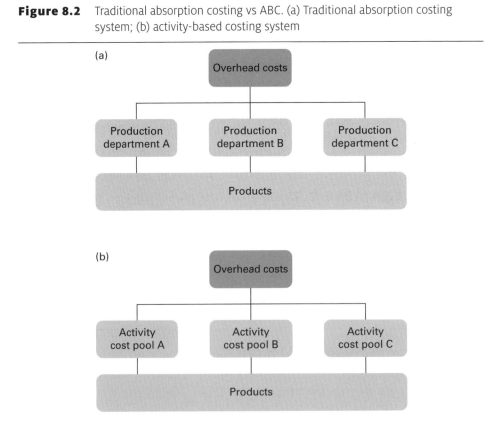

WORKED EXAMPLE 8.3 Activity-based costing and pricing

Pedal Co manufactures a range of different bicycles, including the A-series and the B-series. The A-series is a bicycle aimed at serious sports riders. The company makes and sells 200 of these each year. The B-series is a leisure bicycle. The company makes and sells 5,000 of these each year.

The bicycle frames are made in the company's factory, but all other components, including wheels, are bought in from other suppliers. The factory has a normal production capacity of 10,000 direct labour hours each year.

Production overhead costs relating to receiving raw materials and bought-in components are $240,000 per year. These costs have been identified as relating to the following activities:

Receiving 225 consignments of frame tubing	$90,000
Receiving 250 consignments of components	$150,000

The A-series requires 60 frame-tubing consignments and 50 component assignments. The B-series requires 50 frame-tubing consignments and 75 component assignments.

The direct costs of producing each model of bicycle are as follows:

	A-series	B-series
Direct materials:	450	90
Direct labour:	(2.5 hours@ $16 p.h.) 40	(1.5 hours@ $16 p.h.) 24
	$490	$114

The company applies a standard mark-up on its products of 40 per cent.

Required:
Compare the total cost and therefore the price of the two models of bicycle using traditional absorption costing and activity-based costing.

Answer: Traditional absorption costing
If Pedal Co uses traditional absorption costing, the $240,000 production overhead costs would be absorbed into each model of bicycle using an OAR based upon production time:

$$\text{OAR} = \frac{\text{Total overheads costs}}{\text{Labour hours worked}} = \frac{\$240,000}{10,000} = \$24 \text{ per hour}$$

Therefore the total cost and price of each model would be:

	A-series	B-series
Direct costs	$490	$114
Overhead costs	(2.5 hours@ $24 p.h.) 60	(1.5 hours@ $24 p.h.) 36
Total cost	550	150
Price (40% mark-up)	$825	$210

Answer: Activity-based costing

If activity-based costing is used, the overhead costs will be apportioned based upon cost drivers. In this case the cost drivers are receiving the frame tubing and receiving the components. The absorption rate based upon these cost drivers will be:

Receiving frame tubing = $90,000 ÷ 225 = $400 per consignment
Receiving components = $150,000 ÷ 250 = $600 per consignment

These costs will be apportioned to the two models of bicycle based upon the level of activity which each model generates:

	A-series	B-series
Direct costs	$490	$114
Receiving frame tubing	($400 × 60/200) 120	($400 × 50/5,000) 4
Receiving components	($600 × 50/200) 150	($600 × 75/5,000) 9
Total cost	760	127
Price (40% mark-up)	$1,064	$178

This ABC analysis suggests that more overhead costs should be apportioned to the A-series and less to the B-series. This in turn has a knock-on effect on the prices which the company should be charging for each model of bicycle.

Advocates of ABC argue that this calculation provides a much more accurate analysis of the true cost of producing each model of bicycle because the technique is more sensitive to how activities give rise to the overhead costs.

Life-cycle costing and pricing

With many modern high-technology products, life cycles have become much shorter and more costs are incurred at a pre-production stage in research, development and design. This means that direct production costs can be a relatively small part of the overall cost of the product. In such cases it is more useful to identify the costs across the whole life cycle of the product and use these as the basis of establishing a suitable price.

Figure 8.3 Life-cycle pricing

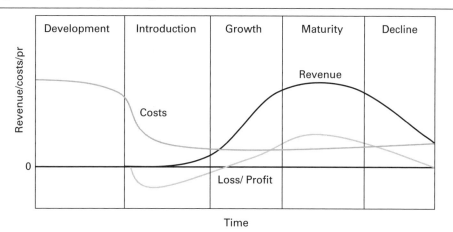

All products can be seen as having a life cycle, from development through to with-drawal from the market. This life cycle, as illustrated in Figure 8.3, has different stages during which costs and revenues will have differing patterns. During develop-ment, costs will be incurred but no revenues are earned yet. At the introduction stage, sales may be slow to pick up, meaning that initial sales revenue will be low. At the same time, costs may be relatively high because there is insufficient sales volume to generate economies of scale. In the growth stage, sales begin to pick up and grow rapidly and the product becomes more profitable. During the maturity stage, sales will stabilize at a maximum level. This is usually the most profitable period for a product. As the product enters its final stage of decline, sales and profitability will fall off until the point where management are forced to withdraw the product from the market.

Life-cycle costing recognizes the fact that in order to make a profit, revenues must cover all costs whether they are incurred pre-production, during production or post-production. This focus on costs across the whole life cycle has many advantages. Firstly, focusing on all costs will help management see opportunities for cost reduc-tions. Secondly, many costs will be linked across the life cycle and therefore oppor-tunities for reducing costs later can be identified at an earlier stage. For example, better design may reduce production costs and changes in manufacturing processes may reduce end-of-life decommissioning costs.

A further dimension of life-cycle pricing is the recognition that different pricing strategies may be adopted at different stages in the product's life cycle. The best choice of pricing strategy at any given stage will depend upon customers' percep-tions, competition and the nature of the product being sold. All of these factors, together with the appropriate strategies, will be discussed as we progress through this chapter.

Extract 8.1: Sony PS3 life-cycle costing

When Sony launched its PlayStation3 it was priced at $499, but it was costing Sony $806 per unit to make. This represented a loss of $307 per machine. Sony launched the PS3 at this price because it expected to reduce its losses over the 5–10-year life cycle of the machine as economies of scale reduced the cost of parts. In fact, over the whole life cycle of the PS3 Sony expected to make a small profit. In addition, the bulk of Sony's revenue comes from selling or licensing software to run on the PS3. The pricing of the gaming platform then needs to be competitive in relation to the main alternatives – Microsoft's Xbox 360 and the Nintendo Wii. Sony's pricing decision was made after considering the full life cycle of both the gaming machine and the software.

Conclusions: costing for pricing

A major disadvantage of all the costing methods examined above is that they are entirely inward looking. That is to say, they ignore the impact which price has on demand. By simply calculating the costs of production and adding a mark-up for profit, one is assuming that the customer will be willing to pay the price that is arrived at through these calculations. In reality, customers are not concerned with how much it costs to make a product. Rather, they are interested in the value the product provides them and they will be reluctant to pay a price which does not offer good value. Furthermore, the internal focus ignores the activities of competitors. If competitors are producing similar products at lower costs, they will be able to undercut the business's price. It is therefore important to consider these external factors and these are the subject of the following sections.

The economist's perspective

From the economist's perspective we look at the competitive environment of the business and how this will impact on pricing strategy. There are two aspects of economic theory which we want to consider in relation to pricing. The first is the concept of the price elasticity of demand. The second concept is that of market type or market context: the competitive conditions in which the business operates.

Price elasticity of demand

Generally speaking, as the price of a product or service increases, the demand for it will decrease. However, the amount by which that demand decreases will vary across different products or services, for a number of reasons (which will be explored later in the chapter). The relationship of this change in demand to a change in price is known as the **price elasticity of demand (PED)**. Economists measure this with the following formula:

$$PED = \frac{\text{Percentage change in demand}}{\text{Percentage change in price}}$$

The greater the percentage change in demand in relation to a given price change, the more 'elastic' that demand is said to be. If a 10 per cent increase in price creates a 30 per cent fall in demand, demand is said to be relatively *elastic*. On the other hand, if a 10 per cent increase in price creates only a 5 per cent fall in demand, demand is said to be relatively *inelastic*.

It is important for a business to understand how elastic the demand is for its products or services, as this price elasticity of demand will have an impact on the success of different price strategies. For example, if a business knows that the demand for its products is relatively inelastic, it would not pursue a strategy of cutting prices in order to try to stimulate demand. The importance of this relationship is explained in the following section.

Price elasticity of demand and total revenue

In order to appreciate the importance of price elasticity of demand upon pricing strategies, it is necessary to understand the relationship between demand, price and total revenue. In Figure 8.4 total revenue is represented by the area enclosed by the lines P_1, A, D_1. This area is a graphical representation of the fact that *price × demand = revenue*:

Figure 8.4   Total revenue

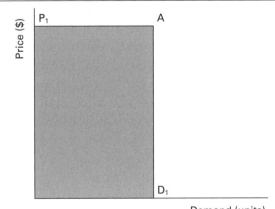

Demand (units)

Figure 8.5 Price inelasticity

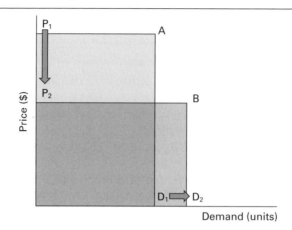

Demand (units)

Figure 8.6 Price elasticity

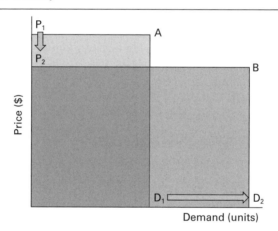

Demand (units)

Now look at Figure 8.5 where the price is reduced from P_1 to P_2. That reduction in price stimulates an increase in demand from D_1 to D_2. In this example, demand is relatively **inelastic** in relation to price so that the decrease in price creates a relatively small increase in demand. Now look at the relative change in total revenue as indicated by the shaded boxes. It can be seen that the decrease in revenue resulting from the price cuts (box P_1–P_2–A) is much greater than the increase in revenue resulting from the increase in demand (box D_1–D_2–B). Therefore, overall revenue falls as a result of the cut in price, even though demand has increased.

On the other hand, in Figure 8.6 a relatively small decrease in price creates a large increase in demand. In this case the loss of revenue caused by the fall in price (box P_1–P_2–A) is more than offset by the increase in revenue from the greater demand (box D_1–D_2–B). As a result, overall revenue will increase due to the price cut.

What determines elasticity?

The graphs above serve to illustrate the way in which the price elasticity of demand can be a hugely important factor when it comes to pricing. Therefore, it is important for a business to understand what determines the elasticity of demand for its products or services. Managers also need to understand how they can take measures to change the price elasticity of demand. Generally speaking, it is more beneficial for a business to have low price elasticity of demand. This means that managers will seek methods for reducing elasticity. In this section we will look at the factors which determine the price elasticity of demand and look at how it may be possible to manipulate those.

The relative price of the goods   The more expensive that something is, relatively speaking, the more elastic demand will be. For example, if a bar of chocolate costs $0.50 and the price increases by 20 per cent to $0.60, this increase is unlikely to have a major impact upon demand. On the other hand, if a car costing $25,000 increases in price by 20 per cent to $30,000, this increase will decrease demand as it will put the car out of the affordable price range of some existing customers.

The price of other goods   Economists identify two different categories of related goods or services, the price of which can have an impact upon the price of other goods or services.

The first category is *complementary* goods. These are products which go together, such as video games and gaming consoles. If the price of a complementary good increases, this may have a negative impact upon the demand of your product. For example, if the price of gaming consoles increases so that fewer people can afford them, then fewer people will be buying games (see Extract 8.1).

The second category is *substitute* goods. These are goods which a customer could buy instead of the item we are trying to price because they can be substituted in its place. An example is two mobile phones from different manufacturers with similar specifications. If the price of a competitor's phone is less than the price of your similar model, a customer will buy the competitor's phone as it represents better value.

Consumer income   Products or services can be categorized in terms of how their price elasticity of demand changes with levels of consumer income. Some items, known as *staple goods*, will have a relatively stable level of demand, regardless of consumer income. A simple example might be a basic foodstuff such as potatoes or rice. Generally speaking, people tend to eat the same amount of potatoes or rice, regardless of their level of income. An increase in income will not increase demand for this type of goods.

A second category of goods, known as *luxury goods*, will be subject to an increase in demand as consumers' income increases. This will include items such as expensive holidays, luxury cars and jewellery.

A third category of goods, known as *inferior goods*, will be subject to a fall in demand as consumers' income increases. These goods may not actually be inferior in terms of quality, but they are in terms of consumers' perception. Therefore, for example, a consumer on a low income may buy a pair of cheap unbranded denim jeans. If that consumer has an increase in income, he or she may stop buying the cheap jeans in favour of more expensive brand-name clothing.

Tastes and fashions   Tastes and fashions can have a significant impact on the elasticity of demand for products and services. It is not unusual to see the latest 'must have' children's toy, usually linked to a recently released film, selling at a very high price and yet parents are falling over each other to buy it. On the other hand, last season's clothes can usually be found in the bargain bin when nobody wants to buy them, even at a fraction of their original price.

Expectations   If customers expect the price of a product to increase in the near future, this can increase demand in the short term. An example of this is seen in the UK each year before the Chancellor's budget. The usual expectation is that the Chancellor will increase taxation on vehicle fuel. This leads to large queues at filling stations the evening before the budget, as drivers rush to fill their vehicles in expectation of an increase in fuel prices.

Obsolescence   Aside from changes in taste and fashions, goods can also become obsolete. This is particularly the case with high-technology products. Once a new version with a higher specification has been released, demand for the older version usually falls off very quickly and customers are not willing to buy that product even at a substantially reduced price. Another issue, related to obsolescence, is how long a product lasts. If a product has a relatively short life before it wears out or breaks, then over a long period customers will buy more of that item. However, this must always be balanced with customer expectations of value. If a product wears out or breaks sooner than the customer thinks it ought to, the customer may boycott that item in the future.

Discussion point

Consider your own purchases over recent months. Which items that you bought were most price dependent for you? Why? (Can you relate your decision to the factors discussed above?)

Pricing within market context

The second aspect of economic theory that is important to pricing is market type, or market context. This refers to the competitive conditions in which the business operates. This can refer to the number and type of competitors and the ability of a business to differentiate itself from competitors.

Economists identity four types of market:

- perfect competition;
- monopoly;
- monopolistic competition;
- oligopoly.

Each of these different types of market has an implication for the business's ability to determine its own pricing strategy, and therefore whether it is a *price setter* or a *price taker*. It is therefore extremely important for a business to understand what type of market it operates in and how this will impact on it.

Perfect competition

Perfect competition describes the situation in which there are many buyers and sellers in a market, none of whom is big or powerful enough to influence the market. New sellers can freely enter the market at any time and all firms operating within the market are selling products or services which are difficult to differentiate, so that they are essentially identical. This means that customers are likely to choose between the products or services of different businesses purely upon the basis of price. The consequence is that an individual business will find it very difficult to set a price which differs from that of every other seller in the market. This situation is illustrated in Worked Example 8.4.

WORKED EXAMPLE 8.4 Perfect competition and pricing

Imagine a large fruit and vegetable market in which there are 30 stalls all selling oranges which were purchased from the same wholesaler and are therefore indistinguishable in quality. If 29 of the stalls sell the oranges at $0.50 each, what will happen if one stall attempts to sell the oranges at $0.60 each? The likely outcome is that the more expensive stall will be unable to sell any oranges, as customers, freely able to see the price and quality of the oranges at all the other stalls, will buy oranges elsewhere. On the other hand, what would happen if one stall dropped its price to $0.40 per orange? Again, because customers are able to compare prices and quality freely, they will all rush to the one stall to buy the cheaper oranges. This will force all of the other stallholders to reduce their price to $0.40. The ultimate outcome is that the original price-cutting stall will have no price advantage and all stallholders will have lost profit by selling their oranges at a lower price.

The implication is therefore that the closer to perfect competition the market conditions are, the more difficult it will be for an individual firm to set its own prices. Each firm selling within that market will be forced to go along with the prevailing market price.

It is interesting that the internet and, in particular, price comparison sites have made information much more freely available to customers and have created a situation very close to perfect competition for many retailers.

Monopoly

A monopoly describes a situation where a market is dominated by one major seller. In this situation customers will have little or no option to buy from an alternative supplier. This gives the monopoly business far more control over pricing. A business can have a monopoly through ownership of patents or copyrights or through access to limited resources. Any aspect of the market which creates a barrier to entry for other firms can result in a monopoly.

Provided that there is not a very high level of elasticity of demand, a monopoly will be able to charge higher prices and customers will continue to buy from them, simply because they have no other option. Because this creates a situation in which the supplier can potentially abuse customers, many jurisdictions have created competition laws to prevent or restrict monopolies. In the UK many industries have been broken up to remove monopolies in an attempt to create more price competition among suppliers. Examples include electricity and gas suppliers, telecommunications and rail transport.

Monopolistic competition

Monopolistic competition describes a market in which there are multiple buyers and sellers, but sellers are able to differentiate their products or services from those of their competitors. This means that if you are able to persuade customers that your product is somehow better than that of your competitors, for example by having better features or being of a better quality, you will be able to charge a higher price.

The market for many common products and services can be seen as falling into this category. Businesses operating in such a market tend to spend a lot of money on marketing to establish brand loyalty and to convince customers that their products should be purchased in preference to those of competitors.

Oligopoly

Oligopoly describes the situation where a market is dominated by a small number of suppliers selling similar products or services. A surprisingly large number of markets are oligopolies: car manufacturers, computer manufacturers, petrol and oil suppliers, gas and electricity suppliers and mobile telephone providers are all oligopolies. When there is an oligopoly, even though there are multiple suppliers in competition, the suppliers are few enough in number to be able to cooperate and work together to control prices. An example of this is OPEC, the group of oil producing nations that work together to control oil prices.

Discussion point

List as many industries as you can that are oligopolies. For each industry, consider the degree to which the sellers work in collaboration.

Extract 8.2: The perils of trading with an oligopoly

The supermarket industry in the UK is a well-known oligopoly, being dominated by four major businesses: Tesco, Sainsbury, Asda and Morrisons. This means that leading food producers must trade with the supermarkets, which consequently dominate their order book and squeeze their profit margins. However, smaller food producers are often unable to deal with the major supermarkets and therefore sell to independent retailers. As this is a more open market, it enables them to charge more reasonable prices and earn higher profit margins.

The marketer's perspective

The marketer's perspective on price is concerned with the impact that price will have upon consumers' perception and purchasing behaviour. Price is therefore one of the 4 P's of the marketing mix, the others being product, promotion and place.

Expert view 8.3: the marketing mix

The marketing mix is that set of factors which are regarded as being crucial in marketing a product or service. Since the 1960s this has been commonly referred to as the **4P's**: *price, product, promotion* and *place* (McCarthy, 1960). However, this model has been refined and developed over time so that there is now a **7P's** model of the marketing mix (*price, product, promotion, place, people, process* and *physical evidence*) which is considered to be more appropriate for marketing services rather than products. Also, more recently a **4C's** model has been proposed as being a more consumer-focused view of the marketing mix. This has two alternative versions, the first being *consumer, cost, communication, convenience* (Schulz *et al*, 1993) and the second being *commodity, cost, communication, channel* (Shimizu, 1973). Regardless of the variation in detail and emphasis, in all these models of the marketing mix the *price* or *cost* to the consumer is highlighted as being a key factor.

Expert view 8.4: Product positioning

In a competitive market it is important to make your products or services stand out from those of your competitors, an activity which is known as *product positioning*. There are several academic models of product positioning which look at different aspects of what is important to customers, but pricing is widely recognized as being key. Generally speaking, businesses will want to charge the highest price they can, but their ability to persuade customers to pay a higher price will depend upon customers' perception of the quality of what they receive for their money. The model in Figure 8.7 illustrates how price maps against quality in product positioning.

The product positioning price/quality model shows four general strategies which a business might follow (A, B, C or D). Of the four quadrants available, only quadrants C and B offer sensible strategies. Strategy A is to charge a lower price for a high-quality product. This strategy will certainly attract customers but it will not be one which maximizes profit for the firm. Strategy B is to charge a high price for a high-quality product. This is a strategy followed by many businesses that sell luxury products. Customers are willing to pay a higher price because they believe that what they are getting is a better product. Strategy C is to sell a lower-quality product at a low price. This is another common strategy. The business will charge a low price and thereby gain a high volume of sales, so that even if the profit per item is low the overall profitability will be high. Strategy D is to sell a low-quality product at a high price. This strategy is unlikely to succeed in the long term as customers will realize that they can get better-quality products at the same price elsewhere.

Many businesses combine strategies B and C by offering a range of products at different qualities and different prices. For example, most major supermarkets have a budget low-cost range, a normal range and a luxury high-cost range of foods.

Figure 8.7 Product positioning

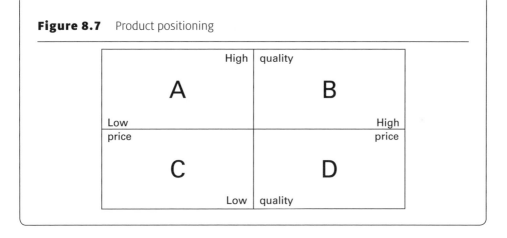

The impact of price on consumer behaviour

From a marketing perspective, price is important because it has an impact on the customer's perceived value of the product. It is therefore not so much the price itself but the customer's perception of that price which is important. If customers can be convinced that a higher price represents good value for a product or service, they will be willing to pay a higher price.

In the section on the economist's perspective we looked at a number of factors which can affect the price elasticity of demand. The marketer is equally concerned with these factors, as good marketing may be able to reduce the price elasticity of demand. That will enable the business either to charge higher prices or to gain more customers at existing prices.

Price perception

Customers are looking for good value from any product or service they buy and will therefore be unwilling to pay a price which they believe does not offer value. The level of sensitivity to price will generally vary with the absolute price being charged. That is to say, most customers will unhesitatingly buy something which is relatively cheap, say $0.50, but will stop and think before buying something which is more expensive, such as $1,000. (As explained in the economist's perspective above, this will also vary according to the level of the consumer's disposable income.)

If customers are looking for value from a product, it can be useful to make customers believe that a product is cheaper than it actually is. It is therefore not unusual to see products priced at $9.99 rather than $10, or $79.99 rather than $80. The objective of this pricing, which is sometimes known as *psychological pricing*, is to overcome any perceived price barriers that customers may have. A customer may consider $10 to be too expensive, so pricing the product at $9.99 makes an important psychological difference.

Perception of quality

If customers perceive a product or service to be of a higher quality, they will be willing to pay a higher price. It is the customer's perception of quality rather than the actual quality itself which is important. This is why many businesses invest in heavy advertising which emphasizes the quality of their products.

Perception of difference from other products

Differentiating your products from those of competitors is another way of persuading customers to pay a higher price. This involves persuading customers to buy based upon other elements of the marketing mix, such as special or unique features of the goods, special promotion activities, brand loyalty, and place (where the goods or services can be obtained).

Consumer ethics

Goods or services which satisfy customers' ethical concerns can command higher prices. For example, customers will be willing to pay higher prices for free-range eggs, fair-trade products, carbon-neutral products, sustainable products or foodstuffs which have been farmed organically in order to reduce damage to the environment.

Differentiating customers

Another important aspect of marketing is the recognition that not all customers will behave in the same way. For a given product within a given market, some customers will have relatively high price elasticity of demand whereas other customers will have relatively low price elasticity of demand. An important skill in marketing is identifying and targeting different groups of customers according to their willingness to pay. An example of this is supermarkets which have a 'value' range of products for thrifty customers, a normal range of products for the majority of customers, and a premium or luxury range of products for better-off customers.

Discussion point

List as many clothing retailers as you can, then place each retailer within the 'product positioning' grid in Figure 8.7.

Combining the three perspectives: establishing an appropriate pricing strategy

Now that we have looked at the different issues which go into the pricing decision and the factors which influence prices, we can look at how organizations should consider these when establishing pricing strategies. Figure 8.8 sets out a range of different pricing strategies. Before we look at these in detail, we need to consider some general principles. Firstly, the long-term pricing strategy of an organization should be in line with the organization's mission and broader strategic objectives. Secondly, any pricing strategy adopted should always be informed by all three C's of pricing discussed above: costs, competitors and customers.

Broadly speaking, there are three considerations that will help the business frame an appropriate pricing strategy. These relate to the following questions:

1 Are we pricing a new or existing product or service?

2 Are we going to a new or existing market?

3 Are we a volume-driven or a price-driven business?

New product or existing product?

If a business is launching a new product or a product with substantial new features (ie one that is not currently offered by any competitor), there will be no competition for that product. This may mean a relatively inelastic demand and a high level of interest in the product. On the other hand, if the business is launching a product which is similar to those already available from competitors, it needs to compare that new product with those already available. Are the features comparable? Are there new or unique features? These factors will impact upon the business's ability to charge higher prices. For example, when Apple launched the iPad there were no comparable products available. This, together with the relative price inelasticity of the market, enabled Apple to charge high prices for their new product. However, as other competing manufacturers launched similar products they had to price more competitively in recognition of the fact that there were several substitute products available.

New market or existing market?

If a business is entering an existing market where other similar products are already on sale, they will need to analyse what competitors are charging and set their prices accordingly. On the other hand, if a business is entering a new market where there is no existing competition, pricing will be based upon expectations of what customers are willing to pay.

Volume driven or price driven?

Businesses that have large fixed overhead costs tend to be volume driven in their pricing strategy. For example, an airline will have a largely fixed cost of operating a flight. It will therefore manipulate its prices in order to fill all the seats on an aeroplane whilst covering those fixed costs. In a similar manner, supermarkets have high fixed costs. They price to sell a high volume of products at a low margin. On the other hand, businesses that are price driven tend to have low fixed overheads. Such businesses do not need high volumes of sales.

Pricing strategies

Having considered these overriding issues, let us look at the range of pricing strategies available. These can be seen as a range of pricing positions in relation to the prices of competitors, as illustrated in Figure 8.8.

1) Market skimming pricing

A market skimming pricing strategy involves launching a new product at a very high price and then gradually reducing the price over time. This strategy is often used to launch a new technology product which has little or no competition. It takes advantage

Figure 8.8   Price-positioning strategies

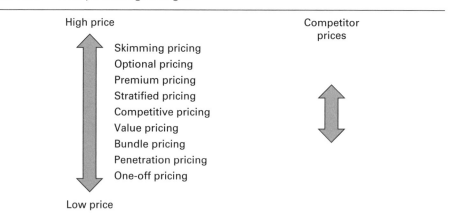

of the fact that demand for the new product will be relatively inelastic for some customers. This strategy is effectively a type of price discrimination which segments the market in terms of how long customers are willing to wait before obtaining the new product. For example, if a new specification of smart phone is launched, some customers, referred to as *early adopters*, will want to buy that new phone immediately, with little regard to the cost. The seller is therefore able to charge a very high price at launch. On the other hand, some consumers will only buy that new phone once the price is substantially lower, and they are willing to wait several months after launch before buying it.

Price skimming is by necessity a short-term strategy applicable only to the launch stage of a new product, as it relies on the uniqueness and novelty of the new product. As competitors launch comparative products this will put downward pressure on prices. A business also has to be careful in the timing of reducing the price. If prices are kept high for too long, a relatively small volume of sales will be achieved and there is a risk that a competitor may develop an alternative product which goes on to take a higher volume of the market.

2) Optional pricing

Optional pricing is another method of segmenting the market in order to maximize profit. This strategy is used by many car manufacturers. Rather than just offering one version of a particular model of car, the manufacturer will offer a basic model with a range of enhancement options at additional cost. These options will include larger and more powerful engines, alloy wheels, leather interiors, more electric and electronic gadgetry and so on. By offering a range of different versions of the car at different prices the business is able to capture a wider range of customers and to make more profit from those customers willing to pay for the higher specifications.

3) Premium pricing

Premium pricing is a strategy of setting prices at the top end of the range offered by competitors. A business using this strategy is not trying to compete on price. Rather, it will concentrate on competing through the other elements of the marketing mix, such as product quality or features, ease of access to the product or service (ie availability) or the way the product is promoted.

Establishing a strong brand name to reduce price elasticity enables a business to charge premium prices. Strong branding also reduces the impact of substitute goods. Coca-Cola is an example of strong product branding.

Ethical products also tend to be premium priced as they are meeting non-price-based consumer needs.

Extract 8.3: Premium pricing at MV Agusta

The iconic Italian motorcycle brand MV Agusta has a reputation built upon a racing heritage, stylish Italian design and high performance. The company opts for a niche marketing strategy that emphasizes this reputation and is enhanced by celebrity customers such as actors Brad Pitt, Tom Cruise and Angelina Jolie, and former Formula One world champion Michael Schumacher.

The company has a strategy of maintaining the essence of this brand and focusing on high-quality product development. Part of this strategy is charging premium prices for its products.

---

4) Stratified pricing: Price discrimination and market segmentation

Price discrimination is the practice of charging different prices to different customers for the same product or service. This practice is common in a number of industries. For it to be successful it is important that the market for the product and service can be successfully segmented such that customers are not able to move between the different price brackets. One example of market segmentation is peak and off-peak travel. Customers are charged different prices for the same service depending on when they use that service. A business using this strategy is taking advantage of the fact that those customers who will need to travel during peak commuting times have little flexibility about when they travel. There is therefore relatively little elasticity of demand, so prices can be increased. On the other hand, customers travelling for leisure generally have more flexibility about when they travel. They can be attracted to use buses or trains during off-peak times by making this cheaper.

A second form of *stratified pricing* involves producing a range of similar products but with different features to meet the needs of different customers. An example of this is the different classes of air travel available. Three passengers may all fly from Paris to New York at the same time on the same aeroplane. However, each will pay a different price (and receive a different level of service) by flying economy class, business class or first class. The airline divides the market for air travel into three different market segments.

Extract 8.4: Stratified pricing wins Apple the US market

The world of mobile phones is dominated by two major players: Apple and Samsung. Apple is known for its premium pricing strategy and perhaps because of this Samsung has achieved a higher volume of smartphone sales across the world. However, towards the end of 2012 Apple ended Samsung's four-year lead in the US mobile phone market. With the launch of the iPhone 5, Apple also offered lower-priced, old versions of the iPhone, shipping an estimated 17.7 million phones to the United States in the last three months of 2012. This **stratified pricing strategy** provided a range of phones to satisfy the needs of more budget-conscious consumers. Apple's share of the market increased from 25 to 34 per cent in one year.

---

5) Competitive pricing

A competitive pricing strategy will be adopted by a business operating in a market that is close to perfect competition. These market conditions make it difficult for the firm to charge prices that are significantly higher or lower than those of competitors. The business will therefore price its products very close to the price of competitors.

6) Value pricing

Value pricing involves selling a product which is of similar quality to that of competitors at a lower price. The aim of this strategy is to attract customers by offering better value than competitors. Although this strategy can mean that the business is potentially not maximizing its profit from each sale, the aim is to increase sales volume so that overall profitability is increased. This strategy uses the consumer psychology in the product positioning model discussed earlier in this chapter.

Extract 8.5: Value pricing at Amazon – a strategy for market monopoly

Amazon, the online retailer, has established a business model that enables it to operate at very low profit margins – often 2 per cent or less – whilst delivering a high-quality service and cheaper products than the competition. It is estimated that Amazon now has over one-third of the entire e-commerce market in the United

States. This strong position has enabled Amazon to undercut new market entrants and increase its dominance of the e-commerce world. In addition, the online retailer has steadily squeezed out high-street bookshops and DVD retailers.

7) Bundle pricing

Bundle pricing is often used by retailers to entice customers to spend more. Typical bundle pricing strategies include 'buy one get one free' (BOGOF) or 'three for the price of two'. Such a strategy decreases the profit margin on each product sold, but increases the volume of sales such that the retailer can achieve an overall higher level of profit. Usually this is a short-term pricing strategy.

Another strategy commonly used by retailers, particularly supermarkets, is that of the *loss leader*. A loss leader is a product which is priced below cost in order to attract customers into the store. The rationale behind the loss leader is that it will attract customers who will then buy other products whilst in the store. This must be a short-term pricing strategy for any one product.

In some cases, prices may be deliberately set very low, even giving away products for free, by a dominant business in the market in order to cut out competitors. This is known as *predatory pricing*, a practice which is illegal under competition law in most legislations.

8) Penetration pricing

Market penetration pricing is the strategy of introducing a new product at a very low price in order to entice consumers to buy that product. In some cases, this may involve selling at a price which is lower than the cost of production. (As mentioned above, this is known as a *loss leader*.) Once the product is established in the market, the price can be brought back up in line with competitors' prices. This is therefore a strategy for increasing market share through sales volume and will only succeed if there is a relatively high level of price elasticity.

This is a good strategy to adopt when launching a new product into an existing market which already contains several similar products. The goal of the business launching the new product is to encourage customers to switch to their product because of its lower price. An example is the launch of a new washing powder. There are already several different brands of washing powder on the market. By launching the new washing powder at a low price the business should achieve two important objectives. Firstly, they will make their product more attractive than that of their competitors. Secondly, by gaining relatively high levels of sales very quickly they will be able to establish economies of scale, thus reducing the cost per unit. Once customer habits have been established in buying the new product, the business can increase the price so that it is in line with those of competitors.

9) One-off pricing

One-off pricing has been kept as a separate category here because it relates to certain unusual pricing situations. It is at the bottom end of the pricing scale in Figure 8.8 because the strategy usually (but not necessarily) involves selling at a very low price. This pricing strategy will be used by a business that has surplus inventory that could not otherwise be sold. Rather than setting a price to recover the full cost of the product, the business recognizes that any price which covers selling costs will put the business in a better financial position than if it kept the otherwise unusable inventory. This principle is illustrated in Worked Example 8.5.

WORKED EXAMPLE 8.5 One-off pricing

Glaze Co manufactures window units. The company took an order for 50 windows from a customer that subsequently went bankrupt and never paid for or collected the windows. The windows cost $20,000 to manufacture. Another customer has placed an order for similar windows. Glaze Co could change the specification of the 50 windows it already has in stock to meet the needs of a new customer at a further cost of $5,000. It has no other use for the windows which otherwise would be scrapped. Glaze Co usually adds a mark-up of 30 per cent to the cost of windows in arriving at a sales price.

What is the minimum price that Glaze Co should accept from the new customer for the 50 windows?

Answer

In this case Glaze Co should ignore the $20,000 it has already spent on manufacturing the windows. If it costs only $5,000 to adapt the windows to the needs of the new customer, any price above $5,000 will put Glaze Co in a better financial position than not selling the windows and having to scrap them. The company should therefore be happy to negotiate any price above $5,000.

Exercises: now attempt Exercise 8.2 on page 313

Target pricing and target costing

Target pricing is an approach to pricing which combines the three elements discussed in this chapter (cost, competitors and customers). It does so in a manner which recognizes the importance of cost on profitability, whilst ensuring that the competitive focus on customers and competitors leads cost considerations rather than being subsumed by them. The technique originated in Japan in the 1960s, but by the 1980s it was being widely used by a range of businesses across the world.

Target pricing involves examining the market and customer preferences in order to determine in advance what the optimum price would be. The business then sets itself the target of producing the goods or services at a cost which will enable a profit at the target price. This process typically involves the following five steps:

1 Develop a new product based upon analysis of customer needs and demands.

2 Set a target price that is based upon customers' perceived value of the product.

3 Set a target profit margin. This will be based upon the required return on investment. (See Chapter 6 for more details of return on investment.)

4 Derive the target cost of production by subtracting the target profit from the target price.

5 In many cases there will be a cost gap between actual cost per unit and the target cost per unit. Techniques such as **value engineering** and **kaizen** (see below) can then be used to bring actual costs as close as possible to target costs.

This process is illustrated in Figure 8.9.

Figure 8.9 The target costing process

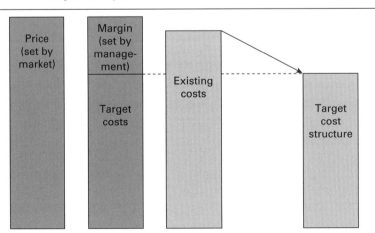

Value engineering

Value engineering is a customer-focused approach to product design. It involves identifying those parts of a product or service that add value and equally importantly eliminating those features which do not add value. The aim of value engineering is to maximize value to the consumer whilst minimizing costs.

Value engineering focuses on the planning and design stage of a product's life cycle and strives to ensure that products are designed in such a way that it is possible to produce them to target costs. Some features, although desirable, may be much too expensive to manufacture. Sometimes minor changes at the design stage can create huge efficiency savings once manufacturing commences. If such matters are not dealt with at the planning stage, it may be impossible to meet target costs no matter how efficient the production process is.

In practice, activity-based costing will be an important tool at the product design stage, as it will help in decision making about how product features will translate to manufacturing costs. By understanding the cost drivers a business will be better able to control its costs.

Kaizen

Kaizen is a Japanese term which refers to a philosophy of continuous improvement in operations. In practice, it means continually examining the manufacturing processes and business systems of the organization in order to identify and implement efficiency changes which will reduce costs. The focus of kaizen is typically on small improvements, rather than large and drastic changes to production processes. An example of a kaizen improvement can be as simple as moving the location of a parts trolley by one metre in order to improve the efficiency and speed at which an operative works.

Exercises: now attempt Exercise 8.3 on page 313

Conclusion

This chapter has examined the factors that go into the pricing decision and has set out a range of pricing strategies used across different industries. In practice, the pricing decision can be very difficult. It may not be possible to obtain the information needed to make some of the evaluations set out in this chapter. Furthermore, many markets are volatile and the factors underpinning pricing are constantly changing. The pace of change of technology and new innovation in many products and services makes the life cycle of a product and the competitive environment extremely uncertain. This means that managers must continually review their pricing strategies and the costing, competitor and consumer factors which underpin them.

COMPREHENSION QUESTIONS

1 Distinguish between the three main perspectives on pricing and identify the main concerns of each perspective.

2 What are the 3C's of pricing and how does each impact upon price?

3 Distinguish between full-cost and marginal-cost pricing.

4 Explain the concept of life-cycle costing and how this relates to pricing.

5 If a product is known to have a low price elasticity of demand and a company reduces its price in order to stimulate demand, would you expect this to lead to increased or decreased overall sales revenues?

6 Publisher Co sells both paper books and e-books. If the company reduces the price of its e-books, should it expect demand for paper books to increase or decrease?

7 Explain how customers' expectations can impact upon the price they are willing to pay for a product.

8 What is price skimming and under what circumstances is it an appropriate pricing strategy?

Answers available at **www.koganpage.com/afm3**

Exercises

Answers available at www.koganpage.com/afm3

Exercise 8.1: Marginal-cost-plus pricing

Printit Co provides rapid printing and design services to the public and small businesses. The business, which has 12 employees, operates out of a high-street shop which includes office space. The company undertakes 400 to 500 jobs each month. It currently operates a full-cost-plus pricing system, and as each job is unique it must be priced individually. The accountant, who works part-time, is struggling to keep on top of the task of pricing each job. She has suggested that the company should move to a marginal-cost-plus pricing system as this would make pricing much easier.

Required:
Discuss the advantages and disadvantages for Printit Co of changing to a marginal-cost-plus pricing system from its existing full-cost-plus pricing system.

Exercise 8.2: Pricing strategy

XTA Co is about to launch a new personal computer called the *Eye* which the user wears like a pair of glasses. Interaction with the computer is through eye movement and voice. No competitors are offering such an advanced product, but two competitors are expected to launch a similar device within the next six months. Market research has indicated that there is a great deal of customer excitement about this new computer and there have been several favourable articles in leading computer magazines.

Required:
Set out a pricing strategy for the new product, explaining why you consider it to be the most appropriate.

Exercise 8.3: Target pricing

ACT Motors, a large vehicle manufacturer, is seeking to launch a new family saloon car. The market for such cars is already well established and highly competitive.

Required:
Explain the main steps ACT Motors should take in developing a target price for the new family saloon car.

References

McCarthy, J E (1960) *Basic Marketing: A managerial approach*, Richard D Irwin, Homewood, IL

Schulz, D E, Tannenbaum, S I and Lauterborn, R F (1993) *Integrated Marketing Communications*, NTC Publishing Group, Lincolnwood, IL

Shimizu, K (1973) *Advertising Theory and Strategies*, Souseisha Book Company, Japan

Investment decisions

09

OBJECTIVE

All organizations have to make investment decisions through the process of acquiring, replacing or upgrading premises, equipment or vehicles, hiring new staff, investing in training, or changing systems and procedures. Such decisions must make strategic sense for the organization, but they must also make good financial sense. It is because of this that managers at all levels find themselves involved in the financial evaluation of investments, whether it be in preparing proposals or evaluating options. This chapter therefore aims to provide the understanding necessary for managers to participate in the financial evaluation of investment opportunities.

LEARNING OUTCOMES

After studying this chapter, the reader will be able to:

- Assess the financial impact of an investment using traditional techniques.
- Evaluate the strengths and weaknesses of the above techniques.
- Demonstrate an awareness of alternative techniques.
- Explain the role of financial assessment within the wider strategic assessment of investment decisions.

KEY TOPICS COVERED

- Traditional investment appraisal techniques.
- The strengths and weaknesses of individual appraisal techniques.
- The use and abuse of investment appraisal techniques.
- Financial analysis within the overall context of investment planning.
- Non-financial factors in investment appraisal.
- Alternative strategic approaches to investment appraisal.

MANAGEMENT ISSUES

- Managers need to be able to interpret and evaluate the results of financial investment appraisal calculations, rather than perform the calculations. This chapter therefore focuses on those skills.
- The apparent sophistication and precision of financial investment appraisal techniques can mask shortcomings and behavioural aspects of their application. This chapter therefore includes evaluation of frequently used techniques within a wider behavioural context.

Introduction

Investment appraisal is the process of deciding which projects or assets to invest in. In this chapter we will look at how to evaluate investments from a financial point of view and how such financial analysis fits into the overall investment decision process. Investment appraisal should always be understood within the wider context of strategic formulation and implementation. Although such matters are beyond the scope of this textbook, this chapter will look at how non-financial factors, risk levels and wider strategic concerns can impinge upon the more traditional concerns of the immediate economic return from an investment.

Investment appraisal, sometimes referred to as capital investment appraisal, is concerned with organizational decisions about investment in equipment, machinery, buildings or other long-term assets. This can include a range of types of decision such as replacement of existing assets, investing in new IT or equipment to reduce operating costs, expansion through purchasing new buildings or equipment, improving delivery service or staff training. However, the principles apply equally to investments in shares in companies, whether made by businesses or individuals. Therefore the techniques looked at in this chapter are equally relevant to both businesses and individuals who are involved in making investments.

The importance of good investment appraisal lies with the strategic and financial importance of the investments made. Investments will shape the future of the organization. Such investments often involve large resources. Wrong decisions can be costly and difficult to reverse and will have a direct impact on the organization's ability to meet its strategic objectives.

From a financial point of view, an investment involves making a cash outlay with the aim of receiving future cash flows in return. At a basic level, assessing the financial viability of an investment involves simply comparing costs with benefits, and ensuring that the benefits outweigh the costs. However, in practice this can prove difficult, as identifying and measuring the costs and benefits from an investment can be a complex task. This chapter will address some of the problems of investment cost–benefit analysis and look at how techniques have developed in order to meet these problems.

In order to help make investment decisions, a common method of appraisal is required; one which can be applied equally to a whole spectrum of investment situations and which will enable the decision-maker to assess individual investments and compare alternative investment opportunities.

Investment appraisal – the basics

In this section we will consider the important questions which should be asked when an investment is being evaluated. Imagine that you are offered an investment opportunity as follows: 'Invest $1,000 with me now and I promise that I will make you rich.' Before you hand over your money, what is the information that you need in order to evaluate this investment opportunity effectively?

Firstly, you would want some clarification on how 'rich' the investment would make you. In other words, you want some information on the *return* that the investment offers.

Secondly, you would also want to know *when* you will become rich. You therefore need more information on the *timing* of returns from the investment. There would be a significant difference between receiving a return immediately and receiving the same return in 10 years' time. This is referred to as the **'time value of money'**. This principle recognizes that the sooner you receive a return, the more valuable that return is to you.

Thirdly, you would also want some more information on the *risks* involved in your investment. If you are going to invest $1,000, what is the risk that the promised return never materializes (or that you lose the whole $1,000)?

Therefore, we can say that in evaluating a potential investment we need information about three key issues: *risk*, *return*, and *timing*.

Having established these basic principles we can now look at the techniques most frequently used in practice by businesses for investment appraisal, and examine how these techniques address the questions raised above.

Traditional evaluation techniques

There are three techniques which are in common usage in evaluating capital investment decisions:

- payback period (PP);
- accounting rate of return (ARR);
- discounted cash flow (DCF).

The last of these techniques, discounted cash flow, can be divided into two different methods of application: net present value (NPV) and internal rate of return (IRR).

In order to examine each of these techniques we will look at how they are applied to a simple investment opportunity, as set out in Worked Example 9.1.

WORKED EXAMPLE 9.1

Soundzgud Co is a manufacturer of hifi equipment. The company is currently considering the launch of a new amplifier called the 'Window Rattler'. Research indicates that the company can expect sales of its new amplifier as shown in Table 9.1.

Table 9.1

	1	2	3	4	5	6
Year	$'000	$'000	$'000	$'000	$'000	$'000
Revenue	600	800	800	700	500	400

The machinery needed to produce the 'Window Rattler' will cost $1,200,000. However, at the end of six years this machinery can still be used for other products and is expected to then have a value of $150,000. The machinery will be purchased as soon as the decision to manufacture has been approved by the board of directors.

The company accountant has forecast the production costs for the 'Window Rattler' (Table 9.2).

Table 9.2

Year	1 $'000	2 $'000	3 $'000	4 $'000	5 $'000	6 $'000
Production costs	320	410	410	350	250	200

The production costs exclude depreciation, which the company normally charges on a straight-line basis. The company uses a discount rate of 15 per cent to evaluate new investments.

Expert view 9.1: Common notation conventions

Because of the importance of timing, any cash flows or profits in relation to an investment must be allocated to a particular accounting period. With the use of computer spreadsheets, an accurate analysis of timing can be made to the nearest month or even week or day. However, as all cash flows used in investment appraisal are forecasts, and therefore by their very nature estimated, it is often not possible to identify when they will occur to such a high level of accuracy. Therefore, the most common convention for investments which will run over several years is to identify cash flows by year and to assume that they will arise at the end of the year. Obviously, this may not be the actual pattern of cash flows.

A significant difference between profit and cash flow is that profit is recorded using the accruals principle. That is to say, sales and purchases are recorded when the transaction takes place rather than when any underlying payment is made. This means that, in practice, profit may be allocated to a different period from the underlying cash flow. However, for simplicity, in this example it will be assumed that cash flows occur in the same period in which accounting costs or revenues arise.

Another significant difference between profit and cash flow is depreciation. This is an accounting adjustment rather than a cash payment.

A common convention in recording the timing of cash flows or profits is to use the term t_0 to denote an item which occurs immediately, t_1 to denote an item which occurs in one year's time, t_2 for two years' time and so on. Hence, the cash flows forecast for the 'Window Rattler' can be recorded as shown in Table 9.3.

Table 9.3

Timing	Cash flow	$'000
t_0 (Immediately)	Cost of machine	(1,200)
t_1 (1 year's time)	Net cash inflow (600–320)	280
t_2 (2 years' time)	Net cash inflow (800–410)	390
t_3 (3 years' time)	Net cash inflow (800–410)	390
t_4 (4 years' time)	Net cash inflow (700–350)	350
t_5 (5 years' time)	Net cash inflow (500–250)	250
t_6 (6 years' time)	Net cash inflow (400–200)	200
t_6 (6 years' time)	Residual value of machine	150

We can now go on to examine how each of the investment appraisal techniques deals with this information.

Payback period (PP)

The payback period is the length of time it takes for an initial investment to be re-paid out of the net cash inflow from a project. The easiest way to calculate this is to establish the cumulative net cash-flow position at the end of each year of the invest-ment. Applied to the example of the 'Window Rattler' the payback period can be calculated as shown in Table 9.4.

Table 9.4

Timing	Cash flow	$'000	Cumulative $'000
Immediately (t_0)	Cost of investment	(1,200)	(1,200)
1 year's time (t_1)	Net cash inflow	280	(920)
2 years' time (t_2)	Net cash inflow	390	(530)
3 years' time (t_3)	Net cash inflow	390	(140)
4 years' time (t_4)	Net cash inflow	350	210

There is no need to take this calculation further than four years as we can see that the initial cost of the investment is paid back sometime between three and four years. At the end of three years there is still another $140,000 to pay back, but after four years the initial cost plus a further $210,000 has been paid back. If we stick with the assumption that all cash flows arise at the end of the year, we would say that this investment has a payback period of four years. However, if we assume that the cash inflows arise evenly throughout the year, we could calculate the payback period to a fraction of year as follows:

Initial cost still not paid back after three years = $140,000
Net cash inflow in year four = $350,000

Therefore the remaining balance of $140,000 would be paid back in $140,000/$350,000 = 0.4 of a year.

The payback period is therefore 3.4 years.

Simply knowing that this investment would take 3.4 years to pay back does not in itself tell us whether this is a good investment. An evaluation has to be made as to whether this is an acceptable payback period. However, if two or more alternative investments are being compared, they can be ranked in terms of their payback period, with the shortest being the most attractive.

Extract 9.1: Payback period in use – Standard Life and Next

In practice, businesses which use this technique have predetermined payback periods. These tend to differ according to type of investment. For example, an investment in IT equipment may be required to pay back within two years. On the other hand, investment in a new building may be required to pay back within 20 years:

- Standard Life, a pensions and life assurance company, set itself a payback period of five years for any new products launched.

- Next, a UK-based retailer, uses a payback period of 18 months when investing in a new clothing store. However, when the business opened its first Home and Garden store, it set a payback period of 25 months.

Evaluation of PP

Having examined how the payback period works as an investment technique, we can evaluate how well it addresses the three questions we set at the beginning of this chapter. The payback period, by its very nature, tells us something directly about *timing*. In doing so, it also tells us indirectly about an important aspect of *risk*, because a shorter payback period can be equated with a lower level of risk. However, the technique tells us very little about *return* other than the fact that the initial outlay is recovered. Payback period can therefore be seen as more of a *risk* appraisal tool than a measure of *return*.

In fact, in terms of addressing return, the technique has some major shortcomings. Firstly, it ignores cash flows outside of the payback period and in doing so ignores total return. Consider Worked Example 9.2 which compares two potential investments.

WORKED EXAMPLE 9.2

Table 9.5

Timing	Cash flow	Investment A $'000	Investment B $'000
Immediately (t_0)	Cost of investment	(600)	(600)
1 year's time (t_1)	Net cash inflow	200	200
2 years' time (t_2)	Net cash inflow	200	200
3 years' time (t_3)	Net cash inflow	200	200
4 years' time (t_4)	Net cash inflow	10	400
5 years' time (t_5)	Net cash inflow	5	600
6 years' time (t_6)	Net cash inflow	5	800

Both Investment A and Investment B have identical payback periods of three years and are therefore equally attractive according to the payback period technique. However, in years 4 to 6 the cash returns of Investment A fall substantially. In comparison, the cash returns of Investment B continue to rise. Looking at this full picture, Investment B is clearly a better alternative, as the same initial investment offers a much greater overall return. But this fact is not revealed by the payback period method of analysis. To take this example a step further, consider the implication of Investment A offering a $400,000 return in year 1. This would make the payback period two years. Investment A would therefore be favoured using the payback period method of evaluation, even though Investment B offers a much higher overall return. An issue to be aware of when using this technique, therefore, is that it favours short-term returns rather than highest overall returns.

A second shortcoming is that the technique ignores the timing of cash flows within a payback period. Consider Worked Example 9.3, again of two investments with identical payback periods.

WORKED EXAMPLE 9.3

Table 9.6

Timing	Cash flow	Investment A $'000	Investment B $'000
Immediately (t_0)	Cost of investment	(600)	(600)
1 year's time (t_1)	Net cash inflow	500	50
2 years' time (t_2)	Net cash inflow	50	50
3 years' time (t_3)	Net cash inflow	50	500

Both investments take exactly three years to pay back the initial cost. However, Investment A has repaid the bulk of this initial cost by the end of the first year. There is therefore a significant difference between the two investments in that we can say Investment A is less risky. Were the investment to stop suddenly for some reason at the end of year 2, the business making Investment A would have already recovered a substantial part of the initial cost, whereas the business making Investment B would have lost most of this money.

Despite the shortcomings, payback period is an extremely popular investment appraisal technique in practice. Several surveys of businesses conducted over the past 40 years have all shown that, despite the rise in popularity of more sophisticated techniques, payback period remains the most widely used means of investment appraisal, being used by around 80 per cent of businesses. Its strength lies in its simplicity – it is not difficult to calculate or to understand. Most importantly, it appeals to a basic human level of psychology. Anyone having made a substantial investment understands that there is an initial period of anxiety concerning the risk of that investment. The point at which the investment has repaid its initial outlay is an important psychological landmark as it means that the initial capital investment has not been lost. It is because of this that payback period becomes an extremely important technique when a company has liquidity constraints or severe limitations on the availability of financing. The technique is also most useful for projects which are known to have a short life and require a quick repayment of investment.

Expert view 9.2: Discounted payback period

Some of the shortcomings of the payback period discussed here can be overcome by applying the technique to a discounted cash flow (see later section 'Discounted cash flows and the time value of money'). However, if this is done, some of the major advantages of the technique are lost, such as its simplicity.

Extract 9.2: Disney buys Star Wars

In 2012 Disney bought Lucasfilm, the company behind the Star Wars films, for US$4bn. How did this purchase price stack up in terms of return on that investment? The main value comes from the potential earning of future films. Disney announced that it planned to release three new Star Wars films, one every three years, starting in 2015. The previous three Star Wars films generated around US$1.5bn each at the box office. Such films usually cost around US$0.5bn to make and market, so that would generate Disney net cash flows of US$3bn. In addition, Lucasfilm has ongoing revenue of around US$0.9 billion per year from existing films, video games and related consumer products. There is an obvious risk in terms of the success of future films, but the previous three Star Wars films were a box office success despite not being well received by many fans. These cash-flow forecasts would suggest a payback period as short as five years. Not bad for a brand that has been financially successful for the past 35 years and looks set to continue long into the future.

Accounting rate of return (ARR)

The term 'accounting' in accounting rate of return refers to the basis of calculation of this technique, which is accounting profits. Unlike the other techniques examined in this chapter which all use cash flow, ARR is calculated on the accruals basis, ie using profit.

The ARR is sometimes referred to by other names. In the United States it is more widely called return on investment (ROI). Other names include average rate of return, book rate of return or unadjusted rate of return. It is also sometimes called return on capital employed (ROCE). However, as will be seen below, this name is more appropriately applied to divisional or overall company performance, rather than the tool for investment appraisal. This multitude of names reflects both the wide usage of the technique and the fact that there is a range of definitions as to its calculation.

Although there are different ways of calculating ARR, which will be discussed below, we will concentrate on the most commonly applied calculation. This takes the 'return' on an investment as being the average accounting profit after depreciation and expressing this as a percentage of the average investment over the life of the project:

$$\text{ARR} = \frac{\text{Average annual profit}}{\text{Average investment}} \times 100\%$$

Applying this formula to our investment scenario in Worked Example 9.1, the average annual profit can be calculated by dividing the total profit for the investment by the number of years over which this profit is earned.

The total profit before deducting depreciation is $1,860,000 ($280,000 + $390,000 + $390,000 + $350,000 + $250,000 + $200,000).

The total depreciation can be calculated as the initial cost less the residual value of the investment = $1,200,000 − $150,000 = $1,050,000.

$$\text{The average annual profit} = \frac{(\$1,860,000 - \$1,050,000)}{2} = \$135,000$$

Because the company charges depreciation on a straight-line basis, the average investment will be the value halfway between the initial cost and the residual value:

$$\text{Average investment} = \frac{\text{Initial cost + Residual value}}{2}$$

$$\text{Average investment} = \frac{\$1,200,000 + \$150,000}{2} = \$675,000$$

$$\text{Therefore the ARR} = \frac{\$135,000}{\$675,000} \times 100\% = 20.0\%$$

Once calculated, this ARR of 20 per cent can be compared with a predetermined minimum acceptable return for the company. For example, if Soundzgud has a predetermined requirement of a return on investments of 15 per cent, the above return of 20 per cent would be acceptable.

Evaluation of ARR

Unlike payback period (and the discounted cash-flow techniques we will look at later in the chapter), the ARR evaluates investments based upon profits. The other techniques use cash flows. There are both advantages and disadvantages to this use of profit.

The main advantage of ARR is that it calculates the performance of an investment in terms of profit returns, which is in line with the most often reported figure for overall company performance. ARR provides a measure which is directly comparable with ROCE, which is the most common measurement of the financial performance of a business as a whole.

ROCE is measured as:

$$\text{ROCE} = \frac{\text{Profit}}{\text{Capital employed}}$$

It can therefore be seen that there is direct comparison between the formula for ARR and that for ROCE. They are both measuring the same thing – the level of profit in relation to the capital invested in order to earn that profit: ARR measures this at the level of the individual investment; ROCE measures it at the divisional or company level.

It makes sense to use a measure for evaluating new investments which reflects the way the performance of the whole business will be evaluated. By comparing the ARR of a new investment with the existing ROCE of the whole business, managers are able to assess the potential impact of that new investment on the financial performance of the business as a whole. If a new investment has an ARR which is lower than the existing ROCE, that investment will reduce the future ROCE of the business. On the other hand, a new investment with an ARR greater than the existing ROCE will increase that ROCE in the future.

Despite the advantages outlined above, ARR suffers from some major deficiencies which have caused the technique to be criticized by many academic commentators. However, it is still widely used in practice, so you need to be aware of these deficiencies and their implications:

- ARR uses the accruals concept, that is to say, it is calculated from profit rather than the cash flow. Profit is far more judgemental and therefore easily manipulated than cash flow. For example, profits from an investment will vary with different methods of stock valuation and depreciation calculation. This means that it is more difficult to obtain an objective measure of performance. If ARR is being used to make comparisons between different organizations, problems will arise in comparing the figures.

- ARR is a relative measure: it measures profit returns in relation to the amount invested. This makes it possible to compare the profitability of investments of different sizes, but it means that if ARR is used to choose between two or more projects, a small project may have a higher ARR than a larger project whilst giving a much smaller absolute profit.

- There is no universally accepted basis of calculating the figures used for either the profit from an investment or the capital invested to earn that profit. This means that, in practice, erroneous comparisons may be made between investments because one is not comparing like with like. One major problem is that there is disagreement over whether the ARR calculation should use average capital invested (as shown in the example above) or initial investment. The argument for using the initial investment is that this is the cost of the investment and therefore reflects the return required to recover that cost. The more widely accepted average capital invested method argues that the ARR calculation should take into account the fact that the initial cost is written off over the life of the investment, and that an average return therefore needs to reflect the average value of the capital investment. Neither method is wrong; they simply reflect different principles.

- The technique ignores the timing of profits, as the averaging used in the calculation of ARR removes all information about timing of receipts and payments. Consider Worked Example 9.4 in which three different investments each last four years:

WORKED EXAMPLE 9.4

Table 9.7

Profits ($'000)	Investment A	Investment B	Investment C
Year 1	850	50	250
Year 2	50	50	250
Year 3	50	50	250
Year 4	50	850	250

All three investments offer an average annual profit of $250,000. However, there are significant differences in both the evenness and the timing of this profit. This information, which may be important in an investment decision, is lost in the ARR calculation through the process of averaging. ARR is therefore blind to the **time value of money**.

- Another problem arises because of this averaging process. It renders the technique unsuitable for comparing investments of different lengths. If an investment offers long-term but diminishing profits, then as each year of a lower profit is added to the calculation the average profit will be pulled downwards. Consider Worked Example 9.5 in which two investments have the same initial cost of $1 million with no residual value. However, Investment A has a life of only three years whereas Investment B has a life of six years:

WORKED EXAMPLE 9.5

Table 9.8

Profits ($'000)	Investment A	Investment B
Year 1	300	300
Year 2	300	300
Year 3	300	300
Year 4	–	200
Year 5	–	150
Year 6	–	100

For the first three years both investments offer the same level of profits. However, Investment B continues to deliver profit for a further three years, albeit at a lower level. Investment B offers a total profit return of $1,350,000 from an initial investment of $1 million, whereas investment A offers a total profit return of only $900,000 from the same initial investment.

However, when we calculate the ARR of each investment, Investment A appears to be the more attractive simply because the average annual profit is higher:

$$\text{ARR (investment A)} = \frac{\$300}{\$500} \times 100\% = 60\%$$

$$\text{ARR (investment B)} = \frac{\$225}{\$500} \times 100\% = 45\%$$

Discounted cash flows and the time value of money

The final two investment appraisal techniques we will examine in this section both involve the use of **discounted cash flows**. Discounting a cash flow involves making adjustments for the time value of money, that is to say, to reflect the fact that *when* you receive money has an impact upon its **value** to you.

Here is a simple example to illustrate this principle: Would you prefer to receive $100 now or $100 in two years' time? I would imagine that you would answer that you would prefer to receive the $100 now, for a number of reasons:

- There is always the risk that you will not actually receive the $100 in two years' time.

- The effect of inflation means that you can buy more with your $100 now than you will be able to in two years' time. Hence it is more valuable to you now.

- You could take the $100 now and invest it for two years, after which you would have more than $100.

We will look at risk and inflation later in this chapter, but at this point we can examine the issue of earning interest in more detail. In the example above, deciding between $100 now or $100 in two years' time was relatively easy. However, what if I offered you a choice of $100 now or $108 in two years' time? You need some means of comparing the two amounts to decide which is the more attractive. One way in which you could do this is to ask: 'What would $100 received now be worth if I invested it for two years?'

Compounding and discounting

Let us assume that you can invest your $100 received now at an interest rate of 5 per cent. At the end of one year you will have $105 ($100 × 1.05). At this point, the principle of **compound interest** starts to apply, because in the second year you will earn interest not only upon your original $100 but also upon the $5 interest you earned in the first year. Hence, at the end of two years you will have $110.25 (($100 × 1.05) × 1.05).

Because the formula calculating this is $100 × 1.05 × 1.05 = $100 × 1.05², we can generalize this as:

$$A = P \times (1 + r)^n$$

Where: A = the amount received in the future
P = the original amount invested
r = the interest rate earned
n = the number of years the investment runs

This technique gives you a way of comparing the $100 offered now with the $108 offered in two years' time. You can calculate that if you take the $100 now and invest it for two years at 5 per cent, you will end up with $110.25. You would therefore be better off taking the $100 now rather than the $108 in two years' time.

This technique works well for a simple investment scenario such as that given above. However, it is not so useful if the investment is a little more complex.

What if you were offered the alternative of $100 now or $55 in one year's time and a further $55 in two years' time? In this case you cannot use the compounding technique shown above, because there is no single time in the future to which you can compound the $100 received now. We therefore need to modify the technique.

The one point in time which we can always use consistently is now (the present moment). So rather than asking the question 'what will $100 received now be worth at some point in the future?', we ask 'what would the money received in the future be worth if received now?' By asking the question this way we can compare monies received at several different points of time in the future.

Let us go back to the choice between $100 received now and $108 received in two years' time. Rather than **compounding** the $100 forward, we **discount** the $108 back to today's date by asking the question: 'What would I need to receive now to have the equivalent of $108 in two years' time?' Another way of looking at this is to ask: 'If I can earn interest at 5 per cent per year, how much do I need to invest now in order to end up with $108 after two years?' We can calculate this by using the formula which we established above:

$$A = P \times (1 + r)^n$$

We used this formula before to calculate the value of A (the amount received in the future) when we already have the value of P (the amount invested now). We simply need to rearrange the formula to start with A, the amount receivable in the future ($108), and calculate the value of P:

$$P = \frac{A}{(1 + r)}$$

An alternative way of stating this formula is:

$$P = A \times \frac{1}{(1+r)^n}$$

If we apply this formula to our example:

$$P = \$108 \times \frac{1}{1.05^2} = \$97.96$$

This means that if we wanted to receive $108 in two years' time we would have to invest $97.96 now. In terms of the time value of money, receiving $108 in two years' time is the equivalent of receiving $97.96 now. We can compare the two alternatives: receive $100 now or receive an amount in two years' time which is the equivalent of receiving $97.96 now. We end up with the same decision as we did before – it is better to take the $100 now.

What of the second scenario in which you were offered the alternative of $100 now or $55 received at the end of one year and a further $55 received at the end of two years? The calculation is a little more complex, but we can evaluate these alternatives using this new discounting technique. We do this by taking each of the future amounts and discounting them back to their present value and then adding them together as follows:

Present value of $55 received in one year's time:

$$= \$55 \times \frac{1}{1.05} = \$52.38$$

Present value of $55 received in two years' time:

$$= \$55 \times \frac{1}{1.05^2} = \$49.89$$

Therefore, receiving $55 in one year's time plus $55 in two years' time is the equivalent of receiving $52.38 + $49.89 = $102.27 now. We are now able to evaluate this choice. In this case we would be better off taking the two future amounts as their present value is more than the $100 offered now. (In fact, we can measure precisely that we would be $2.27 better off in today's terms by taking the future amounts: $102.27 − $100 = $2.27).

Discount tables   The fraction by which we multiply the future cash flow A in order to calculate its present value P is known as the *discount factor*. This, as was shown above, is calculated using the following formula:

$$\frac{1}{(1+r)^n}$$ where: r = the discount rate applied

n = the number of years

Because we use the same formula every time to calculate a discount factor, a standard set of values can be set out in a table which provides the discount factor for common discount rates and time periods. A discount factor table is available in Appendix C.

Net present value (NPV)

The NPV technique uses the principle of discounting cash flows explained above. The NPV of an investment is the sum of the present values of all cash flows which arise as a result of undertaking that investment.

The present value (P) of a single sum, A, receivable in n years' time, given an interest rate (discount rate) of r, is given by:

$$P = A \times \frac{1}{(1+r)^n}$$

Let us now see how this technique works when applied to the Soundzgud Co investment in Worked Example 9.1. The discount rate we need to apply to the cash flow from the project is 15 per cent. The relevant discount factors have been extracted from Appendix C. We can present the NPV calculation as shown in Table 9.9.

Table 9.9

	Cash flow $	Discount factor (15%)	Present value $
t_0 (Immediately)	(1,200,000)	1.000	(1,200,000)
t_1 (1 year's time)	280,000	0.870	243,600
t_2 (2 years' time)	390,000	0.756	294,840
t_3 (3 years' time)	390,000	0.658	256,620
t_4 (4 years' time)	350,000	0.572	200,200
t_5 (5 years' time)	250,000	0.497	124,250
t_6 (6 years' time)	200,000	0.432	86,400
t_6 (6 years' time)	150,000	0.432	64,800
Net present value			**$70,710**

From this calculation it can be seen that the NPV of this investment is $70,710. This can be interpreted as meaning that the company will be $70,710 better off, in today's terms, by undertaking this investment.

There is therefore a simple rule for interpreting NPV calculations: If the NPV is positive, the company will increase its wealth by undertaking the investment, which is therefore financially viable; if the NPV is negative, the company would decrease its wealth by undertaking investment and the investment should therefore be rejected.

The NPV technique can be seen as a more sophisticated means of investment appraisal than the payback period and the ARR. Unlike the payback period, NPV takes account of the entire cash flow of the project; unlike ARR, NPV takes account of the timing of earnings from an investment. The further into the future a cash flow arises, the more it is discounted. This reflects the increased risk and uncertainty of cash flows as they lie further into the future.

Not only is NPV more sophisticated in the way that it takes account of *timing*, *risk*, and *return*, but it is also a technique which is capable of incorporating more sophisticated and subtle analysis of investments. We will see this as we look at more complex investment scenarios later in the chapter.

Internal rate of return (IRR)

Internal rate of return is a second discounted cash-flow technique which works on the same mathematical principles as NPV, but uses discounting to give an answer in a slightly different format.

In the NPV calculation above, we discounted the cash flow from the Soundzgud investment at 15 per cent to produce a positive NPV of $70,710. The implication of this positive NPV is that the actual return of the investment is greater than 15 per cent. The discount rate which we apply in calculating the NPV represents the minimum acceptable return. A positive NPV means that this minimum return has been exceeded and this is why investments with a positive NPV should be accepted.

Another way of using the DCF technique would be to calculate the actual discounted cash-flow return of the investment and compare that to our minimum acceptable return of 15 per cent. This is known as the internal rate of return, as it is the rate of return 'internal' to, ie within, the project.

In practice, the IRR will be the discount rate which gives an NPV of zero. With a computerized spreadsheet, calculating this discount rate is relatively straightforward. But if a computer is not available, the IRR can be estimated as demonstrated below.

Returning to the Soundzgud investment in Worked Example 9.1, the NPV at 15 per cent was a positive value of $70,710. This means that the IRR of the investment must be greater than 15 per cent. We can therefore choose a discount rate greater than 15 per cent and recalculate the NPV to see if we are closer to the IRR. (Remember, the exact IRR would give an NPV of zero.) Let us discount the project again using a discount rate of 20 per cent (Table 9.10).

Table 9.10

Timing	Cash flow $	Discount factor (20%)	Present value $
t_0 (Immediately)	(1,200,000)	1.000	(1,200,000)
t_1 (1 year's time)	280,000	0.833	233,240
t_2 (2 years' time)	390,000	0.694	270,660
t_3 (3 years' time)	390,000	0.579	225,810
t_4 (4 years' time)	350,000	0.482	168,700
t_5 (5 years' time)	250,000	0.402	100,500
t_6 (6 years' time)	200,000	0.335	67,000
t_6 (6 years' time)	150,000	0.335	50,250
Net present value			$(83,840)

This time we get a negative NPV of –$83,840. This means that the IRR must lie somewhere between 15 and 20 per cent. We can establish the IRR more accurately using a mathematical technique called *linear interpolation*. This is done by applying the formula:

$$IRR = A\% + \frac{NPV \text{ at } A\%}{(NPV \text{ at } A\% - NPV \text{ at } B\%)} \times (B\% - A\%)$$

Where: A% = the lower discount rate
          B% = the higher discount rate

Applied to our calculations for the Soundzgud investment we get:

$$IRR = 15\% + \frac{\$70,710}{(\$70,710 + \$83,840)} \times (20\% - 15\%) = 17.3\%$$

So in this case we can say that the investment offers an internal rate of return of 17.3 per cent. We can then compare this to an acceptable minimum level of return in the same way as we did with the ARR technique.

Extract 9.3: EDF – IRR in the energy industry

Investment in energy infrastructure in the UK involves a delicate partnership between the government and the private sector. Adequate returns are critical to attracting suitable private-sector investment. The government is seeking to increase investment in low-carbon energy infrastructure, but this can represent a high risk to investors who consequently require high returns. Investors in gas-fired power plants typically expect an IRR of around 10 per cent, whereas investors in wind generation expect an IRR of 10 to 13 per cent.

The government can reduce the returns demanded by reducing the risk. In 2013 the UK government struck a deal with EDF Energy, the French energy company, to subsidize the building of a new nuclear power plant at Hinkley Point in Somerset. The plant has an estimated build cost of £16bn, which is too high to represent a viable investment. The government is therefore offering various incentives, including guaranteeing EDF's income in order to create an IRR of 10 per cent from the plant. Industry experts estimate that this will add up to a subsidy of £7 per household per year. The complexity of this deal underscores the importance of IRR for investors. Without an adequate return on the investment, no new power plants would be built and the UK would risk facing power shortages.

Evaluation of IRR   The IRR is used in the same way as ARR, by comparing with a predetermined acceptable value. However, the IRR uses discounted cash flows rather than average profits, and therefore has all the advantages we identified when looking at the NPV technique: it takes account of risk, timing and returns.

However, one major drawback of the IRR technique is that it will not work with investments which have what are known as 'non-conventional' cash flows. A conventional investment cash flow is one which involves an initial cash outflow followed by a series of cash inflows. With some investments, net cash flows can flow both inward and outward throughout the life of the project. For example, investment in a nuclear power plant may involve initial cash outflows followed by many years of cash inflows and then substantial cash outflows as the power plant is decommissioned at the end of its life. The IRR technique cannot cope with cash flows such as this, as mathematically it will produce more than one value. It is possible to modify the IRR technique to work around this problem, but such calculations are beyond the scope of an introductory text such as this.

Although DCF techniques are more sophisticated in integrating the factors of risk, timing and returns, they do have some drawbacks which have led to criticism. The process of discounting cash flows inevitably leads to a favouring of investments which offer returns in the shorter term. It has been suggested that this leads to short-termism and a reluctance to make investments which offer strategic benefits which may be more long-term and more difficult to quantify. Also, the techniques have been criticized as being inadequate for evaluating new technology investments as they are unable to evaluate non-quantifiable issues. We will look at some methods for addressing these problems later in the chapter.

Exercises: now attempt Exercise 9.1 on page 351

Incorporating real-world complexities into investment appraisal

So far we have examined the main investment appraisal techniques using a relatively straightforward example. However, in the real world, investment appraisal decisions will be more complex and need to take into account issues such as inflation and the impact of taxation. In this section we will examine some of these real-world complexities and look at how they can be incorporated into our calculations.

Establishing an appropriate discount rate

The discount rate used in an NPV calculation represents the minimum acceptable rate of return for the investor. In practice, a wide variety of methods can be used to determine appropriate discount rates. Most organizations establish a discount rate based upon either the weighted average cost of capital (WACC) or the capital asset pricing model (CAPM). The calculation of WACC is discussed in more detail in Chapter 10. However, whatever method is used in practice, it is based upon certain principles. The rate of return from an investment should be sufficient to cover the cost of financing that investment and should incorporate an assessment of the risk. In simple terms, the more risky an investment is perceived to be, the higher the discount rate used to evaluate it. Hence one important way in which risk assessment is incorporated into investment appraisal is through adjustment of the discount rate used in NPV calculations.

Deciding what to count: relevant cash flows

One of the most common mistakes in investment appraisal in practice involves using the wrong figures. This can mean including costs which should not be counted, or omitting costs or revenues which should be included. These mistakes can lead to inappropriate investment decisions, with disastrous consequences for future business operations.

An important principle in decision making, therefore, is that only those costs or revenues which are affected by the decision should be considered. A frequent error is to include costs which will be incurred anyway, even if the investment were not made. These may include, for example, the costs of employees working on a project, but who would be paid anyway, regardless of whether or not the project goes ahead. In a similar way, factory costs, administration and head office costs which will not change as a result of the project should not be included.

Likewise, costs already incurred, even if they relate to the investment, such as market research or product development already completed, should not be included in an investment appraisal calculation. This is because these costs, having already been incurred, cannot change as a result of making the investment.

Therefore, as a simple rule of thumb, you should include in investment appraisal calculations only those costs or revenues which will change as a result of undertaking the investment (see Worked Example 9.6 below).

Opportunity costs

Opportunity costs are a category of costs used only in decision making. They can be extremely important in assessing the true financial impact of an investment. An opportunity cost can be defined as the cost of an alternative that must be forgone in order to pursue a certain action. Opportunity costs arise from the recognition that committing resources to one project means that they cannot be used on other projects. This may mean that there is a cost to the business in terms of the lost 'opportunity' of using that resource elsewhere. For example, using a production facility to make one product means that that facility cannot be used to make a different product, even though the alternative may be extremely profitable. This example may be obvious, but some opportunity costs are less obvious. For example, opening a new store may draw business away from existing stores in the same area, reducing their profits.

By incorporating opportunity costs into investment appraisal calculations, a business is able to quantify the loss of other potentially profitable opportunities and thereby ensure that the most profitable course of action is taken. To ensure that this is the case, opportunity cost is always measured in terms of lost **contribution** from the use of a particular resource.

Expert view 9.3: Contribution

Contribution = Revenue – Variable (direct) costs

WORKED EXAMPLE 9.6 Relevant costs and opportunity costs

Zebra Co is a paint manufacturer that is planning to launch a new range of fast-drying paints. The directors of Zebra Co have asked you to help evaluate the financial viability of the new paint range. Which of the following amounts would you include in an NPV calculation?

A   A proportion of head office administrative costs calculated at $18,000 per year.

B   Depreciation on the new paint manufacturing plant purchased for the project.

C   Salaries of 10 new workers hired to operate the new plant.

D   Financing costs of $25,000 per year on the loan to purchase the new plant in (B) above.

E   The salary of $35,000 per year of the manager running the new plant. This manager ran one of the other manufacturing plants and has been transferred to this job because of his experience. In his absence, the other plant is being run by a new manager hired as a replacement for the duration of this project. The new manager has a salary of $28,000 per year.

Answers

A   Head office costs will be incurred regardless of whether or not the new range of paints is launched. These costs should therefore not be included in an NPV calculation as they are not relevant.

B   Depreciation is not a cash flow. This cost should therefore not be included.

C   The salaries of new workers are a relevant cost and should therefore be included in the NPV calculation.

D   Financing costs should not be included in the cash flows to be discounted. The cost of financing the investment will be incorporated into the discount rate used to evaluate the investment.

E   This is an example of an opportunity cost. The additional cost to the business of using the experienced manager on this project is the $28,000 it costs to replace him in his old job. The amount which should be included in the NPV calculation is therefore $28,000 per year, rather than $35,000 per year.

Taxation

Tax payments can have a significant impact on investment cash flows and should therefore be taken into account. There are four aspects of taxation which are relevant to investment appraisal:

1 Income tax paid on profits from an investment will represent a cash outflow for a business and therefore needs to be incorporated into the NPV calculation. Because of the importance of timing, when tax is paid can make a difference.

2 Interest on any debt financing is an allowable expense against income tax. The method of financing an investment will therefore impact upon tax cash flows.

3 Any tax losses may give rise to tax relief on other profits which can reduce the amount of taxation payable.

4 Capital allowances are the income tax equivalent of depreciation. They provide tax relief on the investment in assets which will reduce the cash outflows for income tax. For projects involving large investments in buildings, plant or equipment, capital allowances can be significant and can have a major impact upon the cash flows of the investment.

Because these aspects of taxation can have a significant impact upon the cash flows from an investment, it is important to ensure that taxation is always considered and incorporated into investment appraisal calculations.

Inflation

Inflation decreases the purchasing power of future cash inflows, making them worth less. Therefore inflation can create distortions when attempting to assess the time value of money and in calculating returns from investments. For example, a rate of return of 12 per cent could be reduced to 8 per cent in real terms after taking inflation into account. It is therefore important to incorporate the impact of inflation into the return on investments and to be clear whether a quoted rate of return includes or excludes inflation.

To avoid this confusion, different terms are used. If an interest rate includes the effect of inflation, it is referred to as the 'money rate'. Just to add the potential for confusion, this is sometimes also known as the 'nominal' or 'market' rate. On the other hand, 'real' interest rates are stated after adjusting to remove inflation. The adjustment is done as follows:

$$(1 + \text{real rate of interest}) \times (1 + \text{rate of inflation}) = (1 + \text{money rate of interest})$$

Note that the real rate is multiplied by inflation, not added, to give the money rate.

WORKED EXAMPLE 9.7 Adjusting for inflation

a   The real rate of return which a business requires from its investments is 12 per cent and inflation is currently 4 per cent. What is the money rate of return which the business needs to apply for investment appraisal?

   Answer. The money rate of return = 16.5 per cent (1.12 × 1.04 = 1.165).

b   A business experiences a money rate of return of 18 per cent on an investment. Over that same period inflation was 5 per cent. What is the real rate of return on the investment?

   Answer. The real rate of return = 12.4 per cent (1.18 ÷ 1.05 = 1.124).

Dealing with inflation in investment appraisal calculations

There are two ways in which the impact of inflation can be incorporated into investment appraisal calculations:

Money method: the first method is to use 'money' cash flows (ie those cash flows which include inflation) and to discount these using the 'money' discount rate (ie the discount rate which incorporates the effect of inflation).

Real method: the second method is to use cash flows which exclude the impact of inflation and to apply the 'real' discount rate.

Which of these techniques is used in practice will depend upon how the cash-flow forecast for an investment has been compiled. If the cash-flow forecast is in 'today's terms', without consideration of the impact of inflation, it is easier to use the real method. On the other hand, if cash-flow forecasts have been compiled looking at actual amounts payable or receivable in the future (and therefore incorporating inflation), the money method should be used.

WORKED EXAMPLE 9.8 Dealing with inflation

A company is considering investing $100,000 in a project which will give returns of $50,000 in current terms for three years. The money rate of return required by the company is 14 per cent and inflation is currently 4.6 per cent. What is the NPV?

Money method

Table 9.11

Year	Real cash flow $	Money cash flow (inflated by 4.6%)	Money discount factor @14%	Present value $
0	(100,000)	(100,000)	1.000	(100,000)
1	50,000	52,300	0.877	45,867
2	50,000	54,706	0.769	42,069
3	50,000	57,222	0.675	38,625
Net present value				26,561*

Real method

Table 9.12

Year	Real cash flow $	Real discount factor @9%	Present value $
0	(100,000)	1.000	(100,000)
1	50,000	0.917	45,850
2	50,000	0.842	42,100
3	50,000	0.772	38,600
Net present value			26,550*

Real discount rate = 9 per cent (1.14 ÷ 1.046 = 1.09)

*The small difference of $11 between these two calculations (Tables 9.11 and 9.12) is due simply to rounding.

Exercises: now attempt Exercise 9.2 on page 352

Annuities

If the level of cash flow from an investment is the same from year to year, it is referred to as an annuity. If this is the case, there is an easier way of calculating the NPV by using annuity tables. Annuity tables show the present value of $1 received every year, starting one year from now and going on for n years. A set of annuity tables is available in Appendix D.

WORKED EXAMPLE 9.9 Annuity

A company is considering investing in a project which will cost $10,000 and will yield cash inflows of $3,000 per year for five years. No scrap value is expected at the end of the project and the company uses a discount rate of 12 per cent to evaluate investments. Should the investment be accepted?

Answer:

Table 9.13

Year	Cash flow $	Discount factor	Present value $
t_0	(10,000)	1.000	(10,000)
t_1–t_5	3,000	3.605	10,815
NPV			815

As the investment gives a positive NPV of $815, it should be accepted.

Capital rationing: the profitability index

Capital rationing refers to a situation in which there is a limited supply of capital to finance investment projects. In this situation, a company cannot accept all projects with positive NPVs if the costs of implementation will exceed the supply of capital. The company will therefore need to choose between alternative investments.

In practice, capital rationing arises for one of two reasons:

Hard rationing: capital markets will always supply a limited amount of capital. A company therefore may not be able to raise sufficient capital to finance all available projects.

Soft rationing: the company may have sufficient funds available but has chosen to restrict its capital investment for strategic reasons.

When faced with a situation of capital rationing a company should allocate available capital so as to maximize returns on the capital invested. Individual investment proposals should therefore be considered in terms of their rate of return (ie NPV divided by capital required). This ratio is sometimes known as the profitability index:

$$\text{Profitability index} = \frac{\text{Net present value}}{\text{Initial capital cost}}$$

WORKED EXAMPLE 9.10 Capital rationing

A company has $10 million available to fund new projects in the current year. It has identified five potential investments and calculated the NPV on each investment as shown in Table 9.14.

Table 9.14

Investment	NPV	Capital required
A	$2m	$4m
B	$1m	$3m
C	$0.4m	$0.5m
D	$0.5m	$0.75m
E	$1.6m	$4m
Total		$12.25m

The company cannot undertake all five projects because this would require a total capital commitment of $12.25 million. In order to choose where to invest the $10 million available, the company will rank the proposals according to their rate of return, ie the ratio of NPV/Capital required (Table 9.15).

Table 9.15

Investment	NPV/Capital required	Ranking
A	$2m/$4m = 50%	3rd
B	$1m/$3m = 33%	5th
C	$0.4m/$0.5m = 80%	1st
D	$0.5m/$0.75m = 67%	2nd
E	$1.6m/$4m = 40%	4th

Based upon this ranking the company would invest in projects C, D, A and E in that order of preference. This would use a total capital of $9.25 million. Although this leaves $0.75 million unused, it is unlikely that project B could be subdivided such that 0.75/3.0 or 25 per cent of the project could be undertaken.

Replacement decisions

All of the investment scenarios we have looked at so far have involved investing in new assets. However, in reality, many investment decisions involve replacing existing assets. An important decision for a company is how long to retain an asset such as machinery or a company vehicle before replacing it. It is possible to use NPV calculations to determine the optimum time at which to replace an asset.

When using NPV for replacement decisions the technique is modified slightly. Firstly, the NPV is calculated in the normal way, and then the figure is adjusted to determine the 'annualized NPV'. The company should then replace an asset at the point when the annualized NPV is maximized.

WORKED EXAMPLE 9.11 Replacement decisions

A company purchases a machine for $15,000. The machine can be used for up to three years before it will be replaced by an identical machine which will be used in the same production process. The following figures have been estimated (Table 9.16).

Table 9.16

Year	1	2	3
Net revenue $	9,000	7,500	4,500
Scrap value $	6,000	4,500	1,500

The company uses a discount rate of 10 per cent for project appraisal. Should the machine be replaced after one, two or three years?

Answer

If the machine is replaced at the end of year 1, the NPV will be as shown in Table 9.17.

Table 9.17

Year	t_0	t_1	NPV
Cost of machine	(15,000)		
Net revenues		9,000	
Scrap value		6,000	
Total	(15,000)	15,000	
Discount factor	1	0.909	
Present value	(15,000)	13,635	(1,365)

If the machine is replaced at the end of year 2, the NPV will be as shown in Table 9.18.

Table 9.18

Year	t_0	t_1	t_2	NPV
Cost of machine	(15,000)			
Net revenues		9,000	7,500	
Scrap value			4,500	
Total	(15,000)	9,000	12,000	
Discount factor	1	0.909	0.826	
Present value	(15,000)	8,181	9,912	3,093

If the machine is replaced at the end of year 3, the NPV will be as shown in Table 9.19.

Table 9.19

Year	t_0	t_1	t_2	t_3	NPV
Cost of machine	(15,000)				
Net revenues		9,000	7,500	4,500	
Scrap value				1,500	
Total	(15,000)	9,000	7,500	6,000	
Discount factor	1	0.909	0.826	0.751	
Present value	(15,000)	8,181	6,195	4,506	3,882

Each of the NPVs is then 'annualized' by dividing it by the annuity factor for the number of years the investment runs:

Replaced after one year:	($1,365) ÷ 0.909	= ($1,502)
Replaced after two years:	$3,093 ÷ 1.735	= $1,783
Replaced after three years:	$3,882 ÷ 2.486	= $1,562

Replacement after two years gives the highest annualized NPV. This is therefore the replacement strategy which the company should follow.

Investment appraisal within context

So far in this chapter we have looked at the main techniques of investment appraisal and how they can be applied to different investment decisions. We will now look at some of the practical considerations of investment appraisal and some of the problems involved in applying these techniques in practice.

There are a number of problems to be found in the way these investment appraisal techniques are actually used in practice. We will focus on three main aspects of practice:

1 Firstly, the techniques we have examined have a very narrow focus on tangible factors which can be quantified financially. In practice, many investment decisions can involve factors which are difficult to quantify or which are intangible, for example investing in a new computer system in order to improve customer service, or investment in research and development for new product features.

2 Secondly, the highly computational nature of the techniques, particularly NPV, means that, in practice, managers can get lost in the details of the calculations and lose sight of the fact that they are based upon forecasts which may not be accurate and which in all likelihood will not actually work out.

3 Finally, the narrow focus of traditional investment appraisal techniques (typified by the concept of relevant cash flows) means that they can fail to capture the richness of investment decisions within the context of a wider organizational strategy. In reality, managers will not just invest for immediate financial return, but also for wider strategic reasons such as increasing operational flexibility, gaining competitive advantage or providing more strategic options in the future. Furthermore, within today's business context, managers must consider more than just immediate financial returns to the business's owners; the interests and requirements of other stakeholders such as employees, customers, suppliers, wider society and the environment can be equally important in investment decisions.

Integrating qualitative factors

One of the problems with traditional investment appraisal is that it tends to lead to an analysis of tangible financial issues in isolation from other important elements of the investment decision. When qualitative considerations are brought into an appraisal, the exercise becomes more complex, even if all the elements being considered are still tangible.

Let us take the example of a company that is investing in a new computerized customer management system (CMS). This new CMS will be integrated into the existing IT-based financial system and will be available in all offices through a new computer network. When doing a financial investment appraisal, there are a number of questions which may be difficult to answer:

- *What tangible costs should be included?* The tangible costs of new networks and other computer hardware can easily be identified. However, what is not so easy to establish is the proportion of these costs which should be allocated to the CMS investment. The network will be of benefit to all departments and all systems, and any new computers or workstations will be used for a number of other functions.

- *How should intangible costs be measured?* Some of the costs of implementing the new CMS system will be intangible and difficult to measure. For example, management time spent on developing and reviewing the new system will be a distraction from other activities; there may be disruption to existing work as a new system is implemented; staff learning to use a new system will be slower and less productive. In such cases it may be possible to record and measure the amount of time spent on the project, but it is not so easy to record and measure the impact which this has on other activities and productivity levels.

- *Diminishing returns from benefits.* If the rationale for implementing the new CMS is to improve customer services, then how far should this go? More and more features could be added to the CMS at an ever-increasing cost. How many of these features should be adapted? In a similar manner, increased processing power will provide information faster. It may be possible to identify that there is a clear advantage in obtaining information in two hours rather than two days. But would it be better to obtain that information in two minutes, or even in two seconds?

- *How should intangible benefits be measured?* The problem with implementing any new investment (particularly an IT investment) aimed at improving the availability of information or quality of service is that the costs are usually tangible and easily identified, whereas the benefits are intangible. Traditional NPV calculations are not able to capture such intangibles, which means that any investment appraisal will inevitably result in a negative NPV. In many cases, the identification of costs is much easier than the identification of benefits. This is particularly the case where the benefits sought from an investment are intangible. There are therefore three options available in this case:

  1 *Ignore the benefits*: the traditional approach is to ignore intangibles and focus only on that which can be measured in financial terms. Unfortunately, this could result in negative NPVs and the rejection of investments, simply because the benefits are not immediately financially quantifiable.

  2 *Quantify the benefits*: a common approach is to attempt to quantify the benefits so that they can be incorporated into a traditional investment appraisal calculation. Although this may work in some cases, it may be extremely difficult to quantify some benefits or it may result in a loss of richness of information about the benefits of investment.

  3 *Change the approach*: the balanced scorecard. A third alternative is to move away from a purely financial analysis to one which incorporates non-financial benefits. This approach tries to integrate qualitative and quantitative dimensions of evaluation within one exercise and can be termed a balanced scorecard

approach. To use such a balanced scorecard approach in investment appraisal requires the decision-maker to weigh up the various quantitative and qualitative aspects of the investment and to give a 'score' to each aspect so that each investment can be given an overall score, which allows comparison between alternatives.

WORKED EXAMPLE 9.12 Balanced scorecard approach

Investment appraisal of new customer management system:

Financial benefits:

- NPV $x.

Non-financial benefits:

- x per cent of users happy with quality;
- x per cent of users happy with scope;
- x hours saved per month.

> Exercises: now attempt Exercise 9.3 on page 353

Addressing risk: the variability in outcomes

In investment appraisal, risk is about the variability of outcomes. When we talk about investment risk we mean that the actual outcome may not be as we expect. In all the examples that we have looked at so far, calculations have been based upon one 'best guess' set of outcomes. Unfortunately, in reality, 'best guess' will hardly ever be the actual outcome. Therefore, one way of further incorporating risk assessment into investment appraisal is to analyse the range of possible outcomes. There are three main ways of doing this: sensitivity analysis; scenario analysis; and probability analysis.

Sensitivity analysis

Sensitivity analysis is a simple but powerful technique which is used extensively in practice. It examines the impact on the project return of changes in individual variables such as the investment cost, the level of cash flows and the life of the investment.

The technique is applied by adjusting each major variable in an NPV calculation until the NPV equals zero (ie the point at which the investment is no longer financially viable). This gives the decision-maker an indication of how much of a change can be tolerated in each variable. If an NPV of zero is arrived at with a relatively small change in a variable, the investment is very sensitive to the value of that variable. Sensitivity analysis makes it easier to identify weaknesses in forecasts. It is an extremely good way of identifying key factors that will need careful monitoring once the project has commenced. It could also be used to evaluate whether further action should be taken to minimize risk, for example interest-rate hedging or the use of currency derivatives to manage exchange-rate risks.

Scenario analysis

Whereas sensitivity analysis is useful in isolating and identifying changes in individual variables, it is not realistic in its presumptions. In reality, it is more likely that several or all variables will change at the same time, depending upon the circumstances. Scenario analysis addresses this by predicting how multiple variables will change under different conditions, for example under improved economic conditions, or if an economic downturn occurs. It is normal for this type of financial modelling to be done using computer spreadsheets.

Probabilities and expected values

Sensitivity analysis and scenario analysis introduce the idea of using a range of different forecasts rather than a single calculation. However, they can make decision making more difficult because they give no indication of the likelihood that each of a range of different outcomes may occur. A second problem is that a range of different scenarios will give a range of different NPV values, some of which may be negative. Does that mean the investment should not be made? It is no longer possible to use the simple rule that a positive NPV means a financially viable investment.

WORKED EXAMPLE 9.13 Probability analysis

A method to overcome these problems is used by some investment analysts. This involves identifying a range of different outcomes and attaching a probability to each outcome. These probabilities can be used to calculate a weighted average of the NPVs of each different scenario as shown in Table 9.20.

Table 9.20

Scenario	NPV $	Probability	NPV × Prob
A	(100,000)	0.2	(20,000)
B	200,000	0.3	60,000
C	300,000	0.4	120,000
D	500,000	0.1	50,000
ENPV = (NPV × Prob) =			210,000

This weighted average of $210,000 is known as the expected net present value (ENPV). It offers the advantage of once more providing a single figure which can be used to evaluate the investment. If the ENPV is positive, the investment is financially viable. However, care should be taken in using this technique as the ENPV does not reflect the outcome which will actually occur. For example, the decision-maker in Worked Example 9.13 should always remember that there is still a 20 per cent chance that the investment will have a negative NPV of –$100,000.

Other methods of assessing risk

There are a number of other methods which are becoming increasingly popular as means of modelling the uncertainty around investment cash flows as the availability of sophisticated computerized spreadsheets and increased processing power has made possible the use of more complex mathematical techniques.

The Monte Carlo simulation method involves the use of a probability distribution and random numbers to estimate net cash-flow figures. If this is repeated many times, a distribution of possible NPVs is derived from which it is possible to ascertain the uncertainty surrounding the project. Similar methods for modelling uncertainty include the use of Markov chain theory and fuzzy set theory. These methods allow unknown cash flows to be represented by a range of inexact ('fuzzy') numbers for the purposes of modelling NPV outcomes.

Taking a broader strategic view

So far we have looked at investment appraisal as an isolated financial exercise. The techniques we have examined, although widely used, have been criticized for not taking into account wider strategic considerations. In this last section we will therefore look at some recent developments in investment appraisal which have been aimed at integrating a broader strategic focus into the financial evaluation of individual investment decisions.

Real options

The traditional investment appraisal techniques we have examined in this chapter take a very narrow financial focus. This is exemplified by the concept of relevant cash flows, whereby any cost or revenue deemed not to be relevant to an investment is excluded from the calculation. However, when looking at an investment from a wider strategic perspective, a business may wish to build in flexibility which will give it options in the future. For example, if investing in a new production facility, a company may build a new factory which is twice the size of that needed for current production capacity. It will do this in anticipation of future growth. The problem with applying traditional approaches to investment appraisal in this case is that the extra cost of the large factory in relation to the revenues based upon current capacity may result in a negative NPV.

The concept of real options borrows from financial options, which are options to exchange a financial asset such as a share for cash. A real option is the option to exchange a real asset for some other asset. For example, buying a prime plot of land can give a food retailer a real expansion option to acquire the revenues from a new outlet by paying the cost of building a new store on that land. The further option to sell the land in the future, should the new store prove to be less profitable than anticipated, is a real abandonment option.

Value chain analysis

One way of evaluating a project's strategic issues as well as its cash flows is to undertake value chain analysis. This involves identifying strategically important value-creating activities. The 'value chain' is that set of activities which link from basic raw materials through to the ultimate end product. Focusing on these activities involves finding opportunities to enhance customer value or lower production costs. It has been found in practice that value chain analysis can produce very different investment decisions from those using traditional techniques, as the linkages between different activities within the value chain become an important aspect of the decision process.

Cost-driver analysis

Cost-driver analysis borrows from the concepts of activity-based costing which were examined in Chapter 8. It involves identifying those cost drivers which flow from the organization's investment decisions. By making these connections more explicit, the organization is able to identify the impact on future cash flows which an investment will make.

Competitive advantage analysis

Competitive advantage analysis involves evaluating whether an investment's benefits are consistent with the organization's competitive positioning strategy, such as cost minimization or differentiation. Projects can be ranked according to their ability to contribute towards the organization's chosen strategy.

Extract 9.4: Cisco – integrating the wider strategic picture

Cisco Systems is a US multinational corporation based in San Jose, California, that designs, manufactures and sells networking equipment. During the economic boom of the late 1990s and early 2000s, middle managers were given great freedom to acquire business start-ups for the technology and ideas. However, during the economic downturn that followed, Cisco tightened up their investment procedures by creating an investment review board that met monthly to vet potential acquisitions. Managers proposing acquisitions were required not only to demonstrate the potential financial benefits but also to draw up detailed integration plans.

Conclusion

This chapter has examined a multitude of investment appraisal techniques. It has presented those techniques traditionally used for investment appraisal together with some more recent innovations. In particular, we have evaluated each technique, pointing out its strengths and weaknesses. The reader will have noted that all the techniques presented in this chapter have both strengths and drawbacks. It might therefore be concluded that reliance upon one technique alone may lead to sub-optimal decision making or even to failure. On a practical level, therefore, it makes sense for an organization to use a mixture of techniques in order to eliminate or minimize the drawbacks of each individual technique used.

We hope that as a result of studying this chapter the reader will have a better understanding of how different investment appraisal techniques should be applied, will be able to use them more effectively to evaluate investments and will be able to identify and avoid common mistakes in the application of the techniques.

COMPREHENSION QUESTIONS

1 Why is good investment appraisal important to organizations?

2 What are the three main factors that should be considered when appraising a potential investment?

3 What are the main drawbacks of the payback method of investment appraisal?

4 Explain the concept of the time value of money.

5 What is the 'discount rate' used in NPV calculations and how is it arrived at?

6 What is an opportunity cost and why should it be included in an investment appraisal calculation?

7 In what ways can taxation impact upon cash flows from an investment?

8 Explain two ways in which risk assessment can be incorporated into investment appraisal.

Answers available at **www.koganpage.com/afm3**

Exercises

Answers available at **www.koganpage.com/afm3**

Exercise 9.1: Basic computations

A company is considering investing in a new production facility at a cost of $120 million. The new facility is expected to produce annual cost savings as set out in Table 9.21. The facility is expected to have a useful life of eight years, before becoming obsolete and requiring replacement. The company has a policy of depreciating all assets on a straight-line basis.

Table 9.21

Year	Annual cost savings
1	$30m
2	$35m
3	$40m
4	$45m
5	$30m
6	$26m
7	$15m
8	$15m

Required:

Evaluate the investment using the following techniques:

(a) Payback period – the company considers a capital investment to be acceptable if it pays back within four years. Should the company make the investment?

(b) ARR – what is the accounting rate of return on the average capital employed?

(c) NPV – if the capital investment has a required rate of return of 12 per cent, what is its net present value? Should the company make the investment?

Exercise 9.2: Understanding principles

Freshfare Co is a food retailer with 25 stores in the south of the country in which it operates. The board of directors are currently considering expansion into the north of the country by opening a large new store in a major northern city.

The investment in the new store is estimated to cost $40m. This will be financed mainly through a new bank loan of $35m at a cost of 8 per cent a year. The investment is expected to pay back within three years with an IRR of 22 per cent.

You have been asked to make a presentation on the proposed investment at the next meeting of the board of directors. The directors have raised some queries regarding the calculations in the investment appraisal and would like you to address the following points in your presentation:

1 A feasibility study for the new store has already been completed at a cost of $28,000. This cost has not been included in the investment appraisal calculations.

2 The interest payments on the bank loan of $35m will be payable quarterly. These payments have not been included in the investment appraisal calculations.

3 The chief accountant proposes to charge 5 per cent of central office administration costs to the new store. This charge has not been included in the investment appraisal calculations.

4 The company has a policy of depreciating all new investments on a straight-line basis over four years. No depreciation charge has been included in the investment appraisal calculations.

5 When the new store opens, it will be managed by one of the company's most experienced store managers. This manager earns $40,000 per year and this cost has been included in the investment appraisal calculations. When the manager moves to the new store, her assistant manager will be promoted to take over her current job. The assistant manager currently earns $25,000 per year but will receive a salary increase to $30,000 per year when he is promoted.

Required:

Make notes for your presentation to the board of directors which explain the treatment of each of the five issues above. You should state whether you agree with the accounting treatment in each case. If you disagree with the accounting treatment, you should explain why and propose an alternative.

Exercise 9.3: Financial appraisal within context

ANG Co is a manufacturer of high-performance processor chips for smart phones and other mobile devices. The company, based in Europe, has grown rapidly over the last five years. It has been able to compete with global competitors through developing a highly skilled and loyal workforce.

The company forecasts continued growth in existing markets and intends to break into the new markets of China and South East Asia. With this in mind, the directors have been examining options for opening a new factory within the next 18 months.

The directors have identified three possible new sites for the factory. You have been appointed as a business consultant to help the business choose which site to develop.

The financial information for each factory is set out in Table 9.22.

Table 9.22

	Factory A	Factory B	Factory C
Initial cost	$150m	$150m	$140m
Expected production life	5 years	5 years	4 years

The company accountant has calculated the information shown in Table 9.23.

Table 9.23

	Factory A	Factory B	Factory C
Payback period	3 years	2 years	2 years
Accounting rate of return	29%	29%	32%
Net present value	$25.6m	$39.4m	$28.7m

The NPV is calculated using the company's standard discount rate of 13 per cent. The following further details are provided:

Factory A: This factory will be opened next to the existing factory. This will provide more jobs for people in the area and possible promotion opportunities for existing employees.

Factory B: Factory B will be located in a new enterprise development zone which is situated approximately 150 kilometres from the existing factory. By opening the factory here, the company can take advantage of some generous tax breaks and other incentives offered by the government. Opening this factory will involve moving some of the existing production into the new factory. This will mean making 20 per cent of the existing workforce redundant. (The cost of redundancies is built into the figures above.)

Factory C: This factory will be opened in China. The company will benefit from cheaper labour costs (this is built into the figures above). The company will also be in a strong geographic position to grow sales in the newly opened market in China and South East Asia.

Write a report to the directors of ANG Co which evaluates each of the three potential investments using the financial and non-financial information provided above. State what further information the directors might need to consider before making a final decision.

Supplementary reading

Ogier, T, Rugman, J and Spicer, L (2004) *Real Cost of Capital: A business field guide to better financial decisions*, Financial Times/Prentice Hall, Harlow

Smit, H T J and Trigeorgis, L (2004) *Strategic Investment: Real options and games*, Princeton University Press, Princeton, NJ

Financing decisions

10

OBJECTIVE

To provide an understanding of the different sources of finance available to businesses and the theoretical and practical factors that underpin financing decisions.

LEARNING OUTCOMES

After studying this chapter, the reader will be able to:

- Differentiate and evaluate the different sources of finance available to a business.
- Understand the relationship between risk and return and the need for a range of finance products that offer a range of risk levels.
- Identify and evaluate appropriate financing strategies.

KEY TOPICS COVERED

- Types of equity finance.
- Types of debt finance.
- Calculating the cost of capital.
- The capital structure decision.
- Practical considerations of raising finance.

MANAGEMENT ISSUES

Managers need to appreciate the range of sources of finance available to a business and to distinguish which sources are the most appropriate for a given situation. They need to understand the impact that financing can have on the profitability of the business.

Introduction

This chapter is concerned with the capital structure decision of a business. It addresses one of the fundamental questions of financial management, which is: 'How should a business be financed?' In this chapter we address this question firstly by identifying the different sources of finance available and then by examining the factors that determine the optimum mix of finance.

Fundamental dynamics of finance: risk and return

Both investors, that is to say the providers of finance, and those seeking to raise finance will be looking for the best deal they can obtain. Such a deal will be measured in terms of the risk and returns involved. By risk, we mean the risk that the expected level of return is not received. For the investor, the highest level of risk is that not only is a financial reward not received from the investment, but also the amount invested is lost. Return is normally measured as a percentage of the initial investment. For example, if you invest $100 and receive back $120 in one year, you have received a 20% return ($20/$100).

Investors will always want an appropriate level of return for the level of risk to which they will be exposed through providing the finance. The higher the risk of an investment, the higher the return that the investor will demand. For example, an investor lending money to a start-up company that is developing a new and innovative product will require a higher rate of return than an investor lending to a well-established company with a good financial track record of earning stable profits from products that are popular and in demand.

Furthermore, different investors have different **risk appetites**. Some investors will be willing to take high risks for the promise of high returns. Other investors may be happier with lower returns if they carry a lower level of risk. Because of this we find that a wide range of financing products is available in order to meet the different risk appetites of different investors and the specific financing needs of the businesses seeking finance.

Types and sources of business finance

The different sources of finance available to businesses are usually classified by type and by term (duration). The two main types of finance are **equity finance** and **debt finance** (Figure 10.1). There are a variety of sources of each of these two types of finance and we will explore these below.

Figure 10.1 Classification of finance

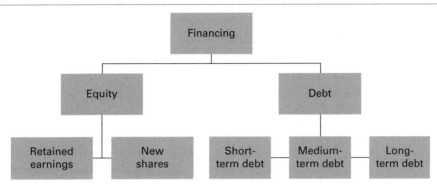

Equity finance is usually open-ended and therefore long term. That is to say, there is no redemption date. Rather, shares will stay in existence for as long as the business. However, debt finance normally has a fixed term with a predetermined repayment date or dates. Debt finance is therefore often classified into three broad categories of term: short term, medium term and long term.

short term = less than one year
medium term = 1 to 5 years
long term = longer than five years

Equity finance

Equity finance is often referred to as **risk capital**. This is because it usually attracts the highest levels of risk for investors and at the same time promises the highest return. The return on shares (**dividends**) is paid after all other debtors have been paid and only if sufficient funds remain. In the event of insolvency shareholders will rank after all other creditors.

There are a number of different types of equity finance, and the variety available reflects the need to provide a wide range of risk levels for different investors and a range of different financing options to meet different business situations. Although many companies will have only one class of shares (ordinary shares), it is possible and increasingly common for even small private companies to have different share classes that confer differing levels of rights and rewards.

Ordinary shares

Ordinary shares are the default class of share and confer ownership rights. That is to say, holders of ordinary shares are regarded as the owners of the business. Ordinary shares will carry voting rights (one vote per share) and are entitled to participate equally in dividends when the company has the financial resources to pay them. If the company is wound up the ordinary shareholders will share the company's assets after all liabilities have been paid.

Some companies, particularly family-run businesses, may have shares with different levels of voting rights. For example, some shares may have no voting rights (for family members or non-family employees) and others may carry extra voting rights (sometimes referred to as **management shares**). Another distinction, increasingly popular with small and family-run businesses is **alphabet shares**. These are categories labelled 'A shares', 'B shares,' etc, such that each category may be awarded different levels of dividend.

Preference shares

Preference shares are classified as equity, but they are designed specifically to reduce the level of risk for the investor and function more like debt. Preference shareholders will have a preferential right to receive a fixed dividend each year, expressed as a percentage return (for example, 8% preference shares). It is usual for preference shares to be **cumulative**. That is to say, the shareholder's right to dividends accumulates if there is insufficient profit to pay the dividend in a given year. Although relatively uncommon, some preference shares may also be **participating**, which means they will receive additional dividends over and above the fixed return if the company has a very profitable year. Preference shares are normally non-voting. Some preference shares are **convertible**. This means that they may be converted to ordinary shares at some point in the future. They may also sometimes be **redeemable** (see below). Such variations represent additional ways of making the shares more attractive to potential investors. Although preference shares were once relatively common they have become less popular in recent years, as there is not the same tax advantage to the company as there is with debt. They have therefore largely been replaced by debt instruments that offer similar benefits to investors.

Extract 10.1: Volvo issues preference shares

In 2018 Swedish car manufacturer Volvo planned to float on the Chinese stock market. In the end this listing did not go ahead, but in preparation for the possibility the company issued $500m of preference shares to investors outside Sweden. The intention was that these preference shares could be swapped for ordinary shares if the company had made the initial public offering (IPO) on the stock market. This move by Volvo enabled them to attract investors with the lower risk preference shares while reducing the risk of shares not being taken up in the initial public offering.

Deferred shares

Deferred shares are not commonly used nowadays, as they have been superseded by other instruments such as restricted stock units (RSUs). They are a means of offering long-term rewards for company founders, executives, and other start-up investors, and are issued as a way of inducing investors to invest in a new company. As the name implies, this class of share is last in line when it comes to a claim on the assets of the company (for example, in the case of bankruptcy). There may also be a restriction on receipt of dividends until dividends have been received by all other classes of shares. However, when profits allow, the dividend levels may be much higher than those of other shares, as holders of deferred shares have access to all the remaining profits after other obligations are met.

Redeemable shares

These are shares that are issued on the terms that the company will buy them back at some point in the future. This may be a fixed date, or a range of time. Such shares may be issued to external investors to provide a clear exit route for that investor. They are sometimes also issued to employees on the understanding that they will be redeemed if the employee leaves the company. Redemption may be at the issue price, a pre-agreed price, or the market price at the time of redemption.

Warrants

Share warrants (or stock warrants) are not strictly a class of share, but because of the way that they operate they are worth discussing here. A share warrant issued by a company to a potential investor acts rather like a share option. The warrant holder will have the option (but not the obligation) to purchase shares in the company, usually at a preferential price, at some point in the future. Warrants are frequently used in conjunction with debt finance as a means of making an investment more attractive, particularly for newer companies that are seen as a high investment risk. An investor may initially make a loan to the company and receive warrants in return. If the company succeeds, the investor has the option to benefit from this and become a shareholder by exercising the warrant.

Retained earnings

Retained earnings are classed as equity finance because they are profits that belong to the shareholders but that have not been returned to them as dividend. Any earnings that are retained within the business remain the property of the ordinary shareholders and effectively represent further investment by them into the company.

Because retained earnings are already held within the business it can appear that it is a costless source of financing. However, this is a misconception, as these funds belong to shareholders who will want a return on any money they have invested in the business, including funds that could otherwise have been used to pay them back as a dividend.

Raising equity finance

There are three main sources for raising equity finance:

Retained earnings

If the company is generating sufficient profits it can retain those profits within the business as an internal source of funding rather than paying them out as dividends. Because the company already holds the funds there will be no cost of raising the finance, as there is with an issue of new capital. This is therefore an attractive option, particularly as relatively small amounts of finance are required.

Rights issue

When a company makes a rights issue it asks existing shareholders to make further investment into the business. It is a requirement that a rights issue must always be made before a new issue to the public. This is in order to protect existing shareholders, as their ownership of the business will be diluted if shares are offered to new shareholders.

The term 'rights' refers to the fact that shareholders have the rights but not the obligation to buy the new shares. Under a rights issue each shareholder will be offered additional shares in proportion to their existing shareholding. For example, in a 1 for 3 rights issue the shareholder will be offered one new share for every three they currently hold. Usually the price will be at a discount to the current market price of the shares in order to encourage shareholders to take up the rights issue. A shareholder may take up their rights and buy the new shares. However, they can also sell their rights to other shareholders if they do not wish to purchase the shares themselves.

New issue

If the company is unable to raise the finance it requires from retained earnings or a rights issue it will make an issue of new shares to the public. It is usual to use an underwriter to manage this process and this will typically be a merchant bank or commercial bank. The underwriter will offer the shares to the public or institutions such as pension funds and insurance companies via a prospectus. This can be an expensive process and is therefore only viable as a means of raising finance if a substantial share issue is being made.

Expert view 10.1: IPO and FPO

Public issues of shares fall into two categories: an IPO or an FPO. If a new company, or more commonly an existing private company, seeks to issue shares to the public for the first time, this is referred to as an initial public offering (IPO). Such a share issue enables the company to raise capital from public investors, thus giving it access to a much greater level of funding. It also allows public investors to participate in the growing success of the business. This move from being a private company to a public company (often referred to as 'going public') is an important transition for a business and is one that typically occurs at the point when the business needs substantial new funding to upscale its activities. By contrast, a follow-on public offering (FPO) is the issue of shares to public investors by a company that is already listed on a stock exchange.

Discussion point

Why is it a requirement that a rights issue must always be made before a new issue to the public?

Debt finance

For the investor, debt financing usually carries a lower risk than equity and as a result the returns are lower. There is normally no right of control, unless the company is in default on the loan agreement.

For the company, debt interest is a business expense that will be paid from pre-tax profits. There is therefore a tax advantage of debt over equity and this can become significant when optimizing financing strategies. We will explore this later in the chapter.

The rate of interest payable on debt financing may be fixed or floating (variable) and the latter may carry special arrangements such as a cap or collar that restricts the range of variable interest rates. Debt is usually fixed term with specific repayment dates. Some forms of **structured debt** (see below) may be sold so that the original debt owner can liquidate their assets before the redemption date.

Expert view 10.2: Measuring gearing

Gearing (sometimes called capital gearing or financial gearing) describes the ratio of debt to equity financing. There are two common ways in which gearing is measured – one using the balance sheet and one using the income statement:

From the balance sheet: gearing ratio = debt/(debt + equity)

From the income statement: interest cover = PBIT/Interest payable

---

Debt security

In the event of insolvency, debt holders rank above shareholders, and those debt holders who have security or collateral will rank above all other creditors. There are two main types of security for debtors: a **fixed charge** or a **floating charge**. A fixed charge is a security against a specific asset of the business, for example a building. A floating charge is against a category of current asset such as accounts receivable or inventory. If the company defaults on the loan the debtor can seize the asset to recover their debt. A charge is therefore a means of reducing the risk for the investor.

Extract 10.2: Norton goes into administration

In January 2020 British motorcycle manufacturer Norton went into administration over unpaid tax bills of £300k. This is an example of the power that creditors have over a company in order to protect their interests. In this case, the problem was not an unpaid loan but unpaid tax. HMRC (the UK tax authority), as an unpaid creditor, has the right to call in administrators who will liquidate the assets of the business in order to repay HMRC and other unpaid creditors. There is a pecking order to how creditors are paid, with secured creditors (with fixed or floating charges) coming first, then unsecured creditors and lastly shareholders, only if sufficient funds are realized.

Structuring debt finance

Expert view 10.3: Debt–asset duration matching

It is important for a company raising debt to match the duration of that debt with the asset or investment it is being used to finance. If there are timing mismatches between the investment and the underlying debt it may cause problems for the business. For example, if short-term debt were used to finance a long-term asset, the company may need to seek further finance before the end of the investment project and the project may be put at risk if suitable financing cannot be found. On the other hand, if long-term debt is used to fund a short-term asset, the company will still be paying interest on the debt when it is no longer required.

Bank borrowing

Banks may make **loans** to businesses or offer them an **overdraft**. An overdraft is a short-term loan that is usually repayable upon demand. However, in practice some companies use an overdraft as a long-term source of financing, which can be a risk if the bank demands repayment. On the other hand, an overdraft is useful as it is a flexible loan. The company will only draw down as much funding as it requires at any given time and therefore will be paying interest only on that balance. Most companies arrange an **overdraft facility** with a bank, which is a predetermined amount of overdraft that is available to them.

The debt market

A company may issue a formal structured debt such as **debenture loan stock** and sell this on the stock market. Such debts usually come in predetermined units, for example $100, which have the advantage of being easily traded on the stock market in the same way as shares. This makes the debt more attractive to investors, which in turn makes it cheaper and easier to raise for the company.

Debt factoring

Debt factoring or accounts receivable factoring is a means of improving cash flow by receiving cash from accounts receivable early. A company may sell on its debt to a **factor** who will typically pay up to 80% of the amount up-front to the company. The balance, less the factor's fee, will be paid once the debt has been collected. This is a common practice among small businesses that have insufficient cash reserves to finance the generous credit terms they are sometimes required to offer. (For a more detailed discussion of debt factoring refer to Chapter 7.)

Convertible loans

A convertible loan is a way of making debt more attractive to investors. The owner of such a loan will have the option to convert their investment into ordinary shares at some point in the future. This means that the investor initially bears the lower risk of debt, but has the opportunity to participate in the future growth of the company by taking up the conversion option. The interest payable is usually lower on such loans because of the conversion option and this results in a lower cost to the company.

Extract 10.3: Primary Health Properties PLC issues convertible bonds

In 2019, Primary Health Properties PLC , one of the UK's leading investors in primary healthcare facilities, announced the launch of an offering of £150 million of Convertible Bonds, at an interest rate of 2.875 per cent per annum, payable semi-annually. This issue enabled the company to repay other more expensive debt and reduce the company's overall cost of capital. This illustrates how convertible debt can provide a company with the opportunity to raise finance at a much lower cost because of the potential future benefits of conversion for the investor.

Leases

Sometimes a company may use a lease to finance assets. There are two main types of lease: an **operating lease** is effectively a rental and is used for the short-term use of an asset; and a **finance lease** is effectively a purchase financed through a loan. (For a more detailed discussion of lease financing refer to Chapter 7.)

Optimizing finance – the underlying principles

The cost of capital

The money used to finance a business will come at a cost. Shareholders expect dividends. Debtors want interest. An important aspect of financial management is therefore not only to ensure that the business has adequate and appropriate finance, but also to minimize the cost of the capital used by the business. In order to minimize the cost of capital we firstly need to understand the cost of each source of capital so that we can put together an appropriate combination of different sources that will meet the business's needs while minimizing the overall cost. Therefore, in this section we examine the financial theory that sets out how to calculate the cost of individual sources of capital and the overall cost of capital for the business.

Discussion point

Why might an investor in a new venture prefer to purchase debt capital rather than equity capital?

The cost of equity

The value of an equity can be measured in terms of the future returns that the investor will receive as a result of owning that equity. As we did for investments in Chapter 9, we can use the net present value (NPV) technique to take the future cash inflows of dividends from an equity and discount them back to their present value – the share price. This technique is known as the **dividend valuation model.**

WORKED EXAMPLE 10.1

A company pays a fixed dividend of $0.50 per share each year. The current market price of a share is $5.00. The cost of equity for this company can be calculated as follows:

Using the NPV technique that was introduced in Chapter 9, the share price will be the present value of the future dividends discounted at the rate of return required by the investor (the cost of equity). This can be expressed using the following formula:

$$P_0 = \frac{D}{K_e} \quad \text{where} \quad \begin{aligned} P_0 &= \text{the (ex-div) share price} \\ D &= \text{the dividend} \\ K_e &= \text{the cost of equity} \end{aligned}$$

As we already know the dividend and the share price, we can rearrange this formula to find the cost of equity (K_e):

$$K_e = \frac{D}{P_0} = \frac{\$0.50}{\$5.00} = 10\%$$

Remember that in this case K_e represents both the return for the investor and the cost for the company of equity finance.

Cum-div and ex-div share prices

If an investor buys a share immediately before the dividend is paid, that investor will receive the dividend. Because of this, the quoted price of the share rises slightly as the dividend payment date draws near to include the dividend that will be received. This is the cum-div price. Once the dividend has been paid, new investors will no longer benefit from that dividend so the share price falls back to its underlying value – the ex-div price. In order to avoid this distortion in the share price, valuation models always use the ex-div price. P_0 is therefore always the ex-div share price. If a share price is quoted cum-div, the ex-div price can be derived by deducting the upcoming dividend from that price.

Dividend growth

The dividend valuation formula above is fine if the dividend remains constant year on year. However, most companies seek to increase their earnings and dividends over time. The valuation model therefore needs to be modified to allow for dividend growth. When this is taken into account the revised formula is as follows:

$$K_e = \frac{D_0\,(1+g)}{P_0} + g \qquad \text{where} \qquad \begin{aligned} &P_0 = \text{the (ex-div) share price} \\ &D_0 = \text{the current dividend} \\ &g = \text{the rate of dividend growth} \end{aligned}$$

This formula is known as the **dividend growth model**. It is sometimes also called the **Gordon growth model** after economist Myron J Gordon.

WORKED EXAMPLE 10.2

A company pays a dividend of $0.50 per share this year. The current market price of a share is $6.00. Dividends are expected to grow by 4% each year. The cost of equity for this company can be calculated as follows:

$$K_e = \frac{D_0\,(1+g)}{P_0} + g \;=\; \frac{\$0.50 \times 1.04}{\$6.00} + 0.04 = 12.7\%$$

The cost of debt

We can use the same NPV technique to calculate the cost of debt. However, the way we apply this will depend upon whether the debt is **redeemable** or **irredeemable**.

Irredeemable debt

Irredeemable debt securities are issued without a provision for repayment. The debt will never be repaid by the company, but interest will continue to be paid in perpetuity. When this is the case, calculating the cost of irredeemable debt is similar to calculating the cost of equity with no growth in dividends. Investors buying such a security are buying a stream of future interest payments:

$$K_d = \frac{I}{P_0}$$ where P_0 = the (ex-interest) price

I = the interest paid

K_d = the return to the investor

WORKED EXAMPLE 10.3

An irredeemable debt pays 8% interest and has a current market price of $90 per cent (this means that the market price is $90 against a nominal value of $100. The interest is always calculated on the nominal value and will therefore be $8 per year). The required return of an investor can be calculated as follows:

$$K_d = \frac{I}{P_0} = \frac{\$8}{\$90} = 8.9\%$$

The company's tax shield

The calculation in Worked Example 10.3 shows the return to the investor. However, because the company pays the interest from pre-tax profits, any interest paid reduces the tax liability. This effectively reduces the net cost to the company and is known as the **tax shield**. When calculating the cost of debt to the company we can incorporate the impact of tax by modifying the above formula slightly as follows:

$$K_d = \frac{I(1-t)}{P_0}$$ where P_0 = the (ex-interest) price

I = the interest paid

t = the tax rate

K_d = the cost of debt to the company

WORKED EXAMPLE 10.4

An irredeemable debt pays 6% interest and has a current market price of $80 per cent (this is also sometimes expressed as $80%). The company pays corporation tax at a rate of 20%. The cost of debt to the company can be calculated as follows:

$$K_d = \frac{I(1-t)}{P_0} = \frac{\$6 \times (1-0.2)}{\$80} = 6\%$$

Redeemable debt

Redeemable debt securities are issued for a fixed period and will have a redemption date. Redemption may be at the current market price (this is unlikely in practice), or at the initial issue price, or at a premium based upon the issue price.

In order to calculate the cost of debt for a redeemable security, we need to identify the relevant cash flows and perform an internal rate of return (IRR) calculation, as was set out in Chapter 9.

WORKED EXAMPLE 10.5

A redeemable loan stock is quoted at $75%. Coupon interest is 9% and this has just been paid. The loan stock will be redeemed in 10 years' time at par (at the nominal value of $100). The company pays tax at a rate of 20%. The cost of debt can be calculated using the IRR technique as follows:

Interest paid will be $9 but the company will benefit from a tax shield of 20%. Therefore, the net cost of interest to the company will be $9 \times (1 - 0.2) = \$7.20*$.

Table 10.1

Time	CF $	DF 10%	PV $	DF 12%	PV $
T_0	(75.00)	1.000	(75.00)	1.000	(75.00)
$T_1 - T_{10}$	7.20	6.145	44.24	5.650	40.68
T_{10}	100.00	0.386	38.60	0.322	32.20
NPV			7.84		(2.12)

*Notice in the example above that tax relief applies only to interest paid. There is no tax effect on the redemption premium.

$$IRR = A\% + \frac{NPV @ A\%}{(NPV @ A\% - NPV @ B\%)} \times (B\% - A\%)$$

Where: A% = the lower discount rate

B% = the higher discount rate

Applied to our calculations for the redeemable loan stock:

$$IRR = 10\% + \frac{\$7.84}{(\$7.84 + \$2.12)} \times (12\% - 10\%) = 11.6\%$$

The weighted average cost of capital (WACC)

If a company is financed through a variety of sources, the overall cost of finance to the company will be the average of the cost of each source, weighted by their relative market value. Therefore, once the cost of each individual source is known, the overall cost of capital can be established through a simple weighted average calculation, as demonstrated below.

WORKED EXAMPLE 10.6

A company is financed partly by equity and partly by debt. The company's current gearing is 30% (ie debt is 30% of total capital, therefore equity is 70%). The cost of equity is 16% and the cost of debt is 10%. The weighted average cost of capital can be calculated as follows:

$$WACC = (16\% \times 70\%) + (10\% \times 30\%) = 14.2\%$$

Discussion point

Why is the cost of capital calculated using market value rather than the nominal (or issue) value of the equity or debt?

The capital structure decision

So far in this chapter we have identified the different sources of capital that are available for financing a business. We have looked at how each source of capital has a cost and how we can identify that cost and the way in which the overall combination of different sources of capital gives us the weighted average cost of capital. In this section we will look at various theories of optimizing the capital structure of the business.

Underpinning the theory of capital structure is the same principle of maximizing shareholder wealth that we examined in Chapter 9 when looking at investment appraisal. In Chapter 9 we learned how shareholder wealth can be maximized by maximizing the return on investment. However, it is also possible for a company to increase its value by adjusting its financing. If the cost of finance is reduced, this will similarly increase shareholder wealth. Theories of capital structure therefore seek to minimize the cost of financing the company.

Different sources of finance carry different levels of risk for the finance provider. Usually, the higher the risk, the higher the level of expected return to the investor, and the higher the cost to the company. Because equity finance carries more risk than debt finance it is usual for debt finance to offer a lower return and therefore carry a lower cost for the company. The logical conclusion from this relationship would therefore be that if a company increases the level of debt finance relative to its equity finance (its **gearing**) it can reduce its overall cost of capital.

In order to understand this relationship between the level of financial gearing and the weighted average cost of capital, it is important to understand that the cost of capital is shaped by three factors:

- the risk-free rate of return;
- business risk;
- financial risk.

The risk-free rate of return

The risk-free rate of return is that rate of return that an investor can expect from an investment that carries no risk at all. This is a theoretical position, as all investments carry some level of risk, even if that is very small. However, it is generally accepted that government bonds represent an investment that is as close as possible to being risk free. The return on Government gilt-edged bonds is therefore usually taken as a good indicator of the risk-free rate of return. The argument from an investment point of view is that if this rate of return can be achieved without taking any risk, then it represents a baseline level of return for any investment that does expose investors to risk. That is to say, any risky investment must offer a return at least equal to the risk-free rate of return.

Premium for business risk

The extent to which the return on a risky investment exceeds the risk-free rate of return will depend upon investors' perception of the risk of that investment. This is usually referred to as business risk. Such risk describes the variability of earnings arising from the business sector(s) in which the company operates. Some business activities are riskier than others in terms of the potential variability of earnings, and would therefore carry a higher business risk premium.

Premium for financial risk

For the equity investor there is an additional tier of risk if the company has borrowings as well as equity finance. That is because interest payments on debt rank before return to equity investors. Consequently, the higher the level of gearing, the higher the financial risk for equity investors (Figure 10.2).

The traditional theory of capital structure

The traditional theory of capital structure uses the three factors explained above to determine how the cost of equity and the cost of debt will behave as the mix of equity and debt (ie the gearing) is changed.

Figure 10.3 illustrates how the cost of equity will increase as the level of gearing increases. When gearing is zero the company is financed entirely by equity and the cost of equity will be made up of the risk-free rate of return plus the premium for business risk. However, as debt finance is introduced gearing increases and this will introduce financial risk for equity investors. Consequently, the level of return that they demand will increase. As gearing approaches very high levels, financial risk will increase substantially and therefore accelerate the rate of increase in the cost of equity.

In Figure 10.4 a similar graph adds the cost of debt. In this case, because the risk for debt investors is lower than that for equity investors, the cost of debt is lower than the cost of equity. It can also be seen from this graph that financial risk will not impact upon the cost of debt until relatively high levels of gearing. This is because most debts will be secured and there is no significant increase in risk for the debtor as

Figure 10.2 The cost of capital

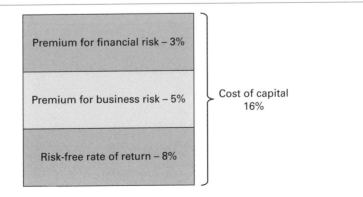

Figure 10.3   Cost of equity

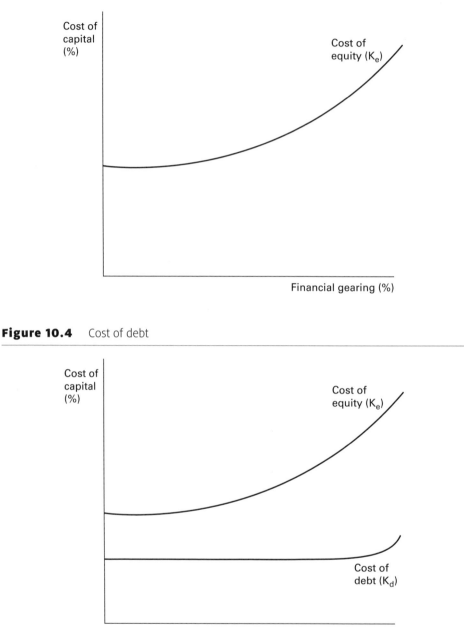

Figure 10.4   Cost of debt

gearing increases. However, at very high levels of gearing even debtors may be at risk of not receiving a return on their investment and therefore a premium for financial risk will be introduced and the cost of debt will start to rise.

If we combine the cost of equity with the cost of debt, we can see how the weighted average cost of capital (WACC) will change at different levels of gearing. This is illustrated in Figure 10.5.

Figure 10.5 shows that when there is no gearing the weighted average cost of capital equals the cost of equity because equity is the only source of finance. As cheaper debt finance is introduced this will pull the average cost downward so that the WACC decreases. However, as gearing reaches higher levels the increased financial risk for both equity and debt investors will cause the WACC to increase again. This means that there will be an optimum level of gearing at the point where WACC is at its lowest cost.

Figure 10.5   Traditional WACC

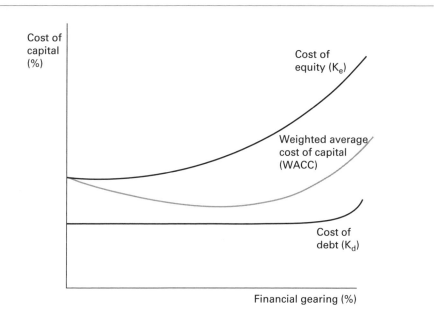

Financial gearing (%)

Extract 10.4: Virgin buys back shares rather than reduce debt

In 2011, Virgin Media announced a share buy-back programme of £625m. Even though the company had very high levels of debt (£5.7bn) management was so confident of cash flows that it chose to use capital to buy back shares rather than reduce gearing. This move effectively reduced the number of shares receiving dividends and maximized the benefit of cheaper debt to increasing the profit available to each shareholder. The move was rewarded with strong share prices.

The conclusion to be drawn from this analysis is that it will be beneficial for a company to have some debt financing in order to take advantage of its cheaper cost. However, although this traditional theory of capital gearing sets out the principles of the relationship between gearing and the cost of capital, it does not provide precise guidance as to what level of gearing a company should aim for. Because of this inexactitude a number of academics have attempted to build models that provide a more precise guidance on optimizing capital gearing. The most famous of these models is that developed in the late 1950s by two US economists, Franco Modigliani and Merton Miller.

The Modigliani and Miller theory of capital structure

In the 1950s, Modigliani and Miller set about modelling the relationship between financial gearing and the cost of capital in order to more accurately prove and measure the relationship. In order to establish a model, they introduced a number of restrictive assumptions. These included the assumption that companies operated within a perfect capital market with no taxes or transaction costs for raising capital; markets consisted of a number of companies operating with the same business risk; and individuals can borrow on the same terms as companies. Based upon these assumptions Modigliani and Miller published a paper in 1958 which set out the relationship between cost of capital and financial gearing as shown in Figure 10.6.

Figure 10.6   MM no tax

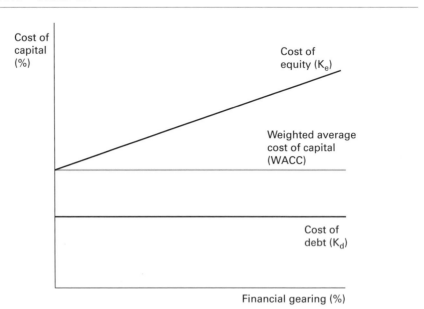

In this model the curves of the traditional view are revised to straight lines. There is no increase in the cost of debt at high levels of gearing and the rate of increase in the cost of equity remains constant at all levels of gearing. Furthermore, Modigliani and Miller suggested that the benefits of cheaper debt are exactly offset by the higher returns required by equity investors to compensate for the increased financial risk. The implication of this model is that the gearing has no effect on the cost of capital. Modigliani and Miller concluded that in a perfect market, the way a business is financed has no impact on its value. It is only the cash flows generated by a company's business activities that determine the value of the company and so a company should focus on generating cash flows and not worry about its level of financial gearing.

Although this theory was revolutionary in establishing precise relationships between gearing and cost of capital, it was heavily criticized for ignoring important real-world factors. The most important of these, critics argued, was the impact that corporation tax has in the cost of debt. Because interest on debt is paid out of pre-tax profits it provides a 'tax shield' for a company. That is to say, the more interest that is paid, the lower the corporation tax bill for the company. It is therefore more tax efficient to pay returns to investors in the form of interest to debtors rather than dividends to equity holders. Therefore, in 1963 Modigliani and Miller published a second paper that incorporated the impact of corporation taxes. This presented a very different view on the benefits of financial gearing, as illustrated in Figure 10.7.

Figure 10.7 MM with tax

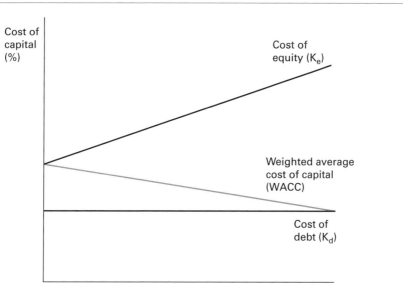

In this revised model the impact of the **tax shield** is such that the higher the level of gearing, the greater the tax benefit to the company. Therefore, the higher the level of financial gearing, the lower the weighted average cost of capital. The implication of this model is that the company should seek to raise gearing levels as high as possible.

Optimizing finance – practical considerations

Although the 1963 Modigliani and Miller model suggests that a company should maximize its level of gearing, in practice there are a number of problems that will restrict the practical level of gearing a company can achieve.

Bankruptcy costs

Although the Modigliani and Miller model suggests that the cost of debt will remain constant at all levels of gearing, in practice there will be an increase in the cost of debt at high levels of gearing as finance providers become concerned that company earnings may be insufficient to service the debt. They will demand an increase in returns to compensate for this increased risk and the cost of capital will rise. As a consequence, companies may have difficulty raising further debt finance if their gearing levels are already very high, or such debt may become too expensive.

Financial flexibility

Interest must always be paid, no matter how well or badly a company is performing. On the other hand, dividends do not have to be paid if the company is generating insufficient cash flows. Many companies will therefore limit their level of gearing in order to give themselves more flexibility in bad times.

Extract 10.5: EDF make rights issue to reduce gearing

French energy company EDF made a rights issue in March 2017 of three new shares for every 10 existing shares in a bid to raise €4bn to reduce gearing and raise further finance to fund new investments. In order to attract investors the new shares were offered at a discount of 34.5% on the market price.

Agency costs

At very high levels of gearing there is an increased risk of financial distress – an inability to meet the returns demanded by investors. If this occurs, the interests of the shareholders and debtholders may not coincide and management may act in a way that favours shareholders to the disadvantage of debtholders. Because of this, debtholders will face higher levels of risk at high levels of gearing and will demand higher returns. This will lower the optimal gearing ratio.

Tax exhaustion

Modigliani and Miller's suggestion that a company should maximize its level of financial gearing is built upon the benefits of the tax shield. However, this benefit only exists so long as there is sufficient profit against which interest can be charged. If there is no profit, or the level of interest exceeds the level of profit, then there is no longer a benefit from increasing the level of gearing. There will therefore be a practical limit on the level of gearing that benefits a company.

When these real-world limitations are considered it is clear that the level of gearing actually does matter and that there will be a practical maximum level of gearing that is beneficial to a company. In practice most companies try to maintain their gearing within a range.

Expert view 10.4: Optimum gearing

There is no absolute optimum level of gearing as appropriate levels will vary across industries and will be affected by issues such as the age of the business, economic conditions and taxation rates. However, a company with more than 50% debt finance is generally regarded as being **highly geared**, and a company with less than 25% debt has **low gearing**. Most businesses aim for a range of 30–40% debt.

Although these real-world limitations may appear to negate the Modigliani and Miller theory and suggest that the level of gearing does matter, the theory is still useful in the way that it focuses attention on why and how financing is important in the real world.

Dividend policy

In this final section of this chapter we will consider the question of dividend policy, as dividends, being the return to equity investors, are closely connected with the financial structure of the business. Unlike the interest payments made on loans, there is no obligation on the company to pay a dividend on ordinary shares. If a company experiences cash flow problems or it requires finance for a large investment, it may reduce or even suspend dividend payments in order to retain the cash within the business.

An important question for the financial manager is: 'Does the level of dividend paid matter?' That is to say, can a company increase or decrease the level of dividends it pays year on year without having a negative impact on the value of the company? A number of theories have developed around this question.

The dividend irrelevance theory

The dividend irrelevance theory was developed by Franco Modigliani and Merton Miller. As the name implies, the theory postulates that the level of dividends paid does not matter, as investors will be indifferent between receiving dividends now or capital gains later. If a company does not pay a dividend, profits will be retained for future growth, which will lead to an increase in the value of shares. An investor requiring cash can therefore generate 'dividends' by selling shares and realizing their capital gains.

Although underpinned by rigorous economic modelling, this theory ignores many of the real-world practicalities that dictate investor dividend preferences. These include the cost and inconvenience of regularly selling small quantities of shares to generate cash flows, and the personal financial and tax position of the investor. The impact of these factors is discussed below.

The 'bird in hand' argument

Developed by Myron Gordon and John Lintner in response to Modigliani and Miller's theory, the 'bird in hand' theory suggests that investors will prefer the certainty of dividends now over the uncertainty of capital gains in the future. The theory, based upon the old adage that 'a bird in the hand is worth two in the bush', suggests that although retained earnings should in theory create capital gains in the longer term, there is simply too much uncertainty around this. The authors suggest that shares with higher dividend payouts are more attractive to investors and command a higher market price. The advice to companies is therefore to maximize their dividend levels.

Although this advice may hold true for some investors, others may be investing for the longer term (retirement, for example) and, because of their current earnings from elsewhere, may not welcome high dividends that would incur high levels of taxation.

The retained earnings theory

The retained earnings, or residual income, theory suggests that a company should refrain from paying dividends as long as it has the opportunity to reinvest earnings at a positive net present value (NPV). If a company has attractive investment opportunities but pays current earnings back to investors as dividends, it will need to raise additional external finance in order to pursue those investment opportunities. As raising external finance is more expensive than using retained earnings, this approach would be inefficient and not most beneficial to investors. Furthermore, unless an investor requires an income from dividends, returning funds to them passes the responsibility for finding new investment opportunities from the company back to the investor. As with the 'bird in hand' theory, this argument may apply to some, but not all investors. Some investors require immediate income from their investments and would prefer dividends now over capital gains in the future.

The clientele effect

In practice, investors will choose to invest in companies that have a dividend policy that meets their investment needs and offers the most tax efficiency for them. If an investor is reliant upon dividends for their income, they will choose to invest in companies that offer high levels of dividends. On the other hand, an investor who has other sources of income and who is already paying higher rates of income tax will favour companies that reinvest earnings into capital growth. This way, the investor can control when they receive returns from their investment (by selling shares and realizing capital gains) in the most tax-efficient manner. This preference of investors for a particular dividend strategy is known as the **clientele effect**, as companies will attract a clientele of investors based upon the level of dividends they pay. For this reason, it is important that companies are consistent in their dividend strategy.

The signalling effect of dividends

There is a further reason why companies need to be consistent in their dividend strategy. Without access to detailed internal information about a company's plans and performance, an investor will use dividend levels as a measure of the financial health of a company. If dividends are consistent with a steady increase year on year, this suggests to the investor that all is well with a company. However, if a company suddenly cuts dividends, even if this is to fund a highly profitable new investment, this may be read as a negative signal by investors. The consequence can be a major fall in the company's share price.

Discussion point

Why might an inappropriate dividend policy have a negative impact upon the company's share price?

Conclusion

In this chapter we have examined the factors that underpin a good financing strategy. We have explored the different sources of finance that are available to businesses and how these different sources provide a range of risk-and-return profiles to meet the needs of both the company and its investors. We have also examined how a company can optimize its financial structure in order to minimize the overall cost of capital.

COMPREHENSION QUESTIONS

1 The cost of capital can be said to consist of three elements. Explain what they are.

2 Why does the cost of equity increase with the level of gearing?

3 Explain the difference between financial risk and business risk.

4 What is the 'tax shield' and how does it benefit a company?

5 What are the practical limits to the level of gearing a company should operate?

6 Why is the 'dividend irrelevance' proposition flawed in practice?

7 What is meant by the 'signalling effect' of dividends? How might this impact on share price?

Answers available at **www.koganpage.com/afm3**

Exercises

Answers available at **www.koganpage.com/afm3**

Exercise 10.1

CanCo's shares have a current market value of $0.80, and the last dividend was $0.10. If the expected annual growth rate of dividends is 4%, calculate the cost of equity capital.

Exercise 10.2

WendCo has in issue 10% debentures of a nominal value of $100. The market price is $90 ex-interest.

Calculate the cost of debt if the debenture is:

(a) Irredeemable.

(b) Redeemable at par after 10 years.

Exercise 10.3

PresCo pays $10,000 a year interest on irredeemable debenture stock with a nominal value of $100,000 and a current market price of $80,000.
What is the cost of debt if the rate of corporation tax is:

(a) 40%

(b) 20%

Exercise 10.4

HomCo is financed partly by equity and partly by debt. The equity portion is always kept at three-quarters of the total. The cost of equity is 16% and that of debt 12%. What is the weighted average cost of capital (WACC)?

References

Modigliani, F and Miller, M (1958) The cost of capital, corporation finance and the theory of investment, *American Economic Review*, **48** (3), pp 261–97
Modigliani, F and Miller, M (1963) Corporate income taxes and the cost of capital: a correction, *American Economic Review*, **53** (3), pp 433–43

Supplementary reading

Gordon, M J (1959) Dividends, earnings and stock prices, *Review of Economics and Statistics*, **41** (2), pp 99–105
Lintner, J (1962) Dividends, earnings, leverage, stock prices and the supply of capital to corporations, *The Review of Economics and Statistics*, pp 243–69

Operational decisions

11

OBJECTIVE

To enable the manager to incorporate financial evaluation into their operational decision making and problem solving.

LEARNING OUTCOMES

After studying this chapter, the reader will be able to:

- Assess the financial consequences of a range of decision-making situations.
- Define the scope and limitations of the financial techniques applied.

KEY TOPICS COVERED

The chapter will examine a range of operational decisions and the financial techniques which can be used to support them:

- setting sales targets;
- predicting the impact of price changes;
- outsourcing vs in-house operation/production;
- operational restructuring/automation of business processes;
- closing a business segment;
- dropping a product/service line.

Introduction

In this chapter we will look at some financial aspects of operational decision making. We introduce some fundamental principles of financial decision making and some core decision-making techniques. Once these techniques are understood, we examine their wider applications and demonstrate their use in a range of typical business decision-making situations. A key skill for managers is understanding which is the most appropriate technique for a given decision.

Operational decision making

All managers are faced with operational decisions. These are decisions concerning the best means of implementing strategies and overcoming problems that are encountered. There is a saying that 'analysis is at the heart of business intelligence': in order to be successful in dealing with the issues they face, managers need a systematic approach towards decision making together with appropriate tools for evaluating the financial impact of different options.

A typical operational decision-making process will involve a number of key steps as illustrated in Figure 11.1.

These steps involve:

- Step 1: recognizing and defining the problem or issue which needs to be addressed.

- Step 2: identifying alternative solutions to the problem and eliminating alternatives that are not practically feasible.

- Step 3: identifying the costs and benefits of alternatives in order to establish their financial feasibility.

- Step 4: assessing qualitative factors in the decision that go beyond the immediate financial benefits.

- Step 5: selecting the alternative which offers the greatest overall benefit when considering both financial and qualitative factors.

Figure 11.1 Decision-making steps

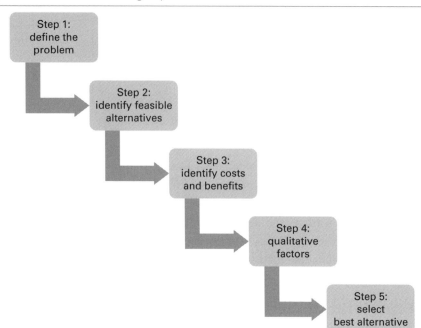

In this chapter we are primarily concerned with step 3: identifying the costs and benefits of alternatives. However, we will also visit some of the qualitative factors in step 4 that will impinge upon decisions.

We will look at a number of typical operational decisions. In order to examine these different business situations we will explore two key areas of financial decision-making theory in this chapter: cost–volume–profit analysis (CVP) and relevant costing. We will introduce each theory in turn and then demonstrate its application through a number of examples which relate to real-world business decisions.

Cost–volume–profit analysis (CVP)

CVP analysis is the study of the interrelationship between costs and revenues (and therefore profit) at various levels of activity.

Economic models which measure changes in costs and revenues as the volume of activity increases can be complex. However, for the purpose of managerial decision making it is possible to simplify these models in a way that makes them easy to use and therefore more readily useful to the average manager. CVP analysis therefore makes a number of assumptions about how revenues and costs behave as the volume of activity within a business increases. We will look at each of these assumptions in turn.

Revenues

Economic models tell us that as the volume of sales increases, the unit sales price will decrease. Although this may be true when looking at the full spectrum of possible levels of sales, when using CVP analysis for decision making we are usually looking at a relatively narrow range of sales volumes. It is therefore possible to make the assumption that unit sales price will remain constant across all levels of activity. In this case we can say that total sales revenue will be the volume of sales (in units) multiplied by the unit sales price:

$$\text{Sales revenue} = \text{Units sold} \times \text{Sales price}$$

This relationship between sales revenue and the volume of activity (units sold) is represented graphically in Figure 11.2.

Figure 11.2  Revenue

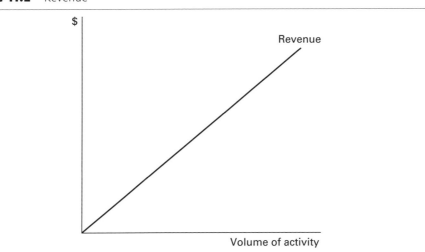

Costs

In financial decision making we usually divide costs into two broad categories: fixed costs and variable costs. This categorization refers to how costs behave in relation to changes in volume of production and sales.

Fixed costs

Fixed costs are unaffected by changes in the level of activity and therefore remain constant or 'fixed' as the volume of activity increases or decreases. An example of a fixed cost is the rent paid on a shop. The rent must be paid even if the shop sells nothing. If the shop does well and sales reach a very high level, the same amount of rent will be paid.

This relationship between fixed costs and the volume of activity is represented in Figure 11.3.

Figure 11.3 Fixed costs`

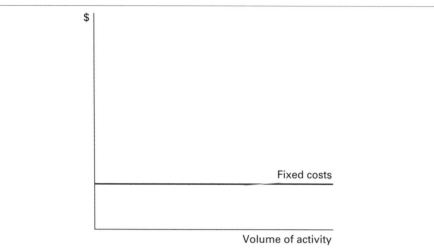

Volume of activity

Expert view 11.1: Fixed costs

Some 'fixed' costs may increase if there is a substantial change in the level of activity. For example, a business may employ a manager in its production department. The manager will be paid a fixed salary and this will not change with the level of production. However, if production is increased substantially, for example by moving to 24-hour operations and running two shifts of workers, the business may employ a second manager so that there is one manager for each shift. In this case the cost is said to be a **stepped cost**, because it remains constant over a range of activity (the cost of one manager for one shift), but then increases by a 'step' once the activity goes beyond a certain level (the cost of two managers for two shifts).

A second point to note about fixed costs is that they are deemed to be fixed in relation to the level of activity, but not necessarily over time. Fixed costs may change over time. For example, the rent paid on a shop may be subject to an annual review, with an increase each year. Similarly, a manager paid a fixed salary may have an annual pay rise.

Variable costs

Variable costs are those costs that are directly related to the level of activity and will therefore change as the level of activity changes. For example, the cost of direct materials will increase with the number of units produced.

Figure 11.4   Variable costs

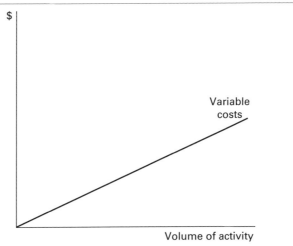

The relationship between variable cost per unit and the volume of activity will vary in different circumstances. For example, in many cases the variable cost per unit will decrease as volume increases, owing to economies of scale. This will be the case when direct labour becomes more efficient as volume increases. It will also be the case if bulk-purchasing discounts are available when buying large quantities of materials. However, in some cases the variable costs per unit may increase as volume increases. For example, higher levels of activity may involve paying employees an overtime premium.

Despite these complicating factors, for financial decision-making purposes we can usually assume that this relationship is linear, as we did with revenues. That is to say, the variable cost per unit will remain the same across all levels of activity. This means that variable costs can be represented graphically, as shown in Figure 11.4.

Total cost

The total cost of an activity will be made up of variable costs plus fixed costs. Therefore we can create a graph to plot total costs by adding these two individual cost elements together. This will give us a graph, as illustrated in Figure 11.5.

Now that we have plotted both revenues and costs on graphs in Figures 11.2 to 11.5, we can incorporate them into one graph as illustrated in Figure 11.6.

Figure 11.5   Total costs

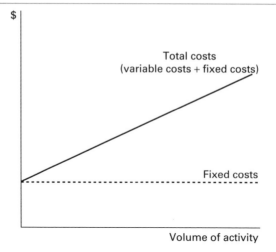

Total costs
(variable costs + fixed costs)

Fixed costs

Volume of activity

Figure 11.6   Total revenue and total costs

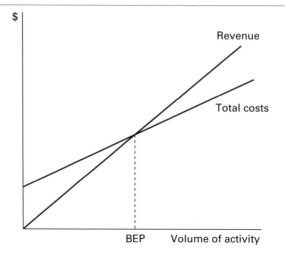

Revenue

Total costs

BEP   Volume of activity

The graph in Figure 11.6 shows that up to a certain volume of activity, costs exceed revenue. However, there comes a volume of activity, known as the **break-even point** (**BEP**), at which total cost equals total revenue. This is the point at which the business makes neither a loss nor a profit. If the business operates at a volume of activity greater than the break-even point, it will make a profit. On the other hand, if the business operates at a volume of activity less than the break-even point, it will make a loss.

Mathematical approach to CVP analysis

Although the relationship between costs and revenues is easy to see and understand using graphs, it is actually easier to apply to managerial decision making using the following profit equation:

$$Profit = PQ - (F + VQ)$$

Where: Q = units sold
P = selling price
V = unit variable cost
F = total fixed costs

We can rearrange this formula to express profit in a way which is more useful for decision making:

$$Profit = Q(P - V) - F$$

Where: P – V = Contribution per unit

We can use this formula to calculate the break-even point. The break-even point will occur at the volume of sales (ie the value of Q) at which profit is nil.

The graph in Figure 11.6 illustrates that this lies at the value of Q where total revenue = total costs. That is to say, where:

$$PQ = F + VQ$$

If we rearrange this formula in order to find the value of Q, we get:

$$Q = \frac{F}{P - V}$$

Put in plainer English, this formula is:

$$\text{Break-even point (in units)} = \frac{\text{Fixed costs}}{\text{Contribution per unit}}$$

(Remember: contribution per unit = sales price – variable cost per unit)

WORKED EXAMPLE 11.1 Computing the break-even point for sales

Isabel wishes to start a business selling ice cream from a mobile van. She can lease a van at a cost of $206 per week. Isabel has estimated that the van will cost around $70 per week to run. She has also obtained the following prices from an ice cream wholesaler:

Tub of ice cream – 100 portions $20.00
Box of 100 cones $10.00

If Isabel sells ice creams at $1.50 each, how many ice creams will she need to sell each week in order to break even?

Answer

We can calculate the number of ice creams that Isabel needs to sell by using the break-even formula. First we need to calculate contribution per unit:

$$\text{Contribution per unit} = \text{Sales price} - \text{Variable cost per unit}$$
$$= \$1.50 - (\$20 + \$10)/100 = \$1.20$$

$$\text{Break-even point (in units)} = \frac{\text{Fixed costs}}{\text{Contribution per unit}} = \frac{\$206 + \$70}{\$1.20} = 230 \text{ units}$$

Therefore Isabel will need to sell 230 ice creams per week in order to cover fixed costs and break even.

Target profit

Obviously Isabel will wish to achieve more than simply break-even with her ice cream business. She will also need to make a profit.

Another application of the CVP technique is to calculate how many units must be sold in order to achieve a target profit. Let's do this for Isabel's business.

WORKED EXAMPLE 11.2 Target profit

Isabel has decided that she needs to earn a minimum profit of $350 per week from her business. How many ice creams will she need to sell each week in order to earn this profit?

Answer

The break-even formula we used in Worked Example 11.1 told us how many ice creams Isabel needs to sell in order to cover her fixed costs. If she wishes to earn a profit of $350, Isabel needs to sell sufficient ice creams to cover fixed costs plus the profit. Hence we can modify the formula we used in Worked Example 11.1 as follows:

$$\text{Target sales (in units)} = \frac{\text{Fixed costs} + \text{target profit}}{\text{Contribution per unit}}$$

$$= \frac{\$276 + \$350}{\$1.20} = 522 \text{ units}$$

Therefore Isabel will need to sell 522 ice creams in a week in order to earn a profit of $350.

Margin of safety

In Chapter 9 we introduced the concept of **sensitivity analysis**. Sensitivity analysis involves exploring how susceptible predicted profit levels are to changes in levels of activity. CVP analysis can be a very useful tool for performing such analysis, and one of the most basic methods of doing this is to calculate the margin of safety.

The margin of safety is the gap in units of sales between the expected or target sales and the break-even point. It is a useful measure in that it tells the business how far sales can fall from their expected level before the business starts to make a loss. This is illustrated in Figure 11.7.

We can apply this analysis of margin of safety to Isabel's ice cream business.

Figure 11.7 Margin of safety

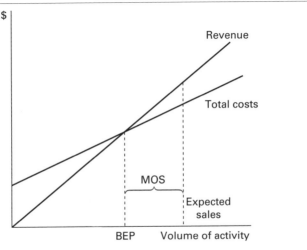

WORKED EXAMPLE 11.3 Margin of safety

Isabel expects to sell 550 ice creams each week. The break-even level of sales is 230 ice creams per week. What is Isabel's margin of safety on her expected sales?

Answer
The margin of safety is 320 ice creams (550 – 230). It is more useful to express this as a percentage of the expected sales:

$$MOS = 320/550 = 58 \text{ per cent}$$

This means that sales must fall by more than 320 units or 58 per cent from the expected level of 550 units per week before Isabel will start to make a loss.

The margin of safety is a useful measure of risk. The smaller the margin of safety, the higher the risk that the business will make a loss if it has a poor week of sales.

Expert view 11.2: Margin of safety and sensitivity analysis

In practice, businesses will usually perform CVP analysis using a computer spreadsheet. The use of a computer allows for easy manipulation of the figures so that managers can quickly identify how sensitive predicted profit levels are to changes in different variables.

Change in selling price

Another application of the CVP technique is calculating the impact on profit from changes in price. In Chapter 8 we looked at the relationship between price and demand. Generally speaking, if a business reduces its prices then this will increase demand. However, increased demand at a lower price will not necessarily increase profits. Therefore, before changing prices it is useful to calculate the predicted impact this will have upon overall profit. We can apply this analysis to Isabel's ice cream business.

WORKED EXAMPLE 11.4   Change in selling price

After selling ice creams for several weeks, Isabel has found that she sells 520 ice creams per week on average at a price of $1.50. Isabel's fixed costs are $276 per week and her variable costs are $0.30 per ice cream sold.

   Isabel is considering reducing the price to $1 per ice cream in order to increase sales.

(a)   What is the minimum number of ice creams that Isabel must sell each week in order to justify the reduction in sales price?

(b)   What will be the impact on Isabel's profit if sales increase to 750 units per week at the new price of $1?

Answer

Isabel currently sells 520 ice creams per week at a price of $1.50. Her weekly profit is therefore:

$$\text{Profit} = Q(P - V) - F$$
$$= (520 \times [\$1.50 - \$0.30]) - \$276 = \$348$$

In order to justify a reduction in the sales price Isabel must make at least the same level of profit at the new price of $1.

At the new price the new contribution per unit will be: $1.00 – $0.30 = $0.70. Therefore the minimum level of sales (in units) will be:

$$\text{Target sales (in units)} = \frac{\text{Fixed costs} + \text{Target profit}}{\text{Contribution per unit}} = \frac{\$276 + \$348}{\$0.70} = 892 \text{ units}$$

Isabel must sell at least 892 ice creams each week at the price of $1 in order to make the same level of profit that she currently makes selling the ice creams at $1.50. This represents increasing sales of 372 units (892 – 520) or 71.5 per cent. This analysis shows us that Isabel would need a substantial increase in sales at the lower price in order simply to make the same level of profit. Unless she can be confident of achieving such a large increase in sales, Isabel should not reduce the price to $1. Otherwise she runs the risk of reducing her profits:

If Isabel's sales increase to 750 ice creams per week at the new price of $1, her profit will fall to $249 per week:

$$\text{Profit} = Q(P - V) - F$$
$$= (750 \times [\$1.00 - \$0.30]) - \$276 = \$249$$

Change in production systems

As well as analysing the impact of price changes on profitability, the CVP technique can be used to analyse the impact of changes in production costs. This is particularly useful for businesses that are making operational changes. For example, the automation of activities is likely to increase fixed costs and reduce variable costs. Because this changes the **operating gearing** (the mix of variable and fixed costs), it will have an impact upon the break-even point, the margin of safety, and profitability at different levels of activity.

Expert view 11.3: Operating gearing

Operating gearing (sometimes called 'operating leverage') describes the relationship between an organization's fixed costs and variable costs:

$$\text{Operating gearing} = \frac{F}{F + V}$$

A greater proportion of fixed costs means a higher operating gearing. Increasing operating gearing makes a business's profits more sensitive to a change in volume of activity. If volume increases, profitability can be greater if operating gearing is higher. However, the effect reverses when volumes fall (see Worked Example 11.5). It is for this reason that businesses with high operating gearing often have to take drastic cost-cutting measures when sales start falling. Managers must be aware of the impact of operating gearing on profits and risk to make good business decisions.

WORKED EXAMPLE 11.5 Change in production systems

Angus Co makes beds. Current production information is:

Materials costs	$80 per unit
Labour costs	$160 per unit
Variable sales costs	$40 per unit
Sales price	$380 per unit
Fixed costs	$1,100,000 per year
Current volume of output	14,000 units per year

The company is considering automating the metal-cutting process, which is the most labour-intensive part of production. This will involve installing a new computerized cutting machine that will have an annual fixed cost of $500,000. However, it is expected that with the new automated cutting, labour costs will fall to $120 per unit.

(a) Compare the annual profit using the current production method and using the new automated production, if annual sales remain at 14,000 units.

(b) Compare the annual profit using the current production method and using the new automated production, if annual sales were to fall to 12,000 units.

Answer

If sales remain at 14,000 units per year:

The current contribution per unit = $380 − ($80 + $160 + $40) = $100
Therefore profit = ($100 × 14,000) − $1,100,000 = $300,000

With the new automated cutting process:

Contribution per unit = $380 − ($80 + $120 + $40) = $140
Therefore profit = ($140 × 14,000) − $1,600,000 = $360,000

At current production and sales levels, the proposed automation of the cutting process will increase profits by $60,000.

If sales fall to 12,000 units per year:

Profit using the current production method:

$$= (\$100 \times 12{,}000) - \$1{,}100{,}000 = \$100{,}000$$

Profit using the proposed new production method:

$$= (\$140 \times 12{,}000) - \$1{,}600{,}000 = \$80{,}000$$

At the reduced level of sales (which represents a fall of less than 15 per cent in sales), the proposed new production method would result in the company earning $20,000 less profit. Therefore, before it goes ahead with the automation, the company should examine its sales forecasts in detail in order to be confident that future sales will not fall. If it cannot be confident of this, it should not change its current production methods.

Advertising campaign

CVP analysis can be used to help managers make decisions regarding discretionary expenditure such as advertising. For example, a company may plan an advertising campaign in order to increase its volume of sales. CVP analysis will help managers assess the potential impact on overall profitability.

WORKED EXAMPLE 11.6 Advertising campaign

Digi Co manufactures laptop computers. The computers sell at $500 and the variable costs of production, sales and distribution are $350 per computer. The company has fixed costs of $9,200,000 per year. Forecast sales for the coming year are 70,000 units.

At a recent board meeting the marketing director argued that Digi Co computers offer good value in comparison to those of competitors. She has therefore proposed an advertising campaign to increase customer awareness of this.

The advertising campaign would cost $350,000 and the marketing director is confident that it would increase sales volume by 4 per cent.

Should Digi Co undertake the advertising campaign?

Answer

If the company undertakes the advertising campaign, fixed costs will increase by $350,000. Total contribution will also increase because of the increase in sales volume:

$$\text{Increase in contribution} = (70,000 \times 4\%) \times (\$500 - \$350) = \$420,000$$

Therefore Digi Co should go ahead with the advertising campaign because the net impact will be an increase in profit of $70,000 ($420,000 – $350,000).

Evaluation of the CVP technique

As can be seen from the worked examples above, CVP is an extremely straight-forward analytical tool. This simplicity is both its strength and its weakness. The strength of the technique lies in the way that it removes many of the complications of the real world in order to provide a sharp focus on the financial impact of decisions. This makes the technique both simple to apply and easy to understand. However, the simplicity of CVP analysis has led to criticism. This criticism focuses mainly on the underlying assumptions. This can be summarized as follows:

- CVP analysis departs from accepted curvilinear models of supply and demand used in economic pricing theory because it uses simple linear formulae for revenues and costs. In other words, CVP analysis ignores price elasticity of demand and economies of scale. Supporters of CVP have responded to this criticism by suggesting that although this is true, the focus of analysis on limited range of activity volumes means that a linear function is a reasonably accurate proxy of the true economic model.

- CVP analysis focuses too much on the short term. It is typically restricted to one accounting period. It therefore ignores longer-term strategic issues.

- CVP analysis usually assumes a single product. The analysis can be used for multiple products but it is necessary to assume a constant sales mix, ie the proportion of different products sold remains the same as the overall volume changes. In practice this rarely occurs. In the real world, changes in volume of sales can result from market conditions that will affect different products or services to differing degrees. This limits the usefulness of CVP analysis for businesses offering a range of products or services.

- CVP analysis assumes a simple, single-stage manufacturing process in which fixed and variable costs can be clearly identified. In the real world, manufacturing processes can be complex, with the interplay of costs being equally so.

- CVP analysis assumes that costs can be categorized into either variable or fixed. It does not allow for costs with more complex behaviour. In the real world, organizations and their activities are complex. It is often difficult to separate costs into clear classifications of fixed and variable.

- CVP analysis assumes that the forces influencing a business are static rather than dynamic. In the real world, changes in volume of sales affect pricing, which in turn can change price elasticity of demand. Changes in volume also affect the cost of materials used in production and the cost of direct labour. CVP analysis ignores these changes and therefore does not reflect the reality that makes up a dynamic complicated market.

All of these criticisms are directed at the simplicity of CVP analysis when used in complex organizations and dynamic business environments. The static nature of CVP analysis means that it must be used with care within a dynamic and complex market. However, this does not mean that the technique is totally without validity. CVP analysis takes a snapshot. This is a useful snapshot provided managers do not think purely in terms of single points in time with nothing changing. There is often great merit in a tool that cuts through the complexities of the real world in order to give simple and straightforward measures for decision-makers.

Cost–volume–profit analysis: summary

This section has demonstrated how CVP analysis can be a useful analytical tool for managers. However, managers must be aware of the limitations of the technique and therefore decide when it is an appropriate tool.

Relevant costing

The concept of relevant costs and opportunity costs were introduced in Chapter 9 in the context of investment decision making. In this chapter we will examine these concepts in more detail and demonstrate how they can be applied to other financial decisions such as: the decision to buy in a product or service or make it in-house, or the decision to drop a product or close a division or segment of the business.

As was the case when we looked at investment appraisal in Chapter 9, it is always assumed when evaluating alternative courses of action that the objective is to maximize the present value of future net cash inflows.

Measuring relevant costs

The relevant costs for decision making are those future costs that will be affected by the decision. Costs that are independent of the decision are not relevant and should not be considered when making that decision.

Figure 11.8   The relevant cost decision

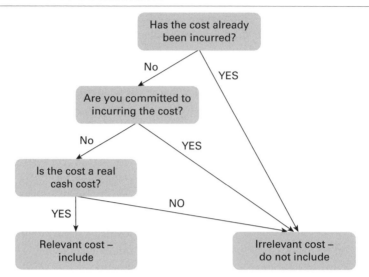

As a general rule, a cost that is avoidable by choosing one alternative over another is a relevant cost. A cost that is unavoidable, no matter which alternative is chosen, is irrelevant and should not be included in the evaluation of the decision. Figure 11.8 sets out a decision tree for deciding whether a cost is relevant to a particular decision.

- The first question to ask is: 'Has the cost already been incurred?' If a cost has already been incurred, it cannot be avoided no matter what decision is made. Such a cost is known as a **sunk cost**; it is irrelevant to any decision and should be ignored. This sounds simple in principle, but often people are confused about the relevance of sunk costs and include them in their considerations.

    For example, a manager may argue that because his organization has invested $500,000 in a new computer system, this expenditure would be wasted if the computer system were abandoned because of problems. Such a manager would argue that the $500,000 is a relevant cost of abandoning the system. However, the reality is that the $500,000 has already been spent, and this cannot change no matter what decision is made now about the future use of the computer system. The only relevant costs in this case would be those future costs incurred to rectify the problems with the system.

- Secondly, you should ask: 'Are you committed to incurring the cost?' In some cases, costs may not yet have been incurred, but the business is committed to those costs no matter what decision is made. If this is the case, the cost is irrelevant and should not be included in the decision-making process.

For example, a business may enter into a five-year lease of a building. After one year the business thinks that it no longer needs that building and faces the decision of whether or not to move out. If the business is contractually obliged to continue paying the rent for the remainder of the five-year lease term, any future rent will have to be paid no matter what decision is made about the use of the building. The rent cost therefore becomes irrelevant to the decision, even though it has not yet actually been incurred.

- Finally you should ask: 'Is the cost a real cash cost?' Some costs are valid accounting costs that should be included on the profitability analysis, but they are not relevant for decision making. This is the category of costs which relate to accounting adjustments rather than direct cash payments. The main example is depreciation. Each accounting period, a cost will be recorded for the depreciation of non-current assets. However, there is no underlying cash payment relating to this depreciation cost. It is therefore not a relevant cost.

    For example, a business owns a machine which is depreciated on a straight-line basis at $5,000 per year. If the business decides to sell the machine, it will no longer incur the depreciation cost of $5,000. However, this is not a relevant cost and should not be included in the decision regarding selling the machine. The reality is that the underlying cash flow represented in the depreciation charge was the initial purchase of the machine. As this occurred in the past, it is a sunk cost and is irrelevant to the decision. The only costs relevant to the decision to sell the machine would be any extra costs incurred in selling it (such as advertising) together with the revenue received from the sale.

Using relevant costing for decision making

There are two basic steps in using the relevant costing approach to evaluate an operational decision: firstly, disregard costs and revenues that are not relevant to the decision; secondly, use the costs and revenues that remain (ie the relevant costs) to evaluate alternatives, choosing that alternative which offers the greatest net benefit.

Costs do not rigidly fit into the category of 'relevant' or 'irrelevant'. What is a relevant cost will depend upon the circumstances of the decision: costs may be relevant in the context of one decision but not in a different situation. For example, the timescale of the decision often impacts on which costs are relevant. We will look at this issue in more detail below when we compare short-term and long-term decisions for outsourcing.

Let us look at how this principle is applied within the context of common operational decisions.

The make or buy decision

Organizations are regularly faced with what is commonly known as the 'make or buy' decision. This is the decision of whether to make a product (or provide a service) in-house, or to buy that product in from some external supplier. There can be many advantages of buying in from an external supplier:

- Management is freed up to concentrate on activities which may be more important to the profitability of the organization.
- Risks are transferred outside of the organization (to the supplier).
- External suppliers can specialize and create economies of scale which enables them to supply at a much lower cost than the organization is able to achieve.
- Buying in from multiple suppliers creates greater security of supply.
- Buying in services when needed may give an organization greater flexibility and save costs during times when those services are not needed.

During the 1980s the concept of **outsourcing** became extremely popular. As a result, many businesses started to buy in from external suppliers those facilities which had previously always been provided internally.

Extract 11.1: Tom Peters – 'stick to the knitting'

One of the best-known proponents of outsourcing is the management guru Tom Peters, who coined the phrase 'stick to the knitting'. Peters' 1982 book *In Search of Excellence* (written with Robert Waterman) is one of the biggest-selling business books ever. Based upon a study of 43 of the world's most successful (at the time) businesses, the book identifies eight common themes to that success. One of those themes was 'stick to the knitting – stay with the business you know'. One interpretation of this principle, which Peters developed in his later work, was the idea that management should concentrate on their core activities and let others take care of the non-core activities by outsourcing them.

Outsourcing became popular and was widespread practice throughout the late 1980s and into the 1990s. It was seen as a way of keeping businesses lean and flexible – non-core activities could be bought in as needed and at a lower cost than doing the work in-house. Many businesses outsourced payroll services, legal services, recruitment and advertising. Businesses also outsourced areas of manufacturing to overseas suppliers, finding that they could take advantage of cheaper (and un-unionized) labour and avoid regulations, high taxes and other operating costs. Outsourcing also became popular in the public sector, with many areas of public service such as public transport, health care and local services being bought in from private-sector suppliers.

This is a trend which continues in the 21st century in both the public and private sectors.

Short-term vs long-term situations

When faced with a decision which covers only the short term, it is often the case that many costs are unavoidable (and therefore relevant to the decision) because reducing or removing those costs requires measures which take a longer timescale to implement. In the long term, more costs become avoidable. This means that the outcome of a 'make or buy' decision will differ according to whether a short-term or long-term position is considered. This principle is illustrated in Worked Examples 11.7a and 11.7b.

WORKED EXAMPLE 11.7A Make or buy decision – short term

Scott Co operates a distillery producing Scotch whisky. The main ingredient of whisky is malted barley, which is produced by processing raw barley in order to convert the starch content into sugars.

Scott Co currently produces its own malted barley. However, the directors are considering the option of buying the malted barley in from an external supplier that specializes in malting.

The estimated cost per tonne to Scott Co of producing malted barley in-house is as follows:

	$
Direct labour	80
Direct materials (raw barley)	260
Direct (variable) overheads	180
Fixed overheads (apportioned)	120
	640

The outside supplier has quoted a figure of $580 per tonne for an order of 500 tonnes of malted barley. This is equal to three months' supply.

The share of fixed overheads apportioned to malted barley production will still be incurred whether or not the company purchases the malted barley from an external supplier. Any redundancies of production staff will be subject to three months' notice.

Should Scott Co continue to produce malted barley in-house or should it buy the malted barley from the external supplier?

Answer
On face value, the buy-in option appears more financially attractive: it currently costs Scott Co $640 per tonne to produce in-house, and the external supplier is offering malted barley at $580 per tonne.

However, in evaluating this decision, the directors need to compare the quoted external price of $580 with the *relevant cost* of producing the malted barley in-house. The relevant cost will be those costs which can be reduced or removed if the malted barley is bought in. The fact that this is a short-term contract has an impact on which costs become relevant.

Because the contract is for three months' supply and direct labour is subject to three months' notice on redundancy, direct labour costs cannot be reduced if the malted barley is bought in. This is therefore not a relevant cost. Likewise, the fixed overhead costs will still be incurred if the malted barley is bought in and so this is not a relevant cost. This means that the relevant costs, ie the costs that will be eliminated if the malted barley is bought in, are:

	$
Direct materials (raw barley)	260
Direct (variable) overheads	180
	440

These figures reveal that the short-term contract is not financially viable for Scott Co. The company would be incurring purchasing costs of $580 per tonne, but only reducing its in-house costs by $440 per tonne. This means that the buy-in option would cost the company $140 per tonne more than manufacturing themselves.

However, the situation may change if the company is able to negotiate a long-term contract for supply of malted barley.

WORKED EXAMPLE 11.7B Make or buy decision – long term

Scott Co is able to negotiate a long-term contract with the outside supplier to deliver 2,000 tonnes of malted barley per year for five years at a cost of $580 per tonne. In the long term the fixed overheads and labour costs can be reduced (with no redundancy costs).

Should Scott Co enter into the longer-term contract for external supply of malted barley, or should it continue to make the malted barley in-house?

Answer

Because Scott Co is able to eliminate both the fixed overhead costs and the labour costs with a long-term contract, all the costs of production become relevant. This means that Scott Co would be saving $640 per tonne by not manufacturing against the cost of buying in of $580 per tonne. This is a net saving to the company of $60 per tonne. In this case, the option of buying in rather than making in-house appears more financially attractive. The final decision should, of course, be made after evaluating wider strategic and qualitative factors. (These are discussed below.)

Extract 11.2: Outsourcing at TagHeuer

TagHeuer, the Swiss watch manufacturer, has a clear 'make or buy' strategy. The company is the world's fourth-biggest producer of luxury watches, after Rolex, Cartier and Omega. Despite this, the company manufactures very little. Watch movements and other components are bought in from external suppliers. Some watch cases are made by a subsidiary, but about half are bought in. Even the final assembly of watches is subcontracted. Only the top-end watches are manufactured internally and that is by a subsidiary.

The company advocates many advantages in this strategy: contracting out manufacturing transfers risk to suppliers; sourcing from multiple suppliers creates security of supply and competitive pricing; management can concentrate on product development and marketing.

Opportunity costs

The concept of an opportunity cost was introduced in Chapter 9. This is a category of cost that will not be found in an income statement. It is used only in decision making. However, opportunity costs can be extremely important in assessing the true financial impact of a decision. This is because, if an organization is operating at full capacity, the decision to engage in one particular activity (for example, to produce a particular good or service) has a cost in terms of not being able to use that capacity for some other activity.

Expert view 11.4: Opportunity cost

An **opportunity cost** is a measure of the opportunity that is lost or sacrificed when the choice of one course of action requires that an alternative course of action be given up. An opportunity cost is always measured financially in terms of lost contribution (Contribution = Sales revenue – Variable costs).

WORKED EXAMPLE 11.7C Opportunity costs

Let us return to the example of Scott Co considering a short-term three-month contract for buying in malted barley (see Worked Example 11.7a).

Scott Co is currently running at full capacity. The production of malted barley internally required 20 hours of production time that could otherwise be used for chill filtering (another part of the whisky production process). Chill filtering yields a contribution of $8 per hour.

Should Scott Co continue to produce malted barley in-house or should it buy the malted barley from the external supplier?

Answer

Returning to the analysis that we did in Worked Example 11.7a, we established that the relevant cost of producing the malted barley in-house was:

	$
Direct materials (raw barley)	260
Direct (variable) overheads	180
	440

However, because Scott Co is now operating at full capacity, there is also the opportunity cost of using production time for malting barley rather than chill filtering. This opportunity cost is measured in lost contribution:

$$20 \text{ hours} \times \$8 \text{ per hour} = \$160$$

When we include this opportunity cost, the total relevant cost of producing malted barley in-house is:

	$
Direct materials (raw barley)	260
Direct (variable) overheads	180
Opportunity cost	160
	600

This means that the cost of buying in malted barley from the external supplier at $580 per tonne is now more financially attractive than manufacturing in-house. Scott Co should therefore buy in the malted barley over the three-month period and use the internal production facility for chill filtering.

The consideration of qualitative factors in outsourcing

The quantitative factors which we have considered above, ie the relevant costs and the opportunity costs of manufacturing in-house as opposed to buying in, do not give the full picture in decision-making situations. Other, non-financial factors should always be considered, both because they are important in their own right, and also because they might have financial effects which are not immediately quantifiable. Examples of factors which can be difficult to quantify financially are:

- *Redundancies*. Outsourcing an activity invariably results in redundancies. These can have an obvious immediate cost. However, there are other costs which can be more difficult to quantify in terms of lost expertise and knowledge. It is relatively easy to outsource an activity, but far more difficult to reverse that decision once the internal expertise has been lost.

- *Employee morale*. Outsourcing which reduces staffing and results in redundancies can have a negative impact on the morale of remaining employees. This can have a knock-on effect on productivity levels and on employee retention. High staff turnover carries additional costs in terms of recruitment and training of new staff and the loss of experience, knowledge and skills of the employees who leave.

- *Reliance on suppliers*. If goods or services are bought in from an external supplier rather than produced in-house, the organization becomes reliant upon that external supplier. Dealing with a third party is always more complex than dealing with issues in-house as it can involve slower communication, formal contracts and far more bureaucracy.

- *Production flexibility*. External supply usually involves formal contracts which stipulate quantities of goods or services supplied. Although this can provide the security in times of stable trading, it can reduce flexibility if the business's situation changes. For example, if production and requirements reduce substantially, a business may find itself contractually bound to purchase large quantities of supplies it no longer needs.

- *Ability to meet customer requirements*. Many industries experience rapid technological development and change. It is therefore important for businesses to be able to modify and develop their products to meet the changing demands of customers. If items are produced in-house, it is more likely that the business will also have in-house research and development facilities. Therefore, outsourcing, although it may reduce short-term costs, may also reduce longer-term product development and innovation.

- *Control over quality*. Any organization needs to ensure that it has control over the quality of what it produces. Often such control is easier if all operations and therefore communications are in-house. Quality problems can be more difficult to resolve when dealing with external suppliers because of communication, cultural and contractual issues between the two separate organizations.

Extract 11.3: Make or buy – did IBM get it wrong?

When IBM launched the PC in 1981 the business was primarily focused on manufacturing computer hardware. Management were faced with the decision of developing an operating system for the new PC in-house, or outsourcing. They decided to outsource to Microsoft, a relatively new and small software development company. If IBM had been able to anticipate the outcome of this decision, they might well have chosen to develop the software in-house.

The shutdown decision: deleting a business segment

In a changing and developing business environment, organizations are often faced with the decision of whether or not to delete a segment of the business. This can cover a wide range of decision-making situations, because a business 'segment' could be a:

- product;
- type of customer;
- geographic region;
- distribution channel;
- or any other identifiable part of a business.

Extract 11.4: Cutting business segments at Nokia

The Finnish company Nokia is known today as one of the world's leading mobile phone manufacturers. However, the business started as a paper manufacturer and developed over a 100-year period into an industrial conglomerate involved in manufacturing paper, tyres, footwear, electrical cables, televisions, personal computers, consumer electronics, military communication equipment, electronic components, plastics, aluminium and chemicals.

When the Soviet Union collapsed in the early 1990s, Finland suffered a huge recession and Nokia faced financial disaster. Management were presented with some challenging decisions and chose to focus on the rising telecommunications business. All non-telecommunication businesses, which represented nearly 90 per cent of revenues, were sold off.

In 1991, more than a quarter of Nokia's revenue came from Finnish domestic sales. However, with the strategic change and refocusing on mobile phones, Nokia expanded into Europe, North and South America and Asia. By 1998 Nokia had grown to become the world's largest mobile phone manufacturer and continued to hold this position until 2012.

Using relevant costing to evaluate the shutdown decision

The decision to drop a business segment will depend upon the impact the decision has on the overall profitability of the organization. The business segment should be closed only if this results in an increase in overall profit. Therefore, in order to assess its impact, it is necessary to analyse the costs carefully and ensure that only relevant costs are included in the evaluation. This should be done as follows:

- Overall corporate profitability should be analysed by business segment.
- In assessing the profitability of individual segments, only those costs that are relevant to the decision should be included.
- The contribution margin that will be lost by closing the segment should be established by comparing the revenue that will be lost with the costs that will be avoided.

This approach is best seen through the use of an example:

WORKED EXAMPLE 11.8 The shutdown decision

Book Co is a book retailer that has three large stores in three different cities. The budgeted income statement for the company for the next accounting period is as shown in Table 11.1.

Table 11.1

	Store A $000	Store B $000	Store C $000	Total $000
Sales	1,000	1,800	1,200	4,000
Cost of sales	480	720	510	1,710
Gross profit	520	1,080	690	2,290
Selling costs:				
Store staff salaries	140	180	150	470
Store running costs	65	95	70	230
Store expenses	25	40	22	87
Advertising	60	60	60	180
Head office expenses	135	243	162	540
Central warehouse costs	120	200	140	460
Total costs	545	818	604	1,967
Net profit/(loss)	(25)	262	86	323

Books are ordered, stored, and dispatched to individual stores from a central warehouse. It is estimated that 60 per cent of the costs of the central warehouse are fixed and 40 per cent are variable.

Store expenses are variable, but store staff salaries and store running costs are fixed. However, all store costs are avoidable if the store is closed. Each store has an advertising budget of $60,000 that is also avoidable if the store is closed.

The directors of Book Co are concerned that Store A is predicted to make a loss. They are therefore considering closing this store. However, before doing so, they have sought your advice as an external business consultant.

Required:
Advise the directors of Book Co on whether they should close Store A, based upon the predicted loss.

Answer
Before a decision is made on closing Store A, the budgeted income statement should be reformatted to clearly identify the relevant costs, ie the costs that would be avoided if the store were closed. This has been done in Table 11.2.

Table 11.2

	Store A $000	Store B $000	Store C $000	Total $000
Sales	1,000	1,800	1,200	4,000
Less variable costs:				
Cost of sales	480	720	510	1,710
Store expenses	25	40	22	87
Warehouse costs (40%)	48	80	56	184
Contribution to all fixed costs	447	960	612	2,019
Store specific fixed costs:				
Store staff salaries	140	180	150	470
Store running costs	65	95	70	230
Advertising	60	60	60	180
Contribution to central fixed costs	182	625	332	1,139
Central fixed costs:				
Head office expenses				540
Warehouse costs (60%)				276
Net profit/(loss)				323

The original budgeted income statement suggests that Store A will make a loss of $25,000. Therefore, if the store were closed, the company would expect overall profit to increase by $25,000 to $348,000.

However, the reformatted budget demonstrates that Store A is making a positive contribution of $182,000 towards the common fixed costs. This means that if Store A were closed, overall company profit would fall by $182,000 to only $141,000.

The conclusion should be, therefore, that because Store A is making a positive contribution to common fixed costs, it should remain open. If Store A is closed, this will have a significant negative impact on overall company profit.

Expert view 11.5: Allocated and apportioned fixed costs

In Chapter 8 we looked at the concept of allocating and apportioning fixed costs when establishing the total cost of a department or product. When decision making, it is important to be aware of the distinction between allocated and apportioned fixed costs, because this distinction usually has an impact upon whether the costs are relevant. In Worked Example 11.8 the allocated fixed costs of running Store A were relevant to the decision because they would be avoidable if the store were closed. On the other hand, the apportioned head office fixed costs were not relevant as these costs would still be incurred even if Store A were closed.

Relevant costing: summary

In this section covering relevant costs in different decision-making situations, we have covered the following important points:

- When decision making, only relevant costs should be considered. Any costs deemed not to be relevant should be ignored.
- Relevant costs are those future costs that will be changed by a particular decision. This may include opportunity costs.
- Whether any given cost is relevant will depend upon the situation.
- The time horizon chosen will impact upon what costs become relevant for a given situation.

Conclusion

In this chapter we have covered two important financial decision-making techniques: CVP analysis and relevant costing. CVP analysis enables managers to identify the levels of operating activity that are necessary to avoid losses and achieve targeted levels of profits. It also enables managers to analyse the impact of organizational changes and the related risks. Relevant costing is a useful technique of focusing management attention on those costs that will be affected by decisions.

COMPREHENSION QUESTIONS

1 Explain the concept of 'margin of safety' in CVP analysis.

2 If a business reduces its fixed costs whilst maintaining the same contribution margin, will this increase or decrease its break-even point?

3 Explain what is meant by 'operating gearing'.

4 If a company increases its operating gearing, will this make its profit more or less sensitive to changes in sales volume?

5 Explain three potential weaknesses of CVP analysis as a decision tool.

6 Alpha Co has 200 units of material x in inventory. This originally cost $40 per unit. Alpha Co no longer needs the material x for its original use. It could sell the inventory for $10 per unit. However, the production manager wishes to use the material x in a new project. What is the relevant cost of using the 200 units of material x in the new project?

7 Give an example of a cost which may not be relevant in the short term, but could become relevant in a long-term decision.

Answers available at **www.koganpage.com/afm3**.

Exercises

Answers available at **www.koganpage.com/afm3**.

Exercise 11.1: Target profit

Huath Co has identified that it can optimize its production costs if it sells 200,000 units of its product. The directors wish to make a profit of $300,000. The following costs have been predicted:

Direct material cost	$15 per unit
Direct labour cost	$10 per unit
Variable production overhead cost	$20 per unit
Fixed costs	$400,000 per annum

Calculate the sales price per unit which the company needs to apply.

Exercise 11.2: CVP analysis and price change

Beath Co makes and sells mobile phone batteries. The variable costs of production are $4 and the current sales price is $7. Fixed costs are $35,000 per month and the annual profit of the company is currently $270,000. The volume of sales demand is constant throughout the year.

The company is considering lowering the sales price to $6 to stimulate sales, but is uncertain of the effect on sales volume.

(a) Calculate the minimum volume of sales required to justify the reduction in price.

(b) What would the percentage change in profit be if sales increased to 300,000 units?

Exercise 11.3: CVP analysis and selling price

Luis Co is a manufacturer of precision parts for electric motors. The company has developed a new brush assembly for large industrial electric motors. The company expects to sell 20,000 units of this new product in the following year, and wishes to make a profit of $90,000. Costs are as follows:

Direct material cost	$25 per unit
Direct labour cost	$10 per unit
Variable production overhead cost	$25 per unit
Fixed costs	$70,000 per annum

Required:

(a) Calculate the required sales price per unit.

(b) Calculate the break-even sales price.

Exercise 11.4: Make or buy?

Nuin Co manufactures a number of different components for the oil industry. The management is considering whether to buy in or continue making one of the components (component A). This component currently has a manufacturing cost as follows:

	$
Direct labour (4hr @ $12ph)	48
Direct materials	24
Variable overheads (4hr @ $2ph)	8
Fixed overheads (4hr @ $5ph)	20
	100 per unit

The direct labour, direct materials and variable overhead costs all relate directly to the production of component A and would not be incurred if production of the component stopped. However, the fixed overheads charge is an apportionment of costs which would still be incurred even if component A were not produced.

Required:
Under each of the three (separate) situations below, advise the management of Nuin Co whether component A should be bought in or made in-house:

(a) The purchasing manager has found an external manufacturer that can supply the component A at a guaranteed price of $90 per unit.

(b) The external supplier can offer component A at $90 per unit. If Nuin Co continues to manufacture component A in-house, it will need to install new computer-controlled manufacturing systems which will have a fixed cost of $50,000 per year.

(c) The external supplier can offer component A at $90 per unit. The manufacture of component A in-house requires the use of specialist skilled direct labour. If component A were bought in, that direct labour could be used in the production of component B which is sold for $180 and has a manufacturing cost as follows:

	$
Direct labour (8hr @ $12ph)	96
Direct materials	18
Variable overheads (8hr @ $2ph)	16
Fixed overheads (8hr @ $5ph)	40
	170 per unit

Reference

Peters, T J and Waterman, R H (1982) *In Search of Excellence: Lessons from America's best-run companies*, Profile Books, London

APPENDIX A
An introduction to double-entry bookkeeping

Double-entry bookkeeping (bookkeeping, for short) is best taught through T-accounts; named thus because of their shape. T-accounts have a left side and a right side. Hereafter these will be referred to as the DEBIT side and the CREDIT side. This links back to the golden rule of accounting: that every debit must have an equal and opposite credit otherwise your ledgers would not balance.

Over the next few pages we will walk you through each of the Mobius Inc examples, completing the T-accounts as we go.

Bookkeeping comes naturally to a small number of people, but to the majority, however, this is something which needs to be practised and given careful consideration. Regardless of whether you 'get it' within five minutes or five years, for almost everyone there is a 'light-bulb moment' where everything clicks into place and you reflect uncomprehendingly on the times you couldn't see how it worked.

Approaching double-entry bookkeeping

Step 1 Set up your T-accounts

A T-account captures the key information about a transaction:

- the date;
- an outline description of the transaction;
  - note that this is normally the name of the account the other side of the journal entry is going to;
- the value.

For example, our first transaction involves two T-accounts: cash at bank and in hand; and share capital. The cash at bank and in hand T-account would appear as shown in Table A.1.

Table A.1 Cash at bank and in hand

Date	Description	$	$	Description	Date

Note that there the '$' or 'value' columns need to be totalled. That is because each T-account needs to 'balance out' at the end of the period of account:

- On the one hand, statement of financial position balances, for example cash at bank and in hand don't stop existing at the end of a period and therefore the amounts left over can be carried forward to the next period.
- On the other hand, income statement accounts, for example rental costs, relate to a period of account and once they have been incurred and paid, they should be closed out.
  - More on this later...

Step 2 Write out your journal entry

Certainly, while you're in the initial learning stages of bookkeeping it is good practice to write out every journal entry. As you progress, you might stop doing this. Note, however, that if you don't write out the entry in full and you make an error (eg a transposition error, post two debits instead of a debit and credit, miss one side of the transaction), tracing the error back is more difficult.

The question states:

Mobius Inc (1)
On day 1, you opt to put financial distance between you and the trading entity and transfer $1,000 from your personal bank account to a bank account you hold in the name of the new enterprise – Mobius Inc.

The journal entry is as follows:

		$	$
Debit	Cash at bank and in hand	1,000	
Credit	Share capital: equity and reserves		1,000

Useful tip

People who struggle with double-entry bookkeeping often don't understand the relevance of posting an entry as either a debit or a credit. The interconnectedness of position and performance provides the clue that we need. The grid below might help you to understand.

First, however, remember the accounting equation:

$$\text{Assets } MINUS \text{ Liabilities } EQUALS \text{ Equity} + \text{Reserves}$$
$$(\text{Assets} - \text{Liabilities} = \text{Equity and Reserves})$$

For this equation to work, an increase in assets would necessarily lead to either:

- a decrease in another asset;
- an increase in liabilities; or
- an increase in equity and reserves.

Examples might be:

- a decrease in another asset, eg swapping cash for inventory;
- an increase in liabilities, eg buying inventory on credit from a supplier;
- an increase in equity and reserves, eg selling share capital for cash.

To continue...

We know that the profit is taken to equity and reserves to close it out at the end of a period. A simple double entry effecting both the statement of financial position and income statement (ie performance and position) might be:

- An operating expense being paid, eg rent.
- Cash would reduce (decrease in assets) and the rental cost in the income statement would increase.
  - Assuming this was the only transaction a business undertook during the period of account, at the end of the year this rental expense would be the loss for the period. This balance would be taken to retained earnings (a sub-heading under reserves).
  - Therefore, our accounting equation holds: a decrease in assets is offset by a decrease in equity and reserves.

The accounting equation tells us that there are two equal and opposite sides to every transaction. This can be summarized as shown in Table A.2.

Table A.2

	Debit	**Credit**
Assets and liabilities (excluding equity and reserves)	Assets increase Liabilities decrease (ie positive effect on financial position)	Assets decrease Liabilities increase (ie negative effect on financial position)
Income statement and Equity and reserves	Expenses increase (Revenue decreases) (ie negative impact on performance; reduce profit) Equity and reserves decrease	Expenses decrease (Revenue increases) (ie positive impact on performance; increase profit) Equity and reserves increase

Or, in shorthand (Table A.3).

Table A.3

	Debit	**Credit**
Assets and liabilities (excluding equity and reserves)	+	−
Income statement and Equity and reserves	−	+

Step 3 Post this journal entry to the relevant T-accounts (Table A.4)

Table A.4

Cash at bank and in hand						
Date	Description	$	$	Description	Date
Day 1	Initial investment capital	1,000			

Share capital						
Date	Description	$	$	Description	Date
			1,000	Bank	Day 1

Step 4 Close out the T-accounts

Assuming that this is the only transaction, you now need to move your closing balances to a trial balance and then into the financial statements (Table A.5).

Table A.5

Cash at bank and in hand						
Date	Description	$	$	Description	Date	
Beginning of day 1	Balance brought forward	–				
Day 1	Initial investment capital	1,000				
			1,000	Balance carried forward	End of day 1	
		1,000	1,000			
Beginning of day 2	Balance brought forward	1,000				

Share capital						
Date	Description	$	$	Description	Date	
			–	Balance brought forward	Beginning of day 1	
			1,000	Bank	Day 1	
End of day 1	Balance carried forward	1,000				
		1,000	1,000			
			1,000	Balance brought forward	Beginning of day 2	

Let's walk through what has happened here.

The original double entry was posted. Both sides were posted correctly and to the appropriate T-accounts.

If this were the only transaction of the day, we need to ask ourselves whether these two balances are position or performance related, ie were they assets or liabilities, or were they revenue or expenses. It is obvious that both cash and share capital are position-related balances. They will continue to be controlled (obligated to settle) by the entity on day 2 given that nothing happened to cancel them out on day 1.

Therefore, these balances have been carried forward (c/fwd) from day 1 to day 2.

You will notice that when the account is closed out, the closing balance which we carry forward is the balancing entry to make the account sum:

- Mobius Inc has $1,000 in the bank at the end of day 1 and none was spent and none generated during that 24-hour period. Therefore, the company has $1,000 at the beginning of day 2.

- Mobius Inc has $1,000 of share capital. No more was sold and none was repurchased during day 1, therefore they close with $1,000 and open the following day with $1,000.

When you open up the account, be careful to bring the brought forward amount down on the correct side, ie the same as it was accumulated; or the opposite of the balancing entry that closed it out. In this case, the cash is c/fwd as a credit to balance the account out, but b/fwd as a debit. Reflecting on the grid above, you'll see that a debit signifies a positive balance and, indeed, we hold $1,000 in the bank. If you had brought this balance forward as a credit, this would mean that you opened with a negative amount of cash (bank overdraft).

Tutor's note: The joy of learning accounting is that it is happening all the time, both to you, with you and all around you. Next time you go into a shop, think about the transaction as a bookkeeping exercise.

- Do you have cash and you want to exchange it for a new pen? If so, you exchange one asset for another (credit cash [reduce asset]; credit equipment [increase asset]).

- Do you pay for your electricity by direct debit? If so, you exchange an asset (credit bank [reduce asset]; debit expenses [reduce profits]).

Step 5 Summarize into a 'trial balance'

A trial balance (TB) is a summary of your T-accounts' closing balances, ie a list of closing balances. Our TB is simple in this instance as we have only two accounts/balances.

Your TB needs to have three columns:

1 account name, eg cash at bank and in hand;

2 debit;

3 credit.

Both debit and credit columns are then summed. If they are not the same value, you have a TB that does not balance and you can therefore conclude that you've made a mistake in your bookkeeping somewhere.

Our TB at the end of day 1 should appear as shown in Table A.6.

Table A.6

	Debit (Dr) $	Credit (Cr) $
Cash at bank and in hand	1,000	
Share capital		1,000
	1,000	1,000

NOTE You will often see debit and credit shortened to 'dr' (DR, Dr) and 'cr' (CR, Cr).

Step 6 Extract the information from the TB and draw up your financial statements

Again in this case, the exercise is straightforward. We only have the statement of financial position entries. We have an asset and the equity (share capital). The statement would appear as follows:

Statement of financial position
For Mobius Inc
As at the end of Day 1

Assets
Current Assets
   Cash at bank and in hand   1,000
Total Assets   1,000

Equity and reserves
Share capital   1,000

Total   1,000

Tutor's Note: These are the basics of double-entry bookkeeping. We have walked through this example slowly and carefully, explaining points of common error as we go. We will now move up a gear and proceed through the rest of the examples at a slightly speedier pace. If you struggle, however, then come back to these basic points.

Mobius Inc

Day 2

The text states:

On day 2, you borrow $500 from a friend to provide further financial help to your business.

The journal entry would be as follows:

		$	$
Debit	Cash at bank and in hand	500	
Credit	Loan (liabilities)		500

The T-accounts would read as shown in Table A.7.

Table A.7

Cash at bank and in hand

Date	Description	$	$	Description	Date
Beginning of day 1	Balance brought forward	–			
Day 1	Initial investment capital	1,000			
			1,000	Balance carried forward	End of day 1
		1,000	1,000		
Beginning of day 2	Balance brought forward	1,000			
Day 2	Loan	500			
			1,500	Balance carried forward	End of day 2
		1,500	1,500		
Beginning of day 3	Balance brought forward	1,500			

(continued)

Table A.7 *(Continued)*

Loan account (liabilities)

Date	Description	$	$	Description	Date
			–	Balance brought forward	Beginning of day 2
			500	Bank	Day 2
End of day 2	Balance carried forward	500			
		500	500		
			500	Balance brought forward	Beginning of day 3

Share capital

Date	Description	$	$	Description	Date
			–	Balance brought forward	Beginning of day 1
			1,000	Bank	Day 1
End of day 1	Balance carried forward	1,000			
		1,000	1,000		
			1,000	Balance brought forward	Beginning of day 2
End of day 2	Balance carried forward	1,000			
		1,000	1,000		
			1,000	Balance brought forward	Beginning of day 3

In other words, no change on the share capital account from day 1.

The revised TB at the end of day 2 should read as shown in Table A.8.

Table A.8

Day 2	Debit (Dr) $	Credit (Cr) $
Cash at bank and in hand	1,500	
Loan		500
Share capital		1,000
	1,500	1,500

Thus, the statement of financial position as at the end of day 2 should read as follows:

Statement of financial position
For Mobius Inc
As at the end of Day 2

Assets
Current assets
    Cash at bank and in hand   1,500

Liabilities
Non-current liabilities
    Loan   (500)

Net assets   1,000

Equity and reserves
Share capital   1,000

Total   1,000

Days 3 & 4

On day 3, Mobius Inc invests $500 of cash by acquiring a new computer.

		$	$
Debit	Non-current assets (computer)	500	
Credit	Cash		500

On day 4, Mobius Inc buys some raw materials worth $400 and holds them as inventories. The cash required to settle the invoices related to these purchases does not need to be found for 10 days as these are the credit terms offered.

		$	$
Debit	Inventories	400	
Credit	Trade payables		400

We now have six T-accounts open:

1 cash at bank and in hand;

2 non-current assets;

3 inventories;

4 trade payables;

5 share capital (remain unchanged during days 3 & 4);

6 loan account (remain unchanged during days 3 & 4).

And they should appear as shown in Table A.9.

Table A.9

Cash at bank and in hand

Date	Description	$	$	Description	Date
Beg of day 3	Bal. b/fwd	1,500			
			500	Inventories	Day 3
			1,000	Bal. c/fwd	End of day 4
		1,500	1,500		

Non-current assets (computer)

Date	Description	$	$	Description	Date
Beg of day 3	Bal. b/fwd	–			
Day 3	Bank	500			
			500	Bal. c/fwd	End of day 4
		500	500		

Inventories (raw materials)

Date	Description	$	$	Description	Date
Beg of day 3	Bal. b/fwd	–			
Day 4	Trade payables	400			
			400	Bal. c/fwd	End of day 4
		400	400		

(continued)

Table A.9 (continued)

Trade payables

Date	Description	$	$	Description	Date
			–	Bal. b/fwd	Beg of day 3
			400	Inventories	Day 4
End of day 4	Bal. c/fwd	400			
		400	400		

Share capital

Date	Description	$	$	Description	Date
			1,000	Bal. b/fwd	Beg of day 3
End of day 4	Bal. c/fwd	1,000			
		1,000	1,000		

Loan

Date	Description	$	$	Description	Date
			500	Bal. b/fwd	Beg of day 3
End of day 4	Bal. c/fwd	500			
		500	500		

The statement of financial position as at the end of day 4 should appear as follows:

Statement of financial position
For Mobius Inc
As at the end of Day 4

Assets
Non-current assets
    Computer   500
Current assets
    Inventories (raw materials)   400
    Cash at bank and in hand   1,000

Liabilities
Non-current liabilities
    Loan   (500)
Current liabilities
    Trade payables   (400)

Net assets		1,000
Equity and reserves		
Share capital		1,000
Total		1,000

Days 5 & 6

Days 5 & 6 introduce performance-related transactions into our accounting. This means that we will need to produce a statement of financial position and an income statement. The bookkeeping remains exactly the same as before.

NOTE: In the interests of economy and ease of reading, we will no longer produce the T-accounts where there have been no changes during the period (in this case, days 5 & 6 eg share capital). We strongly advise that whilst you are in the learning phase, however, you continue to produce all the accounts and get into the habit of opening them up and closing them down.

On day 5, Mobius Inc uses the raw materials to produce 30 units of finished goods stock.

On day 6, half of these are sold for $50 per unit. Cash is received immediately for five of those sold. The remainder were sold to customers on 10-day credit terms.

The first part of this transaction (day 5) is straightforward. We are simply moving an asset from one pot to another. In this case, raw materials are converted into finished goods.

		$	$
Debit	Inventories: finished goods	400	
Credit	Inventories: raw materials		400

The second part, however, is a little more tricky as explained in the main text. We advise you do this in two steps: firstly, the revenue side of the transaction; and secondly, the cost of the transaction (cost of sales), as follows:

		$	$
Debit	Cash	250	
Debit	Trade receivables	500	
Credit	Revenue		750

And then:

Debit	Cost of sales	200	
Credit	Inventories: finished goods		200

See Table A.10.

Table A.10

Inventories (raw materials)

Date	Description	$	$	Description	Date
Beg of day 4	Bal. b/fwd	400			
			400	Transfer to finished goods	Day 5
			–	Bal. c/fwd	End of day 6
		400	400		

Inventories (finished goods)

Date	Description	$	$	Description	Date
Beg of day 4	Bal. b/fwd	–			
Day 5	Transferred from raw materials	400		Transfer to finished goods	Day 5
			200	Cost of sales	Day 6
			200	Bal. c/fwd	End of day 6
		400	400		

Cash at bank and in hand

Date	Description	$	$	Description	Date
Beg of day 5	Bal. b/fwd	1,000			
Day 6	Revenue	250			
			1,250	Bal. c/fwd	End of day 4
		1,250	1,250		

(*Continued*)

Table A.10   (*continued*)

| Trade receivables | | | | | |
Date	Description	$	$	Description	Date
Beg of day 5	Bal. b/fwd	–			
Day 6	Revenue	500			
			500	Bal. c/fwd	End of day 4
		500	500		

Note that these are all statement of financial position accounts and all hold either assets or liabilities which will be carried forward to the next period of account. This is not true of income statement accounts, however. These will be closed out in the period and any balance taken to the income statement (and then through to reserves to be carried forward as a net balance at the end of the period).

The income statement accounts are as shown in Table A.11.

Table A.11

| Revenue | | | | | |
Date	Description	$	$	Description	Date
			250	Cash	Day 6
			500	Trade receivables	Day 6
	Take to income statement	750			
		750	750		

| Cost of sales | | | | | |
Date	Description	$	$	Description	Date
Day 6	Inventories	200			
			200	Take to income statement	
		200	200		

The financial statements would appear as follows:

Statement of financial position
For Mobius Inc
As at the end of Day 6

Assets

Non-current assets
    Computer   500

Current assets
    Inventories   200
    Trade receivables   500
    Cash at bank and in hand   1,250

Liabilities

Non-current liabilities
    Loan   (500)

Current liabilities
    Trade payables   (400)

Net assets   1,550

Equity and reserves

Share capital   1,000
Retained earnings   550

Total   1,550

Income Statement
For Mobius Inc
For days 1 to 6

Revenue   750
Cost of sales   (200)
                                 550

Days 8 to 14

Note: The financial statements are produced in the body of the text and therefore shall not be duplicated here. See Table A.12.

Table A.12

Inventories (raw materials)

Date	Description	$	$	Description	Date
Beg of day 8	Bal. b/fwd	–			
Day 8	Trade payables	800			
			800	Transfer to finished goods	Day 9
			–	**Bal. c/fwd**	**End of day 14**
		800	800		

Trade payables

Date	Description	$	$	Description	Date
			400	Bal. b/fwd	Beg of day 8
			800	Inventories (raw materials)	Day 8
Day 14	Bank	400			
End of day 14	**Bal. c/fwd**	**800**			
		1,200	1,200		

Inventories (finished goods)

Date	Description	$	$	Description	Date
Beg of day 8	Bal. b/fwd	200			
Day 9	Transferred from raw materials	800			
			467	Cost of sales	
			533	**Bal. c/fwd**	**End of day 14**
		1,000	1,000		

Operating expenses

Date	Description	$	$	Description	Date
Day 10	Bank (utilities)	200			
Day 12	Bank (stationery)	50			
Day 14	Bank (web development costs)	750			
			1,000	**Take to income statement**	
		1,000	1,000		

(*Continued*)

Table A.12   *(continued)*

Cash at bank and in hand

Date	Description	$	$	Description	Date
Beg of day 8	Bal. b/fwd	1,250			
			200	Utilities	Day 10
Day 11	Revenue	1,200			
			100	Scanner	Day 12
			50	Stationery	Day 12
Day 13	Trade receivables	500			
			400	Trade payables	Day 14
			750	Web development costs	Day 14
			1,450	**Bal. c/fwd**	**End of day 14**
		2,950	2,950		

Trade receivables

Date	Description	$	$	Description	Date
Beg of day 8	Bal. b/fwd	500			
Day 11	Revenue	900			
			500	Bank	Day 13
			900	**Bal. c/fwd**	**End of day 14**
		1,400	1,400		

Revenue

Date	Description	$	$	Description	Date
			1,200	Cash	Day 11
			900	Trade receivables	Day 11
	Take to income statement	1,800			
		1,800	2,100		

Cost of sales

Date	Description	$	$	Description	Date
Day 11	Inventories	467			
			467	**Take to income statement**	
		467	467		

(Continued)

Table A.12 *(continued)*

Non-current assets (scanner)					
Date	Description	$	$	Description	Date
Beg of day 8	Bal. b/fwd	–			
Day 12	Bank	600			
			600	**Bal. c/fwd**	**End of day 14**
		600	600		

The trial balance as at the end of day 14 should now read as shown in Table A.13.

Table A.13

Day 14	Debit (Dr) $	Credit (Cr) $
Non-current assets (computer)	500	
Non-current assets (scanner)	100	
Inventories (raw materials)	–	
Inventories (finished goods)	533	
Trade receivables	900	
Cash at bank and in hand	1,450	
Trade payables		800
Loan		500
Share capital		1,000
Retained earnings (b/fwd from week 1)		550
Revenue		2,100
Cost of sales	467	
Operating expenses	1,000	
	4,950	4,950

Through to the end of month 1

Mobius (5): Adjustments for non-current assets

The following journal entries relate to the depreciation of the non-current assets which the company acquired during the first two weeks, ie the scanner and the computer:

Depreciation charge against the scanner

Debit	Depreciation (income statement)	5	
Credit	Computer: Accumulated depreciation		5
	(statement of financial position)		

Depreciation charge against the computer

Debit	Depreciation (income statement)	10	
Credit	Scanner: Accumulated depreciation		10
	(statement of financial position)		

Note that the T-accounts for the accumulated depreciation are kept separately to the T-accounts for the original cost of the asset. This is so that later adjustments required – for example, disposal or re-measurement – are simpler.

The entries related to the acquisition of the motor vehicle, the associated loan required to buy the asset and the unpaid interest on that loan would be as follows:

Acquisition of motor vehicle

Debit	Motor vehicle: cost	20,000	
Debit	Motor vehicle costs (additional extras)	3,350	
Credit	Loan (to acquire vehicle)		2,350

Depreciation charge against the motor vehicle

Debit	Depreciation (income statement)	154	
Credit	Motor Vehicle: Accumulated depreciation		154
	(statement of financial position)		

Interest on loan (unpaid) used to acquire the motor vehicle

Debit	Finance costs	90	
Credit	Interest accrual		90

Mobius (6): Period-end adjustments

Telephone line installation unpaid as at the end of the month

Debit	Operating expenses: Telephone line installation	100	
Credit	Accruals		100

Rent paid in advance (prepayment account required)

Debit	Prepayment (rent)	1,000	
Credit	Bank		1,000

Sales and related receivables account

Debit	Trade receivables	20,000	
Credit	Revenue		20,000
Debit	Bank	16,000	
Credit	Trade receivables		16,000

Adjustments for inventories, trade payables and cost of sales

Debit	Inventories (raw materials)	9,000	
Credit	Trade payables		9,000
Debit	Inventories (finished goods)	8,000	
Credit	Inventories (raw materials)		8,000
Debit	Cost of sales	6,000	
Credit	Inventories (finished goods)		6,000
Debit	Cost of sales	533	
Credit	Inventories (finished goods)		533
Debit	Trade payables	800	
Debit	Trade payables	7,000	
Credit	Bank		7,800

APPENDIX B
International Accounting/ Financial Reporting Standards

The following is a list of IFRS Standards and the Conceptual Framework for Financial Reporting. For high-level and non-technical summaries you might like to visit **http://www.ifrs.org/issued-standards/list-of-standards/**

The Conceptual Framework for Financial Reporting

#	Name
IFRS 1	First-time Adoption of International Financial Reporting Standards
IFRS 2	Share-based Payment
IFRS 3	Business Combinations
IFRS 4	Insurance Contracts
IFRS 5	Non-current Assets Held for Sale and Discontinued Operations
IFRS 6	Exploration for and Evaluation of Mineral Resources
IFRS 7	Financial Instruments: Disclosures
IFRS 8	Operating Segments
IFRS 9	Financial Instruments
IFRS 10	Consolidated Financial Statements
IFRS 11	Joint Arrangements
IFRS 12	Disclosure of Interests in Other Entities
IFRS 13	Fair Value Measurement
IFRS 14	Regulatory Deferral Accounts
IFRS 15	Revenue from Contracts with Customers
IFRS 16	Leases
IFRS 17	Insurance Contracts
IAS 1	Presentation of Financial Statements
IAS 2	Inventories

APPENDIX C
Discount tables

Table Appendix C.1

Years	1%	2%	3%	4%	5%	6%	7%	8%	9%	10%
1	0.990	0.980	0.971	0.962	0.952	0.943	0.935	0.926	0.917	0.909
2	0.980	0.961	0.943	0.925	0.907	0.890	0.873	0.857	0.842	0.826
3	0.971	0.942	0.915	0.889	0.864	0.840	0.816	0.794	0.772	0.751
4	0.961	0.924	0.888	0.855	0.823	0.792	0.763	0.735	0.708	0.683
5	0.951	0.906	0.863	0.822	0.784	0.747	0.713	0.681	0.650	0.621
6	0.942	0.888	0.837	0.790	0.746	0.705	0.666	0.630	0.596	0.564
7	0.933	0.871	0.813	0.760	0.711	0.665	0.623	0.583	0.547	0.513
8	0.923	0.853	0.789	0.731	0.677	0.627	0.582	0.540	0.502	0.467
9	0.914	0.837	0.766	0.703	0.645	0.592	0.544	0.500	0.460	0.424
10	0.905	0.820	0.744	0.676	0.614	0.558	0.508	0.463	0.422	0.386
11	0.896	0.804	0.722	0.650	0.585	0.527	0.475	0.429	0.388	0.350
12	0.887	0.788	0.701	0.625	0.557	0.497	0.444	0.397	0.356	0.319
13	0.879	0.773	0.681	0.601	0.530	0.469	0.415	0.368	0.326	0.290
14	0.870	0.758	0.661	0.577	0.505	0.442	0.388	0.340	0.299	0.263
15	0.861	0.743	0.642	0.555	0.481	0.417	0.362	0.315	0.275	0.239
16	0.853	0.728	0.623	0.534	0.458	0.394	0.339	0.292	0.252	0.218
17	0.844	0.714	0.605	0.513	0.436	0.371	0.317	0.270	0.231	0.198
18	0.836	0.700	0.587	0.494	0.416	0.350	0.296	0.250	0.212	0.180
19	0.828	0.686	0.570	0.475	0.396	0.331	0.277	0.232	0.194	0.164
20	0.820	0.673	0.554	0.456	0.377	0.312	0.258	0.215	0.178	0.149

(continued)

Table Appendix C.1   *(Continued)*

Years	11%	12%	13%	14%	15%	16%	17%	18%	19%	20%
1	0.901	0.893	0.885	0.877	0.870	0.862	0.855	0.847	0.840	0.833
2	0.812	0.797	0.783	0.769	0.756	0.743	0.731	0.718	0.706	0.694
3	0.731	0.712	0.693	0.675	0.658	0.641	0.624	0.609	0.593	0.579
4	0.659	0.636	0.613	0.592	0.572	0.552	0.534	0.516	0.499	0.482
5	0.593	0.567	0.543	0.519	0.497	0.476	0.456	0.437	0.419	0.402
6	0.535	0.507	0.480	0.456	0.432	0.410	0.390	0.370	0.352	0.335
7	0.482	0.452	0.425	0.400	0.376	0.354	0.333	0.314	0.296	0.279
8	0.434	0.404	0.376	0.351	0.327	0.305	0.285	0.266	0.249	0.233
9	0.391	0.361	0.333	0.308	0.284	0.263	0.243	0.225	0.209	0.194
10	0.352	0.322	0.295	0.270	0.247	0.227	0.208	0.191	0.176	0.162
11	0.317	0.287	0.261	0.237	0.215	0.195	0.178	0.162	0.148	0.135
12	0.286	0.257	0.231	0.208	0.187	0.168	0.152	0.137	0.124	0.112
13	0.258	0.229	0.204	0.182	0.163	0.145	0.130	0.116	0.104	0.093
14	0.232	0.205	0.181	0.160	0.141	0.125	0.111	0.099	0.088	0.078
15	0.209	0.183	0.160	0.140	0.123	0.108	0.095	0.084	0.074	0.065
16	0.188	0.163	0.141	0.123	0.107	0.093	0.081	0.071	0.062	0.054
17	0.170	0.146	0.125	0.108	0.093	0.080	0.069	0.060	0.052	0.045
18	0.153	0.130	0.111	0.095	0.081	0.069	0.059	0.051	0.044	0.038
19	0.138	0.116	0.098	0.083	0.070	0.060	0.051	0.043	0.037	0.031
20	0.124	0.104	0.087	0.073	0.061	0.051	0.043	0.037	0.031	0.026

APPENDIX D
Annuity factors

Table Appendix D.1

Years	1%	2%	3%	4%	5%	6%	7%	8%	9%	10%
1	0.990	0.980	0.971	0.962	0.952	0.943	0.935	0.926	0.917	0.909
2	1.970	1.942	1.913	1.886	1.859	1.833	1.808	1.783	1.759	1.736
3	2.941	2.884	2.829	2.775	2.723	2.673	2.624	2.577	2.531	2.487
4	3.902	3.808	3.717	3.630	3.546	3.465	3.387	3.312	3.240	3.170
5	4.853	4.713	4.580	4.452	4.329	4.212	4.100	3.993	3.890	3.791
6	5.795	5.601	5.417	5.242	5.076	4.917	4.767	4.623	4.486	4.355
7	6.728	6.472	6.230	6.002	5.786	5.582	5.389	5.206	5.033	4.868
8	7.652	7.325	7.020	6.733	6.463	6.210	5.971	5.747	5.535	5.335
9	8.566	8.162	7.786	7.435	7.108	6.802	6.515	6.247	5.995	5.759
10	9.471	8.983	8.530	8.111	7.722	7.360	7.024	6.710	6.418	6.145
11	10.368	9.787	9.253	8.760	8.306	7.887	7.499	7.139	6.805	6.495
12	11.255	10.575	9.954	9.385	8.863	8.384	7.943	7.536	7.161	6.814
13	12.134	11.348	10.635	9.986	9.394	8.853	8.358	7.904	7.487	7.103
14	13.004	12.106	11.296	10.563	9.899	9.295	8.745	8.244	7.786	7.367
15	13.865	12.849	11.938	11.118	10.380	9.712	9.108	8.559	8.061	7.606
16	14.718	13.578	12.561	11.652	10.838	10.106	9.447	8.851	8.313	7.824
17	15.562	14.292	13.166	12.166	11.274	10.477	9.763	9.122	8.544	8.022
18	16.398	14.992	13.754	12.659	11.690	10.828	10.059	9.372	8.756	8.201
19	17.226	15.678	14.324	13.134	12.085	11.158	10.336	9.604	8.950	8.365
20	18.046	16.351	14.877	13.590	12.462	11.470	10.594	9.818	9.129	8.514

(continued)

Table Appendix D.1 *(Continued)*

Years	11%	12%	13%	14%	15%	16%	17%	18%	19%	20%
1	0.901	0.893	0.885	0.877	0.870	0.862	0.855	0.847	0.840	0.833
2	1.713	1.690	1.668	1.647	1.626	1.605	1.585	1.566	1.547	1.528
3	2.444	2.402	2.361	2.322	2.283	2.246	2.210	2.174	2.140	2.106
4	3.102	3.037	2.974	2.914	2.855	2.798	2.743	2.690	2.639	2.589
5	3.696	3.605	3.517	3.433	3.352	3.274	3.199	3.127	3.058	2.991
6	4.231	4.111	3.998	3.889	3.784	3.685	3.589	3.498	3.410	3.326
7	4.712	4.564	4.423	4.288	4.160	4.039	3.922	3.812	3.706	3.605
8	5.146	4.968	4.799	4.639	4.487	4.344	4.207	4.078	3.954	3.837
9	5.537	5.328	5.132	4.946	4.772	4.607	4.451	4.303	4.163	4.031
10	5.889	5.650	5.426	5.216	5.019	4.833	4.659	4.494	4.339	4.192
11	6.207	5.938	5.687	5.453	5.234	5.029	4.836	4.656	4.486	4.327
12	6.492	6.194	5.918	5.660	5.421	5.197	4.988	4.793	4.611	4.439
13	6.750	6.424	6.122	5.842	5.583	5.342	5.118	4.910	4.715	4.533
14	6.982	6.628	6.302	6.002	5.724	5.468	5.229	5.008	4.802	4.611
15	7.191	6.811	6.462	6.142	5.847	5.575	5.324	5.092	4.876	4.675
16	7.379	6.974	6.604	6.265	5.954	5.668	5.405	5.162	4.938	4.730
17	7.549	7.120	6.729	6.373	6.047	5.749	5.475	5.222	4.990	4.775
18	7.702	7.250	6.840	6.467	6.128	5.818	5.534	5.273	5.033	4.812
19	7.839	7.366	6.938	6.550	6.198	5.877	5.584	5.316	5.070	4.843
20	7.963	7.469	7.025	6.623	6.259	5.929	5.628	5.353	5.101	4.870

USEFUL WEB LINKS

Here, you will find IBM's Q4, 2016 Earnings Announcement and Weibo's quarterly results area of their corporate websites. Alongside a number of other accounting-related documents, you can download results announcements/press releases for free:

IBM (2016) [accessed 28 June 2017] IBM 4Q 2016 Earnings Announcement [Online] www.ibm.com/investor/events (archived at https://perma.cc/JQJ6-LD5J)

Weibo (2017) [accessed 28 June 2017] Weibo's Quarterly Results [Online] http://ir.weibo.com/financial-information/quarterly-results (archived at https://perma.cc/S68D-LPLL)

INDEX